ENVIRONMENTAL ECONOMICS

Second Edition

ENVIRONMENTAL ECONOMICS

Joseph J. Seneca
Rutgers University

Michael K. Taussig
Rutgers University

PRENTICE-HALL, INC., Englewood Cliffs, New Jersey 07632

Library of Congress Cataloging in Publication Data

SENECA, JOSEPH J (date)
  Environmental economics.

  Includes bibliographies and index.
  1. Environmental policy—United States. 2. Cost
effectiveness. 3. Anthropo-geography—United States.
I. Taussig, Michael K., joint author. II. Title.
HC110.E5S45 1979   301.31'0973   78-10372
ISBN 0-13-283291-7

Printed in the United States of America

10 9 8 7 6 5 4 3 2 1

PRENTICE-HALL INTERNATIONAL, INC., *London*
PRENTICE-HALL OF AUSTRALIA PTY. LIMITED, *Sydney*
PRENTICE-HALL OF CANADA, LTD., *Toronto*
PRENTICE-HALL OF INDIA PRIVATE LIMITED, *New Delhi*
PRENTICE-HALL OF JAPAN, INC., *Tokyo*
PRENTICE-HALL OF SOUTHEAST ASIA PTE. LTD., *Singapore*
WHITEHALL BOOKS LIMITED, *Wellington, New Zealand*

To Rozy and Nikki

CONTENTS

III The Economics of Environmental Problems

IV The Vehicles of Collective Environmental Action

V Population, Economic Growth and
Environmental Quality

PREFACE TO SECOND EDITION

This edition of the book has been extensively revised but remains essentially the same as the first edition in coverage, level of presentation, and general point of view. We have made revisions where change was clearly needed. First, we have updated and expanded all factual material wherever possible and have added new evidence bearing on environmental problems available from the many empirical studies published since the first edition of the book. Second, we have moved our treatment of theoretical welfare economics from the text of Chapter 2 to a new Appendix to that chapter. Teachers who use the revised version of the book are thus given the choice of skipping this material without loss of continuity or of including it by assigning the Appendix. Third, in Chapters 3 and 11, we have added extensive new materials on environmental law and its impact on environmental economics. Fourth, in Chapter 5, we have greatly expanded our coverage of the important income distribution aspects of environmental problems. Fifth, in Chapter 10, we have included descriptions of how the Environmental Protection Agency operates and have evaluated the effectiveness of the current regulations covering the air and water quality dimensions of the environment.

Despite the major changes detailed above and numerous lesser changes to improve presentation of the material, the book remains very much what it was in the original edition. We have found the book gratifyingly successful in its use at Rutgers and reports from colleagues using the book elsewhere have also been most encouraging. We are of the opinion that the book does a good job of helping students learn environmental economics within the resource constraints of the typical college semester or quarter course. We can only hope the reader will agree.

We are most grateful to Professors Burley V. Bechdolt, Jr., and Neil Mather for their careful reading of a first draft of the revised manuscript. The book is greatly improved because of their valuable comments and constructive suggestions. We also wish to express our sincere thanks to Helen Martin and Sharin Silverman for their help in preparing the manuscript for publication.

PREFACE TO
FIRST EDITION

The subject of this book is the economics of environmental quality. Our book-length treatment of this subject reflects our feelings about the extraordinary complexity and importance of the topic. We thereby immediately depart from two polar opposing points of view. The first, often expressed by many highly emotional new conservationists, is that economics is completely irrelevant to (if not responsible for) the problems of environmental deterioration. The second, held by some of our purist professional colleagues in economics, is that environmental problems are essentially trivial or "political," and that they can all be solved by the application of simple prescriptions drawn from extensions of traditional economic theory. The latter point of view can be summarized by the following policy recommendation: "Just impose an effluent charge equal to the difference between marginal social and private costs." Although we are conservationists in spirit and loyal economists by profession, we find both positions to be most unsatisfactory. Our own view, as expressed in the book, is that economists have an invaluable potential role to play in helping to solve or alleviate environmental problems. But at the same time we maintain that economists can not undertake this vital role successfully until they first educate themselves both about the very complex physical and biological circumstances of specific environmental problems and about the broader social and legal aspects of these problems.

We therefore take some pains in the book to blend economic theory with environmental facts and social circumstances. The theme of the book is the application of the standard benefit-cost or efficiency criteria of economics to a wide variety of environmental problems. We attempt to make clear to the reader how difficult it is in the real world to apply these criteria to actual environmental problems. We also stress the interaction of efficiency criteria with income redistribution or equity issues. Most important of all, probably, we try to show that environmental policies must take their place in the context of other demands on scarce resources, even in our affluent society.

The book is the outgrowth of a course in environmental economics taught by one of the authors at Rutgers College for the last several years. Thus, the material has been extensively class-tested and refined. The evident success and widespread appeal of this course at Rutgers encourage us to hope that our approach to the subject may have similar appeal outside our own institution. A prerequisite for the course at Rutgers is the micro half of the principles of economics course. Students without this minimum background may find the book beyond their reach. In addition, many students have either taken an intermediate micro-theory course or take it concurrently. Not all of them, by any means, are economics majors. The course has had appeal to students from engineering, the physical sciences, political science, urban planning and other disciplines. We believe that the book can have the same broad audience at other institutions.

The topical organization of the book is detailed in Chapter 1 and need not be duplicated here. Instead let us make some suggestions how the book may best be utilized. At Rutgers, the material in each of the 14 chapters is assigned reading for one week and serves as the main basis for class lectures and discussion. In this way, the whole book fits neatly into a typical college-length semester and can be covered in its entirety without undue haste. We find it useful to supplement the basic core reading in the text with a variety of additional outside readings, and the Selected References at the end of each chapter are intended to guide users of the book to the best available detailed treatments of individual topics. In addition, the Questions for Discussion at the end of each chapter can play a valuable educational role. These questions are designed to help students probe more deeply on their own into the difficult conceptual issues underlying the text discussion. We recognize that our own approach to the subject will not be applicable at all times and places. Users of the book at other institutions will undoubtedly find other ways of utilizing the material to their best advantage.

Many individuals are due our sincere thanks for helping us complete the book. Marshall I. Goldman read the entire manuscript and provided us with a most valuable critique. Professors Paul Gatons, David Fischer, Matthew Edel, and Alan Campbell also reviewed the manuscript and offered sound advice. Our student Sharon Bernstein made many helpful comments on several of the chapters and Jack Worrall also gave us useful assistance. Geraldine Dructor and Irene Matthews typed the bulk of the manuscript with patience and skill. We are also grateful to the Rutgers University Research Council for much needed financial assistance. Finally, we must go beyond our bibliographical citations to make special mention of our intellectual indebtedness to the outstanding pioneers in the new and vital field of environmental economics. We have drawn particularly on the work of J. H. Dales, Allen V. Kneese, John V. Krutilla, Edwin S. Mills and E. J. Mishan. Without their pathbreaking efforts, this book could not have been written.

Joseph J. Seneca
Michael K. Taussig

ENVIRONMENTAL ECONOMICS

I

Introduction

1

THE BASIC CONCEPTS OF ENVIRONMENTAL ECONOMICS

This is a book about the *economics* of environmental quality. A full treatment of environmental problems would include contributions from several different intellectual disciplines: the physical and biological sciences, political science, sociology, the law, and perhaps others. We will attempt to make some use of the insights from these other disciplines. We do insist, however, that economics has its own unique, valuable role to play in the solution of environmental problems. In taking a predominantly economic approach to our subject, we avoid the pitfalls that await those who venture into disciplines in which, unfortunately, they are ignorant, and, more positively, we confirm our faith as practicing economists in the principle that specialization and division of labor generally lead to maximum total output for society.

The theme of this book is that the different aspects of environmental quality are economic goods or, what is essentially the same notion in different words, that they are items of *scarcity*. By scarcity, we mean simply that the demand for a high level of environmental quality (often perceived as the demand for avoidance of environmental pollution) exceeds the supply at a zero price. Unfortunately, nature does not provide enough environmental quality free to satisfy all of society's desires. Contrary to the view often expressed in the popular press, economists tend to agree that most environmental problems cannot be solved by passing a law or by exhorting people to be better behaved. Because aspects of environmental quality such as clean air and water are scarce, society can have more of them only by giving up significant amounts of other desirable consumption goods and services. In the language of economics, environmental quality must be *traded off* against other economic goods and services. The *opportunity cost* of obtaining more environmental quality for any society is the sacrifice of doing without other valuable commodities.

In addition, we shall stress throughout the book that the benefits of the enhancement or preservation of environmental quality will, in general, be distributed unevenly among individuals of the present generation and also between the present and future generations, and that the costs of producing environmental quality almost certainly will be distributed differently from the benefits. In common with all other important economic problems, the issue of environmental quality involves the *distribution* of economic welfare. Therefore, it necessarily will provoke conflicts of interest between potential gainers and potential losers from any specific environmental policy alternative. In such cases, achievement of an optimal level of environmental quality may entail socially unacceptable distributional consequences.

We shall return continually to these central points throughout the book—with appropriate elaboration, of course—and, in doing so, we shall attempt to make clear to the reader the unique contribution of economic principles to the understanding and the solution of various environmental problems.

A GUIDE TO THE ORGANIZATION OF THE BOOK

The present chapter is intended as an introduction to the rest of the book. The theme of the book has been stated in our introduction. Next, we define some basic terminology in Section A below. Section B then attempts to present modern environmental problems to the reader in the proper historical and quantitative perspectives. Section C is an introduction to the economics of environmental problems; it includes a discussion of benefit-cost analysis, the basic mode of thinking that distinguishes the economic from alternative approaches to these problems. Section D contains a brief summary of the chapter.

Following this introductory chapter, Part 2 of the book presents the body of economic theory pertinent to the analysis of environmental problems. The chapters in this part of the book apply basic microeconomic theory to the specific problems involved in achieving environmental quality. The material covered includes the problem of efficiency in the presence of pervasive externalities, the public goods problem, the income distribution effects of government environmental programs, and public versus private sector economic performance.

Next, the three chapters of Part 3 of the book survey the current circumstances of the water (Chapter 6), air (Chapter 7), and assorted amenity (Chapter 8) aspects of the total environment. These chapters attempt to link the technical, physical, and biological aspects of each of these environmental resources to the preceding theoretical analysis. They also discuss the history of policies in each of these areas in the United States.

Part 4 of the book examines alternative courses of government intervention intended to improve environmental quality. Chapter 9 analyzes prohibitions on, and regulations of, polluting activities. Chapter 10 deals with tax and subsidy measures designed to encourage environment-enhancing behavior on the part of individual firms and households through the mechanism of monetary incentives and disincentives. Chapter 11 is concerned with the economics of government investments in environmental resources.

The concluding Part 5 of the book treats the relationship between the growth and distribution of population and general economic growth and environmental quality. Chapter 12 discusses the environmental consequences of growth of population, of changes in *levels* of population in any society. Chapter 13 gives a similar treatment of the environmental implications of urbanization, or the *distribution* of population. The final Chapter 14 consists of a general discussion of the relationship between economic growth and environmental quality. This chapter makes some modest attempts to transcend the intentionally narrow economic focus of the book by considering some broad social implications of continued economic growth.

A. SOME DEFINITIONS OF TERMS

Environmental Science Concepts

Ecology is the science of the interrelationship between man and his living and nonliving surroundings. *Ecosystem* is the term applied to a particular, identifiable set of ecological interrelationships. Typical examples of ecosystems are a lake or a mountain meadow. The *biosphere* consists of the earth, its atmosphere, and all life on the planet. The total *environment* of man includes the biosphere and also the relationship of man to nature and to his own created surroundings. Given this definition, the environment clearly can encompass almost every conceivable aspect of life. We shall confine our use of the term to the relationship of man to the atmosphere and waters of the earth, and to a few other specific aspects of his total environment. In particular, we examine the general issue of the undersupply of environmental amenities. We do not, however, cover the important subjects of natural resource economics or resource use policy, except where they have major effects on environmental quality.

Economic Concepts

The fundamental economic problem is that the goods and services society wishes to consume are generally scarce. Scarcity exists whenever the demand for anything exceeds its supply at a zero price; conversely, any good or service that is free is, by the same definition, not scarce and not an economic good or service. We live, unfortunately, in a world of general scarcity because, with few exceptions, *resources*—the general term applied to anything that contributes to making desired goods and services available for consumption—are limited relative to the desires of man to consume. The welfare of individual consumers is presumed to vary directly with the value of the consumption of economic goods and services over some specified time period. *Efficiency* is defined as maximum consumption of goods and services given the available amount of resources or, what is logically equivalent, the use of a minimum amount of resources to produce or make available for consumption a given amount of goods and services. *Equity* refers to a just distribution of total goods and services among all consumer units.

The *benefit* of any good or service is simply its value to a consumer. The benefits of most goods and services are usually measured directly by the market prices at which consumers show themselves willing to buy them. Benefits of goods not bought and sold in the market must be inferred by some less direct method. *Costs* are essentially foregone benefits and, therefore, are most fundamentally conceived of as *opportunity costs.* The cost of any good or service consists of the foregone benefits from the consumption of some other good or service. The consumption of one unit more of good A implies the shift of some resources away from the production of good B in order to produce the additional unit of A. The true cost of A, therefore, is the foregone B caused by the shift in resources from production of the latter to the production of the former.

Costs, as well as benefits, are typically measured, more or less accurately, by money prices paid in markets.

Pollution

Pollution can be defined either from an environmental science or economic standpoint. By the criteria of the physical or biological sciences, pollution means that certain substances or life forms accumulate in ecosystems because of production or consumption. This concept of pollution rests strictly on man's physical or biological alteration of the natural environment. Economists call such situations pollution only when alteration of the environment is harmful or undesirable. From their standpoint, pollution is a concept involving individual and group preferences as well as technical physical or biological science data. To illustrate the distinction with a trivial example, consider the disposal of a beer can in a natural environment. For the economist, this act is pollution only if people are willing to pay something to prevent this from happening or to have the offending material removed. The extent of pollution is thus measured not by the total weight (or other physical measurement) of accumulated materials but rather by the total amount society would be willing to pay to avoid the damages. The amount society will be willing to pay is equal to the total damages the discarded material imposes on all consumers.

We elaborate on the use of these concepts in Section C of this chapter and throughout the rest of the book. Other, less general economic concepts will be defined in context as they are introduced into our later analysis.

B. ENVIRONMENTAL PROBLEMS IN PERSPECTIVE

The Past

Air and water pollution and other environmental problems are as old as civilized man. Historians of ancient Rome have left us a record of the almost unbearable odors prevailing in the imperial capital. More recently, we have available ample documentation of the obnoxious smoke, noise, and odors that plagued London and other newly industrialized cities of Victorian England. London's "Great Stink" of June 1858 was the result of using the Thames River as a common sewer. Much of the recent popular writing on current pollution problems naively looks back at nineteenth century America as a golden environmental age. Such a rosy view of our past ignores pertinent facts to the contrary, as, for example, the fact that the exhaust system of the predecessor to the automobile created its own unique brand of pollution.

Despite the frequent recurrence of environmental problems throughout human history, widespread concern about environmental quality is a surprisingly recent and localized phenomenon, beginning only in the late 1960s and largely confined to the United States and a few other economically advanced countries. What explains this apparent paradox? From the perspective of economics, the answer is that the unprecedented high levels of output achieved in a few countries in the last half century have transformed environmental quality from a generally free good into an economic, or scarce, good. At the beginning of this century, the supply of clean air, potable water, and other amenities of life generally exceeded the effective demand at a zero price, despite the presence of often serious, localized pollution problems. Today, in many high-income and densely populated areas, demand exceeds supply at a zero price, and formerly free goods suddenly have become scarce goods. For many people, the shock of this unexpected development has added psychic insult to economic injury and health hazards, resulting in widespread public concern about the *new* problem of environment quality.

The reversal of environmental quality supply-demand relationships in just a few years is the result of two, or possibly three, separate factors. First, economic growth accompanied by population increases and urbanization has had the effect of decreasing the available supply of clean air and of other environmental goods through the sheer quantity of effluents generated by high levels of industrial production. Growth in the level of total output has been the cause of growth in the amounts of various effluents. Inevitably, the point has been reached where, in some of the most densely populated and industrialized areas of the earth, the quantity of some effluents has overcome the natural, self-cleansing powers of the atmosphere, waters, and earth, and the waste disposal functions of these environmental media have become incompatible with their use for other purposes. If industrial cities in the nineteenth century were grimy and even dangerous to public health, the pleasant countryside was still easily accessible, especially for the middle and upper classes. Today, pollution problems have increased to the degree that polluted air and water follow the would-be urban escapist to his country hideaway.

A possibly distinct point is that modern pollutants present unprecedented threats to the health and safety of man. The nature of many complex industrial wastes, e.g., nuclear radiation and mercury pollutants, is sufficiently different from traditional pollutants in technological complexity and in long-run danger to the existence of man that the quality, as well as the quantity, of modern pollution problems merits separate consideration. On the more optimistic side, the technical means for dealing with some of these problems are also much more advanced than in the past. In any case, the important point is that economic growth has steadily diminished the available supply of environmental quality.

In contrast, the demand for environmental quality has increased sharply as a consequence of rising levels of affluence, which, in turn, is simply another by-product of sustained economic growth. Men and women at the verge of subsistence care little about the amenities of life, including the various aspects of environmental quality. Once man has assured himself sufficient food and other necessities, plus a good measure of luxuries, he can then turn his attention to satisfying other, less-immediate wants, including the enjoyment of environmental quality. In economic terminology, we hypothesize that environmental quality is a highly *income elastic* or *luxury* good, which means that households with relatively high incomes desire to consume a higher fraction of their income in the form of expenditures on environmental quality than do households with relatively low incomes. Thus, on both the demand and supply sides, the effect of economic growth in the most economically developed countries of the world has contributed to the transformation of environmental quality from a free to a scarce good. The fact that industrially advanced socialist countries are plagued by environmental problems suggests strongly that the basic underlying cause of those problems is the supply and demand relationship outlined above and not the shortcomings of private market economic systems.

The Present and Future

The modern conservation movement—a term we apply to the many individuals and organizations in this country that are demanding more social action to enhance environmental quality—is the intellectual and spiritual heir of the conservation movement of the late nineteenth and early twentieth centuries. The old conservation movement was led by self-styled Progressives, notably Theodore Roosevelt and Gifford Pinchot. The vision of such men was of a country with precious natural resources of all kinds being destroyed by large corporations interested only in exploiting these resources for the sake of maximizing immediate profits. They saw all around them the destruction of great natural beauty and the apparently accelerating depletion of the nation's limited natural resources. Despite the fact that, from today's perspective, the leaders of the old conservation movement were wealthy and staunchly conservative, in the name of conservation they supported the most far-reaching and basic governmental restrictions on the behavior of individuals and business firms within the private market system. This principle of government intervention in private economic activities for the sake of the public interest in conservation is probably the main legacy of the old conservation movement, which now retains little else of its original force.

The modern conservation movement differs from its predecessor in two important respects. First, the present breed of conservationists is much more broadly based, both politically and socially. The old conservation movement mainly represented the interests of the agrarian society that was made obsolete by the industrialization of the United States during the late nineteenth and early twentieth centuries. These interests were largely irrelevant to the major concerns of the entrepreneurs and laborers of the emerging industrial society. Moreover, the major spokesmen of the old conservation movement can be faulted with a lack of concern for the urban working masses. At their worst, the old conservationists appeared to be satisfied, affluent country gentlemen attempting to halt economic progress in order to preserve the traditional amenities of their country estates. The modern conservation movement in the United States is not entirely free of such class bias, but it has now succeeded in attracting broad-based public support, largely due to the fact that sustained economic growth has transformed much of the previously poor working class into a moderately affluent middle class.

Second, the modern conservation movement has largely freed itself of the *exhaustion of resources* fallacy that was the intellectual cornerstone of the old movement's beliefs and has turned its attention, instead, to the more relevant problems of environmental quality. The exhaustion of resources fallacy is the argument that because there exists only a finite amount of any given natural resource in the biosphere, continued economic growth will inevitably exhaust the supply of this resource. The fallacy commonly takes the form of estimating the present annual rate and expected future rates of utilization of some resource, such as coal; then estimating the total amount of coal deposits left in the earth; and, finally, projecting the year in which all coal deposits will be exhausted. Virtually all such projections have proved thus far to be much too pessimistic, and economic growth has proceeded essentially unhindered by raw material shortages.

The flaw in the exhaustion of resources argument is that it fails to take into account the ability of a market system to adapt to the threat of shortages and of continued technological advance in the process of economic growth. As any raw material becomes scarcer, its price rises. This acts as a signal for profit-maximizing firms to devise more efficient use of it or search for alternative resources as substitutes. In the past, technological advance has consistently transformed previously essential resources such as coal into just one of several possible alternative inputs into the productive process. Scientists and economists now envision a future in which the only essential raw materials will be energy and the most basic chemical molecules.

Given the foregoing argument, energy sources remain, in principle, the only exhaustible resource. But many careful studies make clear that even energy sources are available in massive quantities forever or, more precisely, until the sun burns itself out in a few billion years. The important point is that the opportunity costs of developing these scarce resources can be expected to rise sharply in the future as we exhaust the supply of the most economical sources. The consequent rise in the relative price of energy should encourage consumers to find various means of economizing on energy use and producers to develop new forms of usable energy. Energy sources are of interest for our purposes in this book, therefore, not because they are about to run out but, instead, because their exploitation is the root cause of many of our most serious environmental problems. Furthermore, the choice among alternative energy sources should be heavily influenced by their various effects on environmental quality.

The Magnitude of Environmental Problems

Widespread recognition of the problem of deterioration of environmental quality has come, understandably, only belatedly, after many years of steadily accumulating pollution. Some perspective on the magnitude of the problem can be given by citing some estimates of the annual costs of producing present pollution controls in the United States.[1] Public and private outlays on water pollution control were over $15.4 billion in 1977. Total outlays on air pollution control were estimated at $13 billion in 1977. Measures to deal with solid waste disposal, noise, and other environmental problems also run into some billions of dollars each year in the United States. Total annual costs in 1977 were estimated at $40.6 billion for all public and private pollution control activities, but of this, only an estimated $18.1 billion were due to the requirements of existing environmental legislation. The remaining amount would have been spent in any event. The $40.6 billion amounted to about 2 percent of the country's gross national product in 1977.

The estimates above are the best available but are acknowledged by the Council on Environmental Quality to be rough. Although we know too little about the present costs of antipollution measures, we know considerably less about the opportunity costs of producing different specified levels of environmental quality. The relevant technological and economic data are not available to allow us to estimate precisely the costs of achieving a given improvement in the quality of the environment. However, the Council has estimated that the incremental costs of environmental quality control programs caused by current environmental legislation will, by 1985, be $42.4 billion (in 1976 dollars). Of this, $20.6

[1] The source for the figures in the text is *Environmental Quality, The Eighth Annual Report of the Council on Environmental Quality* (Washington, D.C.: Government Printing Office, 1977), pp. 321–334.

billion will be spent to control air pollution, and $18.5 billion for water pollution. Total pollution abatement expenditures, including those expenditures that would occur anyhow (i.e., without the existing legislation), are estimated to rise from the $40.6 billion spent in 1977 to $75.1 billion (in 1976 dollars) by 1985.

At best, the potential trade-off between various degrees of environmental quality and per capita standards of consumption of other economic goods and services can only be roughly estimated at the present time. Given the present state of ignorance on this subject, it is not surprising that views about the gravity of environmental problems differ sharply. Many spokesmen of the modern conservation movement express the doomsday view that our society and the rest of the world face a major crisis, and that only massive social commitments to the environmental cause can preserve human life. In support of their arguments, they observe the widespread serious environmental damage that has already occurred and project present pollution trends into an even more threatening future.

On the opposite side of the question are proponents of the skeptical, business-as-usual view, who deny the overriding urgency of environmental problems and resist all but very modest remedial social actions. They argue that concern with environmental quality is only a fad—just a transitory social cause for youthful idealists. A sophisticated version of this skeptical view argues, first, that Americans, at least, are too materialistic to be willing to sacrifice any significant portion of their high standards of consumption in the long run for the sake of improving environmental quality. In addition, optimistic scientists feel that environmental problems can be reduced to manageable proportions by the application of the same advanced technology that has been so successful in other areas. Granted the validity of both these premises, environmental problems can be expected to fade from the public consciousness, to be replaced by some new cause, and to become the province of technicians and engineers in sanitation and related fields.

The debate between the modern conservation movement and its critics has just begun. Economic growth continues today at customary compound rates in the United States and in most other countries, with the increased flow of output closely matched by increased flows of effluents of all kinds into the absorptive earth, water, and atmospheric media. The full effects of some modern pollutants—fluorocarbons for example—are experienced only with a long lag through complex ecological processes. It remains to be seen whether current policy measures at all levels of government, together with the activities of private parties, will be sufficient to prevent environmental degradation. It is important to recognize that government environmental programs have improved aspects of the environment in the 1960s and 1970s, sometimes dramatically, despite many failures. The environmental policy choices that society makes in the next decade—either consciously or by default—will determine the quality of the environment we shall live in during this century and our children will inherit.

C. THE BENEFIT-COST TO APPROACH ENVIRONMENTAL PROBLEMS

Benefit-cost analysis is the systematic appraisal of all benefits and all costs of a contemplated course of action in comparison with alternative courses of action (always defined to include no action at all as one alternative). The benefit-cost *criterion* for whether to undertake a given course of action is that the additional benefits to be derived from taking the action exceed the corresponding additional costs. In even simpler terms, this criterion means that the course of action be undertaken only if the sum of all the expected advantages outweigh the sum of all the expected disadvantages. Stated in this way, the benefit-cost criterion is nothing more than a description of rational behavior. Who but an irrational man would act in any other way? Despite the deceptive simplicity of this mode of thinking, the benefit-cost approach has proved to be the unique contribution of economics to the solution of social problems; the systematic comparison of benefits and costs and the consideration of all alternatives clearly distinguish the approach of economists to a given problem from the methods of other disciplines. As economists, we believe that this same mode of analysis will prove fruitful when applied to the special problems associated with environmental quality.

A *benefit* is, as we have already defined it, the value of a good or service to a consumer, and a *cost* is fundamentally a foregone benefit. The private market system, in effect, performs complex benefit-cost analyses every day. If consumers value a given consumption good sufficiently to willingly pay the price that makes it profitable for business firms to produce more of it, then the firms will typically respond by doing so. If, on the other hand, consumers are not willing to pay a price high enough to cover the additional costs of further production, then firms will not produce more. Similarly, individuals perform implicit or explicit benefit-cost analyses in making everyday decisions. The man who asks himself whether it is *worth* taking the time to visit his in-laws is implicitly comparing the benefits he expects from the visit to the costs— the foregone time he could have spent watching the football game on television or in some other alternative activity. Benefit-cost types of analyses have been established in many federal government agencies dealing with natural resource development. For our purposes, however, we shall concentrate only on the application of benefit-cost analysis to various activities intended to alleviate or prevent various environmental problems.

The Costs of Waste Disposal

Before presenting a simplified example of applied benefit-cost analysis, let us consider, in some depth, the nature of costs and benefits in environmental problems. Most of the important environmental problems facing man today arise because modern production and consumption techniques of firms and households impose *waste disposal costs* on society.[2] Following the usage of Professor J. H. Dales, we may define waste disposal costs to be the sum of (1) *pollution prevention costs* and (2) *pollution costs.* Pollution prevention costs are those costs incurred, either by firms or individuals in the private sector or by the government, to prevent either entirely or partially the pollution that would otherwise result from some production or consumption activity. The costs incurred by a local government to treat its sewage before dumping it into a river are pollution prevention costs according to this terminology, as are the costs incurred by a firm or by a household to maintain high-efficiency furnaces that minimize the residues emitted to the atmosphere.

Pollution costs, in turn, may be broken down into two categories: (1) the private or public expenditures undertaken to avoid pollution damage once pollution has already occurred and (2) the welfare damage of pollution. Once pollution has occurred, perhaps because of the failure of individuals or government to accept the costs of pollution prevention, society can choose either to avoid the damage of the pollution by undertaking some defensive or remedial actions, or it can simply accept the consequences of pollution. The first alternative line of action may take the form of public expenditures on various kinds of cleanup programs or of private expenditures on air filtration systems or on unpolluted drinking water imported from some area free of water pollution or on vacations to unspoiled (unpolluted) areas. Over the long run, one socially significant cost of pollution avoidance has been the additional commuting costs accepted by surburban dwellers who work in cities. These commuting costs are pollution damage avoidance costs to the extent that

---

[2] The main exceptions to the generalization in the text are the *environmental* problems traceable to human activities that destroy animal and plant life or impair the aesthetic quality of the natural world. The costs due to man's overharvesting a particular species or to the construction of hot dog stands in sites of natural beauty are not waste disposal costs in the usual meaning of the term. They are costs due essentially to the failure of effective enforcement of private or collective property rights, a subject we shall discuss in more detail in Chapter 3.

they are incurred for the purpose of avoiding the environmental quality problems of central cities.]

Finally, pollution that is not prevented or avoided causes welfare damages. Such damage is more or less measurable in money terms, but in any case it is a very real phenomenon. The most tangible pollution damage takes the form of the observable deterioration of both physical assets and of living things, including human beings. For example, air pollution may cause paint to peel and thus impose additional painting costs on the owners of commercial and residential structures.[3] It is also likely to increase everybody's cleaning bills as people attempt to maintain standards of cleanliness established in a less-polluted age. Both air and water pollution probably increase the medical costs of society just to maintain a given level of health. Thus, the explicit money costs of maintenance of physical assets and of human beings will rise as the result of increasing levels of pollution. The more subtle consequences of pollution are the instances of the welfare costs that result from deterioration of physical assets and of human health and are not offset by increased expenditures on maintenance and repair. That is, some physical assets will erode, and some human beings will sicken and even die because of pollution damage that is not counteracted by increased explicit costs. Such costs of pollution damage are conceptually on a par with the explicit money costs of pollution prevention in their effects on human welfare. Lung cancer caused by chronic exposure to pollutants in the atmosphere is a real cost, even if it is not recorded as part of the money costs of producing our gross national product.

The full welfare costs of pollution damage are impossible to measure exactly. How can we evaluate, for example, the welfare cost that results from the polluted water in a stream that once was used for fishing and bathing? Former users and potential users of the stream are *invisible* —they no longer frequent the stream and we can never know how much welfare damage they have suffered from pollution and how much they would be willing to pay to help restore the stream to its former unpolluted state. We cannot measure the full welfare loss of pollution damage in the same way we can measure the costs of pollution prevention or, in many cases, of pollution damage avoidance, but economists have developed sophisticated techniques of approximating pollution damage costs based on how much people would be willing to pay to avoid such damage. We may infer from the stirrings of the modern conservation movement that pollution damage costs have now reached

---

[3] If the *prospect* or *threat* of peeling paint causes the owners of property to apply extra coats of paint, our terminology would call the costs of the additional paint pollution damage avoidance costs. Clearly, the line between pollution damage avoidance costs and the welfare damage of pollution is often hard to distinguish.

large proportions. The following simple equation summarizes the above discussion:

$$\text{Waste Disposal Costs} = \text{Pollution Prevention Costs} + \underbrace{\text{Pollution Avoidance Costs} + \text{Pollution Damage Costs}}_{\text{Pollution Costs}}$$

Some implications of the preceding discussion should be immediately obvious. Waste disposal costs, whatever form they take, are real, or opportunity, costs. They are basically foregone benefits to individual consumers in society. Pollution prevention costs involve direct outlays, by the private sector or by government, to purchase resources to inhibit pollution. The resources used for this purpose are thereby diverted from production of some other good, and the result is less net output for society. The money costs of pollution damage avoidance are comparable to the costs of pollution prevention, with the exception that they may often be more difficult to identify and to quantify in dollar terms. In contrast, the costs of the welfare damage of pollution are imposed directly on individuals in the form of foregone benefits without the intervening mechanism of explicit money outlays. In any form, however, the costs of waste disposal reduce the level of the net output of consumption goods for society.

The analysis in this section suggests two general observations. First, if society's economic goal is maximization of *net* output of goods and services, it should obviously attempt to minimize *total* waste disposal costs, given some level of output of final products. Government programs involving increases in pollution prevention costs make sense only if they cause pollution costs to decline by a greater amount. Similarly, actions involving higher pollution damage avoidance costs make sense for society as long as they reduce the welfare damage costs of pollution at least dollar for dollar. These obvious points are the rationale underlying the benefit-cost analysis presented in the next section of this chapter. Second, the maximization of output net of total pollution costs may call for a different composition of output than would maximization of output gross of such costs. This same point implies that the set of relative prices of outputs and inputs consistent with maximization of gross output will *not*, in general, be the same set of relative prices required to maximize net output. The latter point will be developed at length in Part 2 of the book.

A Simplified Benefit-Cost Analysis Example

Benefit-cost analysis, in the broadest sense, means a systematic evaluation of all the advantages and disadvantages of any actual or hypothetical change in society's production and consumption arrangements. Ideally, all forms of waste disposal costs would be taken into full account in any benefit-cost analysis of any hypothetical course of action that affects environmental problems. In a narrower sense, benefit-cost analysis is an evaluation of the benefits and costs of a government pollution prevention program. The benefits of such a program are the sum of the reduction of pollution costs—both pollution damage avoidance costs and the more elusive costs of pollution welfare damage. The costs of such a program are the total money outlays of the government, a measure of the value in alternative uses of the resources required to carry out the program.

For concreteness, let us consider the application of benefit-cost analysis to a highly simplified problem of determining the proper dimensions of a government pollution abatement program. We shall assume, to keep matters simple, that each additional dollar spent on this program results in one more unit of *output* of pollution abatement, that is, the removal of a given amount of pollutant from the environment. Assume, in addition, that the public generally values the first few units of abatement more highly than subsequent units. Such an assumption is most plausible in that the first few units of pollutant removed will likely significantly lessen health hazards in heavily populated areas, but the removal of the last units will only mean a reduction in annoyance and perhaps also small increments in aesthetic values. Given both these assumptions, we can draw the marginal social benefit (*MSB*) and marginal social cost (*MSC*) schedules for this pollution abatement program as shown in Figure 1–1. The horizontal *MSC* schedule corresponds to our

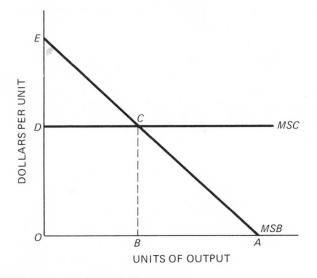

FIGURE 1–1.   Benefit-Cost Illustration.

assumption that every dollar of expenditure on the program yields the same number of units of pollution abatement. The *MSB* schedule represents the sum of all benefits to all households at each level of output of the program, that is, the sum of the amounts each household is willing to pay to remove one more unit of pollutant at a particular level of concentration of the pollutant. The downward slope of the *MSB* schedule reflects our assumption that the first units of abatement output yield more benefits per unit to consumers than do subsequent units. The reader can see immediately that the *MSB* and *MSC* schedules in this simple case are analogous to the demand and supply schedules in competitive private markets.

To concentrate our discussion on the basic principles of benefit-cost analysis, let us make the heroic assumption that the government has full knowledge of the exact quantitative dimensions of both the benefit/unit and cost/unit schedules.[4] From Figure 1–1, it is then immediately apparent, first, that this program is worth undertaking according to the benefit-cost criterion because total benefits (the area under the *MSB* schedule) exceed *total* costs (the area under the *MSC* schedule) at some feasible levels of output. That is, the *MSB* schedule is everywhere above the *MSC* schedule at some levels of output. Second, the optimum level of output is *OB*, because for any lesser level of output, the *additional* benefits of one more unit of output exceed the *additional* costs per unit, and for any greater level of output, the *additional* costs per unit exceed the *additional* benefits per unit. The latter point is especially important, for it contradicts the prevalent notion that society demands complete pollution abatement at all costs (a situation corresponding to output level *OA* in Figure 1–1). The hardheaded, unsentimental view of economists, codified in benefit-cost analysis, is that pollution abatement is justified only up to the point that the additional benefits of more abatement are at least as great as the additional costs per unit. If additional costs exceed additional benefits, as they do at output levels greater than *OB* in Figure 1–1, it implies that households do not value additional pollution abatement more highly than the opportunity costs of the consumption of other goods and services. The implications of this basic point will be developed more fully in Chapters 3 and 4.

Concluding Notes on Benefit-Cost Analysis

As we observed in the introduction to this topic, benefit-cost analysis, in the broad sense, is a term applied to a mode of thinking about social problems. Specifically, it means the systematic appraisal of all the advan-

---

[4] We shall explore the question of how the government may acquire such information in Chapter 4.

tages of alternative courses of action. In the narrow sense, however, benefit-cost analysis is a problem-solving tool, and it is used to help in the making of decisions about the best allocation of government resources. For example, a government economist might very well adopt the methodology described in the previous section and, with a great deal of hard and imaginative work, be able to estimate accurately the dimen- sions of benefits and costs.

The practical application of benefit-cost and analysis is subject to a number of serious limitations that should be made explicit. First, as we have already suggested, the government is, typically, at least partially ignorant of the dimensions of the benefits, and very likely also of the costs. In many cases, decision makers are not even able to specify the nature of the benefits and costs involved in a given program. In addi- tion, many benefits expected from a current budget outlay accrue to society only over various periods of time into the future and therefore must be discounted to make them commensurable with current costs. The choice of the correct discounting technique is one of the most difficult and controversial problems in economic theory, one that we shall take up again in Chapter 11. A closely related problem is that the benefits anticipated from a given government program are subject to various degrees of uncertainty, and, again, this factor complicates life for the benefit-cost analyst.

A more basic difficulty is that applied benefit-cost analysis is most useful in situations in which one problem in the allocation of resources can legitimately be treated as independent of the allocation of resources in general. That is, benefits and costs for a hypothetical course of action can most readily be estimated in a *ceteris paribus*, or, other things equal, framework. In our example of the previous section, the estimation of benefits and costs was a tractable problem in part because of our implicit assumption that the allocation of resources in society was given and only the one particular project under study was in question. Such a partial equilibrium framework is appropriate for some environmental problems but not for others. In general, economists in government will have to learn to cope with the biological, physical, and chemical interactions of the total environment before they can usefully apply benefit-cost analysis to serious environmental problems. To illustrate the nature of the prob- lem with a trival example, suppose that an environmentally naive econo- mist prepares a benefit-cost analysis of a government program intended to alleviate the pollution of a given body of water. If he is careless, he will consider only the outlays of the government as costs and only the value of the pollution abatement in the given body of water as benefits. But if the effect of the government program is simply to cause firms and households to switch from waste disposal into the body of water to waste disposal in some other environmental resource in the ecosystem or biome, this methodology will clearly produce absurd results. The problem of waste disposal costs must ultimately be viewed as a whole, but before this can be done, it will be necessary to understand the basic materials balance theory developed in Chapter 3.

Finally, the most fundamental problem with applied benefit-cost analysis is the analytical treatment of income distribution effects. In brief, a government official cannot limit himself to considering only aggregate benefits and costs. Instead, he must examine the difficult issue of who receives the benefits and who bears the costs of any given program. Because the gainers and the losers from any government action in general will not be identical, the government must determine the magnitude of net gains and losses among various groups and individuals and then somehow balance the desirability of the distributional effects against the pure economic efficiency effects revealed through straightforward benefit-cost analysis. For example, in Figure 1–1, if the optimal level of abatement OB is chosen, costs equal the rectangle $OBCD$ and benefits equal the trapezoid $OBCE$. The people bearing the costs are generally not identical to the people receiving the benefits. The former may be taxpayers and the latter those who live in the vicinity of the affected environmental media. It is not clear that such a redistribution of income is equitable. We shall discuss this point in more depth in Chapter 5.

We have raised several difficulties at this point without any attempt to resolve them. Throughout the rest of the book, however, they will come up repeatedly in several different contexts and will be given more extended treatment. None of the limitations of applied benefit-cost analysis count as arguments against the more broadly conceived benefit-cost approach to environmental problems. The benefit-cost framework is indispensable to the proper conception of these problems and enables economists to ask the right questions even if they are not yet able to provide the correct answers.

D. SUMMARY AND CONCLUSIONS

This is a book about the economics of environmental problems. The theme of the book is that environmental quality is a scarce, or economic, good. It follows then that the study of environmental problems can proceed along the general lines of analysis economists have successfully applied in the past to similar problems involving the allocation and distribution of scarce goods and services.

Pollution problems have always existed to some degree, but only recently has environmental quality become a generally scarce good. The transformation of environmental quality from a free to a scarce good is, paradoxically, the result of man's success in achieving economic plenty. The high levels of pollutants that strain the earth's natural absorptive capacity today are the other side of the coin of the high levels of output in economically advanced countries. The combination of the still higher levels of output anticipated in the future and the lack of effective political response to environmental problems leads us to the gloomy prediction that environmental quality will deteriorate still more in some respects. The major social force for the protection of the environment today is the modern conservation movement, a loosely organized number of individuals and organizations dedicated to the preservation of environmental quality.

Benefit-cost analysis is, in the broad sense of the term, a mode of thinking about problems in the allocation of resources. It is the systematic appraisal and evaluation of all the consequences of a contemplated course of action and of all relevant alternative courses of action.

Most environmental problems today can be linked to the waste disposal costs associated with high levels of production and consumption. Waste disposal costs are the sum of (1) private and public expenditures on the prevention of pollution; (2) private and public expenditures on the avoidance of pollution damage, once pollution has already occurred; and (3) the welfare damage of pollution. For any given level of gross output, society maximizes net output by minimizing total waste disposal costs. This point is the logical basis for a benefit-cost approach to government programs involving pollution prevention or pollution damage avoidance costs. Such costs make sense as long as they result in sufficiently large benefits to society in the form of reduced welfare damage costs of pollution.

Benefit-cost analysis, more narrowly conceived, is a useful problem-solving tool for government decision makers in circumstances where it is feasible and realistic to estimate dollar values for all the benefits and costs of a given government program. In general, the use of applied benefit-cost analysis is limited by a number of complicating factors, the foremost of which are the complex interrelationships between different facets of the environment and the proper analytical treatment of the distribution of benefits and costs.

QUESTIONS FOR DISCUSSION

1. Suppose a body of water A contains m parts per million of a substance X. Is A polluted? Suppose another body of water B contains n parts per million of a substance Y. Is B more or less polluted than A? What criteria are necessary for answering such questions?

2. Spokesmen for less-developed countries have been heard to say that they welcome pollution. What do they mean?

3. Do you think present pollution problems in the United States are serious enough to call for drastic measures such as an additional $100 billion a year in government pollution control expenditures? What kind of information would you want to have to answer this question with confidence?

4. Consider the outstanding pollution problems in your immediate area. Can you classify such problems under the categories (a) pollution prevention costs, (b) pollution damage avoidance costs, or (c) welfare damage costs?

5. Suppose that air quality at your place of residence greatly deteriorates. What costs would this development impose on your community? Outline a benefit-cost analysis of the main alternative courses of action open to the community in response to such a situation. Attempt to specify the various benefits and costs for each alternative. Who would receive the benefits, and who would bear the costs?

SELECTED REFERENCES

BARNETT, HAROLD J., "Population Change and Resources: Malthusianism and Conservation," in *Demographic and Economic Change in Developed Countries.* National Bureau of Economic Research. Princeton: Princeton. University Press, 1960. Contrasts between older and more modern views on the issue of the supply of natural resources.

DALES, J. H., *Pollution, Property and Prices.* Toronto: University of Toronto Press, 1968. An excellent, concise book on the economist's approach to environmental problems. Especially good on the subject of the welfare costs of pollution.

DUBOS, RENÉ, *A God Within.* New York: Charles Scribner's Sons, 1972. A philosophical treatment of the relationship of man to his environment.

Environmental Quality, Annual Report of the Council on Environmental Quality. Washington, D.C.: Government Printing Office, annual. A basic source for any student of the environment. Provides up-to-date information on the state of the nation's environment.

KRUTILLA, JOHN V., "Conservation Reconsidered," *American Economic Review,* LVIII, No. 4 (September 1967). A sophisticated, modern view of conservation.

STEINER, PETER O., "Public Expenditure Budgeting," in *The Economics of Public Finance,* Alan S. Blinder, Robert M. Solow, George F. Break, Peter O. Steiner, and Dick Netzer, Washington, D.C.: The Brookings Institution, 1974. Includes a critical review of benefit-cost analysis.

II

The
Basic Theory
of
Environmental
Economics

2

EFFICIENCY IN A PRIVATE MARKET ECONOMY

This is the first of four chapters of Part 2 of the book, which are devoted to theoretical aspects of environmental economics. The material in this part of the book applies relevant microeconomic theory to the problem of preserving and enhancing environmental quality. Special attention will be given to the theory of externalities of production and consumption. As we shall show, such externalities are intrinsic and pervasive in the functioning of a modern industrial economy and are the root cause of environmental pollution. Microeconomic theory can be adapted to incorporate such externalities and then be applied usefully to the analysis of environmental problems.

This chapter lays the groundwork for all of Part 2 with a discussion of the concept of efficiency in a private market economy. The first purpose of the analysis is to explain the desirable *social* properties of a system of private markets under ideal circumstances. The second purpose is to show why these desirable properties are not realized in a world in which there exist external costs of production and consumption. Chapter 3 then outlines alternative theoretical solutions to the environmental problems caused by extensive externalities: reliance on the common law; extensions of the private market system by more appropriate, comprehensive definitions of private property rights; and government fiscal measures designed to internalize external costs for firms and households by charging for the use of environmental resources. Chapter 4 then extends the analysis by expounding the concepts of common property, public goods, and materials balance. These concepts all help to explain why pollution and environmental degradation are inevitable by-products of economic growth in the absence of countervailing social policies. Chapter 5 concludes Part 2 of the book by going beyond efficiency questions to analyze the income distribution effects of alternative environmental policies and the comparative economic performance of the private market and government sectors.

Our intention, in these four chapters, is to provide a coherent theoretical base for the study of environmental economics. The discussion may appear, at first encounter, to be too abstract for the reader who is anxious to go immediately to the substance of environmental problems. In common with research workers in the natural and social sciences, however, we share the prejudice that a carefully worked out theory is a prerequisite for the successful study of a complex subject. The phenomenal successes achieved by implementation of the scientific method in other fields make a strong argument for explicit, rigorous formal theory as one ingredient of progress in solving complex environmental problems. The second basic ingredient—the subjecting of theoretical hypotheses to the tests of factual verification and the consequent refinement and elaboration of the existing body of theory—is still in a rudimentary state in the infant science of environmental economics, as will be painfully clear throughout the book.

This chapter proceeds according to the following outline: Section A begins with a discussion of the basic problem in modern welfare economics—the relationship of the interactions between individual markets in a private market system and of the efficiency of resource allocation from the viewpoint of all of society. We shall outline, very briefly, in this section, the traditional analysis leading to the conclusion that, under ideal circumstances, the private market system tends to produce optimal *social* results. The discussion in the text is at an introductory level; the Appendix to the chapter treats the subject in more depth. Section B then introduces the concept of *externalities* into the analysis and shows why this result no longer holds even in a system of perfectly competitive markets. Section C adds further qualifications to the analysis by showing the joint effects of externalities caused by environmental pollution and imperfect competition on the efficiency of a market system. Section D then outlines the limitations of the efficiency concept used in the preceding sections of the chapter. A final Section E summarizes the chapter.

A. EFFICIENCY AND PERFECT COMPETITION

This section discusses the *social*, or aggregate, implications of a hypothetical private market economy in which *individual* households and firms take into account only their own, individual welfares. Much of this discussion reviews material covered in the reader's first course in economics.

The *household*, consisting either of individuals or a larger family unit, is the ultimate consumer unit in society. We assume that each household attempts to maximize its welfare (often called utility), which is a positive function of its consumption of goods and services. In other-words, welfare goes up if consumption increases. The *firm*, although owned by households, is, for analytical purposes, best treated as an independent entity whose major goal is the maximization of profits. Firms hire productive services and combine them to produce the goods and services then sold to the ultimate consumers, households.

Firms and households interact as economic units in *markets*—the institutions through which potential buyers and sellers of goods and services deal with each other in the process of exchange. Markets exist both for *outputs* and *inputs*. Firms are suppliers of consumer goods and services to output markets, and households are demanders. In contrast, households supply the services of their labor and capital to firms in input markets, and firms are the demanders of these services. Consumer *expenditures* in output markets are the *revenues* of firms. Wages, salaries, dividends, rents, and other payments by firms in return for household labor and capital services in input markets are the *costs* of firms and the *incomes* of households. *Profits* (losses) are simply the algebraic difference between firm revenues and costs.

Markets may be characterized as *perfectly competitive* if no buyer or seller can affect the market price by varying its own individual supply or demand. Roughly speaking, a market will be perfectly competitive if the number of potential buyers and sellers is sufficiently large to ensure that no one household or firm can affect the market price by varying the amount it demands or offers. If a market is perfectly competitive, it follows from the above definition that every household and firm is a *price taker* in the sense that it can buy or sell all it wants at the going market price.

As explained in every introductory course in economics, equilibrium prices in individual, perfectly competitive markets are determined by the impersonal forces of market supply and demand. In a state of *general equilibrium* in a hypothetical system of perfectly competitive markets, the prices of all goods and services in output and input markets alike are determined simultaneously, with complex interactions occurring between different individual markets, some of them apparently completely un-related. Abstracting from the complex dynamic processes that bring about price adjustments in interrelated markets, let us concentrate on a hypothetical economy in which all adjustments have already occurred and prices in all markets have attained their equilibrium values. That is, we assume that the level of technology, tastes, and other underlying variables affecting the supply and demand of all goods and services re-main unchanged and do not disturb the state of general equilibrium.

Figure 2–1 illustrates industry and firm equilibrium under perfect competition. Market price P_X for good or service X is determined by demand and supply, as shown in the industry half of the diagram. Each firm in the industry takes this price as given and must determine how much to produce. A simple, crucially important rule summarizes the firm's profit-maximizing decision under perfectly competitive conditions. The firm will produce a good or service at a level at which the selling price just covers its incremental or marginal cost of production.[1]

The reasoning underlying this basic relationship is depicted in the firm half of Figure 2–1. The firm in Figure 2–1 faces a market price of

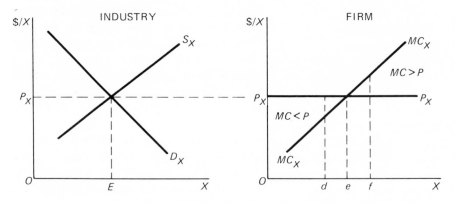

FIGURE 2–1.   Industry and Firm Equilibrium in Perfect Competition.

[1] Over the long run, the selling price must also cover the average, or per unit, cost of production of the firm. This is necessary for long-run equilibrium because otherwise firms will leave the industry for better alternative uses of their resources.

P_X. Note that the horizontal line P_X is the firm's demand curve, which is the geometric representation of our assumption that a firm in a perfectly competitive market can sell as much as it wishes at the going market price without affecting the price. The firm's marginal cost (MC) of production must be increasing at a level of output that is a small fraction of total industry output in order for perfect competition to be viable in the industry. If such were not the case, it would be impossible for many small firms to survive and compete with larger firms, and the industry would be made up of large firms each of which has some control over market price. Thus, the upward slope of the MC curve in Figure 2–1 is necessary for consistency with our assumption of perfect competition.

Given the assumptions stated above, the profit-maximizing firm in Figure 2–1 will produce at an output of Oe units, where $P_X = MC_X$. At any lower level of output, say Od units, $MC_X < P_X$, and each additional unit of X the firm sells yields it a net profit of $(P_X - MC_X)$ per unit. Similarly, a firm will not produce at a higher level of output than Oe units, such as Of, because at this level of output, $MC_X > P_X$, and the firm loses $(MC_X - P_X)$ on each additional unit it sells. Only at output level Oe, where $P_X = MC_X$, does the firm maximize profits. Stated more carefully with proper attention to the internal logic of the theory, the assumption that a firm maximizes profits in a perfectly competitive market *implies* the important result that production of any good or service will be at level at which

$$P = MC.$$

The result derived above holds for every firm in a perfectly competitive economy. That is, every firm in the economy produces its outputs to a point where $P = MC$.

The economic theory underlying the analysis above is somewhat subtle and requires further elaboration. Each firm is assumed to be a price taker. Because the quantity it can produce is small relative to total market supply, it adjusts the quantity it produces to whatever price obtains at the moment in the market and does so without affecting this price. The aggregate of all firms in the industry behaving in this way, however, determines the total market supply for the good or service. The total market supply, together with total market demand, determines the price that clears the market in an equilibrium situation. Each individual firm (and each individual household) is a passive price taker, but the aggregate of the passive behavior of all firms (households) actively helps, together with demand (supply), to determine the equilibrium market price and the total quantity produced (consumed).

Social Welfare in a Perfectly Competitive Economy

What is the meaning of the concept *efficiency* for a whole society? An individual firm or household is said to be efficient if it maximizes output or consumption for a given level of resources or if it minimizes its expenditure of resources to attain a given level of output or consumption. Intuitively, a whole economy may be called efficient if it too can maximize some kind of aggregation of individual welfares for the given amount of resources available to the whole society at any point in time. Individual welfares, in turn, depend on individual household evaluations of the consumption goods and services each is able to consume.[2] Thus, social efficiency is not measured by aggregating physical quantities of goods and services, such as tons or yards, but rather by somehow aggregating the subjective values placed on different goods and services by individual consumer units. Thus, in our usage (maximum) economic efficiency for a society is identical with a term we prefer to use, *maximum social welfare*, or MXSW.

MXSW can be defined tentatively as a situation in which it is impossible, even conceptually, to make any readjustment of production or consumption arrangements that would make even one household better off without making some other household worse off.[3] As long as such a "costless" readjustment can be effected in a society, it has not attained a state of MXSW. This concept of MXSW is usually termed a *Pareto Optimum*, after the famous Italian sociologist Vilfredo Pareto (1848–1923).

With the results we have already derived, it is possible to show that a state of general equilibrium in a perfectly competitive market economy satisfies the necessary conditions for MXSW. To demonstrate this proposition, it is necessary is to prove that the consumption and production relationships established by a perfectly competitive market system are such that it is not possible to make any household better off without making any other household worse off. The full, rigorous proof of these conditions is beyond the scope of this book, but can be found in one of the more advanced texts cited at the end of the chapter. We shall limit our discussion here to the relationship between MXSW and the $P = MC$ result of a perfectly competitive market system. Recall the result established previously that all profit-maximizing firms will produce a level of output at which the MC of the last unit produced will

---

[2] A more complete treatment of this subject would include the value of leisure time, as well as consumption, in individual and social welfares.

[3] We should note immediately that the definition of MXSW in the text is an overly narrow one, and we present it only on the grounds of expository convenience. In Section D we shall reconsider the concept of MXSW within a broader perspective.

be just equal to the market price of its output. To see intuitively the relationship between this profit-maximizing rule for an individual private firm and MXSW, suppose that, for any reason, $MC \neq P$ for some commodity. If, for example, $MC > P$, we could say that the last unit produced of the commodity requires the use of productive input services of greater value than the market price, which is a measure of the subjective value placed on the last unit consumed of that commodity by all households. Therefore, we could say that from the point of view of the whole economy, too much of the commodity is being produced, suggesting that production be cut back to release some of the productive input services employed by the firm for use by some other firm in the production of some more socially valuable commodity. The perfectly competitive market system performs millions of such *benefit-cost* tests simultaneously to determine the optimal levels of production for all goods and services in the economy. These arguments lead to the conclusion that $MC = P$ is a necessary condition for MXSW as well as the outcome of the process of profit-maximizing behavior by individual firms under perfect competition. The appendix to this chapter discusses other necessary conditions for MXSW and shows these are also satisfied in general equilibrium in a perfectly competitive market economy.

To summarize, an idealized perfectly competitive market economy may be viewed as a completely decentralized mechanism that attains the social end of maximum economic efficiency. Each household and firm strives only to maximize its own economic well-being, with the aggregate of all such individual behavior reflected on opposite sides of all output and input markets in supply and demand forces. The impersonal factors of supply and demand interact in the markets of the economy to determine a set of relative output and input prices that satisfy the necessary conditions for MXSW. Adam Smith, the first economist to understand this remarkable social result of apparently uncoordinated private individual behavior, stated his version of the process most eloquently:

> . . . every individual necessarily labours to render the annual revenue of the society as great as he can. He generally, indeed, neither intends to promote the public interest, nor knows how much he is promoting it . . . he intends only his own security; . . . he intends only his own gain, and he is in this, as in many other cases, led by an invisible hand to promote an end which was not part of his intention. Nor is it always worse for the society that it was no part of it. By pursuing his own interest he frequently promotes that of the society more effectually than when he really intends to promote it.[4]

---

[4] Adam Smith, *The Wealth of Nations* (New York: Random House, Modern Library Edition, 1937), p. 423.

B. EXTERNALITIES, SOCIAL COSTS, AND EFFICIENCY

Economists have long recognized that the private market system often produces undesirable *spillover* effects on man's environment.[5] Typical and too familiar examples of such spillover effects are the noxious smoke and polluted water emissions of modern industrial plants. In such circumstances, the technical nature of the production process generates an *output* effect distinct from the final marketed product of the firm. The spillover effects of modern industrial production result in deteriorating environmental quality, an output that the firm does not, and, of course, could not, sell. On the contrary, households and other firms affected by the pollutant spillovers experience real opportunity costs in many different forms and would be willing to pay varying amounts if they could effectively end or lessen the firm's polluting activities.

We define any costs that are additional to the costs resulting from the production outlays of the firm as *external*, or spillover, costs. *Total social costs* (social costs, for brevity) are defined as the sum of the private costs of the firm and any external costs. The use of the word *external* implies that some costs do not accrue to the firm that produces the good but are imposed on all of society or, at least, on a subset of the households or firms in a society. Such costs are outside the market system and are not reflected in relative market prices.

Examples of external costs are easy to find in any modern industrial economy. The paper firm that pollutes a river and destroys the game fish population imposes external costs on fishermen, boaters, and swimmers; so does the chemical plant that plagues the local community with constant stenches. The residential developer who denudes the landscape and constructs row on row of similarly built homes may impose psychic costs on many individuals by affronting their esthetic sensitivities. The individual who misses a number of workdays each year due to illnesses caused by impure air bears a personal external cost, equal to his lost wages. Society, which loses the worker's production for the workdays lost bears an additional external cost, equal to the net difference between the worker's average product and his wages over the relevant time period. Even the charcoal cookout of the suburbanite that soils his neighbor's drying laundry involves a (perhaps) small external cost. The common theme in all of these hypothetical situations is that firms or

---

[5] The classic treatment of this problem is given in A. C. Pigou, *Economics of Welfare* (4th ed.) (London: Macmillan & Co., Ltd., 1960). The term *spillover* indicates that the full effects of production or consumption are not confined to the firms or households directly involved but spill over onto third parties. For a modern, rigorous definition of externalities, see the Baumol and Oates reference cited at the end of Chapter 10, pp. 16–18.

households other than those responsible for the initial act of production or consumption suffer uncompensated monetary or psychic costs.

The Economics of Externalities

A simple, hypothetical example best illustrates the economic effects of an external diseconomy. To begin, let us assume the existence of a small river valley ecosystem in which the land along the upstream portion of the river is unsuitable for cultivation and, initially, lies idle. The downstream land is owned by a single farmer who uses the river water to irrigate his corn fields. The corn yields an average return that is sufficient to keep the land from being used in any alternative use and to keep the farmer from changing his occupation. Now, let us suppose that the upstream land is acquired by a textile producer who proceeds to utilize the river water as a waste disposal resource and, in doing so, degrades the water quality to a point that lessens its productivity for the farmer downstream. We may assume that the decline in the quality of the river water decreases corn yields and may even force the farmer out of the corn production business. The assumed circumstances in this highly simplified example present a relatively unambiguous case of a readily identifiable external diseconomy of production in a private market economy.

Some preliminary general observations may be useful before proceeding to a more detailed formal analysis. Society gains, on the one hand, by the additional textile production and loses, on the other, by the decrease in the farmer's corn crop. The net social gain from the textile production in a fully employed economy is equal to the excess of the value of the textile products over the value of the factors of production used by the textile firm in their best alternative uses. The net social loss associated with the textile production is equal to the decrease in the value of the corn crop net of the value of the land and the farmer's labor in their best alternative uses. (If we make the extreme assumptions that the farmer is driven out of the corn business and that the land is valueless in all other uses and that the farmer becomes unemployed, then the value of the loss is simply identical to the full value of the corn crop.) The external diseconomy of textile production (literally a spillover effect, in this example) is easily measured in any event as the farmer's net income loss. Note that, in this example, the net social gain from the partial or full substitution from corn to textile production is not necessarily greater than zero. The random factor of the upstream geographic location of the textile plant precludes a market test of whether such a substitution makes the most efficient use of the water resource and yields a net social benefit.

The possibility that the switch from corn to textile production results in a net social loss is a form of (potential) market failure. Such a possibility would not arise, of course, if the corn farm and the textile plant were owned by the same profit-maximizing firm. A rational economic calculation by a conglomerate corn farm-textile firm would determine whether the substitution of textile for corn production was, or was not, profitable. Such a calculation would yield the desirable private market solution insuring that river water, like all other productive resources, is allocated to its most socially efficient use. Our assumption of two independent firms is clearly the villain in preventing the invisible hand of profit-maximizing behavior in a competitive market system from allocating resources most efficiently. Also implicit in this example is the crucial assumption that no market exists for the sale and purchase of water rights (that is, that the farmer cannot contract with the textile producer *not* to pollute). This last assumption ensures that the textile producer has no rational (gain versus loss) incentive to include in his cost and profit calculations the amount of external costs he imposes on the farmer as a consequence of his mode of production.

The assumptions in this example are obviously too restrictive to yield insights into more complex real world environmental problems. The possibilities of a viable private market for water rights or various kinds of government intervention in water resource use by private parties would make our simple example much richer and more generally applicable. For the time being, however, we shall postpone consideration of these possibilities and other complexities until Chapters 3 and 4 and shall pursue, instead, the resource allocation implications of externalities in an otherwise ideal private market system.

Price and Quantity Effects of External Diseconomies

As argued in Section A, the goal of profit maximization leads perfectly competitive firms in equilibrium to produce at a level of output at which price equals marginal cost (Figure 2-1). This equality between price and marginal cost is a crucial link in the chain of logic that concludes with the identification of maximum social economic welfare with the outcome of a system of competitive private markets. We are now interested in reexamining the validity of this result once externalities are introduced.

In most contexts, the marginal cost schedule of a firm represents all the additional costs incurred to produce a given unit of output. The implicit assumption is that all costs are borne by the firm and thus may be termed private costs. Given this assumption, then in Figure 2-2 the full incremental costs of production could be shown as the *marginal private cost (MPC) schedule*. Profit-maximizing behavior by the firm then

FIGURE 2-2. Equilibrium of the Firm Reconsidered.

yields the socially optimal output of Oe units. The MPC schedule includes the incremental costs to the firm of labor, materials, and capital.
If these are the only variable costs of production, then MPC is identical
to the full marginal costs of production for the whole economy. By em-
phasizing the word *private* in the firm's marginal cost schedule, we intend
to indicate the possibility that other costs of production may exist. If
we use Figure 2-2 to represent the textile producer in our example, we
know that the MPC understates the full variable costs of its textile production. The net income loss of the farmer is an additional cost from the
standpoint of the whole society, but this cost is not included in the MPC
schedule of the textile firm.

     Thus, we can conceive of another marginal cost schedule that in-
cludes all the costs of textile production, both private and external. We
shall call this alternative the *marginal social cost (MSC) schedule.*
As drawn in Figure 2-2 in accordance with the assumption of our simple
example, it lies above the MPC schedule at every quantity. The vertical
difference between the MPC and the MSC schedules at any given quantity measures the external costs (that is, the farmer's net income loss) per
extra unit of output of textile production. For example, the MPC of
producing the Of^{th} unit of textile is P_2 dollars, but the MSC of this unit
is P_1 dollars. The difference, $P_1 - P_2$ dollars, is the marginal external cost
of producing the Of^{th} unit of textiles. As the two schedules are drawn in

Figure 2–2, the marginal external cost of textile production is a constant per unit of output and does not depend on the level of output. (Geometrically, the vertical distance between the MSC and MPC schedules is equal at all levels of output.) Probably a more realistic assumption is that higher levels of textile production cause at least proportional increases in water pollution with more than proportional damage to the fertility of the downstream land. Under such circumstances, the MPC and MSC schedules would begin from the same point on the vertical axis (at a zero level of output of textiles) and would diverge at higher levels of output. The limit of such a case would be the level of textile production at which water pollution destroyed the whole corn crop. However, the precise relationship between the MPC and MSC schedules does not affect the basic results we are attempting to establish here.

As we are assuming that all markets are perfectly competitive, we know that the textile producer cannot affect the going market price, shown in Figure 2–2 as the horizontal line P_T. Because the manager of the textile firm takes into account only the firm's private costs, he maximizes profits by producing an output of Oe units, where $P_T = MPC$. From society's standpoint, however, all costs—private and external—should be accounted for in determining optimal levels of output. Ideally, the price-marginal cost equality should occur at the output level where $P_T = MSC$, or On in Figure 2–2. This reasoning allows us to conclude that the excess of ne units between the private optimal level of production Oe and social optimal level On represents overproduction of textiles. Society would be better off with On units of textile production than with Oe units because the resources used to produce the last ne units have greater net productive value in other employments. The same reasoning implies, of course, that some other good or goods in the economy are being underproduced, or not produced at all. Thus, the first result of our analysis is simply that an external diseconomy in an otherwise ideal competitive market system distorts the optimal allocation of resources; the quantities produced of some goods are too great, and this implies that the quantities produced of other goods are too small.

The distortion in resource allocation seems trivial in our example as developed thus far because we have assumed that only one small firm's production causes external diseconomies and that the marginal changes in output associated with this one firm's activities have no effects on relative market prices. We shall now extend the analysis one step further by assuming that all textile firms cause exactly the same degree of external diseconomies in their production activities. This assumption permits us to shift our analysis from the firm to the industry level. We may suppose, for example, that the state of textile technology requires water as an input and that the use of the water in textile production degrades its quality. In every case, the pollution discharges of textile producers impose monetary or psychic costs on other firms or households. For example, the discharges of some textile producers may fully or partially destroy commercial fishing grounds. In other cases, the discharges may degrade water quality to the point that downstream communities are forced to spend greater amounts on water treatment plants just to continue to provide their residents with potable water. Or the water pollution caused by textile firms may degrade downstream water used for recreational purposes. With our assumption about the similarity of the polluting activities of all textile firms, we may represent the cost conditions of all textile firms in the economy by the MPC and MSC schedules in Figures 2–2.[6]

The aggregate of all textile firms with similar marginal cost conditions can be summarized in the industry supply schedule. The MPC schedule of each textile firm is its supply schedule at all price levels that exceed average variable costs.[7] The textile industry supply schedule is simply the horizontal summation of the MPC schedules of all the individual textile firms. For example, if each firm produces Oe units at a price of P_T, as in Figure 2–2, then n identical firms will produce $n \times Oe$ units at this price or OM units of output for the entire industry. The reader should see intuitively that any point on the industry supply schedule can be obtained conceptually by adding the quantities that each firm would offer for sale at the relevant price. Such a supply schedule is drawn for the textile industry as its (*private*) *supply schedule* (*PS*) in Figure 2–3.

A similar summation of the MSC schedule of all textile firms is also shown in Figure 2–3 and is labeled SS, short for *social supply schedule*. The SS curve lies above the PS, reflecting the difference between marginal private and social costs for all firms in the industry. The vertical distance between these two industry schedules is the aggregate of the external costs imposed on society for any given level of output by the industry. The reader should note that although the PS curve could be obtained by observing the supply response on the textile industry to different prices, the SS curve locus is dependent on extraneous, nonmarket information. According to our assumptions, firms base all their behavior on private costs alone and are ignorant or indifferent about the external costs of their activities, as reflected in the SS curve.

The PS and the SS schedules, together with the industry demand

---

[6] A more realistic assumption is that textile production results in varying degrees of discrepancy between marginal private and social costs. Our assumption of homogeneous firms with respect to external diseconomies of production is based on simplicity of exposition and does not affect the main line of our analysis. All that is really necessary for our purposes is that a large number of textile firms impose varying amounts of external costs on others.

[7] If the reader is not familiar with this point, he should consult one of the economics texts cited at the end of the chapter.

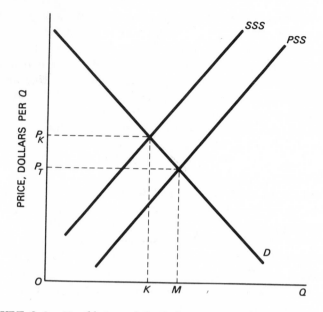

FIGURE 2–3.   Equilibrium of the Industry Reconsidered.

schedule (D) in Figure 2–3, can be used to analyze the full effects of the external diseconomies of textile production on relative prices and resource allocation. The demand schedule intersects the private supply schedule in Figure 2–3 at a price of P_T and a total quantity of OM. The equilibrium industry price P_T is the going market price that faces each textile firm in the industry, as shown in Figure 2–2. Total industry output of OM is just equal to the sum of all firm outputs of Oe in Figure 2–2.

According to our previous assumptions, the SS schedule, not the PS schedule, reflects the social marginal costs of textile output. Embodied in the SS schedule is the value of the foregone corn production and all the other external costs imposed on firms and households in society by textile producers. If SS were the industry supply schedule in Figure 2–3, the level of industry output would be OK units and the market price would be P_K. Comparing this result with the actual industry price and output in equilibrium, we can conclude that the private market for textile leads to too high a production of textiles (by $KM = OM - OK$) units and too low a price (P_T instead of P_K). Also implicit in this conclusion is that some other industries are precluded from producing enough. Society, as a whole, would be better off if textile firms behaved as if SS and not PS were the industry supply schedule. At an output level of OK, pollution costs are reduced to a socially optimal, but not zero level; they will be equal to industry output (OK) times the difference between SS and PS.

As a final observation, we may note that in the absence of any government intervention the external diseconomies of textile production lead, via the invisible hand of the profit incentive, to very visible pollution and the burdensome social costs due to pollution. This conclusion holds, remember, even under the assumption of an otherwise ideal private market system. No evil or sinister motives need be ascribed to the producers in our example in order to explain the malfunctioning of private markets. Given the monetary reward structure of a private market system, the manager of a textile firm in our example simply makes the rational economic calculations required to minimize costs of production that firm managers in all other industries also make. But least cost in the private market framework means least cost to the firm, not necessarily to society. If external costs of production exist but firms are not required to pay the costs of compensating those who suffer from the externalities, then such costs do not enter the rational profit-maximizing calculations of managers. Any individual manager who exhibited *social concern* and did attempt to pay the external costs imposed on others by his firm would be placing himself at a competitive disadvantage relative to other firms and would be risking his own job at the hands of angry stockholders. Indeed, in many cases, it is possible that the manager does not even know that his firm is responsible for generating external costs, and it is generally true that he does not know the exact dimensions of such costs. In later chapters, we shall emphasize methods that provide profit and loss incentives for managers of firms to take into full account their external costs of production, in much the same way that the private market system forces them to account for the private costs of production.

C. MARKET STRUCTURE, EFFICIENCY, AND EXTERNALITIES

Our discussion of the economic effects of externalities in Section B assumed perfect competition in all markets. But what difference does it make to the analysis if we account for the existence of substantial monopoly power in the real world?

Imperfect competition is said to exist if any buyer or seller has *some* power to affect market price. Imperfection of competition and monopoly power are matters of degree, varying greatly among different markets. General Motors, with about half of total sales in the United States automobile market, can obviously influence the price of automobiles. It cannot, despite its best efforts, sell all the automobiles it would like at its established market price. To sell more automobiles, it would have to cut its price, an action it does not ordinarily deem to be most profitable. On the other hand, the local neighborhood supermarket usually has a lesser degree of monopoly power over the prices of various food items, because of the existence of many alternative food retailers in the neighborhood. If the degree of monopoly power in a market is only slight, the assumption of perfect competition is often a useful abstraction from the details of actual market circumstances. In many important problems, the monopoly power of just one or a few buyers and sellers is too significant to ignore, making it necessary for economists to revise theoretical analysis based on the assumption of perfect competition.

Imperfect Competition

The existence of imperfect competition significantly modifies our conclusion in Section A concerning the efficiency results of profit-maximizing behavior in a perfectly competitive private market economy. The fundamental problem is that, with imperfect competition, prices will no longer equal marginal costs. Consider the extreme case of a single supplier—*a monopolist*—who is the only available source of a particular product.[8] The condition that a supplier has monopoly power can be given precise meaning in the assumption that the firm faces a downward-sloping demand curve for its output. That is, the demand curve facing the monopoly firm looks like the one in Figure 2–4 showing that the firm can sell more to its customers only at lower prices. In contrast, under perfect competition, the individual supplier faces a horizontal, or perfectly elastic, demand curve (Figure 2–2); that is, the firm can sell all it wants at the going market price.

We assume that the basic motivation of a firm under monopoly is the same as under perfect competition, the maximization of profits. Therefore, the general rule for determining the output of the firm does not change; the firm should produce and sell a quantity such that the incremental or marginal revenue derived from the last unit of output sold is at least as much as the incremental or marginal cost of producing that last unit.

Given the circumstances that the supplier must, in general, sell all his output at one price to all customers, the profit-maximizing firm with some degree of monopoly power must take into account the fact that an increase of one unit in the amount it sells will always yield it an additional revenue less than the new (lower) market price. This will be the case because in order to sell one more unit of output, the market price

---

[8] This is the exact opposite of the example of the perfectly competitive firm of Sections A and B.

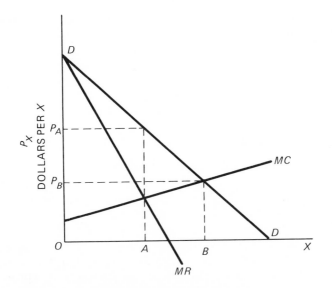

FIGURE 2–4.   Equilibrium of the Monopolist.

the firm charges its customers for *all* items must fall to the new, lower price. The additional revenue need not even be greater than zero. If demand conditions are such that a seller can sell nine units at ten dollars a unit, but can sell ten units at only nine dollars a unit, then the incremental revenue from the tenth unit is zero, because total revenue remains constant at ninety dollars. Thus, in Figure 2–4, we draw an incremental or marginal revenue curve (MR) that lies always below the demand curve, reflecting the fact that a movement down and to the right on the demand curve always adds less to total revenue than the going market price. We can see from Figure 2–4 that the profit-maximizing output level for the firm will be OA, where $MR = MC$, and the selling price in equilibrium, found on the demand curve, will be P_A. The monopoly will not produce an output of OB, where $P_B = MC$, as under perfect competition, for to do so would *spoil the market* and reduce its profits from the maximum possible at output OA. For every unit produced beyond a level of OA, $MC > MR$, which means that the firm loses money on each additional unit sold and that total profits fall. In fact, as Figure 2–4 is drawn, before the firm reaches an output of OB, MR becomes negative, which means that even total revenue falls.

This brief investigation of the implications of imperfect competition is sufficient to give the conclusion that, in general, $P \neq MC$, in contrast to perfect competition. This results because firms with some degree of monopoly power over price will restrict their output below perfect competition levels in order to maximize profits.

Private monopoly power is a fact of life in any economy with a private sector, and much of it is inherent in certain technological and social conditions. The economic rationale for government intervention in a private market economy rests partly on the grounds that, under such circumstances, the private economy, itself, cannot achieve an acceptably efficient solution to some economic problems.

Monopoly and Externalities

We have now developed two separate problems that will distort the efficiency results of private markets. First, external costs cause price to fall below the true marginal social cost of production, and the resulting level of output is too high compared to a situation where all production costs are paid for by the firm. Second, the presence of imperfect competition, as we have just seen, results in a price above marginal costs and an output below that which would be forthcoming from a perfectly competitive industry. The question that suggests itself is, What if both conditions are present simultaneously? The analysis above showed that the two effects work in opposite directions and will tend to offset each other. In theory, either effect could dominate the other. However, to determine which effect is stronger becomes a difficult empirical problem.

Suppose, for example, that a monopolistic firm generates pollution and imposes external costs on society (Figure 2–5). As before, profit-maximizing behavior leads the monopolist to produce where private

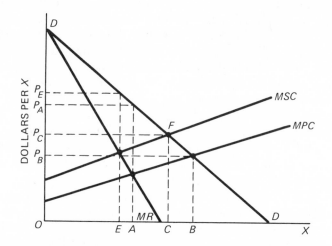

FIGURE 2–5. A Polluting Monopolist.

marginal costs equal marginal revenue at an output of A and a price of P_A.

However, the marginal social cost schedule (MSC) implies that the efficient outcome for society occurs at point F where price equals the true marginal costs of production, including all external costs. This would yield an output of C at a price P_C.

There are two distortions that prevent an efficient result in this market: first, the presence of monopoly and second, the existence of external costs. Correction of both problems is necessary in order to obtain the socially efficient outcome. Economists call such a situation the problem of *the second best*. If either one of the two distortions is corrected—but not both—society will not necessarily be better off in terms of efficiency than if the situation remained unchanged.

In Figure 2–5, suppose a vigorous antitrust campaign is conducted by the Justice Department and competition is restored to this industry but nothing is done to internalize the external costs. Output will expand and price will fall, which is the desired direction of change, i.e., toward C and P_C from A and P_A. However, the correction will be too great. Output will increase beyond C to B and price will fall lower than P_C to P_B. Whether output A is more efficient than B—given that both are inefficient relative to C—is an empirical problem and cannot be answered by theory alone. The conclusion is that in the presence of external costs leaving the monopoly alone may be more efficient than bringing about more competition.

Alternatively, suppose the Environmental Protection Agency institutes an output tax to induce the monopolist to restrict output but does nothing about the presence of monopoly. If the tax per unit of output were exactly equal to the external cost per unit of output, the monopolist would behave as if the marginal social cost schedule were identical to the private marginal cost schedule. The new equilibrium position would be where marginal revenue equals marginal social costs, resulting in a lower level of output E and a higher price P_E compared to the original monopoly position. But an output of E is clearly socially less efficient than output A since it lies even farther away from the most efficient output level, C. Thus, in this situation, given that nothing is done about the monopoly condition, it would be more efficient, from society's point of view, not to internalize the external costs.

In general, the critical factor in determining whether any single course of action in isolation is better or worse than doing nothing depends on the external costs per unit of output relative to the monopolist's margin—the difference between price and private marginal costs. In the example of Figure 2–5, the monopoly margin exceeds the per unit external costs. However, this is just one of several possible situations, and different, but no more clear-cut, conclusions would result from other assumptions.

To summarize the analysis in this section, with the simultaneous presence of both monopoly and external costs, it is no longer unambiguously true that more competition would result in greater social efficiency. In addition, while it would always be desirable to correct for both monopoly and external costs, it cannot be presumed that a more efficient outcome would occur if either condition alone were corrected.

Unfortunately, this problem is more than a textbook complication. It would appear that the joint presence of monopoly and external costs characterizes a large part of the U.S. economy. Table 2–1 lists recent data on expenditures for pollution control equipment by industry and a measure of each industry's monopoly power—the concentration ratio. The concentration ratio is the percent of an industry's market sales which are accounted for by the industry's largest four firms.[9] This ratio is conventionally regarded as a rough measure of monopoly power. While pollution control expenditures—pollution prevention costs as defined in

TABLE 2–1   AIR AND WATER POLLUTION ABATEMENT CAPITAL EXPENDITURES AND INDUSTRY CONCENTRATION

Industry	1973 Expenditures (millions $)	As a Percentage of Total Capital Expenditures	Concentration Ratio
Primary metals	814	23.38	66
Blast furnace, steelworks	230	16.35	80
Petroleum	555	10.26	67
Chemical	416	9.62	74
Paper	355	18.75	45
Transportation	170	5.55	81
Motor vehicles	143	6.37	94
Aircraft	20	3.76	90
Food and beverage	152	4.98	55
Stone, clay, and glass	144	9.58	67
Electrical machinery	129	4.55	57
Machinery (except electrical)	80	2.30	53
Rubber	48	3.06	50
Textile	29	3.68	42

Source: P. Asch and J. J. Seneca, "Monopoly and External Costs: An Application of Second-Best Theory to the Automobile Industry," *Journal of Environmental Economics and Management*, Vol. 3 (April 1976). Reprinted with the permission of the journal and authors.

[9] For example, in Table 2–1, the motor vehicle industry is the most heavily concentrated industry listed with a ratio of 94 percent.

Chapter 1—are not measures of external costs, they do suggest public concern with the potential externalities of these industries; that is, public policy has required these expenditures in order to reduce pollution damages.

Table 2–1 indicates that several important U.S. industries are both highly concentrated and have provoked public policies to control their waste emissions—e.g., motor vehicles, primary metals, petroleum. These industries are characterized by the joint problems portrayed in Figure 2–5, the coexistence of monopoly elements and external costs of pollution.

The overall effect of monopoly *cum* externalities of pollution on efficiency cannot be determined without a case by case empirical examination of the relative extent of both problems. Theory suggests, however, that isolated attempts to improve efficiency may not succeed and that there is a need to coordinate both environmental policy and antitrust activities.

D. PRIVATE MARKETS AND SOCIAL WELFARE: DIFFICULTIES OF INTERPRETATION

Section A reached strong and unambiguous conclusions about the relationship between MXSW and a private market economy. Sections B and C introduced some important qualifications to this result. The purpose of this section is to indicate to the reader some additional limitations of the foregoing analysis. We shall take up in turn three important problems left out of the previous discussions in order to reduce to manageable proportions the complexity of the analysis.

Dynamic Problems and Uncertainty

The microeconomic theory expounded in the previous sections of this chapter is purely static. The analysis is timeless in that it says nothing about dynamic movements of supply and demand conditions over time, such as the introduction of new products, the systematic development of more advanced technology, and sweeping changes in tastes for consumer goods and services. Although we shall not attempt to do so here, it is possible to develop more fully traditional microeconomic theory beyond a purely static framework. Intricate formal theories of markets extending over time have been formulated in a branch of economics called capital theory. The determination of the price called an interest rate in a dynamic market economy turns out to be a problem formally analogous to the determination of the price of apples in a static market economy. In perfectly competitive markets, for commodities to be exchanged either in the present or at some specified time in the future, demand and supply forces serve equally well as the proximate explanatory variables. Useful work in capital theory has done much to clarify aspects of saving and investment behavior, as well as other important topics that require explicit theoretical recognition of the fact of the passage of time.

For our purposes, however, it is sufficient to note only that the link between even a perfectly competitive market economy and the attainment of MXSW holds in a dynamic setting only under strong assumptions, the foremost of which is perfect *certainty* about the course of the future. Once we admit that the future is uncertain, the identity between general equilibrium in a perfectly competitive economy and MXSW cannot be logically demonstrated. In fact, it becomes difficult even to specify the meaning of social welfare in an uncertain, dynamic world. To mention just one problem, a useful definition of social welfare in a dynamic world must include not just the present consumption of existing households but also the consumption of future households, which may include individuals not yet born. Another problem in treating the future theoretically in an uncertain world is that markets for certain essential insurance services in such a world are not viable, so that even individuals who wish to do so cannot deal effectively with all uncertain contingencies. Other, similar complexities are still the subject of much dispute in capital theory. In such a world, government intervention in the private market economy may be necessary to achieve a socially desirable time configuration of production and consumption.

The Problem of the Equity of Income Distribution

In Section A, we defined the concept of maximum social welfare (MXSW) conventionally as a situation in which it is impossible to change the allocation of production or consumption in any way that would increase the economic welfare of any household without decreasing the economic welfare of any other household. As we have already noted, however, the implicit conception of social economic welfare embodied in the conventional definition of MXSW is exceedingly narrow; it is tenable only if the problem of the *equity* of the distribution of income among the households in a society is ignored. Once explicit social concern with the distribution of economic welfare among households is admitted, it becomes immediately evident that government intervention will be necessary in some degree to improve on the outcome of a free, private market economy.

The reader will recall from a first course in economics the simple circular flow model of market relationships in a market economy. The incomes of households are the costs of firms—the payments by firms to purchase the productive labor and capital services owned by households. Each household's money income level is determined in a pure market economy solely by the quantities of productive services it is willing and able to sell to firms and the input market prices of these services. The money income of a household will be higher the more capital services it owns and has available to supply to firms, the more its members of working age are able and willing to work, and the higher the prices of the particular services it offers in the market. The higher its money income, the higher, normally, will be its level of economic welfare.[10]

Now, consider how this briefly sketched analysis of the determinants of the distribution of incomes in a market economy fits into our conventional definition of MXSW. We have shown that, in general equilibrium, in all markets under perfect competition, no household's economic welfare can be improved without diminishing the economic welfare of some other households. To grasp the narrowness of this conception of social welfare, it is sufficient to observe that if all existing property (the legal rights to the proceeds of the sale of productive capital services) were *randomly* redistributed among all households in society, a new state of general equilibrium incorporating the new distribution of income in the economy would also satisfy the necessary conditions for MXSW. Because there are an infinite number of random redistributions of property in any society, it follows that there are also, literally, an infinite number of states of MXSW, each corresponding to a different initial distribution of property rights. Economists have resolved this apparent paradox by recognizing that the conventional conditions for a state of MXSW are only *necessary*, as opposed to *sufficient*, conditions. In a broader view of this very difficult concept, most economists now agree that sufficient conditions for maximum social welfare include some prior specification of the appropriate distribution of income among households as well as the more technical necessary conditions for the *Pareto Optimum* version of MXSW.

In the study of political economy, as opposed to narrowly conceived *value-free* economic theory, the issue of income distribution must be primary. A pure private market economy, without government intervention, will generate a distribution of incomes and economic welfare related only tenuously to the ethical norms of the great majority of the populace. Such a pure market economy has never existed and is inconceivable because of its harsh and inhuman treatment of individuals unable to earn sufficient incomes by selling their productive services in the marketplace. The aged, the disabled and chronically ill, children without parents, and

---

[10] The major qualification of this statement is that differences in the amount of voluntary leisure are also important in determining differences in the economic welfare of households.

the just plain unlucky would literally starve in a pure market economy without the intervention of government and private, nonprofit organizations. Thus, it is neither a controversial nor a difficult point that the private market economy, by itself, cannot attain a state of maximum social welfare that is broadly conceived to take into account the distribution of economic welfare. As we shall see in Chapter 5, government environmental policies inherently raise most complex income distribution issues.

Full Employment of Productive Resources

If government fiscal and monetary policies do not succeed in maintaining aggregate demand sufficiently high to assure full employment of all the productive input services that households are willing and able to supply, then the private market economy will fail to attain a state of MXSW. That is, with unemployed resources, the economy will fail to produce maximum output with available resources. Productive resources that remain idle involuntarily, although households desire the commodities these resources could be used to produce, represent pure social waste. From the whole society's point of view, the opportunity cost of idle resources is literally zero, whatever the market prices of these resources happen to be. We shall not pursue this point further here, other than to observe that full employment of an economy's productive resources is an obvious prerequisite for MXSW.

E. SUMMARY AND CONCLUSIONS

This chapter has analyzed the relationship between the outcome of a private market economy and the concept of (social) efficiency in the allocation of resources. The concept of social efficiency can be defined as a situation in which it is impossible to make any change in the economy's consumption or production arrangements that would improve the welfare of any one household without diminishing the welfare of any other household. The necessary conditions for such a situation—termed either a Pareto Optimum or maximum social welfare (MXSW)—can be shown to be identical to the outcome of a perfectly competitive private market economy. In particular, under perfect competition, $P = MC$ for every firm is a crucial necessary condition for optimal social allocation of resources.

The optimal efficiency results of a perfectly competitive market economy vanish once we allow for the presence of the external costs resulting from the pollution associated with production of goods and services. Such external costs of production must be added to the private market costs incurred by firms to derive the true, total social costs of production. Because firms respond only to private profits and costs, they will ignore the external costs of pollution and produce too much of some goods from the standpoint of MXSW. Thus, the market system fails as a socially efficient resource allocation mechanism in the presence of the external costs of pollution, even if all markets are perfectly competitive.

The problem of attaining MXSW becomes still more complex once the reality of widespread imperfect competition in the economy is taken into account. Monopolistic profit maximization leads to underproduction of the industry's output from the standpoint of MXSW. If a monopolist is also a pollutor imposing significant external costs on society, it is impossible theoretically to say whether this output is too large or too small. The monopolist's restriction of output may either undercorrect or overcorrect for the excessive output level generated by ignoring the external costs of his polluting activities. Empirical evidence suggests that such situations are common in our economy. The policy implication is that neither pollution nor monopoly can be corrected in isolation; both problems must be treated jointly to ensure improvements in social resource allocation.

The desirable social properties of a private market system must be qualified still further. First, a private market system does not guarantee socially optimal results in the allocation of resources over time in a dynamic world rife with uncertainty. Second, a state of MXSW is not unique, and, in fact, an infinite number of MXSWs are possible conceptually, each corresponding to a different initial distribution of the legal rights to productive resources. A *general* state of maximum social welfare must, therefore, involve some specification about the equity of the *distribution* of welfare among individual households. Finally, a private market economy does not necessarily generate full employment of an economy's resources, which is a necessary condition for MXCW.

QUESTIONS FOR DISCUSSION

1. "Individual selfishness results in a socially desirable outcome." Under what circumstances is this statement valid?

2. "The basic cause of pollution is that big corporations have no concern for the public interest." Evaluate this statement critically.

3. What externalities can you think of that are associated with (a) electric power generation and (b) personal services, e.g., medical care, educational services, babysitting? Does your answer lead you

to any generalizations about systematic departures from MXSW in our economy?

4. Consider the example of the polluting monopolist in Figure 2–5. Redraw the diagram with the assumption that the external costs per unit of output exceed the monopolist's margin of price over private marginal cost. Would resource allocation in the economy be more efficient if the industry became more competitive in this situation? Would resource allocation be improved if the monopolist were forced to bear the costs of cleaning up his own pollution?

5. Suppose the monopolist in the preceding question produced a commodity consumed predominantly by poor people. If it is impossible to make the industry more competitive, should the monopolist be forced to bear the costs of cleaning up his own pollution?

SELECTED REFERENCES

Asch, P., and J. J. Seneca, "Monopoly and External Costs: An Application of Second-Best Theory to the Automobile Industry," *Journal of Environmental Economics and Management,* 3 (April 1976). A full treatment of the efficiency problems of a market characterized by the joint existence of monopoly and external cost.

Bator, Francis M., "The Simple Analytics of Welfare Maximization," *The American Economic Review,* XLVII, No. 1 (March 1957). An advanced treatment of the necessary conditions for maximum social welfare.

Baumol, William J., *Welfare Economics and the Theory of the State* (2nd ed.). Cambridge, Mass.: Harvard University Press, 1967. A classic work, which includes good discussions of the output and price effects of externalities.

Meade, J. E., "External Economies and Diseconomies in a Competitive Situation," *Economic Journal,* LXII, No. 245 (March 1952). A discussion of the economic effects of externalities.

Mishan, E. J., "The Postwar Literature on Externalities: An Interpretive Essay," *The Journal of Economic Literature,* IX, No. 1 (March 1971). A survey article containing some of the author's contributions.

Nicholson, Walter, *Microeconomic Theory.* Hinsdale, Illinois: The Dryden Press, Inc., 1972. An intermediate level text that includes a very good discussion of the necessary conditions for maximum social welfare.

Pigou, A. C., *Economics of Welfare* (4th ed.). London: Macmillan & Company, Ltd., 1960. The classic work on externalities.

Scitovsky, Tibor, *Welfare and Competition* (rev. ed.). Homewood, Illinois: Richard D. Irwin, Inc., 1971. Probably the best overall treatment of the topics covered in this chapter.

APPENDIX: Maximum Social Welfare in a Perfectly Competitive Economy

This appendix elaborates on the discussion in the text on the connection between the necessary conditions for maximum social welfare (MXSW) and the allocation of resources in general equilibrium in a perfectly competitive market economy.

HOUSEHOLD EQUILIBRIUM IN CONSUMPTION. First, consider the adjustment of the individual consumer unit, the household, to the pattern of relative prices that exists in output markets—the markets for consumption goods and services. We assume that households behave rationally; that is, that they purposefully attempt to maximize their economic welfare by searching for the largest and best collection of consumption goods and services they can afford. Figure A2–1 depicts the process of rational choice for an individual household allocating its expenditure between just two goods or services—X and Y. Our assumption of perfect competition in all markets implies that the prices of X and Y, P_X and P_Y, are constants for the household (it can buy all of X and Y it desires at these prices). Thus its *budget line*, $Y_M X_M$ in Figure A2–1, is a straight line. Points X_M and Y_M represent the maximum amounts of X and Y, respectively, that it can purchase if it devotes its whole income to just one good or the other. Intermediate points along $Y_M X_M$ represent the various com-

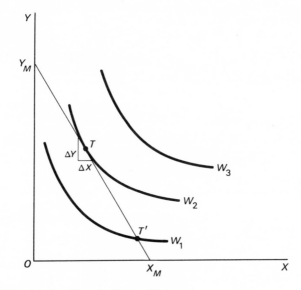

FIGURE A2–1. Household Equilibrium.

binations of X and Y it can buy with the same total expenditures.[1] As shown in footnote 1, the slope of the budget line—the rate at which a household can substitute Y for X in its budget by shifting from the purchase of one to the other in the market—is equal to $-P_X/P_Y$, with the minus sign having the economic interpretation that, with a given income, the household can spend more on Y only by purchasing less of X.

Superimposed on the budget line in Figure A2–1 are three *indifference curves*, W_1, W_2, and W_3. Each of these curves is the locus of a given level of welfare for the household, with the level of welfare increasing as the household moves to the northeast, away from the origin; that is, as it consumes more of *both* X and Y. W_3 represents a higher level of welfare for the household than W_2, and W_2 a higher level than W_1. The slope of any indifference curve, called the marginal rate of substitution (*MRS*), can be given the economic interpretation of the subjective rate of trade-off by the household between X and Y that will leave its economic welfare unchanged. The *MRS* between Y and X (MRS_{YX}) is equal to the ratio of the marginal welfares of X and Y at any point on the curve, or MW_X/MW_Y.[2] The implied negative slope of MRS_{YX} means that an increase in welfare due to an increase in the consumption of either X or Y must be offset by a decrease in welfare due to a decrease in the consumption of the other if the household is to remain at the same level of economic welfare (on the same indifference curve)—an increase (decrease) in both X and Y would make the household unambiguously better (worse) off. Finally, the indifference curves are assumed to be convex in Figure A2–1, which implies a *diminishing* MRS_{YX}. This means simply that we assume that the household's subjective rate of trade-off between Y and X varies systematically

---

[1] The equation of the budget line is $I = P_Y Y + P_X X$, where I is total income or expenditure. Solving for Y as a function of X, we obtain:

$$Y = \frac{I}{P_Y} - \frac{P_X}{P_Y} X.$$

This is the equation of a straight line with $\frac{I}{P_Y}$ equal to Y_M, the Y intercept, and $-\frac{P_X}{P_Y}$ the constant slope. Note that $Y = Y_M = \frac{I}{P_Y}$ when $X = 0$, and $X = X_M = \frac{I}{P_X}$ when $Y = 0$.

[2] A small movement along any indifference curve leaves welfare unchanged. The change in total welfare for any change in X and Y consumed may be expressed as

$$\Delta W = \Delta Y \cdot MW_Y + \Delta X \cdot MW_X$$

where MW_Y and MW_X are the marginal changes in welfare associated with each unit of additional Y or X, and the Δ symbol signifies small changes in the variables. Thus $\Delta Y \cdot MW_Y$ is the change in welfare associated with a small change in the consumption of Y. Along any indifference curve, it follows that $\Delta W = 0$

or

$$\Delta Y \cdot MW_Y = -\Delta X \cdot MW_X$$
$$-\frac{\Delta Y}{\Delta X} = \frac{MW_X}{MW_Y}$$

Note that $-\frac{\Delta Y}{\Delta X}$ is simply the slope of the indifference curve; so we have the result in the text for the MRS_{YX}.

with the relative amounts of Y and X it is already consuming. As we move down and to the right along any indifference curve, the slope, or MRS_{YX}, decreases (in absolute terms), which means that it takes increasingly greater amounts of additional X to compensate the household for the loss of one unit of Y as the household consumes a greater ratio of X to Y.

With the above assumptions and definitions, we can inspect Figure A2–1 to find the mix of X and Y it chooses in order to maximize its welfare. We see that the household can, in effect, move along (or inside) its budget line until it obtains its most advantageous market basket of X and Y. The best combination, given its income, is clearly at point T, where it attains a subjective welfare level of W_2. Welfare levels to the northeast of W_2, such as W_3, are preferable, but it can not attain these higher levels given its current income and the prices of X and Y, as embodied in the budget line $Y_M X_M$.

Note that the crucial result of this analysis is that the best attainable combination point T must occur at a tangency between the budget line and an indifference curve. From our previous results, we know that we can describe this outcome by an equality of the two slope coefficients. At the optimal point, T,

$$\text{Slope of Indifference Curve} = MRS_{YX} = -\frac{MW_X}{MW_Y} = -\frac{P_X}{P_Y}$$

$$= \text{Slope of Budget Line}$$

Rearranging terms, we obtain:

$$\text{either } \frac{MW_X}{P_X} = \frac{MW_Y}{P_Y} \text{ or } \frac{P_X}{P_Y} = \frac{MW_X}{MW_Y}$$

Because our analysis was general for all perfectly competitive markets, we know that this last expression must hold for any household between any pair of goods and services, and, therefore, *all* goods and services in its budget. The allocation of the budget among alternative goods and services will, of course, vary across households, both because of differences in tastes (different indifference curves) and differences in incomes (different budget lines).

In words, *in general equilibrium in an economy of perfectly competitive markets, the maximization of welfare by a household implies that it has a common MW/p for all commodities.*[3]

The logic of this rule can best be understood by observing that if any household does not consume any pair of goods and services so as to meet this maximization condition, it can always increase its level of economic welfare by shifting some of its expenditures from the commodity with a relatively low MW/P to one with a higher MW/P. In Figure A2–1, such a shift would be depicted by a movement from T' to T along budget line $Y_M X_M$, because at point T', $MW_X/P_X < MW_Y/P_Y$, and Y can be substituted for X in the household's budget to increase the household's level of welfare from W_1 to W_2. We re-

[3] The conclusion assumes that all households consume positive quantities of both X or Y. If they do not, corner solutions at Y_M or X_M in Figure A2–1 will be relevant. For the rest of this appendix, we shall not concern ourselves with such theoretical fine points, but the reader may consult the more advanced treatments of this subject cited at the end of the chapter.

mind the reader that this important result holds only under the assumption of perfect competition in which the price ratio P_X/P_Y is a constant parameter for any household.

The result derived above has a very important implication for the interpretation of the role of relative prices in a perfectly competitive economy in a state of general equilibrium. All relative prices, such as $P_X/P_Y = (MW_X/MW_Y)$, measure exactly for every household the relative subjective contributions to its economic welfare of the last units of the goods and services it consumes. The price of every good or service measures the benefit of the last unit consumed—the marginal benefit—for every household in the economy in equilibrium. This result is, in effect, the outcome of individual benefit-cost types of decisions made by millions of households.

FIRM EQUILIBRIUM IN PRODUCTION.   As shown in the text of this chapter, the assumption that a firm maximizes profits in a perfectly competitive market *implies* the important result that production of any good or service will be at a level at which

$$P = MC.$$

The result derived above holds for every firm in a perfectly competitive economy. That is, every firm in the economy produces its outputs to a point where $P = MC$. Because $P_X = MC_X$; $P_Y = MC_Y$; $P_Z = MC_Z \ldots$, it follows that relative prices such as P_X/P_Y will be exactly equal to relative marginal costs for all products. In symbols,

$$\frac{P_X}{P_Y} = \frac{MC_X}{MC_Y}$$

The economic interpretation of this last result is that relative prices in general equilibrium in a perfectly competitive economy exactly measure the relative marginal costs of all goods and services. Combined with our previous result about the interpretation of relative prices from the standpoint of consumers' relative MWs, we are now in a position to put together the pieces of our analysis in order to draw some conclusions about the meaning of efficiency and social welfare in a perfectly competitive economy.

THE NECESSARY CONDITIONS FOR MXSW RESTATED

With the results derived above, we can elaborate on the proposition that a state of general equilibrium in a perfectly competitive market economy satisfies the necessary conditions for MXSW. We shall give the necessary proof very briefly by first establishing the necessary conditions for MXSW, and then showing that these necessary conditions are fulfilled in a state of general equilibrium in a perfectly competitive economy.

The first necessary condition that must hold for MXSW is that all households consume each good and service to the point at which the individual subjective estimation of the trade-off between the last units of any pair of commodities—the ratio of MWs—is equal for all families. If this condition is not met, a reallocation of consumption could make at least one household better off without making any other household worse off.

To see this point, suppose that some households (Group I) are just willing to trade (indifferent between) their last 2 units of commodity X for 1 more unit of commodity Y, and all other households (Group II) are just willing to trade just their last 1 unit of X for 1 more unit of Y. Stated from the opposite perspective, the Group I households are just willing to trade their last 1 unit of commodity Y for 2 more units of commodity X and the Group II households are just willing to trade their last 1 unit of Y for 1 more X. For Group I, then, the $MRS_{YX} = \frac{1}{2}$, and for Group II, the $MRS_{YX} = 1$. (For convenience, henceforth we shall ignore the minus sign in the MRS.) In these circumstances, suppose that A and B were traded on a 1 to 1 basis between Groups I and II. Group II would, by assumption, remain as well off as before the trade in giving up 1 unit of X in exchange for 1 unit of Y; the loss in economic welfare from giving up 1 last unit of X would be just offset by the gain in economic welfare derived from gaining one more unit of Y. By assumption Group I, on the other hand, would be better off as the result of the exchange. The gain in economic welfare from obtaining one more unit of Y would be twice as great for them as the loss in economic welfare from giving up one last unit of X. By the same reasoning, if X and Y were traded on a 2 to 1 basis, Group I would remain just as well off as before the trade, and Group II would be better off. Following the same logic further, if X and Y were traded on a 1½ to 1 basis (or in any ratio between 1 to 1 and 2 to 1), *both* Group I and Group II would be better off as a result of voluntary exchange.

The general conclusion from the foregoing example should now be intuitively reasonable; unless the ratio of individual MWs is the same for all households for any pair of commodities, the reallocation of consumption commodities among households potentially can improve the welfare of some, and perhaps all, households without decreasing the welfare of any other household. In general equilibrium in a perfectly competitive economy, all MW ratios *will* be equal for any pair of goods for all households. Recall that the rule describing the outcome of rational consumer behavior by households is:

$$\frac{P_X}{P_Y} = \frac{MW_X}{MW_Y},$$

for any two commodities, X and Y. Again, the economic logic behind this rule is that all households can maximize their own welfare only if they adjust their expenditures on all commodities until all their MRSs are equated to the relative prices established in output markets. In short, the perfectly competitive market system assures that, in general equilibrium, the ratio of MWs for all households will be equal for any pair of commodities—equal exactly to the general equilibrium relative prices.

A second necessary condition for MXSW to exist is somewhat more complex, because it involves production and consumption relationships simultaneously. What is the economic significance of the ratio of the marginal costs of any two goods and services in equilibrium? Let us suppose that X and Y are the only two outputs in a perfectly competitive economy, and examine the ratio $(-)$ MC_X/MC_Y. We call it the *marginal rate of transformation of X into Y*, or MRT_{XY}. It can be interpreted as the (negative) change in the production of X—the foregone production of X—required to produce one more unit of

Y. (For simplicity, we shall henceforth ignore the minus sign in the MRT.) Suppose that the market price of commodity X is \$3, and the market price of commodity Y is \$1. The fact that X is three times more costly than Y reflects the fact in equilibrium, MRT_{YX}, the ratio of MC_X to MC_Y, is 3 to 1. The economic sense of this ratio is that if the productive input services devoted to producing the last unit of X were reallocated to producing more of Y, 3 more units of Y could be produced. In other words, the MC_X/MC_Y ratio measures the rate at which X can be transformed into Y by means of shifting productive resources from the production of X to the production of Y. If MC_X is 3 times as great as MC_Y, this means that the same productive input services that produce the last 1 unit of X are capable of producing 3 more units of Y.

Figure A2-2 gives the MRT_{YX} a geometric interpretation as the slope of a *transformation* (or production possibilities) curve between X and Y. This curve is a locus of the maximum combinations of X and Y that can be produced with given resources and technology. The slope of the transformation curve $Y_M X_M$ at any point, $-\Delta Y/\Delta X$, can be interpreted as the social marginal opportunity cost of Y in terms of foregone X. From the analysis of the previous paragraph, we know that this slope value must be equal to the MC_X/MC_Y ratio. Superimposed on the transformation curve in Figure A2-2 is a relative price line, PP, with slope $= -P_X/P_Y$, established by the interaction of supply and demand in perfectly competitive markets for X and Y. The optimal production mix of X and Y occurs at point T in Figure A2-2 the point of tangency between the relative price line and the transformation curve; that is, where $P_X/P_Y = MRT_{YX}.$[4] This result is general for *any* two goods or services in a

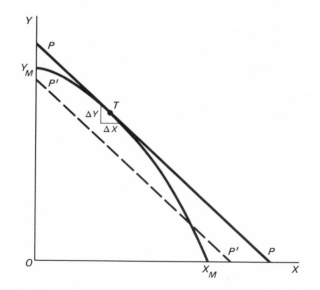

FIGURE A2-2. Maximization of Social Welfare.

[4] Point T is optimal because total product is at a maximum along the transformation curve as measured either in terms of X or in terms of Y. That is, any other price line parallel to PP, such at $P'P'$, that intersects $Y_M X_M$ must lie to the left of PP.

perfectly competitive economy. Relative prices for any pair of goods or services measure the marginal opportunity cost of producing more of one in terms of less production of the other.

The relevance of the result derived above to MXSW can best be brought out by asking the question: What must be the relationship of MRS_{YX} to MRT_{YX}, where X and Y are again any two goods or services, in a state of MXSW. Suppose, for example, that the $MRS_{YX} = 2/(1)$, and $MRT_{YX} = 1/(1)$. Interpreted verbally, this means that all households can trade the last unit of X consumed for 2 additional units of Y (or 1 unit of Y for ½ unit of X) and remain equally well off in their own estimation, and firms can produce one more unit of Y at the cost of producing 1 less unit of X (and of course, one more unit of X at the cost of 1 less unit of Y). Under these assumed circumstances, the economic welfare of all households can clearly be improved by shifting some productive input services away from the production of Y to additional production of X. Households will have 1 less unit of Y available after such a shift in production in exchange for 1 more unit of X, but, by assumption, they value another unit of X twice as much as the last unit of Y consumed, and, therefore, they clearly will be better off. By reasoning closely analogous to the first MXSW condition for the allocation of consumption commodities, it can be demonstrated mathematically in advanced treatments of this subject that a second MXSW condition is that:

$$MRS_{YX} = -\frac{MW_X}{MW_Y} = MRT_{YX} = -\frac{MC_X}{MC_Y}$$

In words, the rate at which all households are willing to trade all consumption goods and services at the margin, must be equal to the ratio of the MCs of all goods and services—the marginal rate at which goods and services can be productively transformed from one to another by the shift of productive input services between alternative uses.

The perfectly competitive market system assures that this second condition of MXSW also will be satisfied. As we have already shown:

$$\frac{MW_X}{MW_Y} = \frac{P_X}{P_Y} \text{ and } \frac{P_X}{P_Y} = \frac{MC_X}{MC_Y}$$

in general equilibrium. By definition, the above equality implies, of course, that

$$MRS_{YX} = MRT_{YX}$$

where X and Y are *any* two commodities. Thus, we have accomplished our purpose of establishing that the necessary conditions for a state of MXSW are identical with the general equilibrium outcome of individual household and firm behavior in a perfectly competitive market system. For a more complete and rigorous treatment of this subject, the reader should consult the references cited at the end of this chapter.

Externalities and Necessary Conditions for Maximum Social Welfare

We have demonstrated that the allocation of resources in an ideal market system without externalities satisfies the necessary conditions for MXSW, or a *Pareto Optimum*. The main link in the reasoning behind this conclusion is that in a competitive market economy in general equilibrium, an equality will exist between the marginal rate of substitution in consumption between any two goods and the marginal rates of transformation in production between the same two goods. For any pair of goods X and Y, this key result can be expressed in symbols as:

$$MRS_{YX} = MRT_{YX}$$

Also, as shown above, the MRT_{YX} is equal to the (minus) ratio of the marginal costs of X and Y:

$$MRT_{YX} = -\left(\frac{MC_X}{MC_Y}\right)$$

Implicit in our previous analysis, however, was the key assumption that the MC_X and MC_Y included all social costs, both private and external. Let us briefly indicate the implications of modifying this implicit assumption.

Profit-maximizing behavior by private business firms will lead to the equalization of price and marginal private cost (MPC), as argued in this chapter. Thus, in general equilibrium, the marginal rate of transformation between any two goods X and Y will be equal to the (minus) ratio of MPC_X and MPC_Y, or

$$MRT_{YX} = -\left(\frac{MPC_X}{MPC_Y}\right)$$

Now, let us suppose that the production of X imposes external costs on society but the production of Y does not. In symbols, these assumptions can be stated as:

$$MPC_X < MSC_X$$
$$MPC_Y = MSC_Y$$

It immediately follows that the ratio of marginal private and social costs of X and Y are not equal:

$$\frac{MPC_X}{MPC_Y} < \frac{MSC_X}{MSC_Y}$$

Thus, the marginal private rate of transformation between X and Y will not be equal to the true social rate at which these goods can be substituted for each other in production, taking full account of externalities. Furthermore, the equality between the MRS_{YX} and the true social MRT_{YX}, including all external costs, will not hold. If the production of X involves external costs, society will not be in an MXSW situation in which a costless improvement in the allocation of resources could not be effected. Under the circumstances assumed in the present example, total economic welfare could be improved by somehow adjusting the MPC of X upwards to reflect the external costs included in MSC. Raising the perceived marginal cost of X would increase its market price and reduce the level of its consumption and production, thus freeing some resources used in its production for more socially valuable employments.

The necessary conditions for MXSW can now be restated very simply. The essential equality between the *MRS* and *MRT* for any two goods must still hold, but all external benefits and costs must be included as well as purely private benefits and costs. As external costs and benefits will not generally be included in private marginal costs, we can restate our previous conclusion that by itself, a private market system will not allocate resources with full social efficiency.

3

ALTERNATIVE
SOLUTIONS
TO THE
EXTERNALITIES
PROBLEM

Externalities result when firms and households do not appropriate the full costs or benefits of their productive or consumptive activities. The benefits or costs that accrue external to the system of private exchange markets do not enter into the rational gain and loss calculus of individual suppliers and demanders. One main theme of Chapter 2, and the point of departure for this chapter, is that in the presence of externalities the private market system fails to allocate resources with maximum efficiency, even under otherwise ideal circumstances.

The purpose of this chapter is to explain the alternative mechanisms that allow society to correct, partially or fully, for the allocative distortions caused by externalities. The first possibility we explore is what may be called the common law solution. This alternative involves defining legal rights to pollute or not to be subjected to pollution.

A second possible solution to the externalities problem is reliance on the private market system to create new markets to internalize what are now external costs of pollution. The basic notion involved in this alternative is simple. If externalities are the consequence of benefits and costs not being incorporated in the market system, then if private firms or households (or profit-oriented public agencies) can appropriate the rights to environmental resources, the possibility of profits should provide the incentive to create new markets for the exchange of such rights. If private markets can be extended in this way, then all benefits and costs initially external to the market system will become internal, just like the benefits and costs of other goods and services already traded in private markets.

A third alternative mechanism of responding to the externalities problem is to use the coercive powers of the government to force private firms and households to take into full account the external costs and benefits that result from their economic activities. Governments can, in effect, establish and enforce property rights to various environmental resources that have previously been treated as commonly owned property or, more accurately, unowned property. This solution may involve relatively crude prohibitions or regulations on the use of such resources or a more subtle system of monetary incentives designed to alter their allocation among different users. In either case, the intent of such government intervention into the private market system is to internalize, for society, benefits and costs otherwise external to private firms or households and in effect impose a market-type solution.

This chapter discusses the above possibilities according to the following outline. Section A begins with an analysis of the concept of property rights and its relationship to the problem of environmental quality. Section B discusses the common law solutions to the externalities problem and the limitations of these solutions with respect to the externalities caused by pollution in a densely populated and highly industrialized modern economy. Section C then demonstrates the tendency of the private market system to internalize externalities by the generation of new markets and the limitations of this mechanism. Section D discusses the rationale of government intervention to inhibit activities that destroy or impair environmental quality. The ideal form of government intervention is a system of charges designed to provide the economic incentives lacking in the private market system for inducing socially desirable results from the aggregate of the many individual activities of firms and households. We demonstrate that, under certain assumptions, the allocative results from such a system of charges are equivalent to the private market solution outlined in Section C. Finally, Section E is a brief summary of the chapter.

A. THE CONCEPT OF PROPERTY RIGHTS

Economists often speak loosely about the private or public ownership of various kinds of property, but the more appropriate legal terminology is ownership of property *rights*. The legal system of the United States, and of other countries sharing the English common law heritage, recognizes only limited and qualified ownership of property. Individuals who own a piece of property are legally entitled to use it only within certain defined limits.[1] For example, any individual who owns a rifle has the right to use it as the law permits, to restrict others from using it without his expressed permission, and to transfer his rights to it to other individuals on mutually agreeable terms. His purchase of the rifle does not entitle him, however, to fire his rifle at three o'clock in the morning in an urban area or to use it to hunt squirrels in a city park. Similar sets of limited rights adhere to all other kinds of property. A large body of law has developed in response to potential conflicts of individual interests related to the exercise of property rights. Such conflicts arise because of what economists term externalities.

From a legal perspective, the private market system may be viewed as a social mechanism for the voluntary transfer of property rights through contracts that are legally enforceable by appeal to the coercive power of the state. Furthermore, externalities may be explained as the consequence either of an incomplete set of property rights or by the inability or unwillingness of the state to enforce public or private property rights.

Consider again the example of Chapter 2. What is the fundamental cause of the external cost imposed by the textile plant on the downstream farmer? In effect, the textile firm in this example simply appropriates a valuable water resource by disposing of its wastes in the river and thereby inflicts heavy losses on the farmer downstream. If the textile firm instead had taken its wastes directly to the farmer's land by truck and dumped these wastes on the farmer's land, our example of the previous chapter would have been patently absurd. The farmer would surely have an overwhelming legal case against the firm in the latter instance because of the prevailing system of enforceable property rights. The textile firm can dump its wastes on the farmer's land legally only if it can first contract with the farmer to transfer the waste disposal rights to the land. Presumably, the firm would be granted such rights only in return for mutually agreeable compensation. We shall explore further this possibility of accommodation between private parties as a possible solution

---

[1] For a fuller discussion of this topic, see J. H. Dales, *Pollution Property and Prices* (Toronto: University of Toronto Press, 1970), Chap. 5.

to the externalities problem in Section C, but, for the time being, let us return to the question of why the two hypothetical alternatives outlined above differ. That is, how is it possible that the textile firm can impose costs on the farmer through the medium of the water in the river when he cannot impose such costs directly by dumping his wastes on the farmer's land?

There are two possible answers to this question. First, if either public or private property rights are defined for the river in such a way as to prohibit waste disposal into the water, then the example of Chapter 2 is simply a matter of nonenforcement of the law. Second, if the river is considered by the legislature and the courts to be a *common property resource*, then the farmer is just an unfortunate victim of the absence of private property rights to the river. The apparently irrelevant circumstance of the direction of water flow in the river allows the textile firm to appropriate the valuable water resource at the farmer's expense. Even if this second possibility is the relevant case, the farmer can still attempt to bribe the textile firm to find another means of disposing of its wastes. That is, he can contract with the firm not to appropriate the river water if both sides find such a transaction mutually profitable. Unfortunately for the farmer, this kind of private market arrangement is unlikely to be of much help. First, it is not clear that the contract between him and the firm can be effectively enforced, a problem we discuss in more detail in Section C. Second, the supply of *potential* polluters is virtually inexhaustible. Any unscrupulous individual can threaten to pollute the water upstream from the farmer and attempt to use such a threat to extort money from him without any violation of law. Such threats are almost costless, and if they are credible, a small number could quickly bankrupt the farmer just as surely as the water pollution from the textile firm's waste disposal. In summary, the externality imposed by the textile firm on the farmer is the result either of the lack of enforcement of property rights to the river (if they exist) or of the failure of society to define adequately property rights to resources like river water. The latter case is the fundamental basis of externalities that lead to perceived environmental problems.

B. COMMON LAW SOLUTIONS

Common law remedies have long been used in the United States and England to resolve disputes involving pollution damages caused by private firms or households. Injured parties have recourse to the common law doctrines of nuisance and, to a lesser degree, of trespass to correct for damages caused by air and water pollution, noise, odors, and other environmental externalities. Such legal remedies can be traced back for centuries in England and have also been used in this country throughout its history because of our inherited English common law tradition.

Private nuisance law is based on a "golden rule" of property; namely, an individual has a right to use his or her own property, but not in a way that injures others. The law of nuisance provides for legal enforcement of the right to enjoy one's own property and to prevent any substantial and unreasonable interference by others in this enjoyment. The courts have used it to define precisely how one may or may not use property. Under certain circumstances, nuisance law can effectively internalize external costs by establishing criteria for (1) whether a violation of property rights has occurred, (2) who is liable for the damage, and (3) how to assess the amount of the liability. The mechanism of a court order can then provide the appropriate remedy for the external costs of pollution damage by imposing sanctions on the violator.

An example of a private nuisance case might involve a private home owner (plaintiff) suing a neighboring cement plant (defendant) for damages to the plaintiff's property allegedly created by the air pollutants emitted by the process of cement production. Not only can the plaintiff ask the court to award damages (to compensate for the depreciation of his property); he can also ask for an injunction against the offending activity, that is, for a court order to the cement company to cease its operations entirely. In nuisance law the prevailing approach of the courts has been "to balance the equities" or to weigh the harm done to the injured party against the economic benefits of the damaging activity. The courts' approach strongly resembles the economist's efficiency test of comparing benefits to costs.

On hearing the evidence the court must determine whether it indeed was the emissions of this particular cement plant that damaged the plaintiff's property and whether this was caused by an *unreasonable* use of the cement plant's property. The court must then decide whether to award damages and whether or not to impose an injunction. The court may find, for example, that the defendant's activities did, in fact, cause the alleged harm and were an unreasonable interference with the plaintiff's rights to use his property. In such a case, the court may award damages but may not grant an injunction since the costs of the economic dislocations that would follow exceed the value to the plaintiff of the relief from the emissions damages. For example, an injunction might cause the cement plant to close down, resulting in the loss of many jobs in the local community, or cause the plant to incur large costs to control its emissions, costs far in excess of the damages its operations impose on the plaintiff. In such a decision, the court's balancing of the equities would be consistent with the economist's efficiency test. However, while the economist can only say that the cement plant should continue operation but pay for the damages it creates, the court can actually provide equity relief by establishing the legal liability of the cement company and by requiring compensation to be paid to the homeowner. In other cases, the court may impose a conditional injunction which orders the offending operation to cease altogether after a specified future date if the defendant does not abate the harmful activity by then. This remedy allows the defendant time to make any necessary adjustments to its production processes, including the installation of pollution control equipment which the court may, in fact, mandate as an explicit condition of the injunction.[2]

Common law remedies for external costs can be an extremely flexible solution to externalities caused by pollution. Under ideal conditions, court orders force the polluting party to internalize all the external costs of its pollution. That is, the firm's private costs of production become identical to the social costs of production after an appropriate common law solution. Unfortunately, there are several problems with any systematic reliance upon the common law to cope with the full range of modern environmental problems.

First, a polluting firm has several legal defenses available to it when charged with nuisance or trespass. For one thing, the courts have been reluctant to find in favor of plaintiffs when suits have been brought against activities that have long gone unchallenged. The courts' attitude is not necessarily unreasonable or without economic justification. Suppose, for example, the homeowner in the case described above had brought vacant land next to the cement plant at a low price reflecting the undesirability of the site for a residence. If he then built a house on the land and sued over the damages caused by the plant's emissions, the cement company could reasonably argue in court that the homeowner "came to the nuisance" and knew full well what to expect.

Common law solutions to the externalities problem involve important costs of their own, and these costs may often be excessive compared to the benefits. Legal costs can be very high in difficult cases. The burden of proof is on the plaintiff. Time requirements, strategic delays, and the defendant's right to appeal are all costly obstacles that discourage potential plaintiffs, even though substantial external costs may be at issue.

Moreover, not all court decisions coincide with an economist's answer to the "balance of equities" test. Many times an injunction will

---

[2] The appendix to this chapter excerpts the actual decision from the cement case outlined in the text. It illustrates the use of injunctions and damage awards in nuisance cases.

be granted even though the resulting economic costs exceed the damage of the nuisance to the plaintiff,[3] and the court's decision will then amount to "overkill" from the standpoint of economic efficiency.

The most fundamental problems with the common law solution arise from the diffuse and pervasive nature of modern environmental problems. The common law remedy is most effective when the externality involves two (or only a few) private parties and the damage is immediately felt, obvious, and clearly traceable to a single source. In such circumstances, the court then has an unambiguous record of evidence before it to establish proof of damages, and it can evaluate the severity of the appropriate sanction. However, as is generally the case with modern environmental pollution problems—e.g., urban air pollution—the causes are many, and they are geographically diffused over a wide area. Also, many parties are affected and with varying degrees of damage.

To make matters still more difficult, pollution damage may be chronic in nature—e.g., cancer induced by exposure to poor air quality for two or three decades. In such cases, it is virtually impossible to establish (legally) a single cause of this health damage and to trace it back over this long time period to a single emitter of air pollutants. The burden of proof is on the plantiff, and for many complex modern pollutants this will be impossible to sustain. Under such circumstances, the common law is an unwieldy and inappropriate mechanism for improving environmental quality. The courts are helpless in attempting to assess blame for pollution damages and redress for those damaged.[4]

Finally, the spillover effects of modern pollutants often cross numerous political jurisdictions. Mercury, PCBs,[5] fluorocarbons, vinyl chloride, and many other hazardous substances follow a complex path to affect human health. Such effects may only be manifested after crossing hundreds and even thousands of miles, distances which transcend most state boundaries and local government jurisdictions. In such situations, determining the appropriate court that has jurisdiction for any common law suit becomes a significant problem.

In summary, when external costs are imposed by one private party on another, and when proof of damages is certain and direct, common law remedies are an effective and useful mechanism for improving resource allocation by forcing polluters to internalize all costs. This can be accomplished because under common law doctrine the courts are able to

---

[3] See, e.g., the dissenting opinion in the appendix for arguments why an injunction should be granted in such a situation.

[4] If there are numerous individuals experiencing damage, it is possible to invoke public nuisance doctrines. These, however, must usually be brought by the state or federal attorney general, and this remedy has not been frequently used for pollution problems.

[5] Polychlorinated biphenyls, a material used as a coolant and insulator.

establish and enforce liability for the unreasonable use of property. Unfortunately, the traditional common law remedies cannot play a major role in coping with the complexities of modern environmental problems. In Chapter 11, however, we shall return to the possibility of legal remedies when we discuss the powerful device of judicial review of public agency performance affecting environmental quality.

C. A MARKET SOLUTION FOR THE EXTERNALITIES PROBLEM

The existence of external effects does not necessarily imply that a private market system will fail to allocate resources efficiently. A central feature of a market system is the existence of property rights and enforceable private contracts for the voluntary exchange of these rights. Contracts are explicit or implicit in any market transaction. For example, a businessman may formally contract to deliver a certain number of goods of specified quality at a given time and place. A casual worker may have an implicit contract to provide labor services for a certain number of hours under specified working conditions in exchange for some mutually acceptable wage. Other, similar contracts are applicable to all other market transactions and are a vital element of a viable market system.

External effects of production and consumption, in contrast, can be viewed conceptually as benefits and costs that do *not* have a market and hence are not transferred between parties through the mechanism of private contracts. Consumer goods and services of all kinds, labor services, and capital goods all are marketed and exchanged between buyers and sellers. Well-defined markets for most of these goods and services aid greatly in providing information about the possibilities of mutually beneficial exchange to all potential buyers and sellers. Households and firms can readily buy or sell goods or services in markets according to clearly established procedures.

In contrast, externalities are not subject to private contractual arrangements within the market mechanism. Consider, for example, an individual who attempts to spend a day of leisure fishing in a nearby lake. A well-defined market exists for him to purchase fishing equipment, as elaborate and varied as his tastes dictate. He can purchase his transportation, picnic lunch, and the fishing bait he needs for the day's activities in readily accessible markets for these items. In the terminology of economics, he can contract with sellers for the purchase or lease of virtually all the complements for a day's fishing. But suppose that when he arrives at the lake ready to begin fishing, he discovers a lifeless, polluted body of water. Let us further suppose that a chemical plant situated on the lake shore is responsible for degrading the water quality in the lake to the point that all or most fish in the lake are destroyed. Initially, we shall make the important assumption that the firm owns exclusive rights to all uses of the lake.

The fisherman obviously values unpolluted water for his day of fishing. The potential benefit to him of unpolluted water may be measured by the amount he would willingly pay to be able to fish in a body of water clean enough to permit the survival of some fish. But, in contrast to the items he can purchase in existing markets, no market exists for him and others to purchase *no pollution* or *less pollution*. Thus, fishermen collectively bear the external costs of chemical production in the form of foregone recreational opportunities. Total external costs will be the sum of the subjective values placed on lost fishing opportunities by all fishermen affected and will, obviously, depend heavily on the accessibility of alternative, unpolluted fishing sites. The losses suffered by the fishermen do not influence decisions of the chemical plant, because its profit and loss incentives are affected only by potential sales and purchases contracted through markets. Thus, the fishermen are economically powerless to better their situation, and the market system apparently fails to allocate resources efficiently.

Our example is critically incomplete, however, as developed thus far. The most important omission the story is that we have neglected the *possibility of the formation of a new market*. Let us suppose that the chemical firm realizes the potential for a market transaction with fishermen who are willing to pay for the opportunity of fishing in an unpolluted lake. It can then attempt to increase its profits by charging an entry fee to fishermen and, at the same time, reducing the pollution of the lake to increase the fishermen's demand for its use. If the management of the chemical firm is economically rational, it will estimate the least-cost combination of the methods of producing no pollution with the available technology. This combination would be derived from the relative costs of different techniques of water treatment, the net reduction in revenue from a cutback in the level of output of chemicals, and, at the extreme, even the cost of relocating the whole plant. The private least-cost combination of producing no pollution in the lake for the firm is also the cost to society measured in terms of the value of treatment equipment and operations, foregone chemical production, or the resources expended in relocating the plant site. If this least-cost method of providing no pollution is less than the maximum revenues that could be obtained from charging admission to fishermen, the firm rationally will elect to produce and sell no pollution and thereby provide fishermen with the opportunity to use the lake.

The profit motive thus may lead to a solution of no pollution. The firm responsible for pollution has an incentive to internalize the external cost it was previously imposing on other firms and households. Once the firm recognizes the possibility of selling clean water, it will see that it is not costless to dispose of its wastes. The cost of waste disposal is the opportunity cost of the foregone revenues it cannot collect if it continues to pollute. The creation of new markets to produce no pollution eliminates the *external* aspect of waste disposal costs and makes them *internal* to the firm, just like the costs of labor and capital services.

Note that it is certainly possible that after the firm in our example estimates the costs of waste reduction and the likely demand for no pollution it may continue to pollute. The continuation of polluting activities under these circumstances would mean that the total social costs exceed the total social benefits of no pollution. In other words, the value of the resources required to end pollution may be greater than the value fishermen place on a nonpolluted lake, perhaps because water treatment costs are prohibitive or because good alternative fishing sites are readily available in the area. Provided that a market can exist for the sale of rights to no pollution, the failure of the two sides to transact a mutually agreeable bargain is, indirectly, an indication that no improvement in the allocation of resources is possible. In our previous language, transactions in pollution rights will tend to take place until it is impossible for any party to gain without loss to the other party, that is, until a *Pareto Optimum* or a state of MXSW is established.

The above analysis has been presented in terms of fixed sum comparisons. That is, we have assumed that the firm makes a simple two-way comparison between the costs of ending pollution and the potential revenue from the fishermen. This comparison results in a decision either to continue pollution with no fishing or to halt waste discharges and provide fishing opportunities. More generally, we can conceive of measuring the degree of water pollution on a continuum. The quality of water is neither *good* nor *bad* in any single dimension, and the number of dimensions of water quality matches the number of potential water uses. The chemical firm may treat its water discharge in degrees and thereby create various levels of water quality. Normally, the higher the water quality in any dimension, the higher will be the costs of treatment. On the other side of the market, we can think of fishermen collectively offering various dollar amounts for different levels of water quality, with more offered for higher qualities than for lower qualities.

These more realistic assumptions are depicted in Figure 3–1. An index of water quality on the horizontal axis represents levels of water quality ranging from zero at point O (polluted, lifeless water) to higher levels of water quality to the right. The horizontal axis is measured in terms of physical units of water that are treated to some given standard

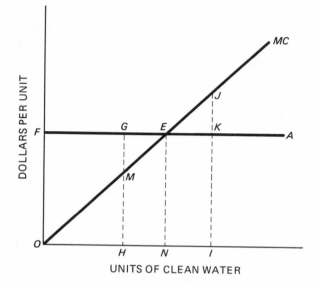

FIGURE 3–1. A Clean Water Market.

of water quality. Thus, increasing levels of water quality are directly related in Figure 3–1 to the number of units of water treated. The marginal cost to the chemical firm of producing different levels of water quality is represented by the marginal cost (MC) schedule. As drawn in Figure 3–1, the marginal cost of producing higher water quality increases with the number of units of water treated.

On the demand side, Figure 3–1 assumes that fishermen are willing to pay a constant amount per unit of water quality. The horizontal line FA implies a constant average and marginal benefit of water quality to fishermen, as measured by their willingness to pay, for each additional unit of water quality.[6] For example, to obtain a water treatment level of OH units, fishermen are willing to pay GH dollars per unit, or a total amount equal to the area $OFGH$. The chemical firm incurs a total dollar cost of OMH (the area under the MC curve) to treat OH units of water. As $OFGH > OMH$, the firm profits by providing at least OH units of treated water.

The relationships shown in Figure 3–1 thus give a simplified de-

---

[6] A more complex analysis, involving monopoly considerations, would be required if we assumed that FA sloped downwards. If such were the case, the chemical firm would have to take into account the fact that the amount of water quality it produces affects the final price it can charge fishermen for admission to the lake. Our assumption of a horizontal FA schedule is probably a good approximation of reality if the lake is just one of a large number of closely substitutable fishing sites within a small area.

scription of a market for clean water or, equivalently, a market for reduced pollution. Such a market is identical, insofar as a firm's profit and loss incentives are concerned, to more conventional markets for goods and services. The chemical firm will be induced, by profit incentives, to provide water treatment up to the point where the marginal cost of producing water quality is just equal to its marginal revenue—the amount fishermen are willing to pay for the last unit of water quality sold. In Figure 3–1, the optimal level of output occurs at point E and a water treatment level of ON. At all levels of water quality less than ON, MC is less than the marginal revenue of the last unit produced, and the firm can increase profits by treating more units of water. At all levels of water quality greater than ON, MC is greater than the marginal revenue of the last unit produced, and the firm can increase profits by treating fewer units of water. At point E, the firm receives a revenue of $OFEN$ and incurs a cost of OEN from its water treatment for a net revenue gain of OFE.

Again, in this more general case, profit incentives lead to the creation of a new market and to the elimination of a previous externality. The firm that can sell reduced pollution will take into account the true social costs of its polluting activities. Once external costs are perceived as potential foregone revenues, the firm fully internalizes them as private opportunity costs. Then, through the market mechanism, the water resource or, more generally, any environmental resource, will be allocated efficiently among alternatives uses.

Note once again the crucial assumption in this example of well-defined and enforceable property rights. If the chemical firm did not have the right to exclude fishermen from the use of the lake, it would have no profit incentive to reduce its pollution. Equally important is the firm's right to exclude others from disposing of wastes in the lake. Without the latter exclusionary right, it could not effectively offer to sell cleaner water to the fishermen. With other potential pollutors of the lake a credible threat, the firm could not guarantee delivery of cleaner water. As explained in the previous section, a market for cleaner, less polluted water would not be viable in the absence of enforceable property rights to the lake.

Nothing in the foregoing analysis refers to the initial assignment of property rights to one party or another. The ownership of property rights to the lake is crucial for the viability of a pollution rights market and to the efficient allocation of resources. But it is not necessary that the chemical firm initially owns the rights to use the lake. Suppose that a fishermen's club had previously bought the lake to preserve it for sports fishing. If such were the case, then the chemical firm would appear in the scene as a potential demander of pollution rights, and the fishermen would now be the prospective seller of these rights. The same prospects for mutual gain would encourage creation of a market for use of the lake, and the optimal result of trading could be (1) sale of the lake to the firm, with the club disbanding or moving on to another site; (2) no sale and continuation of the status quo; or (3) a limited sale of rights to the firm for disposal of wastes, with only minor effects on sports fishing opportunities. Except for considerations of bargaining power, the results of the transactions in the later case are equivalent to the previous results in which we assumed that initial ownership of the lake belonged to the chemical firm.

Indeed, the original owner of the lake could be a third party, who auctions off use of the lake to the highest bidder or bidders. The lake resource would, in any case, be allocated with maximum efficiency, whatever the initial distribution of property rights, provided that market transactions are feasible. One further possibility suggested by our analysis in Chapter 2 is the merger of the two parties affected by the externality. In such an event, the externality is internalized within the same firm and an efficient allocation of resources occurs because the firm's management must now consider all costs and benefits as internal. This possibility of merger is just one good example of how a private market system will tend to internalize externalities.

This conclusion does not imply, by any means, that the initial ownership of the lake is not important to the welfare of its users. Clearly, the initial ownership of the lake puts the original owner in the enviable position of allowing others to attempt to pay him sufficient compensation to relinquish, wholly or partially, his property rights. Much needs to be said on the distributional aspects of environmental problems, but we shall defer a full analysis to Chapter 5. Finally, the reader should not conclude that the establishment of private property rights is necessary for a solution to pollution problems.

The Feasibility of a Market Solution

The analysis of the previous section suggests that the environmental problems traceable to externalities can be corrected within the framework of a private market system. The profit and loss incentives of private firms and households tend to restore efficiency of resource allocation through the establishment of new markets wherever the opportunities of mutual gains are present. This process of market extension tends to provide a comprehensive accounting for all of the economic consequences of production and consumption activities. The market solution essentially requires the existence of enforceable property rights to all environmental resources and the possibility of contractual agreements between the parties affected by an externality and those responsible for its creation. Given these prerequisites, new markets can internalize the costs and benefits of an externality and induce firms and households to include the consequences of their polluting activities in their rational economic calculations. Our discussion, thus far, has been limited to the case of water pollution, but, in principle, similar markets could form for air pollution rights and for other aspects of the environment. The theoretical arguments are perfectly general and apply, therefore, to all environmental problems involving externalities.

The market solution for environmental problems has great appeal, because it appears to involve no basic changes in the organization of economic activities in the private market sector of the economy. The only task for the government would be to extend its traditional role in a market economy by assigning and enforcing property rights to environmental resources. Unfortunately, conditions in the real world are not so simple as our textbook discussion has thus far indicated. Some important considerations argue strongly that private markets for most modern environmental externalities are not viable.

Perhaps the single most important characteristic of environmental pollution as we understand it today is that it involves externalities that are *not* limited to well-defined, and identifiable, individuals or groups. In our previous examples of the effects of externalities, we have assumed explicitly just the opposite, that is, that textile firms impose external costs on downstream farmers or that a chemical firm destroys the fishing potential of a lake. The two-party assumption permits a tractable analysis of the economic implications of externalities in general, but it does not capture the essence of the externalities relevant to *environmental* problems.

In general, pollution in a modern, industralized economy is the consequence of the by-products of consumption and production by innumerable households and firms. The disposal of wastes into the various environmental media becomes diffuse and affects many unrelated individuals by ecological processes that, as yet, are not all well understood. This is particularly true in metropolitan areas where there are large concentrations of people and industrial plants. In modern urban life, the effects of externalities are not generally confined to identifiable and distinct parties. Instead, they are pervasive and collectively form the urban environment affecting millions of individuals. We further elaborate on these points below in our discussion of the materials balance conception of environmental pollution.

Are markets for pollution rights or amenity rights feasible under these realistic conditions of the present-day world? The fact that such markets generally do not exist suggests a negative answer. Even within a single urban area, for example, thousands of air polluters may impose external costs on millions of individuals. Demanders of reduced air pollution could not call forth a corresponding supply unless they could contract with virtually all polluters and potential polluters simultaneously. Furthermore, as we shall show in Chapter 7, *clean air* is a most ambiguous and complex concept. A market for reduced air pollution would have to cope with many different air pollutants. The demand and supply relationships for each dimension of air quality would surely differ significantly, and this fact, too, would be part of the information requirements for a market for reduced air pollution.

A broker for air pollution rights could gather the requisite information and bring buyers and sellers together to sign meaningful contracts only at enormous costs. The costs of organizing and operating private markets for pollution or amenity rights are not unique. Similar costs exist to some degree for every marketed good or service. For an ordinary good, however, say toothbrushes, such costs are comparatively trivial, and private markets are viable. The opposite is true of environmental goods such as air quality because of the diffusion of the various polluting effects of production and consumption. Under such circumstances, too many complex bargains and private contracts are required for a feasible market to operate.

Matters are even more difficult, however, than we have yet indicated. First, consider the problem of sanctions against lawbreakers in any hypothetical market for air pollution rights. That is, suppose that contracts to provide cleaner air were somehow negotiated in spite of the large information and transactions costs discussed above. Successful delivery of clean air to buyers would depend critically on the ability of the police and the courts to enforce the terms of such contracts. Effective enforcement would depend, among other things, on detection of innumberable potential violators on the sellers' side of the contracts. Enforcement probably would be prohibitively expensive, especially if the general public feels that everyone has an inalienable right to burn his garbage or drive his car and refuses to cooperate with law enforcement officials. Indeed, it is the lack of a feasible technology to enforce prohibitions against use of a common property resource such as the air that explains the very existence of socially abused common property resources. A second fundamental problem is how the entrepreneur or any government could possibly obtain *true* evaluations of the value of cleaner air from potential individual consumers. We defer further discussion of these issues to Chapter 4.

We conclude that a private market system can correct efficiently for externalities only under very simple technological conditions. Unfortunately, environment pollution problems involve complex ecological relationships that make the market solution generally inapplicable. The pervasive nature of the externalities of real world environmental pollution problems makes the costs of organizing private markets to provide pollution or amenity rights prohibitive relative to potential benefits.

The Materials Balance Basis of Environmental Problems

In this chapter, we have presented the theoretical common law and market solutions to environmental externalities. Both solutions founder on the same circumstance: the diffuse and pervasive nature of the externalities associated with modern environmental pollution. This is a good point, then, to present the appropriate conceptual framework for analyzing such externalities. Until recently, most economists considered the concept for externalities an interesting intellectual footnote to the main body of economics but one of little relevance to the main public policy issues. This attitude changed only with emergence of serious environmental problems in the 1960s in the United States. The work of Allen V. Kneese and several coworkers at Resources for the Future, Inc. has been especially influential in reshaping traditional views. Kneese and others advanced a new theoretical model of the economy—the *materials balance* approach—that emphasizes that the external effects associated with waste disposal are general and pervasive in a modern economy rather than being trivial or exceptional phenomena.[7]

The point of departure for the materials balance approach is the self-evident relationship between the principle of the conservation of matter and the production process. Because physical matter cannot be destroyed, it follows that any economy will eventually have the same amount of material to dispose of as it initially uses as raw material inputs in production. Indeed, the economist's use of the term *consume* is, strictly speaking, a misnomer, because it suggests that economic goods somehow disappear as they are used. Obviously, as a society, we do not physically consume our output of economic goods. The owner of a car, for example, does not in any physical sense consume the car; he does utilize its services as a means of transportation, but the physical entity of the car remains intact after its useful life as a transport device is over. This is true of all goods, even though some goods (or parts of them) may be transformed from solid matter into gases via combustion processes or become diluted or dispersed in bodies of water instead of remaining simply as solid refuse matter. The disposal of physical goods poses an immense waste disposal problem for an industrialized economy. Ob-

---

[7] The material in this section draws heavily on R. U. Ayers and A. V. Kneese in "Production, Consumption and Externalities," *American Economic Review*, LIX, No. 3 (June 1969).

viously, different mixes of total output between physical goods and what we presently call services (that is, legal and financial services, repair services, medical services, and so on) in our national accounts will result in different magnitudes of waste disposal.

The materials balance approach conceives of the total economic process as a physically balanced flow between inputs and outputs (and the by-products associated with generating outputs). In Figure 3–2, the materials balance view of the production process is depicted to begin with some level of organic and inorganic inputs from the resource base of the economy; then, through the various energy conversion and productive processes (determined by the available technology), the economy generates some output level of final goods. During both the energy conversion and productive processes, various waste residuals are generated that are discharged into the environment. Eventually, the final outputs, after they have been *consumed* (that is, after their services are utilized), also reappear in various waste forms (trash, garbage, sewage, gases, junk, and so on) in the environment.[8]

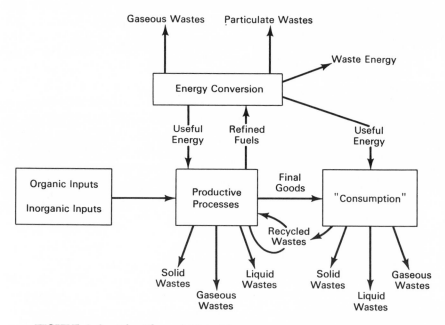

FIGURE 3–2.   The Flow of Materials.

Reprinted with the permission of the authors and the American Economic Review.

[8] We abstract, for simplicity, from the existence of net imports or exports or net changes in inventories of either inputs or outputs.

The laws of conservation of matter and energy tell us that these residual wastes will be virtually identical in amount to the physical masses of all the inputs. Some of these wastes may be recycled into the productive process to reappear as inputs. Natural biological processes also may convert some wastes into inputs after varying periods of time. The amount of recycling of wastes is influenced by the available technology and existing economic incentives. This amount can be altered by appropriately designed policies, a subject we shall discuss in Chapters 8 and 10. However, all of the wastes that are not recycled into inputs must be discharged into the environment in various physical forms (liquids, solids, gases). The essential point at present, however, is that the amount of waste residuals generated as by-products of the production process or at the end of consumption activities is essentially *equal*, in physical weight, to the amount of basic materials entering into the production process over some period of time. The principle of the conservation of matter states that the amount of residuals to be disposed will be roughly of the same order as the amount of basic inputs. Thus, it is certain that the disposal of this material in solid, liquid, and gas form represents a formidable undertaking and one whose effects will be widespread throughout the economy, particularly as the capacity of the environment in any given geographical region to absorb these materials in a costless way is surpassed.

The environment has a large but *finite* capacity to absorb these waste residuals. With increases in the production levels of physical goods in an economy, we can deduce from the law of the conservation of matter that there will be corresponding increases in the waste loads placed on the assimilative media of the environment. As these increases in production (and, hence, potential waste) impinge on the assimilative capacity of the environment, society will begin to incur significant costs associated with environmental pollution. These costs are *external* costs because the individuals and firms that use the waste assimilative capabilities of the environment in the course of production or consumption are not charged for this use. They are, in essence, using a scarce good at a zero price at the expense of the rest of society.

As a final point, we can note that the form in which the residuals are discharged into the environment can be determined, to a considerable degree, by society. Even with a given state of technology for waste disposal, society can choose how it desires to allocate the total amount of wastes between alternative media. Should the wastes be primarily gaseous (that is, use combustion processes); in liquid form, using water resources to dilute and disperse the wastes; or in solid, compressed forms, and disposed of on land? With proper information on the relative costs and benefits, a policy choice can be made of the most efficient disposal solution. Accordingly, it is inappropriate to analyze air, water, or land pollution as separate and distinct problems. For example, if an economy burns most of its wastes, the problems associated with poor air quality will be relatively greater than those of water and land pollution. Thus, the choice of using primarily one environmental medium for waste disposal does affect the qualities of the other media in any ecosystem. The implication of these physical interrelationships of waste disposal is that environmental problems must be considered simultaneously and not as independent problems. Economists working at the frontier of environmental problems are developing complex models that take a systems approach to the interrelated pollution problems of our economy.

D. THE MARKET SOLUTION IMPOSED

This section outlines a public sector analogue to the market solution for externalities presented in Section C. We have shown, thus far, that profit incentives tend to internalize externalities within an extended market system, provided that property rights to the relevant resources can be established and enforced. Given the difficulties of organizing markets for the externalities that cause environmental problems, a natural next step in our discussion is to examine alternative nonmarket solutions. The objective of our discussion remains the same, namely, to find some means of achieving efficient resource allocation in the presence of the externalities that cause environmental problems. The market solution ideally accomplishes this objective by inducing firms to internalize the external effects of their production activities. In our example, the firm becomes aware of the additional profit opportunities available to it from selling reduced pollution to the parties who bear the external costs of its activities. The prospective payments to the firm from potential consumers of reduced pollution thus become an explicit, internal cost to the firm in the form of the foregone revenue that results from its waste disposal practices. Our problem in this section is to devise a similar, nonmarket device that will accomplish the same goal of internalizing, to the relevant decision maker, the external effects of his activities.

Let us consider once more the example of the chemical firm whose wastes impose external costs on individuals who desire to use a lake for fishing. Suppose that the state government owns the lake and all its tributaries and is not willing or able to dispose of its property by sale to the private sector. What actions can it take to assure efficient use of the lake? The perhaps obvious answer is a simple one; it should *charge* the chemical firm for every unit of polluted water that it discharges into the lake. (It should also charge for all uses of the lake perhaps, but this is a separate issue that is not our present concern.) The firm will then take into account (internalize) the previous external costs of the pollution associated with its waste disposal, as it will have to pay a certain dollar amount for each unit of polluted water it produces. The theoretically correct level of this *effluent charge* is the per unit external cost of the untreated water discharge of the firm. We shall pass over, for the time being, the practical difficulties of determining the correct effluent charge amount. The important point for the moment is simply that an effluent charge is an appropriate device for internalizing previously external effects that lead to an inefficient allocation of environmental resources.

We can analyze the effects of an effluent charge by reinterpreting Figure 3–1. Let us assume that the government has a good estimate of the external costs of each unit of pollution discharged by the firm. By our previous assumption, the true value is a constant amount, equal to *OF* dollars. If the government is assumed to know this exact amount, it can charge the firm *OF* dollars for each unit of water discharge that it *fails* to treat. The horizontal line *FA* then will represent the (constant) cost of a unit of untreated water to the firm. Note that the firm must *pay* *OF* dollars per unit of untreated water discharge instead of, as in the market solution, being paid *OF* dollars per unit of treated discharge. The effluent charge thus becomes an internal cost to the firm exactly like the costs of labor, capital, and all other factor inputs into the production process. The firm is induced to make a profit and loss calculation to determine its best response to the imposition of the effluent charge. One alternative open to it is to treat its wastes, incurring the marginal treatment cost given by the *MC* schedule in Figure 3–1. Another alternative is to continue to discharge untreated water and to pay *OF* dollars per unit of discharge. The profit-maximizing (or loss-minimizing) solution for the firm is to treat the water until the cost of treating one more unit would exceed the effluent charge it pays per unit for the discharge of untreated water. In Figure 3–1, this solution occurs at the treatment level of *ON* units, at which point the *MC* schedule intersects the constant effluent charge, *FA*. At all water treatment levels less than *ON*, the effluent charge exceeds the marginal cost of treating more units of water, and the firm can reduce its total costs by further treatment. At all levels of treatment beyond *ON*, it costs the firm more to treat the water than it does to discharge untreated water and pay the effluent charge. Therefore, *ON* is the profit-maximizing water treatment level for the firm, given the *OF* level of the effluent charge.

The imposition of the effluent charge does not mean that pollution will necessarily, or probably, be reduced to zero. Zero levels of pollution will result only when the marginal cost of treatment is less than the effluent charge at all levels of treatment or if the firm's loss-minimizing solution is to close or relocate its plant. The latter extreme response will be appropriate from an economic efficiency standpoint only in cases in which fishing is incompatible with any pollution and the lake is clearly more valuable when used for fishing than when used as a waste disposal resource. The opposite extreme response by the firm would be to continue its previous level of pollution and to pay the effluent charge in full. The latter extreme response would be evidence both that water treatment costs are prohibitively high and that the lake is clearly more valuable as a waste disposal resource than as a fishing site.

The more general response is some degree of treatment of waste water together with some payment of the effluent charge, as shown in Figure 3–1. In this general case, pollution abatement will occur to some degree, probably to a point at which both the chemical firm and fishermen share use of the lake for different purposes. Whatever the firm's response, however, the imposition of the effluent charge of OF dollars assures the most efficient use of the lake, assuming again that OF is a true measure of the external costs of the firm's waste disposal activities.

The reader can easily see that the result of a per unit effluent charge of OF dollars is exactly identical theoretically in its allocation effects to the market solution analyzed in Section C. Indeed, because the two solutions are conceptually identical, they can both be depicted by the same Figure 3–1. Both solutions yield a level of treated water discharge of ON units, which is the optimal amount of pollution abatement for the firm and for society alike. In the market solution, the firm must be paid OF dollars for each unit of treated water. In the effluent charge solution, the firm must pay OF dollars for each unit of untreated water. Thus, the two solutions are equivalent in their allocational effects; both lead to the most efficient use of resources.

On the other hand, the distributional effects of the two alternative solutions are radically different. If the firm owns property rights to an environmental resource, it can in effect sell a new product—pollution abatement—to potential users of that resource and thereby *add* to its previous profits. The users of the environmental resource bear the cost of pollution abatement. If the government owns the property rights, then the firm must compensate the government for the lease of public property rights. The cost of pollution abatement will be borne largely as a capital loss by the owners of the firm. If an entire industry is subjected to an effluent charge, then in the long run, the costs will be shared more widely among factors of production specialized to the industry and the consumers of the output of the industry. The analysis of the long-run incidence of the effluent charge is the same analysis given in most elementary economic textbooks for the incidence of any tax that increases the per unit costs of industry. The supply curve of the industry shifts upward and to the left, but the demand curve is unaffected. In long-run equilibrium, the effect of such a tax is to raise the gross price of output paid by the consumer and to lower the net price received by the industry, with the tax paid per unit of output a wedge between the gross and net prices. Because the gross price to consumers must rise, industry output and sales will fall, as will industry employment of labor and capital. Some firms may be forced out of business as the industry contracts in response to the tax. The reader should note that, in general, the beneficiaries of the effluent charge (the fishermen, in our example) are not the same people who bear its cost. The income distribution consequences of the two solutions are clearly *not* equivalent. We shall further elaborate on this issue in Chapter 5.

The Feasibility of Effluent Charges

The first problem governments face in implementing effluent charges is the determination of the level of the charge appropriate for the use of each environmental medium. The correct level of an effluent charge is a most complex issue once we move away from abstract and highly simplified textbook examples. First, as we have already observed, the pervasiveness and diffuseness of the external costs of pollution make it difficult to estimate the welfare damages attributable to any single source of pollutants. No perfect substitute for the private market has yet been devised to measure accurately the demand for goods and services, such as environmental quality, that cannot be marketed. *Some* measure of the external costs of pollution must be made, for better or for worse, before setting the level of effluent charges.

A second problem is that environmental problems cannot effectively be dealt with on a piecemeal basis. As we have said, an effluent charge for use of one environmental medium such as a lake may merely shift waste disposal to an even more vulnerable alternative medium in an ecosystem with no guarantee of any net social improvement in the allocation of resources. A systems approach, taking into full account the materials balance conception of economic activities, is required to ensure adequate recognition of the interrelatedness of environmental problems and to provide the approximate basis for a *system* of effluent charges.

A related problem in implementing effluent charges concerns the measurement of effluent standards and environmental quality. In Figure 3–1, for example, the horizontal axis is labeled *units of treated water*. The concepts of *unit* and *treated* must be given operational content before implementation of any system of effluent charges. Units of water can be thought of as some quantitative measure, such as 1000 gallons or 55 cubic feet per second. But the determination of an appropriate treatment measure represents considerable difficulty for researchers in both the physical and biological sciences and in economics. Water quality involves such issues as life tolerances, disease levels, toxicity, and esthetic norms. A standardized treatment of the effluent must be determined in conformity with agreed upon quality standards. Quality standards, in turn, may depend largely on subjective attitudes of individuals toward the value of water. This point brings us back full circle to the issue of how we can determine individual valuations of environmental quality in the absence of a market. We shall examine some of the physical properties of various pollutants in Chapters 6, 7, and 8, where we shall also discuss in more detail the problems of determining quality and treatment standards for effluents.

Finally, beyond these technical problems, there remain the considerable problems of administering and enforcing a system of effluent charges. The basic problem is, once again, the enforcement of property rights, which, in this context, are the property rights of the public to various environmental media. The long tradition of free air, water, and public land resources, especially strong in the United States, is a difficult obstacle for effective implementation of effluent charges. Laws cannot be enforced unless the great majority of the people believe in them and see the necessity of enforcing them. A long period of environmental education has just begun in the United States and in other countries. In addition to the problem of enforcement of public property rights, there is a separate issue of whether governments realistically can be expected to administer a sophisticated system of effluent charges through bureaucratic agencies. We shall return to these issues in later chapters.

E. SUMMARY AND CONCLUSIONS

Externalities from environmental pollution arise when property rights are not defined for certain scarce resources or when nominal rights are not enforced. This chapter has examined alternative theoretical mechanisms for correcting for (internalizing) these externalities: (1) resort to common law remedies against nuisance or trespass, (2) extension of private markets to appropriate and trade rights to the use of environmental resources, and (3) imposition of effluent charges for the private use of publicly owned environmental resources.

The common law solution depends on the courts to impose sanctions on one private party that imposes external costs on another private party through its polluting activities. The common law remedies of monetary reimbursement for damages incurred and of injunctions against continuation of unreasonable polluting activity can internalize for the offending firm or household the otherwise external costs of pollution. The court's doctrine of "balancing the equities" can be a sophisticated mechanism for assessing and balancing the relative magnitudes of benefits and costs for society. Thus, the common law solution can correct for the externalities of environmental pollution in simple cases. Unfortunately, this solution fails for most modern pollution problems in which it is generally impossible to prove that a single party is responsible for a given amount of damage to another.

An alternative theoretical solution involves the extension of the system of private markets. When private property rights can be enforced, externalities tend to disappear because profit opportunities for firms encourage them to internalize the externalities. Once a firm recognizes that its use of a resource such as water prohibits others from using it, the possibility of selling pollution abatement will be taken into account in the firm's profit and loss calculations. The foregone revenue from not being able to sell the rights to an unpolluted or less-polluted resource to others becomes an internal opportunity cost for the firm and induces it to ration the resource efficiently among alternatives uses.

The market solution, like the common law solution, is not of much help for the kinds of externalities relevant to real world environmental problems. The market solution is feasible in simple cases of externalities, in which markets can be readily created among just a few easily identifiable buyers and sellers. The market solution is not feasible when externalities are pervasive and diffuse throughout society and the costs of organizing a market become prohibitive. But this means that the extension of the market is not a realistic solution to actual environmental problems, which by application of the materials balance approach, clearly must involve the most complex kinds of externalities.

An alternative nonmarket solution is for governments to assert their sovereign rights to environmental resources by charging private parties for their use. Effluent charges are essentially rents charged for the lease of rights to dispose of wastes in publicly owned environmental resources. The theoretically correct level of effluent charges is the external cost of the marginal unit of unpolluted air or water or some other environmental resource, which is equal to the sum of the marginal valuations of the unpolluted resource to potential consumers. The ideal effluent charge solution theoretically is equivalent in its allocational or efficiency effects to the ideal market solution but differs greatly, of course, in its distributional effects.

The effluent charge solution is no panacea for environmental problems. Like the common law and market solutions, it is most feasible in the simplest cases of externalities, not in the more complex cases relevant to modern environmental problems. The most fundamental problem is the determination of the correct effluent charge in the absence of the information provided automatically in a viable market. Another serious problem is effective coordination of a number of effluent charges into an overall system in a world of interrelated environmental problems. In addition, the technical complexities of defining quality standards for various environmental resources have yet to be fully solved.

QUESTIONS FOR DISCUSSION

1. Ordinances in most communities prohibit individuals from using their own backyards as dumping grounds for refuse. Some libertarians argue that such ordinances are examples of *big brother* government infringements on the individual's rights to use his own property as he sees fit. What is your own view, and why?

2. Suppose that the kind of ordinance described in Question 1 does not exist in a community. Is individual A helpless if his neighbor B uses his property as a free dumping ground for his garbage? If individual A burns his garbage on his own land?

3. Analyze how the variability in the useful economic life of durable goods and structures—automobiles, machinery, houses, and factories—qualifies the simple materials balance model described in the chapter. Can you think of any public policies that would lengthen the useful life of such durables and thereby reduce the amount of waste?

4. Professor J. H. Dales has proposed that a government agency in Ontario set up a market for water pollution rights. (See the Selected References.) What would be the purpose of such a government-created market? How do you think such a market would work in practice in the United States?

5. Spokesmen of the modern conservationist movement have sometimes argued against an environmental policy based on effluent charges on the grounds that "such charges are licenses to pollute and the environment is not for sale." Evaluate this argument critically.

6. Explain how, in the chemical firm—fishing example in the text, the level of external costs imposed on the fishermen is related to the following: (1) the number of fishermen; (2) the availability of alternative fishing sites; (3) the incomes of the fishermen; and (4) the preferences of the fishermen for alternative leisure activities.

SELECTED REFERENCES

COASE, R. H., "The Problem of Social Cost," *The Journal of Law and Economics*, III (1960). A classic article on the nature of externalities.
CROCKER, THOMAS D., "Externalities, Property Rights and Transactions Costs:

An Empirical Study," *Journal of Law and Economics*, 14 (October 1971). An interesting example of the use of merger to internalize externalities.

DALES, J. H., *Pollution, Property, and Prices*. Toronto: University of Toronto Press, 1968. An excellent treatment of the importance of property rights in pollution problems. Presents a detailed proposal for the sale of pollution rights.

DAVIS, O. A. AND M. I. KAMIEN, "Externalities, Information and Alternative Collective Action," *The Analysis and Evaluation of Public Expenditures: The PPB System*, Vol. I. U.S. Joint Economic Committee. Washington, D.C.: Government Printing Office, 1969. A discussion of many of the issues raised in this chapter.

KNEESE, A. V., AND B. T. BOWER, *The Economics of Regional Water Quality Management*. Baltimore: The Johns Hopkins Press, 1968. Discusses the issues of this chapter thoroughly.

KNEESE, A. V., AND R. U. AYRES, "Production, Consumption and Externalities," *American Economic Review*, LIX, No. 3 (June 1969). A generalized analysis of the full implications of production activities, with the presentation of the materials balance approach to the economy.

KRIER, J., *Environmental Law and Policy*. Indianapolis: The Bobbs-Merrill Company, Inc., 1971. An environmental law text that uses air quality issues and cases to develop the legal approach to environmental problems.

RUSSELL, C. S., *Residuals Management in Industry*. Baltimore: The Johns Hopkins Press, 1973. An advanced analysis of the emissions problem in petroleum refining. Uses an integrated systems approach for the simultaneous consideration of interrelated pollution problems.

SCHULTZE, C. L., "The Role of Incentives, Penalties and Rewards in Attaining Effective Policy," *The Analysis and Evaluation of Public Expenditures: The PPB System*, Vol. I. U.S. Joint Economic Committee. Washington, D.C.: Government Printing Office, 1969. A discussion of the basic issues of the use of effluent charges.

TIETENBERG, T. H., "The Design of Property Rights for Air Pollution Control," *Public Policy*, 22 (Summer 1974). A discussion of a workable market permit system to reduce air pollution.

APPENDIX: A Common Law Case Decision

We have excerpted below the decision in a nuisance law case that closely coincides with how an economist might evaluate an external cost problem between individuals. We present it only as an example of the use of, and problems with, the common law in the environmental area. As the reader will see, many cases can be cited which give an opposite or conflicting decision for seemingly similar circumstances. Interested students are encouraged to read the common law sections in the Krier environmental law text cited in the Selected References in order to understand more fully the complexities of this legal approach as a general solution to external costs.

BOOMER v. ATLANTIC CEMENT CO.*
26 N.Y.2d 219, 257 N.E.2d 870, 309 N.Y.S.2d 312
New York Court of Appeals 1970

BERGAN, J.   Defendant operates a large cement plant near Albany. These are actions for injunction and damages by neighboring land owners alleging injury to property from dirt, smoke and vibration emanating from the plant. A nuisance has been found after trial, temporary damages have been allowed, but an injunction has been denied.

The public concern with air pollution arising from many sources in industry and in transportation is currently accorded ever wider recognition, accompanied by a growing sense of responsibility in State and Federal Governments to control it. Cement plants are obvious sources of air pollution in the neighborhoods where they operate.

But there is now before the court private litigation in which individual property owners have sought specific relief from a single plant operation. The threshold question raised by the division of view in this appeal is whether the court should resolve the litigation between the parties now before it as equitably as seems possible, or whether, seeking promotion of the general public welfare, it should channel private litigation into broad public objectives.

A court performs its essential function when it decides the rights of parties before it. Its decision of private controversies may sometimes greatly affect public issues. Large questions of law are often resolved by the manner in which private litigation is decided. But this is normally an incident to the court's main function to settle controversy. It is a rare exercise of judicial power to use a decision in private litigation as a purposeful mechanism to achieve direct public objectives greatly beyond the rights and interests before this court.

Effective control of air pollution is a problem presently far from solution even with the full public and financial powers of government. In large measure adequate technical procedures are yet to be developed and some that appear possible may be economically impracticable.

It seems apparent that the amelioration of air pollution will depend on technical research in great depth; on a carefully balanced consideration of the economic impact of close regulation, and of the actual effect on public health. It is likely to require massive public expenditure and to demand more than any local community can accomplish and to depend on regional and interstate controls.

A court should not try to do this on its own as a by-product of private litigation, and it seems manifest that the judicial establishment is neither equipped in the limited nature of any judgment it can pronounce nor prepared to lay down and implement an effective policy for the elimination of air pollution. This is an area beyond the circumference of one private lawsuit. It is a direct responsibility for government and should not thus be undertaken as an incident to solving a dispute between property owners and a single cement plant—one of many—in the Hudson River valley.

The cement making operations of defendant have been found by the court at Special Term to have damaged the nearby properties of plaintiffs in these two actions. That court, as it has been noted, accordingly found de-

---

* Some portions omitted as well as citations and footnotes.

fendant maintained a nuisance, and this has been affirmed at the Appellate Division. The total damage to plaintiff's properties is, however, relatively small in comparison with the value of defendant's operation and with the consequences of the injunction which plaintiffs seek.

The ground for the denial of injunction, notwithstanding the finding both that there is a nuisance and that plaintiffs have been damaged substantially, is the large disparity in economic consequences of the nuisance and of the injunction. This theory cannot, however, be sustained without overruling a doctrine which has been consistently reaffirmed in several leading cases in this court and which has never been disavowed here, namely that where a nuisance has been found and where there has been any substantial damage shown by the party complaining an injunction will be granted.

The rule in New York has been that such a nuisance will be enjoined although marked disparity be shown in economic consequence between the effect of the injunction and the effect of the nuisance.

The problem of disparity in economic consequence was sharply in focus in Whalen v. Union Bag & Paper Co. (208 N.Y. 1). A pulp mill entailing an investment of more than a million dollars polluted a stream in which plaintiff who owned a farm, was "a lower riparian owner." The economic loss to plaintiff from this pollution was small. The court, reversing the Appellate Division, reinstated the injunction granted by the Special Term against the argument of the mill owner that in view of "the slight advantage to plaintiff and the great loss that will be inflicted on the defendant" an injunction should not be granted (p. 2). "Such a balancing of injuries cannot be justified by the circumstances of this case," Judge Werner noted (p. 4). He continued: "Although the damage to the plaintiff may be slight as compared with the defendant's expense of abating the condition, that is not a good reason for refusing an injunction" (p. 5).

Thus the unconditional injunction granted at Special Term was reinstated. The rule laid down in that case, then, is that whenever the damage resulting from a nuisance is found not "unsubstantial," viz., $100 a year, injunction would follow. This states a rule that had been followed in this court with marked consistency (McCarty v. Natural Carbonic Gas Co., 189 N.Y. 40; Strobel v. Kerr Salt Co., 164 N.Y. 303; Campbell v. Seaman, 63 N.Y. 568). . . .

Although the court at Special Term and the Appellate Division held that injunction should be denied, it was found that plaintiffs had been damaged in various specific amounts up to the time of the trial and damages to the respective plaintiffs was awarded for those amounts. The effect of this was, injunction having been denied, plaintiffs could maintain successive actions at law for damages thereafter as further damage was incurred. . . .

This result at Special Term and at the Appellate Division is a departure from a rule that has become settled; but to follow the rule literally in these cases would be to close down the plant at once. This court is fully agreed to avoid that immediately drastic remedy; the difference in view is how best to avoid it.

One alternative is to grant the injunction but postpone its effect to a specified future date to give opportunity for technical advances to permit defendant to eliminate the nuisance; another is to grant the injunction conditioned on the payment of permanent damages to plaintiffs which would compensate them for the total economic loss to their property present and future caused by defendant's operations. For reasons which will be developed the court chooses the latter alternative.

If the injunction were to be granted unless within a short period, e.g., 18 months, the nuisance be abated by improved methods, there would be no assurance that any significant technical improvement would occur.

The parties could settle this private litigation at any time if defendant paid enough money and the imminent threat of closing the plant would build up the pressure on defendant. If there were no improved techniques found, there would inevitably be applications to the court at Special Term for extensions of time to perform on showing of good faith efforts to find such techniques.

Moreover, techniques to eliminate dust and other annoying by-products of cement making are unlikely to be developed by any research the defendant can undertake within any short period, but will depend on the total resources of the cement industry nation-wide and throughout the world. The problem is universal wherever cement is made.

For obvious reasons the rate of the research is beyond control of defendant. If at the end of eighteen months the whole industry has not found a technical solution a court would be hard put to close down this one cement plant if due regard be given to equitable principles.

On the other hand, to grant the injunction unless defendant pays plaintiff such permanent damages as may be fixed by the court seems to do justice between the contending parties. All of the attributions of economic loss to the properties on which plaintiffs' complaints are based will have been redressed.

The nuisance complained of by these plaintiffs may have other public or private consequences, but these particular parties are the only ones who have sought remedies and the judgment proposed will fully redress them. The limitation of relief granted is a limitation only within the four corners of these actions and does not foreclose public health or other public agencies from seeking proper relief in a proper court.

It seems reasonable to think that the risk of being required to pay permanent damages to injured property owners by cement plant owners would itself be a reasonably effective spur to research for improved techniques to minimize nuisance.

The power of the court to condition on equitable grounds the continuance of an injunction on the payment of permanent damages seems undoubted.

The damage base here suggested is consistent with the general rule in those nuisance cases where damages are allowed. "Where a nuisance is of such a permanent and unabatable character that a single recovery can be had, including the whole damage past and future resulting therefrom, there can be but one recovery." It has been said that permanent damages are allowed where the loss recoverable would obviously be small as compared with the cost of removal of the nuisance. . . .

JASEN, J. (dissenting)—I agree with the majority that a reversal is required here, but I do not subscribe to the newly enunciated doctrine of assessment of permanent damages, in lieu of an injunction, where substantial property rights have been impaired by the creation of a nuisance.

It has long been the rule in this state, as the majority acknowledges, that a nuisance which results in substantial continuing damage to neighbors must be enjoined. To now change the rule to permit the cement company to continue polluting the air indefinitely upon the payment of permanent damages is, in my opinion, compounding the magnitude of a very serious problem in our state and nation today.

In recognition of this problem, the Legislature of this state has enacted the Air Pollution Control Act (Public Health Law, secs. 1264–1299-m) declaring that it is the state policy to require the use of all available and reasonable methods to prevent and control air pollution (Public Health Law, sec. 1265).

The harmful nature and widespread occurrence of air pollution have been extensively documented. Congressional hearings have revealed that air pollution causes substantial property damage, as well as being a contributing factor to a rising incidence of lung cancer, emphysema, bronchitis and asthma.

The specific problem faced here is known as particulate contamination because of the fine dust particles emanating from defendant's cement plant. The particular type of nuisance is not new, having appeared in many cases for at least the past sixty years. It is interesting to note that cement production has recently been identified as a significant source of particulate contamination in the Hudson Valley. This type of pollution, wherein very small particles escape and stay in the atmosphere, has been denominated as the type of air pollution which produces the greatest hazard to human health. We have thus a nuisance which not only is damaging to the plaintiffs, but also is decidedly harmful to the general public.

I see grave dangers in overruling our long-established rule of granting an injunction where a nuisance results in substantial continuing damage. In permitting the injunction to become inoperative upon the payment of permanent damages, the majority is, in effect, licensing a continuing wrong. It is the same as saying to the cement company, you may continue to do harm to your neighbors so long as you pay a fee for it. Furthermore, once such permanent damages are assessed and paid, the incentive to alleviate the wrong would be eliminated, thereby continuing air pollution of an area without abatement.

It is true that some courts have sanctioned the remedy here proposed by the majority in a number of cases, but none of the authorities relied upon by the majority are analogous to the situation before us. In those cases, the courts, in denying an injunction and awarding money damages, grounded their decision on a showing that the use to which the property was intended to be put was primarily for the public benefit. Here, on the other hand, it is clearly established that the cement company is creating a continuing air pollution nuisance primarily for its own private interest with no public benefit. . . .

I would enjoin the defendant cement company from continuing the discharge of dust particles upon its neighbors properties unless, within eighteen months, the cement company abated this nuisance.

It is not my intention to cause the removal of the cement plant from the Albany area but to recognize the urgency of the problem coming from this stationary source of air pollution, and to allow the company a specified period of time to develop a means to alleviate the nuisance.

I am aware that the trial court found that the most modern dust control devices available have been installed in defendant's plant, but, I submit, this does not mean that *better* and more effective dust control devices could not be developed within the time allowed to abate the pollution.

Moreover, I believe it is incumbent upon the defendant to develop such devices, since the cement company, at the time the plant commenced production (1962), was well aware of the plaintiffs' presence in the area as well as the probable consequences of its contemplated operation. Yet, they still chose to build and operate the plant at this site.

In a day when there is a growing concern for clean air, highly developed industry should not expect acquiescence by the courts, but should, instead, plan its operations to eliminate contamination of our air and damage to its neighbors. . . .

4

ENVIRONMENTAL QUALITY AS A PUBLIC GOOD

Government intervention into a private market system for any purpose raises many difficult theoretical and practical issues. This chapter explores a few of these issues relevant to the public provision of environmental quality. The purpose of our discussion is to make clear to the reader the complexities involved in collective, nonmarket, economic activities. The market system by itself fails to allocate environmental resources efficiently, but corrective action by government agencies does not *necessarily* make things any better.

The discussion of alternative solutions to environmental problems in Chapter 3 emphasized the role of property rights in achieving an efficient allocation of society's resources. In relatively simple cases of externalities from pollution, efficiency can be achieved by internalizing the costs of pollution either by enforcing traditional common law rights to property through the courts or by private appropriation of rights to environmental resources and the extension of the market system to exchange these rights. We observed, however, that these solutions were generally not feasible in the real world of complex, pervasive pollutants emitted by our industrial economy. Thus some kind of nonmarket solution for environmental problems is required.

This chapter continues this line of thought by summarizing the basis of the serious environmental problems facing society under the rubric of the problem of *common property* resources. Section A explains that the all-important environmental resources such as the atmosphere, major bodies of water, and some valuable land sites have traditionally been owned in common by all members of society. The common property characteristics of these resources is shown to be the basis of pervasive environmental degradation. Since private ownership of such resources is not feasible or desirable, public ownership must be resorted to, and public property rights must be defined and enforced. Section B discusses the theoretical problems arising from the assertion of public property rights to common property resources. The basic problem is that environmental quality is either a pure *public good* or has important public good characteristics. This means that once a given level of environmental quality is provided, it is freely available for all to consume in equal amounts. Indeed, it is virtually impossible for any one individual to avoid consuming the same level of, say, air quality as everyone else in a given air shed. Section B spells out the important efficiency implications of the public good characteristics of environmental quality. Section C then goes on to discuss the effectiveness of the government as an alternative to the market system in the provision of environmental quality. Our analysis leads to the conclusion that the government solution to environmental problems does not necessarily enhance efficiency of resource allocation. Any government will encounter formidable difficulties in obtaining adequate information through the mechanism of voting about the demand for environmental quality and in achieving specified environmental objectives at an acceptable cost.

In brief, then, this chapter is intended to provide an overview of efficiency problems associated with government environmental policies. Chapter 5 will take up the equally complex and important *equity* or income distribution aspects of these same policies.

A. THE COMMON PROPERTY BASIS OF ENVIRONMENTAL PROBLEMS

As observed in Chapter 3, environmental degradation occurs because of incomplete ownership of rights to the use of valuable resources. To put this same point in another perspective, it may be more illuminating to say that the rights to use some scarce resources are held in common by everyone in society, or at least by very large numbers of people. The atmosphere, all large bodies of water, and large amounts of public lands have traditionally been commonly owned property, and access to their use for most purposes has long been open to all comers. That is, historically individual A "owned" Lake Michigan in the sense that he could sail his boat in it with few, if any, restrictions, but his rights to use this common property resource did not extend to prohibiting its use by individual B for swimming or by individual C for dumping his garbage. If common property resources have sufficient capacity relative to all demands on them, then no economic problem arises when the community shares in their use. When demand rises to the point where users inflict external costs on each other, however, then economic efficiency inevitably suffers. For example, two centuries ago the dumping of garbage into Lake Michigan did not appreciably affect the quality of the water for use in boating and swimming; today it clearly does. Environmental problems such as air and water pollution have resulted from the historical tradition of treating the atmosphere and waters as common property resources. Unfortunately, with many people using common property resources for many purposes, the environmentally damaging uses—e.g., for a community dump—dominate the nondamaging uses—e.g., swimming. Only recently has the law begun to place limits on certain uses of these resources.

Economists have long recognized that there is a strong tendency toward overexploitation and degradation of common property resources. Common ownership may be better characterized as effectively *no ownership*. The individual who burns his trash and pollutes the air reaps the full benefit of free trash disposal but bears only a tiny fraction of the welfare damage costs of his pollution. His own private benefit-cost test is simple: The benefits of burning his trash exceed his costs. In the absence of some offsetting consideration such as (1) a social conscience, (2) informal community sanctions such as his neighbors' overt disapproval of his inconsiderate behavior, or (3) formal, *effectively enforced* legal sanctions such as fines or imprisonment, it is rational for him to ignore the external effects of his pollution on the quality of the common property of the atmosphere. If everybody else follows the same private benefit-cost logic, air quality will deteriorate, and everybody may end up worse off, in the sense that the total benefits of "free" trash disposal are less than society's welfare damage costs of air pollution. This is the kind of perverse social situation that Garrett Hardin has termed "the tragedy of the Commons." [1]

---

[1] Garrett Hardin, "The Tragedy of the Commons," *Science*, Vol. 162, pp. 1243–1248 (1968).

The reader should note the ironical implication: The "invisible hand" does not work when common property resources exist; all individuals could be *better off* if they all refrained from attempting to maximize their own self-interest.

Some familiar examples of the overuse of common property resources will help illustrate the general idea outlined above. National parks used to be common property resources in the absence of entry fees and charges for camping privileges or other nonprice restrictions on use. (To the extent that such fees and charges are too low, they still are, although to a lesser degree.) When demand for the use of national park resources was still relatively low, this did not matter because any one person's use of the parks did not detract from the benefits enjoyed by other users. As demand grew, however, overuse of these valuable common property resources became all too evident. The individual visiting the parks took into consideration only his own personal benefits and costs and ignored the external costs of crowding and pollution his visit inflicted on other visitors. The National Park Service now imposes some fees and charges, but these are nominal and are generally not intended to control access. Common ownership of the ocean makes it costless for tankers to flush their fuel tanks at sea. The oil slicks impose external costs on firms and households that also attempt to use the ocean either as a commercial or recreational resource.

The common property resource problem also explains the phenomenon of "endangered species." Nobody owns the rights to whales. If any one country delays in getting its fair share of the available supply of whales, other countries may not be so slow. Thus, there is a strong incentive for overharvesting of the whale population and a consequent threat to the survival of the species. What is true on an international scale for whales is true also for other species within individual countries. Note that the endangered species are all wild and undomesticated; there is no concern about the survival of privately owned livestock. Nationalistic concerns for appropriating the ocean's resources—minerals, oil, fish stocks—have led recently to declarations of 200-mile limits of exclusive use off the coastline of many countries, including the United States.

Finally, common ownership of community resources, such as city parks, streets, and public buildings, is the source of other environmental problems. People who litter in public parks and public thoroughfares do not, in general, dump trash on their own real estate holdings. The lack of enforceable property rights to commonly owned resources explains much of what John Kenneth Galbraith has termed "public squalor amid private affluence."

Common property resources are held in the form of common, rather than private, property for understandable historical and technological reasons. The appropriate social response to the common property resource problem is *not*, in general, to convert common property into private property. For both efficiency and income distribution considerations, common property should in general be transformed into *public* property. The transition from common to public property requires some mechanism for rationing the use of a resource, that is, ending free access to all. The problem for society is how to create some institutional process to ensure allocating these resources efficiently among alternative uses. This is a most complex problem because one alternative use of these resources is to provide *public goods* (or services) for society. The nature of the efficiency problems with public goods is the subject of Section B.

B. ENVIRONMENTAL QUALITY AS A PUBLIC GOOD

A (pure) public good may be defined as the limiting, or extreme, case of externalities. That is, a public good is one that is enjoyed in equal amounts by everyone in society. To put the same idea in a different perspective, individual A's consumption of a public good is necessarily equal to individual B's consumption of that good and to every other individual's consumption as well.

Consider an array of all possible goods and services along a continuum running from pure private goods to pure public goods. At one end of the continuum are such pure private goods as most personal services, e.g., television repair services. At the other end are pure public goods such as national defense. The characteristic distinguishing these and all other goods and services in the economy along this imaginary continuum is the degree of externalities involved in their production and consumption. Television repair services involve a minimum of externalities, as do many other personal services. Most goods possess some degree of externalities, because of disposal problems. In contrast, national defense involves maximum externalities of consumption because all the benefits from the provision of national defense accrue automatically to everybody in society. Once a given level of protection is provided for any one individual in society, the same level of protection is available for more than 200 million other individuals without additional cost. The marginal cost of providing national defense services for one more individual is literally zero. Indeed, society can exclude any individual from sharing the consumption of these services only by incurring costs to remove him beyond its protected boundaries.

Thus, the degree of externalities inherent in goods and services, and, therefore, the degree of *publicness*, varies over an extremely wide range. It is difficult to conceive of more than a very few goods or services

that are either purely private or purely public on the basis of our definition. For our purposes in this book, however, it is sufficient to note that
environmental quality lies near the extreme public end of the private
good-public good continuum. This is the case because, like national defense services, once a given level of environmental quality is provided
for any one individual, it can be enjoyed by others in society at virtually
zero additional cost. The best example of this point is the provision of
clean air; once provided for one person, it is also available automatically
to everyone else within the same air shed. Again in common with national
defense services, any individual can be excluded from the benefits of
purer air only by expelling him from a given area.[2] Of course, the scope
of publicness can vary from one small community to the entire world,
depending on the aspect of environmental quality in question.

A well-developed literature on the economics of public goods may
be applied directly to the problem of environmental quality. As we shall
argue, although it is futile to expect any form of adequate private market
solution to the provision of environmental quality or of any other pure
public good, the alternative of government provision is not free of grave
problems of a different sort.

Let us assume, for our discussion in this section, that the government recognizes the inability of private markets to function efficiently
with relation to environmental problems and that it decides to intervene
to provide higher levels of environmental quality directly. The particular
methods the government uses to achieve its environmental objectives—
prohibitions, regulations, effluent charges, or others—need not concern
us here, for this policy choice problem is the subject of all of Part 4. Instead, we shall concentrate for the present on some general theoretical
aspects of government provision of environmental quality.

In Chapter 3, market failure in the provision of environmental quality was shown to be due in part to the problem that information costs
and transaction costs are too high for mutually advantageous private
contracts to be negotiated for the rights to environmental resources.
Ideally, the government can use its fiat powers to cut through the maze
of information and transaction costs and enforce any given environmental
quality standards it establishes as its proximate goals. At issue here is the
economic *efficiency* of any hypothetical government-imposed solution.

[2]Any particular good is not a public good because of the *impossibility of exclusion.*
It is almost never impossible to exclude individuals from sharing in the consumption of any good
or service. The more fundamental point is that, in the case of public goods, exclusion is too
costly to be *worth* enforcing on the basis of the efficiency criterion. As we emphasize in the
text, for example, an individual *can* be excluded from the benefits of air pollution control,
but it is not worth enforcing exclusion when the marginal costs of providing such benefits to any
individual are zero or very close to zero.

The basic allocation problem is the determination of the socially optimal level of environmental quality in all relevant dimensions. The general efficiency rule is that more environmental quality should be provided only up to the point at which additional social benefits are equal to the additional costs. Problems arise, however, in determining the magnitude of the relevant benefits and costs in the absence of price information provided automatically in market transactions. Once the government abandons the market as an allocation mechanism for environmental resources, it must find some other means of obtaining information on the benefits and costs that result from its actions.

We have defined a pure public good to be the limiting case of externalities and have observed that environmental quality fitted well into this conceptual category. The case of clean air was cited as perhaps the best example of an environmental good meeting the pure public good criterion. Once a given quality of air is provided for any one individual, it is automatically available without additional cost to all other individuals in the same air shed. Recognizing this technological fact, how can a government estimate a demand or benefits schedule for clean air in determining the efficient dimensions of an air quality program? The possible conceptual demand schedules for a public good are outlined below; the estimation of either one raises profound problems for public policy.

Demand as the Sum of Willingness to Pay

Let us begin by attempting to give precise meaning to the concept of the demand for a given level of air quality. We might define the *demand price* for any air quality level by appeal to the private market analogy, that is, as the sum of the amounts all individuals are willing to pay per unit of output. In markets for private goods, the demand price (P_i) for the ith unit of output (Q_i) is simply the price at which the sum of all individual demands exactly equal Q_i. That is, for a given level of output Q_i, the average value of output to consumers is the price P_i at which consumers are collectively willing and able to buy the total amount Q_i. Figure 4–1a illustrates the conceptual derivation of a private market demand curve for the three-person case. Total quality Q_i corresponds to the *horizontal* summation of individual demands OA, OB, and OC at price P_i. All consumers pay the same price but buy different amounts. The locus of all such (P_i, Q_i) points is the market demand curve D_T.

For a pure public good, however, individuals cannot choose to vary the amount they consume independently of each other. If any individual consumes a given amount Q_j of a pure public good, then everybody necessarily also consumes exactly Q_j. Figure 4–1b shows the conceptual

FIGURE 4–1a. Private Good Demand Curve: Horizontal Summation.

FIGURE 4–1b. Public Good Demand Curve: Vertical Summation.

derivation of a pure public good demand curve, again for the three-person case. The demand price P_j corresponding to a given quantity Q_j is the *vertical* summation of individual valuations (willingness to pay) OP_A, OP_B, and OP_C. Everyone consumes the same amount, but they differ in how much they are willing to pay for any given quantity. The locus of all such (P_j, Q_j) points is the demand curve for a public good, D_T. We would expect this public good demand curve to slope downwards just like an ordinary private good demand curve. For either public or private goods, the law of diminishing marginal utility states that individuals are willing to pay more for the first few units of consumption of any good than they are for additional units. For example, most individuals value clean air highly if they see a direct relationship between very polluted air and their ability to breathe. Once the air is clean enough to allow breathing without great difficulty, the relationship between air quality and health is less obvious, and the willingness to pay for clean air therefore diminishes.

How *good* an estimate of the demand for a pure public good such as clean air can the government hope to obtain? If a government agency attempts to ask directly for individual valuations of different air quality levels through some sort of survey, it will undoubtedly obtain a very poor estimate. First, it may find that the costs of gathering such information are unacceptably high. The private market is an efficient instrument for generating high-quality information, and nonmarket substitutes such as questionnaires are distinctly inferior. A more fundamental problem, however, is that individual valuations of a public good cannot be trusted as true valuations if individuals see any systematic relationship between their answers to hypothetical questions and the amounts they may be charged (through taxes or prices) to pay for the provision of the good. Any intelligent individual realizes that the total estimated demand price for a given air quality level will be virtually unaffected by his own individual valuation and therefore that his failure to reveal his own true valuation will not affect the demand price for the whole population. He also knows that if the government does proceed to provide better air quality in the area, he will share it equally with everyone else as a *free rider* regardless of the amount he pays to help finance antipollution measures. If he suspects that his share of the cost of any government programs will be related to the amount he says he is willing to pay, he will have a strong monetary incentive to understate his true valuation. (Note that he cannot conceal his true valuation of a private good. If he does not pay the going market price for a private good, he is excluded from consuming it.) Even if he is otherwise a public-spirited citizen, he knows that all other individuals are aware of the situation and are subject to the same incentives to understate their true valuations. He may therefore consider himself foolish to reveal his true preferences if he has reason to believe that others will not be so forthright.

The competition of all individuals to minimize their share of total payments in these circumstances is not coordinated by a benevolent invisible hand to lead to an optimum result. Thus, it seems almost inevitable that total demand for public goods would be greatly understated if the government attempted to obtain demand information by means of sample surveys or by other nonmarket devices. Alternatively, if people believe that their responses to hypothetical questions cannot affect their tax burdens, they may *overstate* their true valuations of public goods. Thus, public opinion polls often find large majorities in favor of all kinds of social welfare programs when they are presented in a costless guise.

This analysis helps explain why the dominant mode of government provision of public goods takes the form of largely *noneconomic* legislative and administrative determinations of quality and quantity levels together with financing through general taxation. The political process thus substitutes for the private market system as a resource allocation device for public goods. Everyone in society shares in the financing of the costs of any public good according to his position in the total tax structure, but his tax share of the total cost may be far from his own individual valuation of any particular public good. At best, an individual's total tax burden may correspond roughly to his valuation of the total package of public goods provided by the government, but even this weak correspondence does not necessarily hold. In general, nothing in the political process guarantees that the total package of public goods provided meets the test of efficiency of resource allocation.

Demand as the Sum of Willingness to Sell

The *willingness to pay* approach to the determination of the demand for public goods, outlined above, is explicitly based on the analogy of the determination of private market demand. Private market demand curves, in effect, measure the value of a good by the amount of income individuals are willing and able to give up to obtain it. Thus, in our previous discussion we implicitly treated the demand curve for clean air as a measure of the willingness and ability of the population to give up income for cleaner air. This approach to the determination of demand for a public good follows the private market analogy so closely and naturally that it may tempt the reader to believe that it is the one correct approach. But if we probe deeper into the question, we can see that the willingness to pay approach to demand determination yields only a *minimum* estimate of the value of a given level of environmental quality to the public. More fundamentally, it depends on the assumption that the public must pay for the property rights to environmental resources.

Suppose that we begin, instead, from the plausible assumption that property rights to the air and to other environmental common property resources reside in the general public and cannot be appropriated by any private parties without adequate compensation. With this assumption, it no longer makes sense to value a given level of air quality by asking how much individuals in society are collectively willing to pay for it, as they already own it. Instead, it is natural to ask for the minimum amount all individuals collectively would be willing to accept as compensation to give up their rights to all higher-quality levels. The latter approach yields a *maximum* estimate of the value of a given level of air quality, and of the quality of environmental resources in general.[3] Why does the latter approach give a higher valuation than the willingness to pay approach? The answer is that the original assignment of property rights to the public gives it greater financial ability to achieve a higher standard of consumption, including consumption of environmental quality. In other words, if the public owns common property resources such as the atmosphere, it is wealthier than if it has to pay private parties to relinquish their use of these resources.

A specific example can illustrate this point. A man's willingness to pay for a minimum level of air quality just sufficient to sustain life is bounded by his current income, his net assets, and his ability to borrow. But *no* conceivable price could compensate him for the loss of his life if air quality is his to sell. A great gap may exist between the two alternatives of the willingness to pay and the willingness to sell, as measures of the value of environmental quality.

The reader should note that the *willingness to sell* approach to the valuation of environmental resources poses the same basic information problems as the willingness to pay approach. In either case, the government cannot count on the self-interest of individuals to obtain an unbiased measure of total demand for environmental quality. If the government attempted to use direct survey methods to obtain individuals' valuations of environmental quality according to the willingness to sell concept, individuals would be tempted to overstate their true valuations if they believed that their tax liability might be reduced according to their response. The analogy to our previous discussion of the willingness to pay approach should be obvious without further elaboration. The important difference between the two approaches lies in the assignment of property rights to environmental resources and not in the fundamental difficulty of obtaining true evaluations in the absence of private market transactions.

Thus, it should now be evident to the reader why resource allocation in the public sector is determined largely through the political process. Political judgments have been supplemented in recent years by formal benefit-cost analyses that make use of information derived indirectly from market transactions. However, the role of market-type information is still relatively insignificant. We shall take up the subject of the political and administrative processes as mechanisms of resource

---

[3] This point is developed more fully in E. J. Mishan, "The Postwar Literature on Externalities: An Interpretive Essay," *The Journal of Economic Literature*, IX, No. 1 (March 1971).

allocation in Section C. First, however, we shall discuss selected international environmental problems as important illustrations of the points in this and the preceding section.

International Environmental Problems

As noted previously, the scope of public goods varies enormously. Some environmental problems transcend all national boundaries because the environmental resources involved—the oceans and the atmosphere—are the common property of all mankind. The degradation of these crucial resources occurs because national governments as well as private individuals and firms treat them as common property. Although global environmental quality is a global public good, no international government exists to provide effective environmental protection.

The global environment has deteriorated significantly in many respects in recent decades. The international treatment of the oceans as common property resources has permitted locally devastating oil spills and ocean dumping of highly toxic and exotic forms of wastes. The survival of whales and other species of ocean life is threatened because of failure by national governments to limit their harvests of these valuable, renewable resources. The technological feasibility of ocean mining in the near future threatens the oceans with immense environmental degradation, similar in nature to the effects already evident from conventional mining on land.

Similarly, nuclear radiation does not respect national boundaries. The advent of nuclear power on a mass basis threatens the survival of all of mankind. One small nation's failure to provide adequate protection of its nuclear facilities against accident or sabotage could doom millions of people within and beyond its own borders.

Perhaps the most interesting case of environmental degradation on a global scale is the gradual, insidious buildup of carbon dioxide in the earth's atmosphere. Carbon dioxide is a natural and necessary component of the atmosphere and plays a vital role in the life cycle of all plants and animals. In normal amounts it is readily absorbed by plant life and by large bodies of water. Unfortunately, the enormous releases of carbon dioxide by the combustion of fossil fuels, especially coal, cannot be absorbed by natural processes. As a result, carbon dioxide levels have been rising steadily over past decades. A National Academy of Sciences study has documented the past buildup of carbon dioxide in the atmosphere and has projected even faster increases in its atmospheric concentration in the future. For example, the report projects a doubling of carbon dioxide levels between now and the year 2050. These projections are the result of a massive increase in reliance on fossil fuels and of economic growth throughout the world. The individual user of coal or oil contributes a negligible amount of carbon dioxide to the atmosphere, but heavy and continued worldwide use of these fuels results in dramatic, if gradual, changes in the composition of the earth's atmosphere.

The welfare damages of carbon dioxide "pollution" of the atmophere are subtle and long-term in nature. Increases in carbon dioxide levels in the atmosphere exert what is called a "greenhouse" effect on the earth. The amount of solar energy reaching earth is not reduced; however, the increased carbon dioxide concentration does absorb some of this energy, thus interfering with the normal process of its radiation back through the earth's atmosphere. This leads to an increase in temperatures on earth unless the "greenhouse effect" is offset by some other temperature-reducing force. The consequences of projected temperature increases due to carbon dioxide buildup stagger the imagination. The earth's climate would be transformed with unpredictable, but likely devastating, effects on the earth's population through natural disasters such as floods and famines. The ultimate irony of the world "energy shortage" thus may turn out to be the limited capacity of the atmosphere to absorb the carbon dioxide emissions from combustion of fossil fuels without severe consequences for mankind. The only way to avoid the projected carbon dioxide buildup in the amosphere is to cut down drastically on the use of fossil fuels, especially coal. This could be accomplished, perhaps, in any one country by determined government measures to force firms and households to use much more costly alternative forms of energy. Such measures within one country would be futile, however, unless other governments did the same. But such a situation is an excellent example of a public good problem in the absence of a government authority that can effectively protect a common property resource. Any one country can enjoy the benefits of environmental protection measures by other countries as a free rider while continuing to use relatively cheap fossil fuels itself. International competition will induce all countries to attempt to be free riders in the absence of any coercion or enforced cooperation.

It is difficult at this time to envisage any form of international government cooperation that would induce many countries to switch away from cheap fossil fuels to much more expensive alternatives. Indeed, more reliance on coal is the heart of the current U.S. energy program. Thus, the prognosis for atmospheric degradation throughout the world must be very pessimistic.

C. GOVERNMENT AS A PROVIDER OF ENVIRONMENTAL QUALITY

Thus far in the book, we have paid a great deal of attention to the economic reasons for *market failure* with respect to environmental problems. We have argued that, even under otherwise ideal circumstances, the private market system fails to allocate environmental resources efficiently because of the pervasiveness of pollution costs external to private decision makers. This chapter has carried the basic argument one step further to show that environmental quality is an important example of a class of goods appropriately termed *public goods,* the extreme case of externalities in which private market failure is most complete. Granted these arguments, the goal of economic efficiency in environmental resource allocation calls for collective action through some form of government intervention. We now must face the issue of the efficiency of government in its role as a producer of environmental quality. Is it realistic to expect that any government can increase efficiency of environmental resource allocation for a society by its intervention in private markets? If so, what are the appropriate limits, if any, on the degree of public intervention?

Our discussion of these questions proceeds in the following order: First, we examine the role of voting as a mechanism for determining the public interest in environmental issues. That is, how good a substitute for the private market system is voting in providing basic information about individual valuations of different environmental alternatives? Second, given the outcome of voting and the determinations of the public interest in environmental problems, how well do government agencies function in achieving agreed-upon objectives? In other words, how good a substitute is the typical bureaucratic government agency for the typical profit-maximizing firm in the private market? Finally, we briefly examine the issue of the appropriate balance between the public and private sectors of the economy in the provision of environmental quality.

Voting and Efficiency

Economists often observe that consumers in a private market system vote with dollars instead of ballots. Under ideal conditions—an acceptable distribution of income (or dollar votes) and perfect competition—the market is the most sensitive of electoral mechanisms. The consumer is said to be sovereign because each dollar vote in the market has equal weight in its claim upon scarce resources. Of particular importance is the fact that the system gives the dollar votes of minorities equal weight with the dollar votes of the majority. The interests of the majority prevail, but not at the expense of minorities. Under ideal conditions, such a system of market voting results in an efficient allocation of society's resources.

For a public good such as environmental quality, however, the market system of dollar voting breaks down as an efficient social resource allocation mechanism. The government must take responsibility for the provision of public goods, and, inevitably, the decisions of government officials, guided in a democratic system more or less by the wishes of the electorate, replace the decisions of the market.

Voting becomes the mechanism for revealing individual preferences about alternative allocations of environmental resources. Remember that efficiency, in the economic sense of the word, is not just an engineering concept; it is defined in relation to individual preferences. Therefore, we take up the issue of how well the mechanism of voting serves the cause of economic efficiency in comparison to a private market system of dollar voting.

The political process, as it exists today, gives public officials only the loosest set of guidelines to the true aggregation of individual preferences about environmental alternatives. Not all potential consumers of environmental quality are eligible to vote, and even the eligible voters often do not participate in elections. Those individuals who do vote do not participate in numerous referenda on individual issues but, instead, generally select one of two candidates, each of whom embodies an intentionally vague stance on a wide variety of issues. Furthermore, voters do not choose candidates solely on the basis of rationality or self-interest but are also influenced by such considerations as the television personalities of the candidates and often also by their race, religion, and even the sexual attributes of their spouses. Minority votes do not stand on an equal footing with majority votes in determining the allocation of resources. The refusal to vote does not convey an important and unambiguous message in politics as does a refusal to spend on consumption goods in the private market system. Finally, in general, individual votes differ fundamentally from market dollar votes in that the former do not directly reveal the *intensity* of individual preferences for alternatives. Intensity of preferences can only be expressed outside the polling place by a variety of activities of varying effectiveness.[4]

Without belaboring the point any further, it should be obvious that the present political system is not a sensitive mechanism for translating individual preferences into economically efficient social decisions, especially not on issues as narrow as those that arise in the provision of environmental quality. At best, the existing political process places some broad constraints on elected public officials by not allowing them to deviate too far from the majority views of their constituencies on any particular set of issues. Even granted that this ultimate veto on unpopular decisions by government officials does exist and does operate effectively, the burden of formulating public interest about economic efficiency

---

[4] For example, groups such as the Sierra Club and Audubon Society help express the intensity of the feelings of environmentalists through lobbying and educational activities.

in the provision of environmental quality largely must reside with the relevant elected and appointed government officials.

On a more abstract level, voting is deficient as a mechanism for articulating the public interest even under ideal circumstances. Suppose that a society consisted of as few as three individuals, each of whom had unambiguous preferences between any two of as few as three alternatives states of the world. Would majority voting generally lead to an un-ambiguous collective ranking of the three alternatives? In a classic study of this and related issues, Kenneth Arrow has demonstrated that the general answer to this question is *no;* unambiguous collective rankings of the alternatives do not necessarily result from the aggregation of un-ambiguous individual rankings.[5] Thus, voting cannot be counted on as a mechanism for determining the public interest in the environmental area even if we could ignore all the practical problems of our present political system.

In summary, some very difficult practical and conceptual problems arise in attempting to relate voting to the concept of economic efficiency. The issues in this area of political economy are deep and cannot be treated adequately in this book. But the reader should understand the basic point that voting does not necessarily lead to a clear articulation of the public interest in environmental issues.

Government Bureaucracy and Economic Efficiency

Let us now take as given the broad environmental decisions of the legislature, which, hopefully, reflect the preferences of the general public. To be more concrete, suppose that the Congress has appropriated funds to some agency for the administration of various environmental programs specified in previous legislation. How well can the bureaucracy of the agency be expected to function according to the criteria of economic efficiency? Will the allocation of society's resources really be improved relative to the private market as a result of the agency's activities?

Only general answers can be given to these important questions despite the existence of a huge literature on the characteristics and per-formance of bureaucracies. Economists, typically, approach the problem of the functioning of bureaucracies—either private or governmental—by observing that, in general, bureaucrats should be expected to pursue their own self-interest (maximize their utility) in their jobs, very much like workers and entrepreneurs in the private sector. This presumption about individual bureaucratic behavior is neutral and is not biased toward the

---

[5] Kenneth J. Arrow, *Social Choice and Individual Values* (2nd ed.) (New York: John Wiley & Sons, Inc., 1963).

view that bureaucrats are either any better (more altruistic) or any worse (more selfish) than people in nonhierarchical positions. The reader will recall that the self-interest of individual firms and households in the private sector is coordinated by the checks and balances of the market system and that the invisible hand of the market will, under ideal circumstances, make the sum of individual self-interest lead to maximum social welfare. Analogously, we may ask whether a similar mechanism operates in bureaucratic structures to coordinate the self-interested behavior of individuals to produce socially desirable results.

The answer depends on whether the perceived private benefits and costs of a bureaucrat's activities correspond to *social* benefits and costs in some kind of normal, or equilibrium, state. (The analogous question for the private market is, of course, whether equilibrium market prices correspond to social benefits and costs.) Unfortunately, there are strong presumptions for believing that bureaucratic incentive structures do not foster economic efficiency. Specifically, the major incentive facing a bureaucrat usually is to maintain or increase the agency's budget appropriation. Toward this end, he will go by the book in carrying out his duties and will above all avoid fiscal scandal or some similar malfeasance in office. In contrast, achieving efficiency of resource allocation for society is only vaguely understood and poorly motivated. Unfortunately, the social costs of use of scarce bureaucratic time and effort to achieve these goals is likely to be vastly different from the perceived individual costs of the average bureaucrat. However abhorrent on moral grounds, individual dishonesty in the use of government funds and failure to observe strictly directives from superiors generally involve trivial social costs, but the costs of a severe misallocation of society's resources can be enormous.

We can summarize this complex subject with the generalization that the incentives facing government bureaucrats, whatever their other advantages, do not, in general, promote socially optimal behavior according to economic efficiency criteria. The bureaucratic structure of rewards and penalties does not correspond to market prices in an ideal market system, and, therefore, no mechanism analogous to the invisible hand of the market operates to assure efficiency in the allocation of society's resources. The efficiency problem inherent in bureaucratic structures has been recognized by government administrators, and valiant first attempts were begun in the late 1960s to develop *Planning, Programming, Budgeting Systems* (PPBSs) in federal government agencies. The basic goal of PPBSs was to promote economic efficiency by inducing each government agency to subject its own activities to a systematic analysis of the relationship of resources expended to program aims. PPBS quickly passed into oblivion, however, and government agencies generally carry on today according to traditional bureaucratic procedures.

The Optimal Balance of Private and Public Economic Activity

The preceding discussion should dispel any illusions that the solution to all instances of private market failure is government intervention. Just as a perfect private market system is a textbook ideal, so is the kind of government activity outlined in Chapter 3, in which the divergence between the private and social costs of some market activity is perfectly offset by a scientifically calculated effluent charge. Government economic intervention may be quite imperfect, in general, for two reasons:

1. Individual preferences are likely to be weighted incorrectly, or even overridden altogether in the process of formulating the public interest at the administrative and legislative levels of government. The prevailing system of majority voting is not an adequate substitute for dollar voting in an ideal private market for the purpose of economic efficiency.

2. Once the public interest is determined by the government, however accurate the weighting of individual preferences, the bureaucratic agencies of government that are entrusted the task of carrying out policies are not engines of economic efficiency, whatever their other merits may be. The problem of efficiency in government primarily is concerned with the optimal allocation of scarce resources relative to social economic goals and not just the avoidance of waste of government funds or cost minimization within an agency. The structure of bureaucratic incentives inevitably pushes government agencies toward the latter goals at the cost of neglecting the optimal allocation goal.

The foregoing points have led some economists to suggest the concept of *government failure* as an analogy to the concept of *market failure*. Government failure, like market failure, is not total, but rather a matter of degree, and it does not necessarily extend to other important dimensions of government beyond the attainment of economic efficiency. But it is a key concept because it correctly implies that not all government intervention is an improvement on the private market—at least on efficiency grounds—in cases where market failure is apparent. In our imperfect world, this means that society must somehow choose in each specific case between the better of two less than ideal solutions to the allocation of resources, or perhaps more accurately, between the lesser of two evils. The specific form of government intervention to deal with any environmental problem is also an important issue. The government may be much more effective in dealing with pollution problems through one kind of intervention than with some alternative measures.

Our discussion in this section may help to clarify the reasons for what Marshall Goldman has called *the convergence of environmental disruption* in societies as different in their economic structure as the United States and the Soviet Union.[6] Why should environmental problems exist in the centralized Russian economy in which externalities in private markets surely cannot be blamed for the failure of the economic system to account for all pollution costs? Because the Soviet government owns all the important property rights, it would seem that it would allocate environmental resources efficiently by balancing all marginal productivity gains against all marginal pollution costs. But, as Goldman makes vividly clear, such is not the case. Russian environmental problems are similar to those in the much more decentralized American economy, despite the large discrepancy between the levels of total output in the two countries. Russian bureaucrats appear to pay little more attention to broad issues of economic efficiency than do American bureaucrats. The Russian environment suffers from the results of the monument-building mentality of Soviet government officials just as the American environment often suffers from the single-minded activities of the U.S. Army Corps of Engineers and the Bureau of Reclamation. The message of this discussion should be the disillusionment of any notion that government intervention *automatically* provides a solution to environmental problems.

The foregoing discussion is narrow in focus in that is assumes implicitly no ideological preferences for either the private sector or the public sector. Many economists fervently believe that there is always a strong presumption in favor of the private sector over the public sector on the grounds that greater government economic activity always results in a curtailment of precious individual freedoms. Other economists argue just the opposite position and contend that the conception of *freedom,* in the arguments of the private market advocates, is naive and overly narrow. Such noneconomic considerations obviously will play an important role in society's choice of how best to deal with environmental problems in the absence of any clear-cut presumption that either the private or public sector is a superior mechanism for attaining an efficient allocation of resources.

D. SUMMARY AND CONCLUSIONS

This chapter has discussed the efficiency aspects of government provision of environmental quality. Most environmental problems are traceable to the common property nature of environmental resources. Common property ownership of resources such as the atmosphere has traditionally

---

[6] Marshall I. Goldman, "The Convergence of Environmental Disruption," *Science,* CLXX, No. 3953 (October 2, 1970), pp. 37–42.

meant no ownership at all and free access to all users. Environmental degradation of such resources has occurred when demand has risen to overwhelm their limited capacity to absorb wastes. Individual maximizing behavior becomes perversely inefficient when property rights to resources are held in common and government assertion of public property rights is required to assure efficient resource allocation. Extreme examples of this inefficiency are evident from some serious and threatening international environmental problems.

Government provision of environmental quality involves serious efficiency problems of a different kind. Environmental quality is a public good in that the benefits of environmental improvement are shared in equal amounts by all who live in a given area. For example, improvement of air quality provides cleaner air for everyone in a given air shed. The benefits of cleaner air are equal to the sum of all the individual evaluations of the improvement. Following this reasoning, demand curves for environmental quality can be derived conceptually with benefits commensurable with costs. Unfortunately, the government has no means of obtaining the information necessary for estimating the true demand functions and must resort to rough approximations based on public preferences expressed through voting and other political activities. Thus, the efficiency of the government solution to environmental problems is inherently subject to a large degree of error.

Finally, some very simple points about the workings of government reveal the sobering and not surprising conclusion that government intervention in the environmental area is not a panacea for private market deficiencies. The problems of defining the public interest through the mechanism of voting and of achieving agreed-upon goals efficiently through the actions of bureaucratic agencies are of comparable importance to the problems of market failure, suggesting the analogous concept of government failure. The realistic choice society faces, in meeting its environmental problems, is between two quite imperfect mechanisms for achieving efficiency, and it does not necessary follow that, in every instance of private market failure, government intervention in any form results in a net social gain.

QUESTIONS FOR DISCUSSION

1. Eagles in the United States are an endangered species. Conservation groups have been successful in having laws passed prohibiting the killing of eagles. Western ranchers ignore these laws, however, and

kill eagles to protect their livestock. The government has not been able to enforce these laws, and the eagle is in danger of extinction. Can you think of any solution to this problem within the constraints of narrowly limited resources? What social arrangements might reconcile the interests of conservation groups and ranchers?

2. Consider a pollution problem in your own area. Indicate the methods you might use to obtain quantitative measures of the demand schedule for pollution reduction. How good are the measures you think you could obtain at reasonable costs?

3. How much are you willing to pay to improve air quality in your own community? Does your answer depend on how much others have to pay? Suppose that the air quality in your community were ideal. How much would the government have to pay you to obtain your permission to pollute it to its present state?

4. Solar energy has no significant effects on the environment but is considered much too expensive compared to fossil fuels and nuclear energy to be practical as an alternative. When costs of energy sources are compared, how are external costs considered? How does this affect the perceived relative cost of solar energy?

5. Suppose that your own local government were given funds to improve the quality of the environment. Based on what you know about its performance in providing other services, predict how well it would carry out its new environmental responsibilities. Specifically, would you expect it to improve significantly the overall efficiency of resource allocation?

SELECTED REFERENCES

AMACHER, R. C., R. D. TOLISON AND T. D. WILLETT, "The Economics of Fatal Mistakes: Fiscal Mechanisms for Preserving Endangered Predators," *Public Policy* (Summer 1972). An interesting approach to making common property private property to save wild animal species from extinction. Provides a possible answer to Question 1 above.

ARROW, KENNETH J., *Social Choice and Individual Values* (2nd ed.). New York: John Wiley & Sons, Inc., 1963. A classic fundamental study in political economic theory. Very advanced.

BOHM, P., "An Approach to the Problem of Estimating Demand for Public Goods," *Swedish Journal of Economics*, LXX (March 1971). Proposes a method of handling the dilemma of obtaining true valuations for public goods.

BUCHANAN, JAMES M., "Individual Choice in Voting and the Market," *Journal of Political Economy*, LXII, No. 4 (August 1954). A classic discussion of the relationship between voting and economic efficiency.

CHRISTY, F. T., JR., "Property Rights in the World Ocean," *Natural Resources Journal* (October 1975). A review of the status and issues of property rights for various uses of the oceans' resources.

GOLDMAN, MARSHALL I., *The Spoils of Progress: Environmental Pollution in the Soviet Union.* Cambridge, Mass.: The M.I.T. Press, 1972. A fascinating account of environmental problems in the Soviet Union.

HAVEMAN, ROBERT H., AND ROBERT D. HAMRIN (eds.), *The Political Economy of Federal Policy.* New York: Harper & Row, Publishers, Inc., 1973. An excellent review of the efficiency performance of federal policy in many areas—defense, agricultural, natural resources, transportation, and urban problems.

HEAD, J. G., "Public Goods and Public Policy," *Public Finance,* No. 3 (1962). A treatment of the relationship between externalities and public goods.

KRUTILLA, JOHN V., "Efficiency Goals, Market Failure, and the Substitution of Public for Private Action," *The Analysis and Evaluation of Public Expenditures: The PPB System,* Vol. I. U.S. Joint Economic Committee. Washington, D.C.: Government Printing Office, 1969. A good source on the effects of the government sector on efficient resource allocation.

SAMUELSON, PAUL A., "Diagrammatic Exposition of a Theory of Public Expenditure," *The Review of Economics and Statistics,* XXXVII, No. 4 (November 1955). The pioneering study of the economics of pure public goods.

STEINER, PETER O., *Public Expenditure Budgeting.* Washington, D.C.: The Brookings Institution, 1969. A survey of many of the topics covered in this chapter.

5

INCOME DISTRIBUTION ASPECTS OF ENVIRONMENTAL POLICY

Government environmental programs raise complex issues of distributional justice, or *equity*. As observed in Chapter 2, maximization of efficiency in resource allocation can be defined concretely in the Pareto Optimum sense: a situation in which it is impossible to reallocate resources in such a way as to make anybody better off without making anybody else worse off. This conception of efficiency must assume, however, a given distribution of income among all households. But there are an infinite number of Pareto Optimal states—at least one for each of an infinite number of different income distributions. Intervention by the government in economic affairs will not be distributionally neutral. Some individuals will always enjoy windfall gains as other individuals suffer windfall losses. Government environmental programs, in common with all other government economic activities, cannot, therefore, be judged solely on the basis of pure benefit-cost or efficiency criteria. Considerations of distributional justice should also count to some degree in the decision-making process of a government environmental protection agency.

Efficiency is a deceptively simple and attractive objective for government economic policy. Who can oppose the principle that more of every good for everybody is desirable. Economists are careful to point out, of course, that greater efficiency in the Pareto Optimum sense means only that more of everything is potentially available for everybody. The distribution of the actual gains from efficient changes in society's mode of resource allocation often is quite unequal. As a rough generalization, many government programs result in large gains for a few beneficiaries and small losses for the general public, with the total value of gains perhaps somewhat larger than the total value of losses. In an attempt to separate efficiency from equity considerations, economists have devised various compensation tests that say, in effect, that any given change is socially desirable (more efficient) if the gainers *could* fully compensate the losers for their losses and still come out ahead. Unfortunately, these compensation tests suffer from a large degree of theoretical ambiguity. More fundamentally, the hypothetical compensation of losses is, in general, impossible in the world outside the covers of economic textbooks. We may conclude, then, that equity and efficiency effects of government programs are inextricably interrelated in practice and must be considered jointly in the formulation of economic policy.

This chapter takes up the equity issue according to the following outline. Section A discusses the main analytical issues concerning the distributional effects of governmental environmental policies. The criteria for desirable distributional effects are much less concrete and therefore much more controversial than the Pareto Optimum criterion for efficiency in resource allocation. Tracing out and quantifying the full distributional impact of specific government programs is a challenge both from theoretical and empirical standpoints. Section A attempts to illustrate these points with a carefully worked out example of a hypothetical case with familiar real world counterparts. Section B then goes on to summarize the empirical evidence now available on the income distribution effects of government environmental programs and on the distribution of environmental quality within the United States. Section C then briefly reconsiders the possible trade-offs between efficiency and equity in environmental policy. Section D is a summary of this chapter and of the main points of all of Part 2.

A. EQUITY ISSUES IN ENVIRONMENTAL POLICY

The meaning of efficiency can be defined with precision in the Pareto Optimality sense, but what are the criteria for distributional equity? Moral philosophers have long debated this issue without, unfortunately, reaching any consensus. Let us venture two relatively simple criteria acceptable to many but not to all:

1. A redistribution of income is socially desirable, other things equal, if it raises the incomes of the very poor closer to the average level of income in society. A more controversial extension of this criterion would deem any change desirable, other things equal, if it reduces the inequality of the whole income distribution, that is, if it narrows the gap between very high and average incomes as well as the gap between very low and average incomes. This is called the *vertical* equity criterion.

It is important to add that other things are often *not* equal with government programs that reduce the inequality of incomes. Such programs generally involve some reduction in efficiency through their effects on incentives, and therefore they achieve greater equity only at the expense of loss of potential output. We shall return to the equity-efficiency trade-off problem in Section C.

2. In contrast to the above vertical redistribution criterion, no comparable general rule applies to what are largely *horizontal* redistributions of income, that is, transfers of income between individuals at the same level of income. Horizontal redistribution may be said to occur when income is transferred between two groups differentiated *principally* by characteristics other than size of income, even if the average income of the two groups is not precisely equal. We can only suggest the criterion that gains and losses from such horizontal redistributions of income should not be arbitrarily bestowed or imposed on minorities in the population unless other considerations of government policy are of overriding importance. Insofar as possible, the losers should have recourse to the full procedural protections traditionally afforded them by our common law traditions.

As the reader should recognize, distributional equity is a thorny issue that is not easily susceptible to analytical treatment. Indeed, no completely satisfactory method of making the efficiency and equity effects of government programs commensurable in the social decision-making process has ever been devised. A dollar's worth of greater efficiency cannot readily be compared with a dollar's worth of redistribution between the rich and the poor or between, say, the East and the West. Such an agnostic view is cold comfort, however, to public officials, who *must* make decisions between various options involving complex mixtures of efficiency and redistributional effects, including the option of making no changes at all from the status quo. With these general considerations as background, we turn to equity problems related to government environmental programs.

The Impact of Environmental Programs
on the Distribution of Income

If an environmental program is effective in abating pollution, it results in benefits in the form of less welfare damage for all persons affected. The value of these benefits may differ greatly among the beneficiaries. The same population will bear the costs of the program in the form of lower incomes, higher prices, extra taxes, or foregone private or public consumption opportunities. As in the case of benefits, the costs may vary greatly from person to person. The *net benefit* of the program for each person is his or her benefits net of costs. This can be a net cost if personal costs exceed benefits. The distribution of net benefits (and costs) among the population may alter the original distribution of income significantly.

Some simple examples will help to illustrate the income distribution effects of environmental programs. Suppose that the government prohibits a firm from dumping its wastes into a neighboring river and the firm is forced to close down for lack of an alternative disposal site. The benefits of this action accrue to the users of the river; the costs fall on the owners and workers of the firm and perhaps also on its customers if there are no close substitutes for its products. Suppose, for a somewhat different example, that the government decides to clean up a polluted river. The main benefits remain with the users of the river, but the costs in this case are borne primarily by those who pay the taxes to finance the cleanup program. In the latter case, the costs will be shared much more widely among the population than in the first case. Such income distribution comparisons of alternative government programs to enhance environmental quality are of the utmost importance for policy decisions; they stand on an equal footing with benefit-cost tests of relative efficiency.

Short-Run Equity Effects

Most popular interest in the distributional effects of government environmental programs centers on their short-run employment impact. Often, government environmental regulations threaten the closing of a local factory or a severe cutback in its scale of operations. If full employment exists in the area, workers can make transitions to new jobs without great difficulty. In many instances, however, the impact of a plant closing can be devastating, especially for older workers with minimal skills or specialized, nontransferable skills. Such employment effects, however serious they may be in individual cases, are commonly exaggerated beyond their true importance. First, there are few cases where it can be shown that environmental regulations have actually resulted in large numbers of layoffs. The owners of firms and unions find the threat of such layoffs a useful political weapon to fight against the implementation of costly regulations. Indeed, the automobile industry and the United Auto Workers union have skillfully used the threat of mass shutdowns and layoffs to persuade Congress to postpone again and again the effective date of implementation of tough auto emission standards. Also, plants which do close may blame environmental regulations when the real reason lies elsewhere, e.g., obsolete plants and equipment or poor management.

The prevailing view of the threat of environmental programs to jobs neglects the fact that environmental programs taken together as a package create as well as destroy employment opportunities. When environmental regulations force firms to invest in pollution abatement devices or in new, less polluting equipment, new employment is created. There is no good a priori reason to expect environmental programs to be job-destroying or job-creating on balance. The empirical evidence on this issue is inconclusive, and much depends on the timing or phasing in of pollution control requirements. Monetary and fiscal policies should be relied on, in any event, to maintain aggregate demand and overall employment at high levels. Specific employment assistance such as retraining programs or special unemployment benefits should be used to deal with severe local impacts of environmental programs—just as they are used to alleviate the similarly disruptive employment effects of a large volume of new imports from our trading partners abroad. In summary, too much attention has been given to the short-run distributional impact of environmental programs and too little to their more general, permanent impact on income distribution.

Gains and Losses from Environmental Programs

We turn now to consideration of the full distributional effects of environmental programs, taking into account all the gains and losses—direct and indirect, short-run and long-run. The identification of gains and losses can be extremely complex in the general case in which the parties affected by an environmental program are large in number and geographically diffuse. We shall attempt to bring out the essential points by use of a relatively simple example, however, in which the benefits and costs of an environmental program can be readily identified.

Let us assume that a metropolitan airport authority acquires some land in a convenient site located in a previously peaceful suburban community, Jetportville, and proceeds to construct an airport. The noise from jet aircraft landing and taking off from the airport turns out to make life very unpleasant for the inhabitants of Jetportville. In response to the anguished complaints of its constituents, the local government success-fully asserts its sovereign local air rights and institutes a schedule of landing and takeoff fees—called *noise control* fees—designed to reduce the noise pollution problem of the community. The mayor of Jetport-ville fortunately happens to be an economist, and recognizing that the noise control fees are a variety of effluent charge, he sets up a complex schedule of fees that vary with type of aircraft and time of day. Because of his cleverness, the program turns out to be a great success. Who gains and who loses from Jetportville's noise reduction programs?

The most obvious gainers are the residents of Jetportville. The noise control fees not only reduce the psychic costs from noise pollution but also raise additional revenue for the local government. The additional revenue can be used either to finance additional local services or to lower local property taxes that finance the existing level of services or to sub-sidize soundproofing of homes. Both the reduction in noise pollution levels and the additional revenue will result in higher real incomes (including psychic benefits from noise reduction) for the residents of Jetportville. Probably the best direct measure of the increased welfare of the citizens of Jetportville is the observed increase in property values in the com-munity. The impact of noise control fees should, at least, offset the initial loss in property values caused by the construction of the airport and the excess noise problems associated with it. The *worst* Jetportville could do would be to set the noise control fees so high as to close down the airport, but it is likely that the residents could do better by trading off some peace and quiet for the additional revenue that could be derived from the noise reduction fees.[1]

Who are the other gainers and who are the losers from Jetport-ville's noise reduction program? Let us assume for this discussion that the situation in Jetportville holds more generally for all airports in the country. In the short run, the airlines and, perhaps, the airport authority are likely to suffer a reduction of profits, because they cannot avoid the extra costs of the noise reduction fees and of the shifting of flight schedules in response to the fee schedule. In the longer run, however, the price of airline tickets must rise to include the costs resulting from the noise reduction fees so that the return to capital invested in the air-line industry will not fall below the normal level for the industry. The eventual higher price of airplane tickets will impose additional costs on

---

[1] Our previous discussion of distribution effects should make it clear to the reader that the gains and losses from the government's noise control fees are just the opposite of the gains and losses that would result if the city had to compensate the airport authority for any noise reduction. To restate our previous fundamental point, the distribution of gains and losses from environmental programs turns on the assignment of property rights to one side or the other.

all airline travelers, however, including those business firms for whom air travel is a business expense. If we can presume that the demand curve for airplane travel is downward sloping, the higher price for airplane tickets will reduce the amount of air travel and, therefore, will also indirectly reduce the demand for all the resources hired by the airline industry. Resources that are highly specialized to the industry—airline pilots and skilled jet engine mechanics, for example—may experience a reduced demand for their services, and many individuals in those groups will suffer a loss in income. Other resources, such as unskilled labor and basic raw materials, that are not highly specialized to the airline industry will, in general, be reabsorbed into other industries at much the same prices and will suffer relatively small losses, if any.[2]

Even in this simple example, the analysis of the full redistributional effects is not yet complete. The rise in the price of airplane tickets implies an increase in demand for alternative forms of travel and communication as substitution away from airline travel occurs, and the increased demand will result in some indirect gains for the resources employed in alternative transportation industries. For exactly the same reasons discussed above, resources specialized to, say, the railroad industry will experience gains comparable to the losses suffered by the resources specialized to the airline industry. Of course, all of these indirect gains and losses may be quite small, depending on the size of the noise reduction fees and the elasticity of supply and demand schedules for the airline industry.

Finally, we should observe that the direct gainers from the noise reduction program, the residents of Jetportville and other airport communities, will, in general, share the gains unequally. The big gainers will be the individuals who initially suffered the most from noise damages, those who enjoy the largest actual reduction in experienced noise levels, and those who derive the most benefits from the additional fee revenue, either through expansion of local government services or from tax reduction. Note also that the set of gainers may overlap with the set of losers. The resident of Jetportville or some other community who gains from the noise reduction program in the form of reduced noise damages and higher property values may also lose in his role as an employee of the airline industry or as an airline passenger.

In general, the best economists can do is to trace out the likely major gainers and losers from environmental programs; benefit-cost analysis will rule out the high costs of attempting to specify in any detail all the indirect distributional consequences of environmental programs.

[2] This discussion assumes full employment of all resources.

More complicated cases than the example considered in this section will involve correspondingly more complex redistributional effects. The most useful contribution an economist can make in this area is to present to the policy decision makers comparisons of the major distributional differences expected to result from major environmental policy alternatives. Much of the popular literature on environmental problems suggest that only the *bad guys* or the *interests* lose when the government intervenes in the private market system to improve environmental quality and that the public gains. Unfortunately, the truth is much more complex. Let us now attempt to apply the two distributional criteria suggested in the introduction to this section to problems that face society in choosing between environmental policy alternatives.

To begin, let us first examine more deeply the noise reduction example presented above. As the example stands, most readers probably would not question the noise reduction fee program on distributional equity grounds, because the gains to the residents of Jetportville largely go to reimburse them roughly for the psychic and dollar losses of noise pollution arbitrarily imposed on them by the construction of the airport. In addition, it is well established that the typical airline passenger enjoys a much higher than average income. In comparison to the residents of Jetportville, then, the direct losers from the noise reduction fees are likely to be able to afford their losses, which, in any event, probably are very small for any individual because of their wide dispersion among the many thousands of passengers using the airport facilities. Thus, the most direct redistributional effects of the noise reduction program appear to violate neither of our two suggested criteria; both vertical and horizontal redistributional effects appear to be acceptable and, perhaps, even desirable.

The reasoning above is faulty, or at least incomplete, on two grounds. First, the example implicitly assumes that the residents of Jetportville at the time the noise reduction program takes effect are identical to the people who initially suffered losses. Such a situation is possible, but it should be recognized realistically as an extreme case. To take an equally extreme counterexample, suppose that all the original residents of Jetportville responded to the announcement of the site of the airport by selling their properties to large industrial corporations at prices that fully reflected the capitalized losses in property values due to the anticipated noise pollution. If each original resident of Jetportville valued the expected psychic loss of noise pollution from the airport at, say, $500 per year, he would have been willing to sell his property at the previous market value minus the present value of a perpetual annual flow of $500 per year (about $10,000 at a 5 percent rate of discourt).[3] Given this admittedly extreme assumption, the full loss from the location of the airport is borne by the original residents who sell their properties and move away. Other people, the owners of corporations in this example, acquire the affected property at reduced prices that fully capitalize the cost of noise pollution and can suffer losses only if the level of noise pollution turns out to be greater than expected at the time the properties are purchased. Thus, the gains from the noise reduction program accrue to the *new* owners of property in Jetportville and are obviously pure windfall gains. These gains are just as arbitrary a redistribution of income as the losses originally imposed on the previous residents. In reality, the gains from the noise reduction program will undoubtedly be some mix of more or less justifiable compensation for previous losses and of windfall gains, with the degree of the mix depending on specific factors such as the extent of capitalization of the losses in value due to noise pollution and the volume of turnover of properties after the airport site is first announced.

The second complicating factor in our simple noise reduction example has already been raised in our previous discussion. The losses due to the noise reduction fees are borne in part by the consumers of airline

---

[3] The value or market price of any asset traded in a competitive market tends to equal the present discounted value of the expected income flows from that asset. In symbols,

$$P_A = \sum_{t=o}^{n} \frac{Y_t}{(1 + r)^t} ,$$

where P_A is the market price of the asset, Y_t is the expected net income yield of the asset in time period, t, r is the rate of discount, and n is the number of time periods in the expected life of the asset. If n is very great—a realistic assumption for a long-lived asset such as real estate—and if Y_t is a constant over time, then the above equation can be approximated by the following simplification:

$$P_A = \frac{Y_t}{r} ,$$

which is the basis for the example given in the text.

For some assets, bonds, for example, Y_t is simply expected money income. For an asset such as real estate, however, Y_t is the sum of any net money income (rent, for example) and the value of the housing services enjoyed by the owner of the real estate. Even if Y_t consists entirely of nonmoney income, it can be reduced by any phenomenon, such as noise pollution, that lowers the value of the housing services from a real estate property in a given location. The loss from noise pollution is a real loss, as can be established by observing that if the owner rented out his house instead of living in it himself, the noise pollution problem would force down the rents he could successfully charge potential tenants. The money equivalent of the noise pollution loss must be subtracted from the initial value of Y_t to obtain the postpollution value. Then, by the above formula for the market valuation of an asset, the income loss is said to be *capitalized* in a corresponding change in the capital value of the real estate. In reality, the extent of capitalization will depend on such factors as the degree of uncertainty about the actual effect of noise pollution and in various, specific real estate market circumstances in Jetportville.

services, but additional indirect losses fall on resources specialized to the airline industry. The latter indirect losses may take the form of lay-offs of pilots and skilled mechanics, who can find no comparable employment opportunities in other industries, even if the labor force is fully employed.[4] These unfortunate individuals and their families are likely to judge the redistributional effects of the noise pollution program as arbitrary horizontal redistributions of income and as a violation of our horizontal equity criterion.

The points raised thus far in this discussion are difficult to generalize because the redistributional effects of various environmental programs will vary greatly according to the circumstances special to any given environmental problem. We can observe, however, that often and, perhaps, in a majority of cases, a conflict will arise between the efficiency and equity criteria that should guide government environmental policies. An environmental program that passes a benefit-cost efficiency test is likely to violate both of our equity criteria. First, the redistributional effects of many environmental programs may be regressive or favor the rich because the benefits will be more highly skewed toward upper income classes than the tax burdens that finance such programs. Our basis for this speculation is that many environmental goods—air and water quality, peace and quiet, and natural recreation facilities—are apparently highly income elastic goods, yet the total tax structure of all governments taken together in the United States is, at best, very mildly progressive. If environmental programs are financed at the state or local level of government, the net regressivity of benefits and taxes will be even more pronounced because the slight progressivity of all taxes is the net effect of the modest progressivity of federal government taxes and the regressivity of state and local tax structures.

Two factors, not yet mentioned, complicate the above analysis. First, if the mechanism for improving environmental quality is effluent charges rather than government expenditures, we would have to know the distributional impact of a general system of effluent charges rather than the distributional effects of marginal changes in the existing tax structure. In the absence of evidence to the contrary, we would take the neutral position that effluent charges are similar in their distributional effects to a proportional tax on consumption. But because consumption declines as a percentage of income at higher levels of income, it is likely that such a tax is slightly regressive. Thus, we see no reason on this count to alter our analysis substantially. On the other hand, the existing

---

[4] In an economy of fully flexible prices and wages, the adjustment would take place through a general fall in wages for skilled airline employees. In the real world of wages that are downwardly sticky, however, some unemployment is the more likely occurrence.

burden of some kinds of pollution costs may fall very unevenly on the poor. In particular, the worst air quality is generally to be found in central cities. So, under some circumstances, antipollution measures may well have an important effect in equalizing the real incomes of rich and poor. The above point does not contradict our original hypothesis that the rich are willing to spend a greater fraction of their income on environmental quality than the poor, but it does substantially modify our generalizations about the distributional effects of environmental programs in a world in which existing pollution costs are currently distributed unequally.

Second, the largely horizontal redistributional effects of many government environmental programs will inevitably impose arbitrary losses on people who are no more to blame in any ethical sense for pollution problems than the general public. Many of the gains apparently accruing to firms and individuals from using scarce air, water, and land bodies as free waste disposal resources are almost entirely illusory because the cost savings from such polluting activities are, by this late date, largely capitalized and incorporated into the economy's relative price structure. The typical individual who owns some small fraction of a firm that pollutes the air paid a price for his shares of stock in the company that fully reflected the cost advantages to the firm from using the air as a free waste disposal resource. Any government program that takes away the assumed air pollution rights of the company will cause a reduction in profits and in the value of the common stock of the company. In addition, as observed in our previous example, environmental programs that force industries to bear explicit costs for the use of environmental resources lead to a contraction of the output of the industries, with indirect losses consequently borne by specialized labor and other resources. None of these losses can be justified on the grounds of the moral responsibility of the affected individuals for the state of environmental quality. For the most part, the original sinners responsible for our current environmental pollution problems have gone to their graves completely unaware of their guilt in a simpler age before the existence of such problems was even recognized.[5]

To summarize, theoretical analysis suggests that many environmental programs that pass a benefit-cost efficiency test will have undesirable equity effects. In such circumstances policy decision makers must somehow attempt to balance efficiency and equity considerations. We shall discuss this problem in Section C; first, however, in Section B we

---

[5] This point does not apply, of course, to new industries that attempt to claim rights to the use of scarce environmental resources. For example, it does not sanction the redistributional effects of the supersonic transport (SST).

discuss the empirical evidence available on the distributional effects of environmental policies.

B. EVIDENCE ON DISTRIBUTIONAL EFFECTS OF ENVIRONMENTAL POLICY

The theory of the last section suggested that environmental programs will have a pro-rich or regressive effect on the distribution of income. Theory by itself is not sufficient, however, and this section presents a summary of the available evidence on this issue. The reader is cautioned in advance that economists began only very recently the immense job of gathering evidence on the distribution of pollution prevention costs and pollution damage and damage avoidance costs. The greater part of this long story still remains to be told.

National Estimates

Three studies have attempted comprehensive estimates of the distributional effects of national pollution abatement programs. As in all empirical work of such ambition, many critical assumptions are required, and the results of any one study must be treated with considerable caution. Nevertheless, the weight of the evidence allows a tentative conclusion that the net benefits of governmental programs to improve environmental quality are regressive, or at best, proportional.

In an ambitious study, N. Dorfman and A. Snow examined the incidence of the pollution control (prevention) costs of existing and proposed environmental standards from 1972 to 1980.[6] Three separate components of the distribution of costs were analyzed: (1) auto emission control costs, (2) general price increases resulting from required pollution control expenditures by industry, and (3) the additional taxes (at all levels of government) assumed to be necessary to fund environmental control programs. The estimated total of all three effects together appears in Figure 5–1. The vertical axis measures the cost of pollution control as a percent of family income, and the horizontal axis shows the cumulative size distribution of income. For each year, pollution control costs are regressively distributed—the percentage of income they represent declines as income rises. Moreover, it appears that this regressivity increases with time, and the 1980 results are the most markedly regressive of all three years.

[6] N. S. Dorfman assisted by A. Snow, "Who Will Pay for Pollution Control? The Distribution by Income of the Burden of the National Environmental Protection Program, 1972–1980," *National Tax Journal*, 28, No. 1 (March 1975).

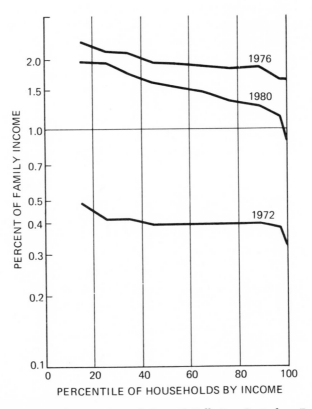

FIGURE 5–1. Distribution of Total Cost of Pollution Control as Percent of Family Income 1972, 1976, and 1980.

Source: N. S. Dorfman assisted by A. Snow, "Who Will Pay for Pollution Control? The Distribution by Income of the Burden of the National Environmental Protection Program, 1972–1980," *National Tax Journal,* 28, No. 1 (March 1975), p. 102. Reprinted with the permission of the journal and authors.

Figure 5–1, however, represents only half the incidence story. It does not measure the distribution of the benefits—the value of pollution damages avoided—of the national pollution control program. Conceivably, if the benefits of pollution control were very progressive, this could outweigh the regressive pattern of control costs, and net incidence (benefits minus costs) could be progressively distributed.

Unfortunately, national estimates of pollution control benefits by income class are even more elusive than those for pollution control costs. However, Professor Robert Dorfman has attempted to integrate the above results on pollution control costs with an estimate of the distribution of environmental benefits derived from a consumer survey on environmental quality.[7] The survey, sponsored by the National Wildlife Federation, questioned individuals on how much they would willingly pay in additional taxes to clean up the natural environment. Willingness to pay was then taken as a proxy for benefits received, and the answers to this question were related to income levels. Figure 5–2 shows this relation for four different income groups. As expected, a greater percentage of higher-income individuals are willing to pay for any given increase in the costs of pollution control.

After merging the previous results on pollution control costs with this estimate of benefits, Dorfman concluded that the distribution of net benefits remains regressive. That is, for low-income families as a whole, the costs of pollution control exceed the benefits they receive. For high-income families, on the other hand, benefits exceed costs. His results suggest that families with incomes below $6000 experience negative net benefits, while families above an income level of approximately $11,500 receive positive net benefits.

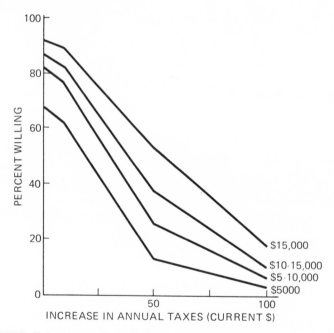

FIGURE 5–2. Asserted Willingness To Pay Taxes for Environmental Improvement, 1971 Survey.

Source: R. Dorfman, "Incidence of the Benefits and Costs of Environmental Programs," *American Economic Review,* Vol. 67, No. 1, February, 1977, p. 336. Reprinted with the permission of the *Review* and the author.

[7] R. Dorfman, "Incidence of the Benefits and Costs of Environmental Programs," *American Economic Review,* 67, No. 1 (February 1977).

As already observed, great caution must be taken before accepting these estimates. The methodology in this study of asking a direct question about willingness to pay involves all the *free rider* problems discussed in Chapter 4. Moreover, the "cleanup" question asked was very general and encompassed all types of program benefits—air, water, recreation, etc. Nevertheless, the results suggest that the regressive distribution of pollution control costs persists even after an estimate of program benefits is taken into account.

An entirely different approach to incidence was taken by Gianessi, Peskin, and Wolff. They combined micro industry data and air quality information to estimate the distributional effects of achieving the ambient air quality standards of the Clean Air Act of 1970.[8] Their study estimated the distribution of both benefits (damages) and control costs. Estimates of the pollution damage by industry were allocated to local geographic areas throughout the United States according to the employment distribution of each industry. Damages were assumed to be proportional to emissions, and the geographic and population size of the local area was also taken into account. Pollution control costs were divided into three components: industrial, household, and government. Industry costs were distributed according to recent evidence on the relation between consumption expenditures and income class. Government costs were assumed to follow the incidence of the average tax burden, while household costs (essentially auto emission controls) were allocated according to the income distribution of automobile ownership. Table 5–1 summarizes the distribution of benefits, costs, and net benefits from this

TABLE 5–1   DISTRIBUTION OF NET BENEFITS OF AIR POLLUTION CONTROL BY INCOME CLASS
(percent of income)

	Income Class ($000)									
	< 3	3–4	4–6	6–8	8–10	10–12	12–15	15–20	20–25	25+
Pollution control costs	8.2	6.0	5.1	4.4	3.9	3.6	3.4	3.0	2.7	1.8
Benefits	8.0	5.1	4.1	3.5	3.4	3.0	2.9	2.5	2.2	1.3
Net benefits	−0.2	−0.9	−1.0	−0.9	−0.5	−0.6	−0.5	−0.5	−0.5	−0.5

Source: H. M. Peskin, "Environmental Policy and the Distribution of Benefits and Costs," in P. Portney, *et. al.* eds., *U.S. Environmental Policy*, (Baltimore, Johns Hopkins Press, 1978). Reprinted with the permission of the author.

[8] L. P. Gianessi, H. M. Peskin, and E. Wolff, "The Distributional Effects of the Uniform Air Pollution in the United States," *Quarterly Journal of Economics*, forthcoming.

study. As in the Dorfman and Snow study, pollution control costs turned out to be regressively distributed. Here, however, benefits were progressive, and the net benefits of achieving the federal air quality standards were neither clearly progressive nor regressive. Net benefits were progressive to an annual income level of approximately $8000 and proportional for all higher income levels.

Pollution Exposure

A number of other studies have examined the distribution of air pollution according to physical measures of pollutants. They have not attempted to translate pollution levels into estimates of dollar damages but instead have examined the spatial distribution of pollution exposure.

Asch and Seneca matched annual particulate matter levels in 1972 at 76 air pollution monitoring sites in three U.S. cities with the incomes of the population residing in the census tracts where the monitoring sites were located.[9] Each census tract was categorized according to whether the annual level of particulates violated or complied with the federal standard for this pollutant, that is, an annual average of no higher than 75 micrograms per cubic meter of air (mg/m^3). Table 5–2 summarizes the results for the three cities: Chicago, Cleveland, and Nashville. The cell values in row 1 are the number of families in each income group exposed to particulate levels which meet the federal standard (i.e., levels below 75 mg/m^3), divided by the total number of families in the city in that particular income class. Row 2 gives the number of families in each income group residing in tracts where the standard is violated (i.e., greater than 75 (mg/m^3), again divided by the total number of families, city-wide, in that income class. If air quality were randomly distributed with respect to income, the values in both rows would all tend to be equal to 1. For example, if 10 percent of the families in the city had annual incomes below $3000, we would expect to find that of those families living in areas where the air quality standard was violated, 10 percent of them would have income below $3000. An income group is overrepresented in any cell if the ratio exceeds 1 and underrepresented if it is less than 1.

A consistent pattern emerged for each city; the poor were underrepresented in areas where the air quality standard was met and overrepresented in areas where it was violated. Conversely, higher-income

---

[9] Particulate matter is any solid or liquid particles suspended in the air (dust, ash, soot). The principal sources of particulates are stationary combustion processes (e.g., power generation) using solid fuels (coal). Particulates are responsible for the aggravation of respiratory diseases (leading to increased mortality), soiling of property, and crop damage. P. Asch and J. J. Seneca, "Some Evidence on the Distribution of Air Quality," *Land Economics*, 54, No. 3 (August, 1978).

TABLE 5–2   POLLUTION EXPOSURE INDEX:
PARTICULATE MATTER (primary standards)

Particulates	Income ($000)						
	< 3	3–5	5–7	7–10	10–15	15–25	25+
Chicago							
1. < 75 mg/m³	0.688	0.889	0.955	0.940	1.008	1.084	1.209
2. > 75 mg/m³	1.477	1.169	1.071	1.091	0.988	0.870	0.680
Cleveland							
1. < 75 mg/m³	0.526	0.689	0.635	0.861	1.081	1.342	1.613
2. > 75 mg/m³	1.280	1.218	1.257	1.098	0.944	0.759	0.568
Nashville							
1. < 75 mg/m³	0.713	0.776	0.762	0.895	1.061	1.269	1.703
2. > 75 mg/m³	1.282	1.220	1.234	1.103	0.940	0.735	0.310
All three cities							
1. < 75 mg/m³	0.659	0.815	0.867	0.912	1.025	1.147	1.329
2. > 75 mg/m³	1.428	1.233	1.169	1.112	0.969	0.815	0.589

Source: P. Asch and J. J. Seneca.

groups were overrepresented in good air quality neighborhoods and underrepresented where air quality was poor. The conclusion is that for this large urban sample, including 76 census tracts and almost 100,000 families, particulate matter air pollution was regressively distributed.

Freeman noted a similar regressive pattern for sulfur dioxide as well as particulates for three different U.S. cities—Kansas City, Washington, D.C., and St. Louis—using earlier (1966) pollution data.[10] Zupan, employing an air quality simulation model for air pollution in the New York metropolitan region, also concluded that low-income groups were located in areas of relatively poor air quality.[11]

Thus, these studies all show that the welfare damage costs of poor air in urban areas are borne disproportionately by low-income persons. These results imply that the benefits of pollution prevention programs to improve air quality would accrue predominantly to these same low-income people. Of course, higher-income people outside the worst polluted areas would also benefit to the extent that they worked or otherwise spent time

[10] A. M. Freeman, III, "The Distribution of Environmental Quality," in *Environmental Quality Analysis*, A. V. Kneese and B. T. Bower, eds. (Baltimore: The Johns Hopkins Press, 1972).
[11] J. M. Zupan, *The Distribution of Air Quality in the New York Region* (Baltimore: The Johns Hopkins Press, 1973).

in these areas. However, this conclusion does not necessarily mean that the net benefits of pollution prevention programs for improving air quality would be progressively distributed. The distribution of net benefits would depend on the distribution of the costs as well as the benefits.

C. THE BALANCE OF EQUITY AND EFFICIENCY IN ENVIRONMENTAL POLICY

How can the government balance equity and efficiency considerations in formulating its environmental policies? Environmetal programs that pass the benefit-cost test improve efficiency of resource allocation, which translates roughly into a potentially greater total output of goods and services (including environmental quality) to be shared among the consuming public. But does potentially more for everybody justify actual, arbitrary gains and losses for specific individuals and groups and a widening of the economic welfare gap between the rich and the poor? No general answer can be given to these hard questions. Efficiency and equity trade-offs differ from one policy issue to another, and indeed, in easy cases, no trade-off need exist as both criteria point to the same policy decision. To some extent, the terms of the trade-off can be influenced by judicious choices of policy instruments, e.g., by use of the more progressive of the alternative taxes to finance a given environmental program. When a trade-off cannot be avoided, however, equity considerations should not be neglected in favor of the deceptively simple and uncontroversial criterion for economic efficiency.

Some economists argue that distributional effects of environmental programs *should* have little influence on policy decisions. They base their argument on the observation that government measures to protect environmental quality are taken to correct the misallocation of resources that would result in the absence of government intervention in the private market economy, that is, for *efficiency* reasons. The distributional effects of such measures are largely unintentional side effects of attempts to achieve greater efficiency of resource use. They argue further that it would be a great mistake to insist that all environmental programs satisfy equity criteria. To do so would inevitably eliminate environmental programs that could significantly improve society's use of its scarce resources. If many efficient programs were not undertaken for this reason, total output would be lower and the intended beneficiaries of an equity test for environmental programs could end up worse off than without an equity test. That is, low-income groups might be better off in the long run with no equity criteria for environmental programs because they would share in a larger total output. Furthermore, according to another variant of this same argument, environmental programs are poor vehicles for redistributing income; such programs should be designed to maximize efficiency, and income redistribution should be dealt with through separate tax and transfer programs. Even if environmental programs taken together have a net regressive impact on the distribution of income, measures such as a negative income tax and a progressive tax system can fully offset any adverse distributional effects and indeed can be used to attain any distribution of income society desires.

The above argument has much merit, but it ignores crucial problems and is incomplete. The tax and transfer system in the United States has not been well suited, historically, for rectifying regressive effects of other government programs. Decisions about environmental policy are taken separately from decisions on taxes and transfers in our government. Such decisions have never been coordinated and probably never will be. Furthermore, it is unrealistic to consider the distributional effects of government tax and transfer policies as the result of some well-defined consensus about the just distribution of income. Individual preferences about distributional equity differ sharply among voters, and, for the reasons discussed in Chapter 4, the aggregation of such preferences through voting behavior provides only the roughest kind of guide to legislators and administrators in charge of tax and transfer decisions. In brief, the distributional effects of environmental programs are most unlikely to be offset or corrected by general tax and transfer programs; therefore, they can either be ignored or balanced somehow against efficiency effects in the making of environmental policy.

The equity-efficiency trade-off problem in environmental policy becomes even more complex when we extend the equity concept to include the welfare of future generations relative to the welfare of the current generation. Many environmental measures taken today reduce the consumption levels of those alive now and raise the potential consumption levels of those too young to participate in political decisions and of those not yet born. The point has often been made that under such circumstances the interests of future generations must be represented by the current generation acting as a kind of trustee. One appealing notion of equity in this intergenerational context is that each generation should pass on to the next a stock of wealth per capita—including the value of environmental resources—at least equal in value to what it itself inherited. On the other hand, some economists argue that future generations will be richer than the current generation anyway and that there is no good reason to worry about the amount of wealth passed on to them. The deep ethical nature of this issue should be obvious. Environmental policy is intimately involved in the general issue because the quality of the environmental resources passed on to future generations will be one of the major components of their legacy from us.

In summary, the equity-efficiency trade-off is a fundamental problem in environmental policy. Each environmental program and the whole set of programs jointly must be evaluated by using both equity and efficiency criteria. When a program meets the benefit-cost test of efficiency but is undesirable on equity grounds, equity and efficiency must somehow be balanced. To insist that no efficient program be undertaken unless it meets the test of equity is too strict a standard and might even end all hope of improving environmental quality. On the other hand, to ignore equity criteria entirely is just as wrong and probably more of a danger today. A judicious compromise between these extreme alternatives is required together with persistent efforts to improve the terms of the equity-efficiency trade-off.

D. SUMMARY AND CONCLUSIONS

This chapter concludes our presentation in Part 2 of the economic theory relevant to environmental problems. We began in Chapter 2 with a discussion of the concept of economic efficiency and the distortions created by external costs. The additional complication of the simultaneous presence of both externalities and monopoly power makes any statement on the efficiency of resource allocation in private markets extremely difficult. Chapter 3 developed the underlying foundation of externalities—the impossibility of establishing and enforcing property rights to environmental resources—and analyzed several appealing solutions. Reliance on the common law and an extension of the market system to define and provide for the exchange environmental rights offer effective means to improve resource allocation by internalizing costs. Unfortunately, both approaches are most useful only in relatively simple cases of externalities. They encounter serious problems when confronting the pervasive nature of modern environmental problems. In fact, the physical laws of the conservation of matter and energy ensure that environmental external costs will be a major and growing problem in industrial society. A tax on waste discharges imposed by the government represents a more realistic alternative to internalizing all costs, although this also encounters formidable information and enforcement difficulties.

Chapter 4 returned to the theme of property rights and explored the historical common property bases of most major environmental resources. The rational incentives in situations of common property readily explain the overuse and deterioration of existing common property resources. Many environmental problems involve the limiting case of a pure public good and the associated difficulties of obtaining accurate measures of demand. Several severe international environmental problems provide worrysome real world examples of the overuse of common property resources.

While the uncontrolled activities of private individuals and firms using public goods for waste disposal lead directly to environmental deterioration, reliance on the government to correct this situation unfortunately does not necessarily result in an improvement in resource allocation. Voting preferences can only be vaguely translated into efficiency objectives, and the government bureaucracy is not likely to regard efficiency as an important goal.

Finally, the present chapter investigated the equity implications of government environmental quality programs. The central point to emerge from this discussion is that environmental programs entail complex redistributional effects that are difficult to trace out, let alone measure. The available, preliminary evidence suggests that pollution control costs are regressively distributed. Moreover, a rough measure of the distributional *net* benefits also points to a regressive pattern. For government agencies, facing daily decision problems, equity considerations must clearly carry weight alongside the efficiency criterion in environmental policy making. Hard cases inevitably arise in which efficiency and distributional equity criteria clash, and society must then make trade-offs between goals that are not easily compared.

QUESTIONS FOR DISCUSSION

1. Suppose that the only factory in a small town pollutes the air in the area. To solve this externalities problem, the federal government bans all emissions of pollutants. In response, the firm shuts down, and 50 percent of the town's population lose their jobs. Does the solution to the externalities problem in this example involve any externalities of its own? Does it involve any important equity issues?

2. Consider a subsidy scheme in which polluters are paid not to pollute. What are the equity effects of such a policy? Compare them to the equity implications of an effluent charge.

3. In our example in this chapter, the existing city of Jetportville imposes effluent charges on the airport authority for use of the *new* airport. In your opinion, are the effluent charges in this example equitable?

Would your answer to this question differ if we had assumed that the airport predated the existence of Jetportville?

4. Suppose a successful national clean air program made central cities attractive places to live once again. Also suppose that, as a result, upper-income groups eventually return from the suburbs to live in the cities. The current residents of central cities, the urban poor, are displaced by the resulting higher rents. Analyze the short-run and long-run distribution of benefits from the clean air program.

5. The Clean Air Act of 1970 requires that a new car in rural Montana have the same emission control equipment as a new car in New York City. The act also states that the intent of the law is to "protect the health of persons regardless of where such persons reside." Do these two isolated facts suggest anything about the relative weights Congress places on efficiency versus equity?

SELECTED REFERENCES

Asch, P., and J. J. Seneca, "Some Evidence on the Distribution of Air Quality," *Land Economics*, 54, No. 3 (August 1978). A discussion of measurement issues for environmental quality distribution with empirical evidence of a pollution exposure measure of equity.

Baumol, W. J., "Environmental Protection and Income Distribution," in *Redistribution Through Public Choice*, H. Hochman and G. Peterson, eds. New York: Columbia University Press, 1974. A theoretical treatment of the likely incidence implications of environmental quality improvement.

Bromley, D. W., "Economics and Public Decisions: Roles of the State and Issues in Economic Evaluation," *Journal of Economic Issues*, X, No. 4 (December 1976). A discussion of the role of efficiency and equity in influencing government policy making.

Dorfman, N. S., and A. Snow, "Who Will Pay for Pollution Control," *National Tax Journal*, XXVIII, No. 1 (March 1975). A systematic investigation of the distribution of costs of the entire pollution abatement program.

Freeman, A. M., III, "The Distribution of Environmental Quality," in *Environmental Quality Analysis*, A. V. Kneese and B. T. Bower, eds. Baltimore: The Johns Hopkins Press, 1972. A treatment of distributional aspects of environmental quality with a review of available empirical evidence.

Harrison, D., *Who Pays for Clean Air: The Costs and Benefit Distribution of Federal Automotive Emission Controls*. Cambridge, Mass.: Ballinger Publishing Company, 1975. An analysis of the incidence of the federally required auto pollution control program.

MUSGRAVE, R. A., *The Theory of Public Finance.* New York: McGraw-Hill Book Company, 1959. The best overall treatise on public finance, with good analyses of the concept of incidence and the distributional effects of the government budget.

OKUN, A. M., *Equality and Efficiency. The Big Tradeoff.* Washington, D.C.: The Brookings Institution, 1975. A very readable discussion of the efficiency versus equity issue.

III

The
Economics
of
Environmental
Problems

6

WATER
RESOURCES
AND
WATER
QUALITY

The next three chapters provide an overview of the technical, physical, and biological aspects of specific environmental problems. Emphasis is given to the *economic* significance of these technical facts of life. This chapter is concerned with the nature of water use, the existing quality of this nation's water resources, and the economic implications of different levels of water quality. Chapter 7 deals with the analogous interplay of technical and economic relationships as they apply to air quality. Finally, Chapter 8 discusses what may be termed broadly *quality of life* problems, including such varied topics as solid wastes, pesticides, noise, the supply of outdoor recreation, and other amenity issues.

Before becoming immersed in the complex details in these three chapters, the reader should have some perspective on how this material fits into the overall study of environmental economics. Part 1 of the book outlined the benefit-cost framework within which economists approach environmental problems. Part 2 discussed the concepts of efficiency and equity and pinpointed externalities—the divergence between private and social costs or benefits—as the common thread linking a wide variety of environmental issues. We demonstrated that externalities were the cause of inefficient allocation of environmental resources, even in an otherwise ideal market system, and outlined the theory of how government policy could cope with the efficiency and equity problems associated with externalities. If we now wish to use the theoretical framework constructed in these earlier chapters not only to understand the causes of environmental deterioration but also to deal effectively with real world environmental problems, we must provide empirical content to such concepts as benefits, costs, and the nature of environmental externalities. This is the purpose of Part 3.

The common theme, therefore, in the next three chapters is an attempt to identify the causes of divergence between private and social costs with respect to different environmental media and to assess the quantitative significance of these externalities. To do this properly, we must, first, identify the physical or biological factors responsible for the deterioration of environmental resources; trace these factors back to their sources in the economy; then, quantify the relationship between each source of pollution and the environmental damage associated with it; and, finally, translate the physical or biological effects in each case into dollar measures of economic damage.

With such a measure of environmental damage, we could then use the benefit-cost framework of Chapter 1 to evaluate the net social gains to be derived from preventing environmental damage in any particular case. We could also begin to assess the distributional effects of various types of pollution damage. Unfortunately, as we shall soon see, measures of damage for most environmental problems are elusive because the empirical basis of environmental economics is still in a rudimentary state. Without such information, much of which must be provided by the research of physical and biological scientists, it is impossible to give precise operational content to the concepts of benefits and costs, and environmental policies must operate in an empirical void. Nonetheless, we shall survey what empirical knowledge is available as of this date and at least make a beginning toward a fuller, more satisfactory treatment of this subject.

This chapter covers the economics of water use. Section A surveys the quantitative dimensions of water quality problems in the United States and reports on the extent of pollution in the nation's water resources. Section B analyzes the nature of the water cycle and considers alternative definitions of the term *water use*. Section C then classifies and describes the major types of pollutants found in water resources, concentrating on the physical characteristics of these pollutants and their impact on water quality. Section D examines the economic effects of deteriorating water quality. Finally, Section E summarizes the key points of the chapter.

A. THE QUALITY OF WATER RESOURCES IN THE UNITED STATES

The United States has enjoyed significant and, on average, steady economic growth throughout its history. Since 1910, our national product has grown at a 3 percent average annual compound rate of growth. Real GNP rose from $314.7 billion in 1929 to $1256.0 billion in 1976 (stated in 1972 prices). Economic growth has been accompanied by increasing demands on the nation's natural resources, including an ever-growing utilization of water resources.[1] The role of water in economic activity is apparent from casual observation. Besides its obvious uses for household consumption, water is a vital input in almost every industrial and manufacturing activity, in agriculture and mining, and in the generation of electrical energy. In addition to these uses directly related to production, substantial uses of water are associated with the enormous growth in outdoor recreation activities. This upsurge of recreational activities is also a by-product of economic growth, as a wealthier population begins to take increasing proportions of productivity and real income gains in the form of leisure time and leisure activities.

Table 6–1 provides estimates of projected water withdrawals for different purposes in the United States. The magnitude of the projected increases is noteworthy. Total water withdrawals are expected to almost double between 1980 and the year 2000 with the major increases attributable to self-supplied industrial needs, steam-electric utilities, and publicly supplied municipal uses of water. It should be stressed that projections of water withdrawal requirements are not independent of economic factors. Changes in production techniques and the relative cost of water may significantly affect the amount of future water withdrawals. Nevertheless, the data in Table 6–1 demonstrate the relationship between economic activity and water use.

When water is withdrawn from a water source for a given purpose and used, it may escape from the control of man. For example, a steel plant may use water to cool burning coke and, in the process, convert the water into steam. In this situation, the steam escaping into the atmosphere would represent a *consumptive* use of water as it is no longer directly

---

[1] The relationship of economic growth to environmental problems is treated in detail in Chapter 14.

TABLE 6–1 ESTIMATED WATER WITHDRAWALS
AND PROJECTED REQUIREMENTS,
UNITED STATES (million gallons daily)

Type of Use	Projected Requirements		
	1980	2000	2020
	Withdrawals		
Rural domestic	2,474	2,852	3,334
Municipal (public-supplied)	33,596	50,724	74,256
Industrial (self-supplied)	75,026	127,365	210,767
Steam-electric power:			
Fresh	133,963	259,208	410,553
Saline	59,340	211,240	503,540
Agriculture:			
Irrigation	135,852	149,824	160,978
Livestock	2,375	3,397	4,660
Total	442,626	804,610	1,368,088

Source: *The Nation's Water Resources,* Water Resource Council, Washington, D.C., 1968, p. 4–1.

available for subsequent uses. If, however, some water is returned to the water source and remains available for subsequent uses, then the amount of water withdrawals can exceed the amount of *consumptive water use* as the same water can be reused for several purposes. However, as water may be used or lost in this obvious quantitative sense, it may also be lost or used qualitatively. Section B will pay particular attention to the economic implications of this distinction. The existence of this important quality dimension with respect to water use gives rise to general concerns of water quality and the relationship of water quality to economic activity. In many instances, the uses of water listed in Table 6–1 involve certain quality effects. For example, some uses raise water temperatures, while other uses result in the discharge of organic wastes, toxins, inorganic substances, pesticides, and other pollutants into the water. This deterioration in water quality may reduce, or entirely preclude, further uses of the water, or it may necessitate substantial treatment costs before the water can be reused.

Because the issue of water quality deterioration is the central theme of this chapter, some indications of the magnitude of the problem will be useful. The projected growth of organic wastes created by municipal uses of water is of the order of about 300 percent for the United States as a whole between 1970 and 2020.[2] In addition to the wastes associated with domestic and municipal water uses, even larger amounts of organic

[2] We shall treat the technical aspects of organic wastes in detail in Section C.

wastes are generated by various industrial water users. In particular, the food processing, chemical, and paper industries are major sources of organic wastes, contributing approximately 90 percent of all organic wastes created in manufacturing. Agricultural wastes from feedlot run-offs are a further source of organic wastes.

However, the level of organic wastes in the nation's waters is by no means the complete picture of present and future water quality problems. Although some rough national estimates of organic wastes exist, there is no comprehensive national inventory of the extent of inorganic substances entering water supplies. Yet we know industrial and agricultural uses of water add many inorganic substances to water resources. For example, a *partial* list of substances found in a cup of water dipped from the Ohio River near the city of Cincinnati included, in addition to organic wastes, ammonia, arsenic, barium, boron, cadmium, chloride, copper, fluoride, iron, lead, magnese nitrates, phosphorus, selenium, silver, sulfate, zinc, organic chemicals, and radioactive substances.[3] In various degrees, these materials and others are present in many major water systems in the country. The diffuse presence of such substances in water discharges involves further considerable water quality problems. We shall treat these issues in more detail in Sections B and C.

The overall picture of water quality improvement is not encouraging. Although there has been a measure of progress in some watersheds and for some pollutants, a recent Council on Environmental Quality study concluded that, for the United States as a whole, water quality, at best, is only holding at former levels in the major drainage basins of the country.[4]

What are the economic implications of the water quality deterioration? Because property rights and water law with respect to assigning the full costs or benefits of the use of water are imperfect, significant external diseconomies result from the many competing uses of water. These externalities, together with the extensive role of water in economic activity, imply that important efficiency and equity issues are involved in the use of the nation's water resources.

B. TECHNICAL ASPECTS OF WATER USE

Before we can analyze the specific environmental consequences associated with the use of water resources, it is necessary to discuss certain technical aspects of the nature of water supplies and the alternative uses

[3] See *Fortune Magazine,* February 1970, p. 102.
[4] See *Seventh Annual Report, Council on Environmental Quality,* Government Printing Office, Washington, D.C., 1976.

of water. A complete investigation of water and water supplies would involve many complex issues in the physical, biological, and engineering sciences beyond the scope of this book. Our purpose in this section is to present an overview of certain physical phenomena associated with water in order to provide a basis for understanding the economic problems arising from water use.

Water is continually in movement, flowing over land, evaporating from water bodies, transpiring from vegetation, or moving in cloud and vapor form in the atmosphere. This movement is a continuous flow and forms the basis of what hydrologists call the *water cycle*. The intuitive aspects of this concept are fairly straightforward. If the water cycle is entered at a given point, for example, when rains fall on the earth's surface, we can trace this water through various routes that lead back into the atmosphere. Some of the routes will afford possibilities for withdrawal of water from the natural water cycle. One avenue for this water is quick reevaporation back into the atmosphere from the land surface or water bodies on which it falls. Alternatively, the water may enter the soil and percolate into underground water supplies or be taken into vegetation and transpired back into the atmosphere. The water may run off land surfaces into surface bodies of water. Finally, water may fall in solid snow form and be stored as ice to await melting before rentering the cycle. When water is in liquid form in freshwater bodies or in underground storage, man is able to withdraw it for various uses before it returns to the oceans or atmosphere.

The United States, as a whole, has a relatively plentiful supply of water with an average annual precipitation of 30 inches over the 48 continental states. However, this rainfall is not equally distributed. The amount of water in surface sources (streams, lakes, rivers) is relatively small compared to the amount available in underground storage areas (acquifiers), but withdrawals from surface sources represent about 67 percent of total water withdrawals in the United States. Groundwater sources account for only 22 percent of water withdrawals.[5] Rough estimates of the extent of groundwater indicates that it surpasses the amount of water in all the Great Lakes. The current low percentage of use of groundwater supplies is, in part, due to the location of the acquifiers relative to the location of the users of water and the currently lower relative costs of surface sources. This relatively unused source of available water is a valuable national asset and one which will be increasingly used in the future. Obviously, the proper management of groundwater

---

[5] We have omitted the ocean as a withdrawal source. However, at present, 11 percent of withdrawals are saline in nature, and, with advancing desalting technology, the ocean can be expected to increase in relative importance as a water source.

sources is an important policy concern, and considerable caution is required to avoid the relatively easy degradation of water in underground sources.[6]

While water is in rivers, streams, lakes, and underground reservoirs, it becomes economically feasible to withdraw water and put it to economic use. The notion of the *use* of water may appear to be an intuitive and simple concept. However, we shall see that a careful definition of this concept is necessary in order to obtain a proper understanding of our basic concern, the economics of water quality. Hydrologists speak, in a technical sense, of the consumptive use of water occurring when water escapes from the land phase of the water cycle into the sea or atmosphere and is no longer physically available for further use. From this technical definition, a nonconsumptive use of water would imply water that not only is used in a given activity but also physically remains in the land phase of the water cycle and, hence, is available for further uses.

This technical distinction between consumptive and nonconsumptive water use is incomplete for our purposes. The essential economic implication of the term *use* is that the water is no longer suitable for subsequent desirable uses. Costs must be incurred before the water can be used again. Whether the water does or does not remain in the liquid-land phase of the water cycle is not necessarily the crucial distinction in defining an economic use of water. If we consider a quality dimension to water use within the land phase of the water cycle, it is then possible to have economic uses of water even though the water remains quantitatively the same in terms of physical availability. Once subsequent uses of water are hindered by a given preceding use of water, the water has been used, or partially used, in an economic sense. For example, if stream water is used for waste disposal purposes, then downstream uses of the water for recreation purposes may be impaired. Alternatively, if a river is to be devoted to trout fishing, it cannot be readily used as a disposal site for toxic waste or as a source of cooling water because both of these uses would destroy, or greatly reduce, the trout population (in the absence of incurring costs to remove the toxins from the discharged water or to lower the temperature of the returned cooling water).

If one use of a water supply creates quality deterioration that partially or wholly precludes another potential use of the water, then the water has been used consumptively in an economic sense. Only at some costs can the water be rendered fit for various other uses. This

[6] For example, local legislation in the city of Akron, Ohio has prohibited the use of phosphate detergents in this community entirely dependent on well water supplies. See *The New York Times*, Dec. 13, 1970. Similar policies have recently been implemented in a number of other localities; e.g., New Jersey is considering land use legislation to protect the extensive underground water resources in the southern part of the state.

definition of water use presents the familiar economic problem of choosing between the alternative uses of a scarce resource.

An important aspect of this problem, as it concerns water use compared to many other economic resources, is that water has a wide quality dimension and various qualities of water are called upon for various uses.[7] For example, recreational use of water requires certain biological purity characteristics; waste disposal draws on the assimilative capacity of water and the size and flow characteristics of the water body, and use of water for cooling purposes relies on the heat absorption property of water. We could extend this list to include many other uses and their associated quality demands on water.

Once the nature of the economic use of water is understood, then it follows that *pollution* can take the form of any action that impairs the necessary water qualities needed for subsequent and/or competing uses of the water. Given this definition, pollution, at times, can become an extremely elusive concept. For example, suppose an upriver industrial plant uses a river flow for cooling purposes and restores the water to the river without adding any type of waste discharge. However, the water temperature of the downstream flow of the river is raised, on average, by 5 degrees. Does this represent pollution? Is this an economic use of water? To answer these questions, we need considerably more information than the fact that the average river temperature has increased; that is, the plant has *used* some of the heat absorption capacity of the river. Suppose this particular river is the site of a considerable annual salmon run that affords both extensive commercial and sports fishing opportunities. If the increase in water temperature lowers the oxygen level in the stream sufficiently to prevent the salmon from using this river, or at least decreases their number and hence reduces fishing on the river, then there is an economic use of the water. The physical nature of the quality impairment of the water can be called thermal (or heat) pollution.

The point to be emphasized is that the issue of whether there has been an economic use of water depends on whether there are actual or potential subsequent uses of the water and if these have been impaired. Suppose the river was not a salmon fishing river but flowed past a downstream city and then into the ocean. The increased temperature of the river did not affect the city's use of the water for domestic and industrial purposes nor did it damage the ecological system of the river or preclude any fishing opportunities. In this situation, no economic use of

---

[7] Of course, other economic resources also have quality dimensions. Unskilled labor and skilled labor are not perfect substitutes in production, and degrees of labor skill may vary just as widely as the quality of different water requirements.

the river water results from the water being used in the upstream plant. Does thermal pollution exist in this case? In a physical sense, yes, because the river's water is heated to the same extent as before and, accordingly, the heat absorption capacity of the river is reduced. In the economic sense, however, no pollution has occurred because no other uses of the water are precluded.[8] Thus, it is not always true that changes in the physical characteristics of water imply an economic use of the water. We must ask whether other potential uses are prevented by the use of water qualities in question. If they are, then problems of external costs arise together with the associated problems of the efficient use of the water resource.

Before we further examine the implications of the economic use of water in Section D, we shall give a brief survey of the major causes of water quality deterioration. In terms of the above discussion, we shall treat pollution in the physical sense of the factors that adversely affect water quality.

C. POLLUTANTS: AN OVERVIEW

The technical aspects of the deterioration of the physical characteristics of water are numerous and complex. This section surveys some broad classifications of the physical agents responsible for water quality deterioration.

1. Degradable Pollutants

As an initial distinction, pollutants can be categorized as either *degradable* or *nondegradable*. The term degradable implies materials that are organic in nature and undergo physical changes through the chemical and biological processes occurring in water. The most common component of degradable wastes is the sewage associated with domestic uses of water. In addition to domestic sewage, however, numerous industries, particularly paper, food processing, oil refining, and chemical plants, produce large amounts of organic waste materials that are discharged, in various stages of treatment, into water bodies. When organic wastes are deposited in a river or stream, the bacteria present in the water begin to break down the unstable organic waste into stable inorganic

---

[8] In fact, consider a third case, where the increased water temperature stimulates bacterial action and provides in this instance a *beneficial* effect on fish population and hence on fishing activity. Has pollution occurred here? The water is physically identical to the other situations, that is, a 5-degree increase in temperature, but here a *beneficial* effect is associated with thermal "pollution."

elements, primarily phosphates, nitrates, and sulfates. Through this process, water bodies are said to have a *self-cleansing* quality whereby they convert organic wastes into more stable components.

In clean water, the bacterial degradation of organic wastes will occur with the use of the oxygen dissolved in the water. The process whereby bacteria utilize the free oxygen dissolved in the stream to break down organic wastes is called an *aerobic* process. A measure of the extent of the organic waste in any water body is found in the amount of dissolved oxygen used by bacteria. The higher the given level of organic waste load, the more dissolved oxygen will be needed. The oxygen requirement of bacteria needed to break down the organic wastes is called the *biochemical oxygen demand* (or BOD). As the amounts of organic wastes discharged into water increase, the BOD will also increase. In addition to the amount of the organic waste load, BOD is also affected by the temperature of the water. Because warmer water temperatures stimulate bacterial processes, BOD increases with the temperature of the water for any given waste load. Warm water temperatures are also associated with lower levels of dissolved oxygen due to the lowered capabilities of warmer waters to assimilate oxygen. The result is that in periods of warm weather, oxygen in the water is drawn up more rapidly from a base that is already relatively low. If the BOD in such conditions is sufficiently great, the level of dissolved oxygen in the water falls to extremely low levels for a considerable length of time. When this occurs, many forms of fish life may be destroyed. In addition, if the BOD is so large that the dissolved oxygen level approaches zero, then bacterial degradation continues without the use of free oxygen; that is, it occurs *anaerobically*. As a result, a series of gases are given off by the water (hydrogen sulfide and methane), and the water has both a disagreeable look and a noxious smell. Water bodies with extreme organic waste loads and subsequent consistent anaerobic conditions are reduced to the simple functions associated with a sewage depository.

As noted above, the aerobic action of bacteria on organic wastes produces inorganic components, primarily nitrates and phosphates. These by-products of bacterial degradation form a base of plant nutrients in the water and stimulate algae growth. Although some algae growth may be desirable for fish life, excessive growths of algae, resulting from abnormal plant nutrient levels, alter the taste and odor of water and may prove toxic to fish life, obstruct navigation, and hinder recreation activities.

Due to the relatively low water circulation rates, the problems of organic waste loads in lakes and other standing bodies of water are, in some respects, more severe than those involving flowing rivers and streams. The excessive growth of algae from the abnormal levels of nutrients created by high amounts of BOD combined with large amounts of detergent-related phosphates can remove much of the dissolved oxygen from a lake. Indeed, in extreme forms lakes become devoid of oxygen over large areas. This accelerated reduction in the dissolved oxygen content of a lake represents artificial aging of the lake, or what is called *eutrophication.* Lake Erie has become the unfortunate showcase example of the problems associated with high levels of organic waste loads and the subsequent severe problems of low dissolved oxygen levels, excessive algae growth, and accelerated eutrophication. The other Great Lakes are threatened by the same series of events. Recently this problem has been the subject of extensive technical research efforts spurred on by deep concern on the part of government and private conservation groups.

2. Nondegradable Pollutants

The second major group of pollutants are those classified as nondegradable. These are substances that are not changed by the bacterial processes in water. Many industrial wastes such as various metals, metallic salts, chlorides, and toxins of various kinds are nondegradable pollutants. These substances are dispersed and diluted but are not physically altered by natural processes in water. Another related group of pollutants that are not strictly nondegradable can be called *persistent pollutants.* These substances, though organic in nature—DDT and synthetic detergents are two well-known examples—deteriorate very slowly over time. Certain insecticides, herbicides, and phenols from oil products are persistent and resist both treatment processes and natural bacterial action. Radioactive wastes represent an extreme form of persistent pollutants.

D. WATER POLLUTANTS AND THEIR ECONOMIC EFFECTS

Examples of severe water pollution abound throughout the United States. Perhaps one of the most dramatic occurred in the summer of 1970, when the Cuyahoga River, flowing through industrial Cleveland, actually caught fire. Used as a receptacle for numerous industrial and municipal discharges, the wastes in the Cuyahoga burst into flames, and the resulting floating fire threatened several bridges. Witnesses to this event were confronted by the incredible sight of fire control efforts directed at a river!

The destruction of once large and commercially valuable fish populations in the estuaries and rivers of the Potomac, Delaware, Hudson, Connecticut, and other East Coast rivers provide ready examples of the ecological disruptions of water pollution.

Although the Great Lakes are the largest surface source of freshwater in the world, they are being increasingly degraded by human and industrial wastes. Pollution in Lake Erie has worsened to such a degree that not only is swimming prohibited by many shore communities, but typhoid inoculations are required for persons desiring to boat on the lake for protection against the unhappy prospect of falling in!

New York City draws its water supply from a complicated upstate reservoir system while the polluted Hudson, one of the largest rivers in the United States, flows directly past the largest city in the country.

We could easily extend this chronicle of noteworth pollution problems for many pages. The essential point, however, has been made. Water pollution is pervasive throughout the country, from rural Maine through the industrialized middle Atlantic area to the rivers of Washington and Oregon. We turn now to a systematic evaluation of the economic effects of water pollution.

1. Health Effects

A once common effect of organic pollutants in water was the threat to public health. Disease-causing bacteria are present in domestic sewage and other organic wastes. Outbreaks of dysentery and typhoid associated with organically polluted water supplies were, in the past, common occurrences in this and other Western countries. In fact, even today the problem is not completely eliminated in the United States. The U.S. Public Health Service recorded almost 26,000 cases of waterborne disease in the United States from 1946 to 1960. However, over half of the disease outbreaks were associated with untreated surface or groundwater sources, and public water systems are now relatively secure from this problem.

In less-developed countries, the disease menace to public health remains a real danger. The periodic appearance of cholera in Africa and Middle and Far East countries is an example of public health problems related to water pollution. Water supplies destined for domestic use that contain unsafe coliform counts—the index conventionally used to indicate the presence of wastes from the human intestine—are treated with chlorine to destroy bacteria and prevent disease epidemics. The use of chlorine treatment in this country has successfully eliminated the major epidemic dangers of organic pollutants in public water supplies. Obviously, chlorine treatment is not costless, and the economic effects of bacterial pollutants are reflected in the costs of treatment incurred to avoid the vast potential dangers associated with epidemic bacterial diseases.

Inorganic toxins and persistent organic toxins also present significant dangers to public health, and water containing these substances requires treatment to established tolerance levels. The immediate dangers in terms of mortality are known for the conventional poisons and inorganic toxins. Tolerance levels for domestic water supplies accordingly reflect significant safety margins for these pollutants. However, conventional water treatment processes are often unable to remove many inorganic pollutants, viruses, pesticides, and other complex compounds. In fact, surveys by the Public Health Service found significant amounts of such substances in the water systems of numerous communities throughout the country. As in the case of bacterial pollutants, when treatment is undertaken, the costs incurred to control the levels of these inorganic pollutants in domestic water supplies represent another economic cost of their initial discharge into water sources.

Much less easily measured are the welfare damage costs of inorganic pollutants in terms of human health; that is, the long-term consequences of the human ingestion of these substances following the failure of treatment methods to remove them from the water supply. Medical science has the difficult problem of determining the long-run health effects of continued human ingestion of low, *safe* levels of inorganic toxins, other inorganic pollutants, and the growing number of synthetically produced organic substances that also end up in water. For example, researchers have found statistically significant relationships between cancer deaths and domestic use of the Mississippi River.[9] A study of the Hudson River revealed that large quantities of toxic chemicals and known carcinogens were present in the river, posing a health threat to the 150,000 people who rely on the Hudson for drinking water. New York State has banned commercial fishing in the Hudson because of the presence of PCBs and other toxic pollutants in fish life. An Environmental Protection Agency study found organic chemicals, including the suspected carcinogen chloroform, in the water supply of each of 79 cities surveyed. Moreover, the presence of chloroform is suspected, in part, to be caused by the conventional water treatment chlorination process, a vital and effective method to prevent the immediate catastrophes of epidemics of waterborne diseases such as typhoid, cholera, and dysentery.

The ability of commonly used toxins and organic chemicals to enter the food chain via the medium of water presents unknown, and potentially significant, dangers to human health. Identifying the complex reactions of these substances with the human body processes over extended lengths of time is an enormous but critically important problem for toxicology and the biochemical sciences. The potential human health costs of these effects threaten to be of enormous magnitude.

In addition to treatment methods designed to eliminate the threats

---

[9] See T. Page, R. H. Harris, and S. S. Epstein, "Drinking Water and Cancer Mortality in Louisiana," *Science*, 193, No. 4247 (July 2, 1977), pp. 55–57.

to public health associated with bacterial diseases, viruses, and various toxins, domestic water supplies are also treated to provide acceptable taste, odor, and other esthetic characteristics. The costs of this treatment must also be included as part of the social costs resulting from the introduction of pollutants into water sources in addition to the welfare costs of water that still tastes poor, even after treatment, or *because of* treatment. The Environmental Protection Agency estimates that over $157 billion in public sector capital and operating costs will be required between 1975 and 1984 to provide acceptable water treatment for domestic and municipal uses. This involves the upgrading of existing treatment facilities and the construction of new facilities to complement population growth and provide treatment services where none currently exist.

2. Industrial Effects

Manufacturing uses of water are numerous and differ widely with respect to the necessary quality characteristics of water used as an input of production. However, corrosion damages resulting from a natural high mineral content of water are common in many industrial uses of water. The presence of additional inorganic substances, such as chlorides and manganese, increase this type of damage. Water that meets the quality standards for domestic uses may require treatment for certain industrial uses in order to remove such economically damaging characteristics as hardness, acidity, alkalinity, or salinity. For example, water used in high-pressure boilers, a common industrial use, should be essentially free of corrosive materials such as manganese and iron, although these minerals are tolerated or even favored in public water supplies. Alternatively, the quality of water used in paper production can be low in terms of human consumption standards but should also contain only small concentrations of corrosive elements. A measure of the pollution costs associated with these effects can be given by the expenses undertaken to avoid these industrial damages plus the damages that can actually be attributed to these pollutants. More significantly, in terms of industry's water discharges, the Environmental Protection Agency estimates that industry will have to spend over $90 billion between 1975 and 1984 to comply with existing federal water pollution control requirements.

3. Recreational Effects

Beyond the effects of water pollutants on domestic and industrial uses, we can identify a category of effects related to recreation, esthetics, and conservation. The rapid growth of public participation in outdoor recreation activities in this country is a well-documented phenomenon. Table

TABLE 6–2   PROJECTED PARTICIPATION IN MAJOR
WATER-BASED RECREATION ACTIVITIES
(millions of activity days)

Activity	1980	2000
Swimming	2,676	4,697
Fishing	738	1,020
Boating (all types)	774	1,353
Water skiing	146	296
Ice skating	183	325
Total of major water-based activities	4,517	7,691
Total of 25 recreation activities including the above	18,342	29,774
Water-based as a % of total	25%	26%

Source: *The Nation's Water Resources*, p. 451.

6–2 presents some projections for participation in several popular water-based recreational activities. Swimming is, by far, the most popular outdoor recreation activity and is projected to be almost double its 1980 level by the end of this century. The other water-based activities also have large projected rates of growth, with the total of all water-based sports indicating a growth from 4.5 to 7.7 billion activity days by the year 2000. In addition to these obviously water-oriented pursuits, many other recreational activities—camping, picnicking, sightseeing—also, at times, require the use of water resources. If these projections are to be realized, sufficient amounts of water, and water of appropriately high qualities, will be necessary to support society's demands for recreation.

Of the water-oriented outdoor activities listed in Table 6–2, swimming obviously requires a relatively high level of water purity in terms of coliform count. Fishing requires various levels of dissolved oxygen and relative freedom from toxins, depending on the species. Although boating has relatively low biological water quality requirements, a lack of corrosive materials and certain esthetic qualities of water—lack of odor, turbidity, and suspended solids—significantly increase its enjoyment.

Section C has already discussed the effects of organic wastes on the dissolved oxygen levels of lakes and streams. At low levels of dissolved oxygen (DO), water bodies become incapable of supporting fish life. The minimum DO level necessary to sustain fish life varies over types of fish (for example, trout, bass, and other sport fish require higher DO levels than rough fish such as carp and suckers), but all fish species are damaged or destroyed when certain minimum dissolved oxygen levels are reached. Excessive levels of inorganic and persistent toxins also eliminate fish life and preclude fishing. Thermal water effects created by industry operations, primarily in the generation of electrical energy and also by cooling processes in many industries, lower the dissolved oxygen levels in water and may have adverse effects on fish populations.

The heavy algae growths associated with high BOD levels also may hinder swimming and fishing. Unpleasant anaerobic conditions may deter various types of recreational boating in addition to eliminating fishing and swimming opportunities. Further, these anaerobic characteristics reduce the amount or the quality of other recreational activities that occur near water areas.

The value of the resulting reduction in outdoor recreation activity is a pollution damage cost that must be attributed to those pollutants responsible for the deterioration of the water quality. Given the large numbers measuring the extent of recreational activities that involve water, it is evident that the implicit economic costs of pollutants that deter or destroy recreational opportunities are quite significant.[10]

4. Commercial Fishing Effects

Finally, substantial economic losses in commercial fishing activity have occurred as a result of both organic and inorganic pollutants. For example, commercial fish catches in Lake Erie have declined from over 26 million pounds in 1955 to eight million pounds in 1975. This decline is general for several other Great Lakes and many other inland waters. The virtual elimination of a once substantial shad fishery in East Coast rivers is a further example of this effect of pollutants on commercial fishing. A more recent extension of the same phenomenon is the closing of many shellfish beds in East Coast estuaries and tidal areas. Even some open ocean fishing activities are threatened by the ocean dumping of wastes.

5. Assessment of Total Effects

We have now discussed a number of the potential effects of deteriorating water quality on human and economic activity. All of these effects impose pollution prevention costs, pollution damage avoidance costs, or actual pollution damage costs on society. However, the potential magnitudes of the various costs differ considerably.

A number of studies of specific industries indicate that production costs are inelastic with respect to relatively large changes in water

---

[10] Additional considerations in this area would involve the loss due to water pollutants of unique, irreproducible, natural water environments (such as wilderness rivers). We shall discuss this and similar issues in Chapter 8.

quality.[11] This conclusion implies that relatively small cost savings for industry would be realized with improved water quality. As a result, only minor amounts of the expenditures on water pollution abatement programs can be justified by the pollution damage costs saved by industry. Similarly, other studies indicate that, in general, relatively little of the costs of water quality improvement can be matched by the resulting cost savings in public water treatment. However, this conclusion does not account for the potentially enormous long-run health perils associated with the ingestion of a variety of inorganic substances in *safe, potable* domestic water supplies.

Nevertheless, it appears that the burden of justifying the bulk of water pollution control costs falls on the recreational and esthetic values associated with high water quality. In terms of the analysis in Part 2, this implies that the major part of the external costs caused by water pollution are associated with foregone recreational, esthetic, and ecological values. Moreover, several studies have indicated that the magnitude of the value of high-water-quality-oriented recreation is quite capable of equaling the expenditures needed to achieve and maintain such high-quality water. We tentatively can conclude that, in the specific case of water resources, it is essentially the recreational and esthetic values of water that are highly sensitive to improvements in water quality rather than the use of water in production activities or for household consumption.

E. SUMMARY AND CONCLUSIONS

This chapter has surveyed the technical aspects of water resource problems and has emphasized the link between water use and economic activity. The incomplete ownership rights of water and the extensive and multipurpose uses of water in the economy combine to generate considerable externalities associated with water use. These externalities are an important illustration of the general problem of externalities discussed in detail in Chapters 3 and 4. A brief overview of the dimensions of water use indicated the vital role of water resources in the economic growth process. The major conclusion from available data was the strength of the relation between the level of economic activity and the demands on the water resources of the nation.

Because water resources serve such varied economic functions, it is

---

[11] In part, the conclusion represents the fact that a large amount of industrial water is used for cooling purposes and this use requires water of relatively low quality. Therefore, improving water quality will not significantly lower the costs of the major use of water in industry.

important to understand the quality dimensions of water. Different uses of water depend on differing qualities of water. A given use may, by destroying or damaging a particular quality characteristic, preclude subsequent uses of the water. This important distinction forms the basis of a careful definition of the *economic use* of water and provides a precise clarification of the economic meaning of water quality.

With this definition of water use, we surveyed the technical aspects of some major factors that affect water quality. A broad distinction was made between *degradable* and *nondegradable* pollutants. Both kinds of pollutants have important impacts on water quality. Pollutants of water can be related to particular water uses and to the economic effects of various water quality conditions. Some cost estimates associated with water quality provide a basis for assessing the social significance of water quality problems. Such cost estimates are the basic data for estimating the magnitude of the benefits in benefit-cost analyses of alternative programs to improve water quality.

QUESTIONS FOR DISCUSSION

1. This chapter details numerous cases of water quality deterioration. Who makes the decisions that are responsible for this deterioration? Who bears the costs of these decisions? Could public-spirited individuals do anything effective to alleviate the problem of water pollution?

2. "Water pollution can be solved very simply. Just put an effluent charge on the emission of water pollutants." Comment critically.

3. Suppose that a given body of water can be used for two purposes only: (a) as a cooling agent for industrial firms or (b) as a fishing resource. Fishing does not affect the use of water by industry. Unfortunately, industrial use of the water destroys all the fish. Do these assumptions imply anything about the most efficient allocation of the water resource? Explain.

4. "The use of water by industry is vital to the economic health of the country. Recreational uses of water are just luxuries. Therefore, when industrial and recreational uses of a given water resource conflict, government should generally give preference to industry." Evaluate this statement critically.

5. It is possible to place a dollar value on the welfare damage costs of long-run human consumption of drinking water containing "safe" concentrations of various complex inorganic substances?

SELECTED REFERENCES

DAVIS, R. K., *The Range of Choice in Water Management: A Study of Dissolved Oxygen in the Potomac Estuary.* Baltimore: The Johns Hopkins Press, 1968. A sophisticated synthesis of economics and engineering in a case study of the Potomac.

ECKSTEIN, O., *Water Resource Development.* Cambridge, Mass.: Harvard University Press, 1958. A discussion of benefit-cost analysis as applied to water investments.

HIRSCHLEIFER, J., F. DEHAVEN, AND J. MILLIMAN, *Water Supply, Economics, Technology and Policy.* Chicago: University of Chicago Press, 1972. A detailed treatment of the economic considerations in water supply. Provides a useful overview of both the technical and economic problems of water use. The basis of the discussion in Section B.

KNEESE, A. V., AND B. T. BOWER, *Managing Water Quality: Economics, Technology, and Institutions.* Baltimore: The Johns Hopkins Press, 1968. A most comprehensive study of the economics of water. Emphasis is given to the evaluation of policy alternatives. The study also provides extensive references to applied water studies.

SAX, J. L., *Water Law, Planning and Policy.* Indianapolis: The Bobbs-Merrill Company, Inc., 1963. A comprehensive survey of water law and its interface with economic issues.

Water Resources Scientific Information Center, *Selected Water Resources Abstracts,* Office of Water Resources Research, National Technical Information Service, Dept. of Commerce, Washington, D.C. The vast water literature from many disciplines is summarized in this semimonthly publication of abstracts of relevant water articles. The abstracts are classified by several categories: nature of water, water cycle, water supply augmentation and conservation, water quantity management and control, water quality management and protection, water resources planning, and others. A ready and valuable source for pursuing detailed investigations into specific areas of water research.

7

THE
PROBLEM
OF
AIR QUALITY

The most serious being "foot odor." The effects are devastating.

The atmosphere is the life blanket of the earth, the essential ingredient for all living things. Air covers every part of the 200 million square miles of the earth's surface. In the course of a day, a single person breathes between 30 and 35 pounds of air in a constant automatic response to extract life-giving oxygen. The atmosphere extends upward from the earth's surface for hundreds of miles, although it thins rapidly, and man can breathe with ease only within the first 10,000 feet. The air is composed of nitrogen (78 percent), oxygen (21 percent), and various other gases: argon, carbon dioxide, helium, hydrogen, krypton, neon, and xenon. The supply of air in the atmosphere is estimated to be 6 quadrillion tons and is constantly in movement about the earth's surface in both horizontal and vertical directions.

These facts suggest that the atmosphere is, truly, the closest man can come to possession of an effectively infinite and free resource. Over long periods of time, the atmosphere was, in fact, a free good, and human and economic activities proceeded essentially unconstrained by air quality considerations. It is true there were, even before modern times, references to the poor air conditions over such places as London in the fifteenth century due to the emissions of thousands of home and trade fires burning at once. Also, instances of natural air pollution for volcanic action, thermal inversions, dust storms, and other natural phenomena did (and still do) occur and, at times, disrupted economic activity. In fact, long before the advent of industrialized society, the automobile and mass electric power generation, thermal inversions and natural pollutants created the Indian summer conditions well known in certain sections of this country. This condition is an inversion of the normal weather patterns and results in the trapping of particulate matter, dust, and smoke from combustion processes. This natural atmospheric event, by itself, does not cause air quality deterioration. However, when combined with heavy industrial and domestic discharges, thermal inversions have led to human fatalities and widespread illness in several air pollution catastrophies. In less severe forms, eye-stinging and lung-irritating conditions accompany thermal inversions in urban areas as man's activities greatly aggravate a situation of natural air pollution potential.

Increasing industrialization and urbanization have created growing demands to use the atmosphere, whether consciously or not, as a waste disposal medium. Thus, in certain areas at certain times, the accumulation of waste gases and particles from combustion, production, and other economic activities exceeds the natural dispersion capacity of the atmosphere. When air movements are unable to disperse wastes at a rate equal to or exceeding the rate they enter the atmosphere, air quality deteriorates. At such times, the seemingly infinite supply of clean air becomes used up by man over broad areas.

Conditions of deteriorating air quality have grown more severe as urbanization and mass consumption have become standard ways of life throughout large parts of the world. Economic growth—generating more products, greater demands for power to run the economy, and, ultimately, more wastes—is the underlying factor behind the emergence of serious air pollution problems. The decline in air quality in megalopolis areas throughout the world signals the end of free air resources. Although use of the air largely remains free to each individual disposing wastes into the atmosphere, the social costs of poor air quality in the form of dangers to human health, agricultural damages, property destruction, and many other (including presently unknown) effects are considerable for society as a whole.

The purpose of this chapter is to detail the factors responsible for air quality deterioration and to indicate the economic consequences of air pollution. Section A provides a survey of specific air pollutants and estimates the quantitative dimensions of the air pollution problem in the United States. Section B reviews the evidence concerning the effects of air pollutants on human health, agriculture, property, safety, work efficiency, and climate. Emphasis is given to established research findings, and, where possible, estimates of the dollar costs of air pollution are provided. Section C summarizes the important points of the chapter.

A. THE NATURE AND SOURCE OF AIR POLLUTANTS

Primary Pollutants

Particulate matter suspended in the air is one of the most noticeable of air pollutants and consists of chemically stable substances such as dust, soot, ash, and smoke. These pollutants are classified as *primary pollutants*, indicating that they do not change form after entering the atmosphere. Primary pollutants are dispersed and diffused by natural air movements but remain structurally unaltered within the air.

At one time, particulate matter was the most common form of air pollution in this country. It remains a large factor in some sections of the United States and in many industrialized areas of Europe. The incomplete combustion of coal is a major source of primary pollutants, and home heating by coal, formerly the predominant type of domestic heating in this country, once was the single largest cause of primary pollutants. In addition, extensive industrial use of coal, as in the steel and electrical power industries, presently contributes significant amounts of particulate matter to the atmosphere. Technological and relative price changes caused the introduction of liquid and natural gas fuels that have replaced coal as the primary home-heating fuel. This substitution has contributed to a decrease in the amount of particulate pollutants, and the United States, as a whole, has experienced a decline in the tonnage of particulate matter in the atmosphere. Part of this decline can also be attributed to the use of particulate pollution abatement devices in heavy metal industries and power plants that continue to consume large, and growing, quantities of coal. However, recent energy plans call for a swing back to relying on coal for energy generation and raise the possibilities of a growing primary pollutant problem.

Secondary Pollutants

Although the general decline in the level of primary pollutants is an encouraging development in itself, the switch to liquid and gas fuels has not led to an overall decline in the level of air pollution. Instead, new gaseous pollutants, of a more complex nature in terms of their structure, stability, identifiability, and effects, have emerged with the basic changes in both fuel and transportation technologies. The new pollutants, called *secondary pollutants,* cause considerably more difficult control problems and pose perhaps even greater health and economic dangers than primary pollutants.

The emission of an array of gases from a large number of sources is the main basis of the air quality problem in the United States. As in the case of water pollutants, almost all air pollutant emissions are directly related to economic activity and the high mass consumption standards of the economy. In particular, millions of motor vehicles, industrial production, and electric power generation are the major sources of gaseous pollutants. Later in this chapter, we shall examine the relative quantitative contributions of these sources to the air quality problem. First, however, it is useful to describe, briefly, the general nature of these secondary pollutants.

Hydrocarbons are organic gases composed of carbon and hydrogen. Inefficient combustion in motor vehicles is the major source of hydrocarbon emissions. Hydrocarbons, by themselves, are nontoxic gases and do not pose immediate health hazards unless absorbed in extreme concentrations. The major problem with hydrocarbons is their ability to unite with nitrogen oxide via a photochemical reaction in sunlight to produce that well-known phenomenon *smog.* Visibility problems and breathing difficulties are the two major results of smog. In combination with carbon monoxide emissions—again, primarily from motor vehicles—trapped particulate matter, and other gases, smog poses serious health hazards.

Discharges of nitrogen combine with oxygen in the atmosphere to create *nitrogen oxides.* As in the case of hydrocarbons, nitrogen oxide is primarily the result of the incomplete burning of gas and oil fuels, and, once again, the motor vehicle is the major source. These oxides of nitrogen make up the other gaseous component that contributes to smog formation. In addition, organic substances in the atmosphere combine photochemically with nitrogen oxides to create *ozone,* a bluish gas that has devastating effects on vegetation, causes rubber to deteriorate, and is responsible for significant amounts of other property damage.

Sulfur oxides are another major pollutant. To various degrees, fossil fuels all contain sulfur. When these fuels are burned, the sulfur produces sulfur dioxide and sulfur trioxide. Both of these gases have serious health effects. In addition, sulfur trioxide combines with water in the atmosphere to create sulfuric acid. At times, in certain areas, it has literally rained sulfuric acid, which corrodes, deteriorates, and weakens structures and results in considerable property damage. The major source of sulfur oxide emissions is electrical power generation via the combustion of large quantities of coal and oil.

Finally, *carbon monoxide,* a colorless and odorless gas produced by the inefficient combustion of carbon fuels, can pose a serious health problem. It is highly toxic at significant levels of concentration and can cause decreased human efficiency in low but chronic doses. Although motor vehicles are the major source of carbon monoxide emissions, other economic activities are also responsible for significant contributions of this pollutant.

Quantitative measures of the extent of air pollution in the United States are perversely impressive. Table 7–1 provides rough estimates of the

TABLE 7–1   TOTAL AIR POLLUTANT EMISSIONS BY TYPE (1974)

Type	In Millions of Tons	Percent
Carbon monoxide	94.6	47.68
Sulfur oxides	31.4	15.82
Hydrocarbons	30.4	15.32
Particulates	19.5	9.82
Nitrogen oxides	22.5	11.34
Total	198.4	100.00

Source: Environmental Protection Agency.

total tonnage of various pollutants from all sources entering the atmosphere in 1974. An estimated 198.4 million tons is the sum of the discharges of millions of motor vehicles, hundreds of thousands of industrial plants, thousands of large and small power generating plants, numerous refuse disposals and individual heating systems, and a miscellaneous collection of combustion and production activities. The data indicate that carbon monoxide represents approximately 47 percent of the total pollutant emissions, and sulfur oxides and hydrocarbons together contribute approximately 30 percent more. These three gases, therefore, compose almost 80 percent of the total emissions of major air pollutants.

The relative contribution of pollutants by source is indicated in Table 7–2. Corresponding to the large share of carbon monoxide in total emissions it follows that transportation, and, in particular, the automobile, is the single largest source (51 percent) of air pollutants. Stationary fuel combustion is responsible for an additional 22 percent of total emissions. This reflects electric power operations using coal as the basic power-generating fuel. Industrial processes account for approximately 16 percent, and waste disposal and miscellaneous activities (primarily residential heating) are the source of 10 percent of total emissions.

The relative contributions of air pollution sources by type of pol-

TABLE 7–2   AIR POLLUTANT EMISSIONS BY SOURCE (1974)
(quantity in millions of tons per year)

	Quantity	Percent
Transportation	102.0	51.41
Stationary fuel combustion	44.2	22.27
Industrial processes	32.5	16.38
Refuse disposal and miscellaneous	19.7	9.92
Total	198.4	100.00

Source: Environmental Protection Agency.

lutant appear in Table 7–3. Transportation is the source of almost 80 percent of total carbon monoxide emissions, 43 percent of hydrocarbons, and 51 percent of nitrogen oxides but makes only minor contributions to sulfur oxides and particulates. In contrast, power generation (stationary fuel combustion) is a major factor in both of the latter categories (responsible for 80 percent of sulfur oxides and 33 percent of the particulate emissions). Power generation is also a large source of nitrogen

TABLE 7–3   AIR POLLUTANT EMISSIONS BY TYPE AND
SOURCE (1974)
(quantity in millions of tons per year)

Source	Type Quantity				
	Carbon Monoxide	*Sulfur Oxides*	*Hydro-carbons*	*Partic-ulates*	*Nitrogen Oxides*
Transporation	75.0	1.0	13.0	1.5	11.5
Stationary fuel	0.7	25.0	2.0	6.5	10.0
Industrial processes	14.5	5.0	2.5	10.0	0.5
Refuse disposal and miscellaneous	4.4	0.4	12.9	1.5	0.5
Total	94.6	31.4	30.4	19.5	22.5
	Percent				
Transportation	79.28	3.18	42.76	7.69	51.11
Stationary fuel	0.73	79.61	6.57	33.33	44.44
Industrial processes	15.32	15.92	8.22	51.28	2.22
Refuse disposal and miscellaneous	4.65	1.27	42.43	7.69	2.22
Total	100.00	100.00	100.00	100.00	100.00

Source: Environmental Protection Agency.

oxides (44 percent) and, together with transportation, is responsible for over 95 percent of this pollutant. Industrial processes are a significant source of sulfur oxide and particulate emissions (16 and 51 percent), reflecting self-supplied industrial power generation capabilities in addition to the discharges associated with regular production activities.

This brief summary of pollutant sources and types suggests the diversity of air quality problems. Some cities, relying on motor vehicles for the bulk of daily commuting transportation and offering few public mass transportation facilities (for example, Los Angeles), suffer from extreme carbon monoxide and other transportation-related emissions. This major air quality problem arises despite stringent controls on particulate matter emissions and stationary combustion processes. In contrast, a city such as New York is more troubled by sulfur dioxide problems from electrical power and heating activities than from carbon monoxide and automobile-related pollutants. This diversity of pollutants and their sources suggests that a uniform national air quality policy may be exceedingly difficult to formulate and enforce.

Widespread private ownership of motor vehicles has been the modern symbol of American affluence and today almost 80 percent of all U.S. households own at least one car. Mass ownership of the automobile combined with an extensive public highway system makes the American public the most mobile in the world. However, the automobile has not been an unmixed benefit to our society. As we have seen, transportation sources are responsible for the creation of significant amounts of pollutants from the incomplete combustion of motor vehicle fuel. A perfectly operating engine would create only water and carbon dioxide discharges. However, real world conditions of imperfect engines, improper fuel grades, lack of regular maintenance, and the physical aging of machinery ensure that motor vehicle combustion is far from ideal. The result is carbon monoxide, hydrocarbons, and nitrogen oxide emissions escaping from the exhaust system and engine parts of the vehicle. Incomplete fuel combustion combined with the vast number of motor vehicles of all ages, types, and conditions being operated in the United States is responsible for a major share of the air pollutant data in Tables 7–1 through 7–3 and for the atmospheric conditions we observe in everyday life in our automobile-dominated urban environments.

Registrations of motor vehicles have increased from 49 million in 1950 to 133 million in 1975; this is more than a 4 percent compound average annual growth rate. The time may not be too distant when motor vehicle registrations equal the population of the United States. Along with the increase in the number of vehicles, estimates indicate that motor vehicles are being used more extensively and operated somewhat less efficiently. Data indicate the average miles per vehicle and average gallons of fuel consumed per vehicle have increased in the last three decades. The average mileage per gallon of fuel consumed has declined until very recently. Since 1974, however, mileage per gallon has increased, due to smaller vehicles, higher gas prices, and changed car buying habits. The magnitude of the increase in the level of fuel consumption and total number of motor vehicles obviously results in increases in automobile pollutant emissions. The rise in miles traveled per vehicle further compounds the problem.

Recent concern about motor vehicle air pollution has resulted in the imposition of stringent federal emission controls on automobile manufacturers. This legislation and the movement to less-polluting motor fuels is likely to help the air pollution problem. We shall discuss the particulars of automobile emission standards and some general air quality policies in Part 4. However, at present we can note a number of factors that may counteract improvements resulting from automobile emission standards and the increasing use of nonpollutant motor fuels. First, and most obvious, is the steady growth in the number of motor vehicles being operated in the United States. If each vehicle contributes less pollutants but there are more vehicles each year, it is clearly possible to have deteriorating air quality levels. Thus, some of the reduction in motor-vehicle-related air pollutants due to the federal emission standards may be offset by continued growth in the number of vehicles and the increase in travel miles and total fuel consumption.

In addition, the age structure of vehicles means that many vehicles even in the late 1970s and 1980s will be operating altogether without emission controls. Moreover, the fact that new vehicles must meet the federal standards today does not ensure that these same vehicles will comply with the standards 5 years, or 3 years, or even 1 year later. Proper and regular maintenance stimulated by periodic local enforcement must accompany these broad-based federal standards. The installation of anti-pollution devices cannot be a once-and-for-all policy. As vehicles age, the engines, the exhaust system, and the emission control equipment of the vehicle must be serviced regularly to preserve the effectiveness of the emission controls. Unless incentives exist to promote regular servicing of antipollutant equipment, the federal controls are not likely to be as effective in the long run as intended.

Finally, there has been considerable government and private research aimed at the development of alternative engines that are relatively pollutant-free. This research promises potential major changes in motor vehicle manufacturing and a vast reduction in motor vehicle emissions. The obvious question is the relative costs of new engine designs compared to the costs of the conventional vehicle engines. However, this benefit-cost comparison should reflect not only the relative production costs of new and standard engines but should also include the net environmental costs caused by conventional engines.

Another major source of air pollution stems from stationary fuel combustion in the generation of electrical power. Like the automobile, electrical power is a basic ingredient in the mass consumption standard of living U.S. economy. Table 7–4 presents energy use data for the recent past and projections to 1990 of what the Federal Power Commission (FPC) calls *energy requirements*. The 100 percent increase in electrical energy use from 1960 to 1970 is impressive but is dwarfed by the projected electrical use in 1990, when almost 5000 billion kilowatt-hours (kWh) will be consumed (compared to the 764 billion used in 1960). Furthermore, Table 7–5 indicates that most of the electrical energy produced by utilities in this country results from the combustion of fossil fuels (75.5 percent) rather than from hydropower or nuclear sources. Thus,

TABLE 7–4 UTILITY ELECTRIC ENERGY USE AND PROJECTED REQUIREMENTS

Year	Energy Use (billions of kilowatt-hours)
1960	764
1965	1060
1970	1534
1975	1916
1980	2717
1985	3687
1990	4980

Source: Federal Power Commission.

TABLE 7–5 ELECTRICAL ENERGY PRODUCTION BY UTILITIES BY FUEL BASE (1975)

Source of Energy	Percent
Coal	44.7
Oil	15.1
Gas	15.7
Hydro	15.8
Nuclear	8.9

Source: Federal Power Commission: *Electric Power Statistics* most of the electrical energy generated by utilities is accomplished by the burning of fossil fuels, and the largest fuel source is coal (45 percent of the total). Although the percentage of coal used of total coal equivalents has decreased (as oil, gas, nuclear, and hydropower have increased their relative fuel shares), the magnitude of the absolute increase in coal consumption has significant implications for air quality. As we observed in Table 7–3, the combustion of coal in electric generation and industrial processes results in considerable sulfur oxide, nitrogen oxide, and particulate matter emissions. The projected growth in electrical energy use and the promise of further heavy reliance on coal as the fuel for power generation makes this area another prime concern for public policy.

The large projections of energy consumption for the rest of the century imply corresponding increases in the capacity and number of power generating plants. Recently, the location of new power plants has become a major environmental issue. Typically, new plants are built on rural sites, although the generated power is transmitted hundreds of miles away for use in urban-suburban regions. The result is air quality deterioration in relatively unspoiled natural areas with damaging esthetic and ecological effects. This pattern is justified by utilities on the basis that the pollution damages would be much higher if the plants were located near, or actually in, the more populous using areas. Many environmentalists disagree.

Some environmentalists and economists have argued that the projections of energy requirements and the need for ever more power plants are grossly overstated. Energy consumption levels are not fixed absolutes but are dependent on economic incentives. Because the price of electricity does not reflect the true social costs of energy generation due to the existence of external costs caused by air quality deterioration, the quantity of energy demanded exceeds the efficient level of energy production for the society. Further, not only is the price of energy below its social costs, but the conventional practice of utilities offering *lower* rates to large industrial and commercial users encourages the use of electricity. Ending these discounts would create direct incentives to use less electricity. The results would be a substantial decline in so-called *energy requirements*. In fact, projections of electrical energy use in 1990 made only a few years ago showed a need for almost 6000 billion kWh. The FPC has revised this estimate downward by 1000 billion kWh, as shown in Table 7–4. In part this new, lower estimate reflects the sharp rise in energy prices and associated reductions in demand. Further price rises, rate structure revisions, and other national conservation policies can be expected to reduce this revised projection even further. The overall effect of such programs would be improved air quality as the efficient pricing of energy reduces the quantity demanded and results in fewer pollutants discharged into the atmosphere.

This summarizes the main point of the environmentalist's view of the energy problem, although it should be recognized that a final result of implementing such policies would be higher prices and lower production levels for goods requiring significant energy inputs. This result would be consistent, however, with pricing goods at their full social costs of production and represents a direct example of the theory presented in Part 2.

Industrial sources represent a considerable component of air pollutants and reflect the discharges caused by self-supplied electric power generation in addition to the discharges from daily production activities. Once again, this particular component of the air pollution problem is an intrinsic part of economic activity.

Finally, the burning of refuse represents another aspect of air pollution. The increasing production of goods, the relatively low levels of recycling of materials, and the law of the conservation of matter combine to result in increasing amounts of junk and solid wastes. Estimates are that the United States generates over 5 pounds per day per person of solid wastes. Much of this waste material is disposed of by burning, which contributes to air pollution problems. Refuse, junk, and other solid wastes are obviously not high-grade fuels and, when burned, burn inefficiently. The result is a discharge of a variety of pollutants. Economic growth promises even greater amounts of goods in the future, and if increasing reliance is made on the burning of waste material, then we can expect a rise in the contribution of refuse disposal to air pollution.[1]

In summary, the obvious lesson from the discussion of the sources of air pollution is that the problem of deteriorating air quality is inherent in economic activity and has a broad base in terms of the direct or indirect contribution of each individual in the society. Driving a car, heating a home, running an air conditioner, and, generally, sharing in the high standard of living in the United States are the basic causes of poor air quality. Next, we turn to the problem of what poor air quality means in terms of damages to human life and economic activity.

B. THE CONSEQUENCES OF DETERIORATING AIR QUALITY

This section presents some of the major identifiable economic effects of poor air quality and singles out the specific air-polluting agents responsible for these effects.

---

[1] We shall discuss the details of the solid waste disposal problem in Chapter 8. It should be noted that technological advances in solid waste combustion techniques promise to reduce the air quality problems associated with refuse disposal.

1. Human Health Effects

Spectacular catastrophes stemming from poor air quality conditions have been infrequent but, unfortunately, real events. Incidents of poor air quality leading directly to human fatalities warn us of the potentially devastating health impact of air quality deterioration. For example, in early December 1930, a stationary air mass together with dense fog engulfed the Meuse Valley of Belgium. This thermal inversion trapped normally heavy amounts of industrial emissions in the air over the valley and inhibited natural dispersion processes. Industrial discharges of particulate matter and sulfur dioxide in conjunction with the thermal inversion resulted in poisonous air conditions. During the 5 days of the inversion, 63 deaths were directly attributable to the poor air, and thousands of other individuals became ill.

Another thermal inversion accompanied by fog trapped the industrial town of Donora, Pennsylvania on the Monongahela River in a killer air mass in October 1948. Stagnant high pressure, again in combination with substantial particulate and sulfur dioxide industrial discharges, killed 20 people and made nearly 6000 others ill.

London, England has a legendary history of fogs and misty low ceilings. These atmospheric conditions have not always contributed to the colorful history of the city. A thermal inversion in early December 1952 together with the coal smoke discharges of millions of household furnaces created disastrous air quality conditions. Estimates indicate that the resulting smog caused nearly 4000 deaths above the normal rate for an equivalent winter period, and countless other individuals were made ill. Essentially the same ingredients combined again in December 1962 to kill an estimated 300 Londoners. Both of these episodes occurred during winter months when widespread home heating with coal resulted in heavy smoke discharges that were then trapped by thermal inversions. These events led to strict air pollution control measures which have recently resulted in dramatic improvements in London's air quality.

As alarming as these events are, evidence suggests that more widespread, and ultimately more damaging, effects may accompany persistent human exposure to poor air quality over long time periods. The connection between air quality and respiratory diseases has received increasing attention. Although medical evidence has established that a general relation exists between air quality and human health, an important problem is to quantify this relation and to adjust for the multitude of other factors that determine human health. Empirical research efforts have attempted to isolate the relation between air quality and such specific diseases as bronchitis, asthma, lung cancer, and emphysema, in addition to general mortality and morbidity rates. The overall weight of this evidence leaves little doubt that widespread and adverse human health effects are associated with poor air quality. For example, rough but conservative estimates of the dollar costs of environmentally related cancer deaths—to which air quality deterioration makes large contributions—are placed at $53 billion annually.

A number of medical studies have investigated the relationship between bronchitis mortality and air quality. The disease of bronchitis manifests itself in breathing difficulties and increased susceptibility to infection that may lead to death. Studies done in Great Britain suggest that a strong association exists between bronchitis mortality and various air quality indices. A correlation analysis across county boroughs in England and Wales indicates a statistically significant and direct relation between bronchitis deaths (for male and female subgroup) and air pollution and smoke indices. The effect of air quality on the incidence of bronchitis seemed to be independent of the sex of the subgroups. A similar type of study of geographic areas in the Buffalo, New York region indicated that for white males between 50 and 69 years of age, the mortality rates from asthma, bronchitis, and emphysema increase by 100 percent with significant increases in an associated air quality index. Alternatively, estimates from these studies indicate that decreases of 25 to 50 percent in bronchitis mortality rates can be realized if air quality is improved to levels reflected by the conditions in the highest air quality areas included in the samples.

Lung cancer in this country is annually responsible for over 50,000 deaths. Recent intensive investigations have demonstrated the association between lung cancer incidence and smoking habits. However, a number of further studies, controlling for the personal smoking factor, indicate, in addition, that a significant difference exists for lung cancer death rates between individuals living in urban versus rural areas. The weight of this evidence is considerable and suggests the association of poor air quality conditions in urban areas with increases in deaths attributable to lung cancer (even after adjusting for smoking habits).

Other studies have pointed to an association of nonrespiratory cancers with air quality indices and/or urban versus rural residency.[2] There is further, but less extensive, evidence relating cardiovascular diseases to air pollution. Various infant mortality rates, total mortality rates, emphysema, pneumonia, and pulmonary tuberculosis diseases also show increases with higher levels of air pollution and/or urban residence. Finally, several studies indicate that work absences are significantly higher when atmo-

---

[2] Urban residence is taken as a proxy for poor air quality because, in fact, urban areas do have lower air quality conditions than rural areas. However, a problem of interpretation in this kind of social science research is to separate the effect on health of poor air in urban areas versus all other urban factors affecting health.

spheric conditions reflect poor air quality than when the air is relatively clean.

The type of air quality measures used in many of these studies reflects the amount of sulfates, particulate matter, carbon monoxide, and hydrocarbons in the air. Combining the various air quality measures into an index number poses complex technical problems, but the evidence is enough to suggest that, even for several definitions of air quality, the incidence of a variety of serious diseases increases markedly as the indices reflect progressively deteriorating air conditions.

Further qualifications to these studies would cite the possible need to control for a variety of other circumstances in addition to age and smoking habits before attempting to isolate air quality effects on human health. Such factors as the individual's general health condition, exercise habits, diet, or psychological strain also may enter systematically into a statistical association with overall health and disease incidence. Although this is a valid caveat, the results of the entire body of health studies are too one-sided to suggest that only a spurious relation has been uncovered between air quality and disease.

Further health effects of poor air quality elude efforts to place dollar estimates on their damages. Loss of efficiency on the job due to air-pollution-related health effects is obviously a difficult item to measure, although it is well established, for example, that carbon monoxide reduces response time of the nervous system. Sickness induced by air pollution may not be recognized as responsible for work days lost or above-normal absenteeism. Some on-the-job injuries and industrial accidents also may be attributable to air pollution although they are not recorded as such. In addition, there may be significant human health effects of persistent exposure to what is now believed to be safe levels of air pollutants. Ideally, all of these items should be included in any dollar measure of the costs of air quality deterioration. Therefore, present estimates of these costs, however large they seem, must be accepted as only a rough underestimate of the true human health costs of air pollution.

2. Agriculture and Air Quality

Agricultural damage to crops and livestock is a second major effect associated with poor air quality. The total extent of agricultural damage caused by air pollution in this country is unknown, but already there is considerable evidence to suggest that it is extensive. Biological studies have isolated the effects on vegetation of a variety of pollutants such as ozone, sulfur dioxide, and fluorides.

Ozone, for example, affects plant cells beneath the surface of the leaf and ultimately damages or destroys the plant. Studies have demonstrated that extensive ozone damage to agricultural corps exists in several industrialized states. *Sulfur dioxide* in the atmosphere is taken into plants through the respiratory process and, in combination with water naturally contained within the plant, becomes toxic to plant cells. Basic cereal crops, such as wheat and barley, are severely attacked by sulfur dioxide. Damages from sulfur dioxide can be extensive enough to result in a total destruction of the entire market value of a crop. Sulfur dioxide also adversely affects trees, and there have been recent instances of damages to forested areas resulting from power plant discharges of sulfur dioxide.[3]

Fluorides adversely affect the photosynthesis of plants when absorbed through the plant's leaves. For fruit trees, fluoride damage results in losses in the number and in the weight of fruit produced. Fluorides that becomes stored in forage foods also have devastating effects on livestock. The consumption of forage containing heavy concentrations of fluorides results in fluorosis, causing deteriorating health, reduction in growth, loss of weight, immobility, and, ultimately, the death of the animal. An extensive case of fluoride damages occurred in Polk County, Florida in the 1950s and 1960s, when increases in phosphate fertilizer manufacturing created widespread and, at times, devastating damage to citrus and beef cattle activities in the area.

Considerable scientific evidence exists to demonstrate the causal relationship between poor air quality and deteriorating agricultural performance. However, it is not always a simple task to establish this relationship in a legal sense in any given instance of air pollution. Numerous common law cases in which affected parties have attempted to recover damages have met with frustration. Private companies or utilities responsible for the emission of pollutants and subsequent air quality deterioration have readily found *expert* witnesses to testify that many factors could have caused the Christmas trees to yellow, the citrus crop to fail, or the cattle to sicken and waste away. The complex and myriad factors determining plant, animal, and, of course, human health make successful legal proceedings for the recovery of air pollutant damages an involved, costly, and often frustrating experience. This difficulty is largely a result of the current structure of property rights and the law rather than a true questioning of the causal relation between a pollutant and, for example, plant damage.

In summary, air pollutants have direct harmful effects on agricultural activities. Their damages probably involve hundreds of millions of dollars annually for the U.S. economy. Available studies estimate large

---

[3] For example, the Virginia Electric and Power Company generating plant at Mount Storm, West Virginia has been accused of destroying a nearby thriving Christmas tree industry as a result of sulfur dioxide discharges.

losses in field and vegetable crops on the eastern seaboard caused by air pollution damage. Other studies estimate a substantial loss in citrus fruits and other crops in California. Although no systematic estimate of the aggregate national effects of agricultural damage has yet been attempted, one advantage in this area is that market prices of agricultural products provide an indication of the agricultural costs of air quality effects.[4]

3. Property Damages

Air pollutants are also responsible for extensive damages to property. Ready examples of this type of damage would be the emission of particulate matter that soils clothes, automobiles, homes, and buildings. The blackened facades of buildings in urban centers are obvious testimony to particulate, hydrocarbon, and sulfur pollutants. This soiling causes cleaning expenditures considerably in excess of those that normally would be undertaken. Beyond its apparent soiling effect, air pollutants corrode, crack, and weaken materials. Ozone, for example, in addition to its damaging agricultural effects, cracks and breaks rubber. In urban areas, there is extensive ozone damage to automobile tires and telephone and electrical wires. Sulfur dioxide emissions also result in substantial property damages, adversely affecting a wide variety of property from the hardest of materials (iron and steel) to domestic furniture, synthetic fabrics, and clothing. Sulfuric acids, formed from a combination of emissions of sulfur oxides and water, weaken and wear building surfaces.

Statistical studies also indicate that air pollutants have a systematic and negative impact on residential property values. Studies have related the sale or rental prices of residences to variables such as family income, number of rooms, age and condition of the property, distance from center city, and other socioeconomic variables. Even after including these variables, statistically significant and negative correlations were found between sales or rental prices and two indices of air pollution. In part, the observed reduction in property values may represent market reaction to the adverse health and general amenity effects of air pollutants rather than actual physical property damages. It also may reflect general market responses to a mix of unmeasured urban ills. Whatever the reason, the loss in residential property value that can be attributable directly to air pollutants is a real economic cost to the owners of homes and buildings and properly should be included as part of total air pollution damage. Dollar estimates of residential property losses for 85 U.S. cities due to

---

[4] Some adjustment of actual agricultural prices may be required to account for government support programs and other market imperfections in order to arrive at the true social value of lost production.

sulfur oxide and particulate matter damages total over $600 million. As in the case of agriculture, the actual market prices of residential houses and property provide reasonable indicators for the costs of air pollution damages. Once again, the main research problem in this area is to identify and quantify the actual extent of air pollution property damages. Crude estimates put the total annual costs of air pollutants to all types of property in the United States at a figure of $13 billion.

Beyond these damages to conventional forms of property, air pollution has endangered unique and historic buildings—e.g., famous European cathedrals, ancient classical structures, and medieval Oxford colleges. So threatening is this pollution damage that there have even been serious proposals to place a glass dome over the Parthenon in Greece to protect it from further air pollution damage. Such sites cannot of course be replaced, and measures of the monetary loss of their destruction are not meaningful. Nevertheless, their destruction or substantial decay clearly represents a major social cost.

4. Safety and Amenity Effects of Air Pollution

Air pollutants may be responsible for a number of automobile, air, and industrial accidents. Decreased visibility due to smog and smoke conditions contributes to the frequency of highway accidents. Smog-related poor visibility is a common condition in urban freeway driving. There have been a number of smog-induced chain car highway accidents on high-speed turnpikes in recent years. The costs of these automobile accidents in terms of lives, injuries, and property should be included as an additional cost of air pollution. In addition to auto accidents, Civil Aeronautic Board studies indicate that a sizable number of air accidents are caused by situations involving adverse weather conditions. Although the extent of the responsibility of air pollution in air accidents is unknown, some of these weather-related accidents may be the result of pollutant-induced smog or haze that further complicates air navigation in existing natural weather difficulties.

Finally, we have already noted that some on-the-job industrial accidents may be the result of poor air quality conditions. High levels of carbon monoxide, for example, inhibit the response time of the nervous system, reduce coordination ability and alertness, and, accordingly, may contribute to increasing the incidence of on-the-job industrial accidents. These same factors may result in the loss of efficiency in urban office workers. At the present time, measurement of the total costs of air-pollutant-induced accidents and dollar losses in terms of worker efficiency is only a speculative exercise. However, these costs, whatever the magnitude, are a real component of the costs of air pollutants, and there is a considerable need for research efforts to identify the exact role of air pollutants in the areas of travel, safety, and work efficiency.

Above and beyond the health, agricultural, property, and safety effects, further damages of air pollutants exist in the form of general amenity costs. The unpleasantness of foul odors, the dreariness of daily views of soot-dirtied buildings, and the overall disagreeability of poor air quality, as perceived by individuals, are all added costs of air pollution. Although accurate measurement of these costs are probably the most difficult of all, the willingness of individuals to pay for the avoidance of the general disamenities of air pollutants should properly be included as another cost.

5. Air Pollution Control Costs

All the air pollution costs cited above occur despite substantial air pollution prevention costs incurred by industry and government. In 1976, for example, private industry in the United States spent $3.6 billion on air pollution control investments. This figure is only part of the total social costs of air pollution prevention. These costs are expected to increase rapidly over the next decade. How much society should spend on air pollution prevention depends, of course, on whether the additional costs of more pollution prevention are equal to the benefits of the welfare damages avoided. The magnitude of the benefits to be expected are suggested by the rough estimates of various types of air pollution damages cited in this chapter.

C. SUMMARY AND CONCLUSIONS

Unrestricted use of the atmosphere as a disposal medium has made the previously unlimited supply of air a scarce economic resource. This scarcity is manifested in deteriorating air quality conditions in many areas of the United States. Deterioration of air quality is the result of the continual injection into the atmosphere of enormous amounts of particulate matter, sulfur oxides, hydrocarbons, nitrogen oxides, and a myriad of other gases and substances. Unfortunately, these undesired pollutants are the by-products of a desired high mass consumption standard of living and are traceable to certain broadly based sources such as transportation and power generation.

Air pollutants have adverse human health effects and have been consistently associated with increases in the incidence of numerous respiratory diseases and the general mortality rate. In addition, considerable agricultural and property damages can be directly attributable to poor air quality conditions. Safety, work efficiency, esthetic reactions, and long-run weather effects are other areas of air pollution concern.

The large (if imprecisely estimated) magnitude of air pollution damages and the promise of steady growth in air pollutants create an obvious need for air quality control policies. Essentially, the job of public policy is to internalize, to each user, all the social costs of discharging pollutants into the atmosphere. If this task were accomplished, it would represent a marked change from the historically costless and unrestricted use of the atmosphere as a disposal medium.

QUESTIONS FOR DISCUSSION

1. What are the most important differences between air and water resources from the standpoint of the economic problems associated with the quality of each? Which do you judge to be the more difficult problem for society, and why?

2. Many of the air quality problems facing this country today are due to the combustion of gas and oil fuels. Would it help solve the problem of air quality if we switched back to coal or perhaps accelerated the switch to nuclear power as alternative sources of energy?

3. "Most of our air quality problems would vanish if the government would just force the big automobile manufacturers to produce perfectly clean engines immediately." Evaluate this assertion critically.

4. What are the fundamental difficulties involved in estimating the dollar value of the welfare damage costs of air pollution? Are the estimates in Table 7–1 of tons of emissions useful estimates of these welfare damage costs? Can you conceive of ideal experiments that would enable a researcher to resolve these difficulties?

5. What has happened to air quality in your area in the last decade? Can you identify the causes of improvement or deterioration? Does it seem to you that the benefits of any air quality improvement were worth the costs?

SELECTED REFERENCES

ANDERSON, R. J., AND T. D. CROCKER, "Air Pollution and Residential Property Values," *Urban Studies*, No. 8 (October 1971). An empirical study of the negative impact of air pollution on property values.

FREEMAN, A. M., III, "On Estimating Air Pollution Control Benefits from Land

Values," *Journal of Environmental Economics and Management*, 1, No. 2 (May 1974). A critique and assessment of attempts to measure the damage to property values caused by air pollution.

KNEESE, A. V., AND W. D. SCHULZE, "Environment, Health and Economics— The Case of Cancer," *American Economic Review*, 67, No. 1 (February 1977). Evidence on the association of cancer and exposure to various pollutants. The source of the $53 billion estimate of cancer costs cited in the text. Highly recommended.

LAVE, L. S., "Air Pollution Damage: Some Difficulties in Estimating the Value of Abatement," in *Environmental Quality Analysis*, A. V. Kneese and B. T. Bower, eds. Baltimore: The Johns Hopkins Press, 1972. Highlights the thorny problems of benefit measurements of air pollution control.

LAVE, L., AND R. SESKIN, *Air Pollution and Human Health*. Baltimore: The Johns Hopkins Press, 1977. Research results on the association between air pollution and human health. Comprehensive.

SMITH, V. K., *The Economic Consequences of Air Pollution*. Cambridge, Mass.: Ballinger Publishing Company, 1976. An excellent survey of the literature on the relationship between air quality and human health and property damages. Also contains additional contributions. Advanced but highly recommended.

STERN, A. C. (ed.), *Air Pollution* (2nd ed.). New York: Academic Press, Inc., 1968. A comprehensive treatment of the technical basis of air quality in three volumes.

U.S. Environmental Protection Agency, *The Clean Air Act*, 92d Congress, 1st Session, Document 92-6. Washington, D.C.: Government Printing Office, March 1971. A detailed economic analysis of the effects of air pollutants and the development of the air quality standards of the act.

U.S. Environmental Protection Agency, *Monitoring and Air Quality Trends Report*, annual. Washington, D.C.: U.S. Government Printing Office. A useful source of data on emission levels and trends for the United States.

8

THE
QUALITY
OF LIFE
AND OTHER
ENVIRONMENTAL
PROBLEMS

The problems of air and water quality listed in the previous two chapters have attracted considerable public attention and resources. Unfortunately, environmental deterioration is not confined exclusively to situations involving air and water quality. The emphasis on pollutants of water and air reflects their pervasive presence and the relatively advanced technical knowledge we possess concerning these problems. Other environmental problems may involve social costs of equivalent magnitude. Thus far, these other problems have received little attention because of their more subtle nature and the paucity of information concerning their long-run environmental effects (for example, pesticides, toxic substances, solid wastes, noise). In addition, environmental concerns extend beyond the effects associated with particular types of effluents. Orderly land use, preservation of unique natural environments, and ample opportunities for outdoor recreation are all important elements involved in maintaining the quality of life.

This chapter provides a brief overview of a variety of these other environmental problems. The problems are diverse and, therefore, difficult to discuss within a common framework. Our objective in the treatment of each is to give the reader a basic understanding of an important aspect of the wide scope of environmental deterioration.

Sections A and B present the difficult and alarming problems of pesticides and toxic substances. The end result of a high mass consumption society, solid wastes, is treated as another environmental problem in Section C. Section D discusses the largely unexplored area of noise and its effects. Finally, Section E extends the scope of our analysis to include land use problems, the supply of outdoor recreation opportunities, and the general issue of conservation. Section F is a brief summary of the chapter.

A. PESTICIDES

In the long-run perspective of history, the development and extensive use of effective pesticides have made a major contribution to human welfare. Pesticides are responsible for enormous increases in agricultural yields and for the control of once widespread and debilitating diseases. However, to balance attention given to the benefits of pesticides, recent concern has focused on their adverse effects on other aspects of human health and fish and wildlife populations. Pesticide research findings again reveal the recurring theme of environmental problems—a difficult, benefit-cost type of decision: whether, and to what degree, to continue pesticide use and gain protection of crop yields and lower incidences of some human diseases at the cost of considerable long-run damages to environmental conditions and increased risks to human health.

Pesticide use stems from the natural competition between man and insect. Insect pests destroy crops, transmit disease to humans and animals, and, in general, plague human existence. Man and his technology have fought these pests with increasingly sophisticated devices, moving from the soap, lye, kerosene, nicotine, and arsenic applications of the nineteenth century to the complex chlorinated hydrocarbons and organic phosphate compounds of the present.

Unfortunately, in this war against pests, it is not always easy to isolate and destroy only the problem-causing pest and to contain the effects of this destruction within known and narrow limits. Most insects are not harmful to humans, and, in fact, many have benefical effects. In addition, all insect life is intimately related to a natural ecological equilibrium. Recent research has uncovered exceedingly complex environmental ramifications associated with man's attempts to eradicate or control certain forms of insects. This new knowledge has resulted in a redirection of thinking into what were previously regarded as *safe* pesticides and generated further research to develop alternative forms of pest control.

Meanwhile, as this research goes on, the production and use of pesticides increase in both the United States and the world. For some time, pesticide use was dominated by the chlorinated hydrocarbon pesticides —DDT and related compounds. Recently, however, there has been a decline in the use of chlorinated hydrocarbons and a subsequent increase in the use of organophosphates and other pesticides. We shall discuss both the chlorinated hydrocarbons and organophosphates in greater detail below. Herbicides are compounds used to combat weeds and control undesirable plant growth and are another significant and growing component of pesticide production. Weed control has always been vital for many agricultural crops, but there are additional, growing uses of herbicides associated with maintaining roadways and other public property.[1] Fungicides combat those plants that are parasites or saprophytes on living or dead organic material. Fungi are responsible for damage to wood and structures, and some types of parasitic fungi cause disease in man, animals, and certain plants (cereal crops and fruit being particularly susceptible).

Most careful studies into the question of pesticide use acknowledge the necessity of the agricultural protection afforded by pesticides. Department of Agriculture estimates indicate that a 25 to 30 percent decrease in U.S. crop and livestock yields would follow a ban on the use of all pesticides. The U.N. Food and Agricultural Organization projection of the sources of additional world food supply requirements relies on a 20 to 30 percent contribution to crop yields from controlling pest-related food losses. The implication of this estimate is that without the use of pesticides starvation would threaten many poor countries.

Today, over 60,000 pesticides are registered for sale in the United States. One of the most important single groups in this vast number are the chlorinated hydrocarbons (for example, DDT, DDE, TDE, dieldrin, endrin, benzaine, aldrin, chlordone, methohexachloride). This group is the prime example of the pesticide dilemma. The foremost among them, DDT, once was regarded as an ideal pesticide. DDT first was used extensively for insect control during World War II, although the compound was known as early as 1874. The initial use of DDT was directed at control of typhus, malaria, and other diseases. The use of DDT for these purposes was a great success. Countless lives were saved, the war effort

---

[1] In addition, much of the recent herbicide production increase was due to their use during the Vietnam War.

improved, and all without any observable adverse effects. DDT administered in low concentrations was found to be deadly to insect life and had persistent toxic effects over a considerable time period. The success of DDT in disease control encouraged its use for agricultural purposes where it increased the yields of many crops. This record, combined with relatively low costs, resulted in the extensive use of DDT and other chlorinated hydrocarbon pesticides. In the 1950s, however, growing evidence of severe environmental effects generated concern over the widespread use of DDT, and its former safe and harmless reputation came under attack.

Chlorinated hydrocarbon pesticides are persistent compounds that retain their toxicity in soil and marine sediments over long time periods. They are absorbed by natural life processes into the food chain and become stored in the tissues of living creatures, concentrating principally in the organs containing fatty substances. The effects of this concentration became distressingly apparent when research traced a series of spectacular and extensive fish and wildlife kills to the use of chlorinated hydrocarbon pesticides.

A now-famous example of the deadly food chain effects of pesticides occurred in Clear Lake, California.[2] Located in the mountains to the north of San Francisco, Clear Lake is a popular recreation area that, unfortunately, harbors a large gnat population. In 1949, an effort was made to control the gnat population by a careful application of DDD (a DDT-related substance, but less toxic to fish). The dosage of DDD used was not thought to be particularly excessive, and given the volume of water in the lake, the DDD amounted, on the average, to only 0.015 part per million. Once applied, the DDD sank to the lake bottom and, as planned, destroyed the gnat larvae. In 1949, and again in 1950, the gnat population was negligible, and the control program seemed to be successful with no apparent lasting ill effects on wildlife and fish. However, by 1954, there were large-scale deaths of the lake's waterfowl. The cause of the decimation of the waterfowl population was not immediately understood. Meanwhile, the gnat population again boomed, and further applications of DDD were made, subsequently followed by further bird deaths. After considerable puzzling over the possible causes of the bird deaths, an examination of bird fat tissues revealed deadly concentrations of DDD in excess of 1000 parts per million (ppm). Incredibly, what began as an initial 0.015-ppm application of DDD to the lake ended up in enormously greater concentrations in the fat tissues of the birds. The path of the DDD led from the lake bottom to absorption by

[2] Rachel Carson's The Silent Spring dramatized the devastating effects of hydrocarbons on fish and wildlife. The Clear Lake case is eloquently presented in her book.

the plankton life of the lake in the amount of 5 ppm. Plankton, the basic food supply of the ecosystem, passed on the DDD to small fish and other aquatic life, up to 400 ppm. Larger predator fish had even higher concentrations of the DDD, and, ultimately, the bird life dependent on the lake's fish population for food became subject to toxic concentrations of DDD. Thus, the food chain of life from plankton to large predators increasingly concentrated the DDD pesticide.

Once understood, other examples of this deadly food chain effect were uncovered. Different types of bird species were fatally affected after feeding on insects, soil life, or seed treated with chlorinated hydrocarbons. Hydrocarbon concentrations were found to impair and, at times, eliminate breeding in many species, including robins, eagles, and certain fish. Residues of DDT showed up in milk from cows fed on pesticide-dressed forage. Human fat tissues revealed alarming concentrations of about 8 ppm of DDT in the body of an average American. Research evidence suggests a relation between some pesticide levels and the incidence of degenerative diseases such as cancer, birth defects, and other genetic damage. Finally, pesticides were found in animal life in areas of the world, such as the Arctic and Antarctic, where no pesticides had ever been applied, indicating the persistent properties of the chlorinated hydrocarbons and their ability to invade almost all life forms.

In response to considerable public outcry and legislation resulting from the concern over environmental consequences of the chlorinated hydrocarbons, some substitutions were made, using organophosphates and other pesticides. In general, the substituted pesticides are less persistent and break down into harmless components relatively rapidly. Being less persistent, repeated applications are often necessary with the result that the use of organophosphates is generally relatively expensive. Organophosphate pesticides are, however, extremely toxic. Parathion and TEPP, for example, are highly poisonous, and a number of human fatalities occur annually due to their improper handling and use. Of course, this toxicity also applies to wildlife, although the relatively nonpersistent nature of these pesticides means that they do not have the severe food chain concentration effects of the chlorinated hydrocarbons.

An additional problem with pesticides in general is the ability of insects to develop immunity to pesticide compounds. For example, there is considerable evidence of the mosquito's adaptation and resistance to a wide range of pesticides. This experience characterizes geographically diverse ecological systems from the Central Valley of California to tropical areas.[3] Insect immunity results from the fecundity of the life cycles of most insects. Resistance to pesticides may lessen considerably the

[3] See, for example, R. Garcia, "The Control of Malaria," *Environment*, XIV (June 1972).

effectiveness of a given application. Stronger pesticides, in terms of toxicity or persistence, must then be used to achieve the desired degree of protection. The resulting implications for soil life and higher-order life forms, therefore, are likely to be more severe than those associated with the initial pesticide administered in its original dosage, although the degree of insect protection has not been improved. The prospect of a treadmill race between new pesticide development and resistant insect populations casts doubt on the continued reliance on pesticides for insect control.

Human health hazards and the other deleterious environmental effects of pesticides have led to the federal government's funding a great deal of research. Much of this research is aimed at isolating the long-term health effects of chronic exposure to pesticides, uncovering the ecological ramifications associated with specific pesticide use, and the development of alternative means of pest control. A number of federal agencies are involved in these research activities: The Department of Health, Education and Welfare, the Bureau of Sports Fisheries and Wildlife, the Environmental Protection Agency, and the Department of Agriculture. This considerable research effort hopefully will be the source of the technical information necessary to design proper pesticide policies.

Pesticide policy is in a state of flux, although all the present and proposed policies rely on methods of prohibition and regulation. Pesticides moving in interstate commerce must be registered with the Environmental Protection Agency. The EPA can cancel a registration if there is improper labeling of the pesticide. It also has suspension powers to halt interstate shipments when an *imminent hazard* exists. Other proposed legislation develops a classification scheme of pesticides by uses covering pesticides suitable for *general use, restricted use,* or *use by permit only.* Pesticides would be registered by the EPA according to category, and application of the pesticide would require increasing technical supervision over the three classifications.

The EPA has used its powers to cancel the registration of DDT and several other related pesticides and effectively to eliminate their use in the United States. This decision represents a landmark in pesticide policy and follows extensive hearings on the benefits and dangers of DDT use. The prohibition ruling was based on the evidence of DDT's persistent toxic effects to wildlife and its long-run dangers to human health. The costs of this prohibition are likely to be increases in insect damage to crops and in insect control costs as more expensive pesticides are used more frequently to achieve the protection once provided by DDT.

Because approximately 80 percent of the pesticides are directed toward the control of only about 100 pests, additional research efforts have concentrated on the development of nonchemical pest controls.

For example, alternative methods rely on destruction by natural predators and diseases, sexual sterilization of the insect population, the use of attracting and destroying devices, and different crop culture practices. Further research is directed at producing pest- and disease-resistant crops. Stringent quarantine laws exist and are tightly enforced in an attempt to control the imports of products that might contain pests (over 120 of the several hundred major pest species in the United States are "imports"). Finally, the Food and Drug Administration establishes limits for pesticide residues on both human and animal foods in interstate commerce.

No policies involving the use of economic incentives have yet been employed in pesticide control. However, possibilities do exist for their use. One major problem in pesticide policy is the present low cost of the various pesticides relative to nonpesticide control methods. Government taxation and subsidy policies could be devised to encourage the use of less-damaging pesticides. For example, assume that a number of possible pesticides are available for a specified use and that all are capable of providing essentially the same degree of protection. Furthermore, assume that the pesticides vary in price and also in their estimated environmental impact but that none is deemed dangerous enough to warrant a total ban or suspension of use. Given enough information on the respective environmental effects and costs, appropriate use of tax or subsidy policies could create economic incentives favoring those pesticides with less damaging environmental consequences.

However, the realistic outlook in pesticide control is for continuation of policies stressing government regulation. This regulation will rely on prohibition and tight control over specific pesticides with respect to extent of use, location, and purpose. Heavy government research expenditures in pesticide problems are likely to continue. At least for the time being, therefore, sophisticated economic policies, in the form of taxes and subsidies, are likely to make only minimal contributions to efficient use of pesticides.

B. OTHER TOXIC POLLUTANTS

Over the last 30 years massive amounts of chemical substances have been introduced into the environment. The pesticide problems discussed in Section A are only an example, albeit a dramatic one, of the complex health and economic issues that have resulted from the extensive use of chemicals. The Council on Environmental Quality estimates that 6000 new chemical substances are discovered each year, and a large number of these are subsequently marketed commercially in various forms. The chronic effects of many of these on human health and ecological systems are only poorly understood.

What is suspected, with varying degrees of evidence already accumulated, is that the exposure of individuals to numerous toxic substances is linked to a variety of degenerative diseases. For example, most cancers are now believed to be environmentally caused with a delay between exposure and the appearance of the disease of 20 or more years. We noted in Chapter 7 that a conservative estimate of the health damage costs of environmentally related cancer deaths is $53 billion. Other diseases—of the respiratory tract, of the circulatory system, of the central nervous system, and sterility problems—are also suspected to be due, in part, to environmental causes.

Table 8–1 provides a partial list of suspected carcinogens along with their uses and estimates of the number of workers potentially at risk due to routine exposure to these substances at their place of work. Moreover, the introduction of such chemicals into the ambient environment creates uncertain, long-term, chronic risks for the population at large. Other substances, such as lead, arsenic, and vinyl chlorides, also

TABLE 8–1   SUSPECTED CARCINOGENS IN THE WORKPLACE

Substance	Uses	Estimated Number of Workers Potentially at Risk
Chloroprene	Production of synthetic rubber	2,500
Trichloroethylene	Industrial solvent, extraction of caffeine from coffee, anesthetic	200,000
Ethylene dibromide (EDB)	Leaded gas additive, dyes and pharmaceuticals, some pesticides	659,000
Coke oven emissions	Smelting	5,000
Asbestos	Brakes and clutch assemblies	908,000
Beryllium	Metal alloys, rocket fuel	30,000
Chromate compounds	Paints and anticorrosives	453,000
Hexamethyl phosphoric trimide (HMPA)	Solvent used in research labs	5,000
Polychlorinated biphenyls (PCBs)	Coolants, insulators, hydraulic fluids, pesticides, ink, etc.	12,000
4,4-Diaminodiphenyl methane (DDM)	Polyurethane production	2,500
Chloroform	Production of fluorocarbons, dyes, drugs, pesticides; contained in cough and cold preparations, laboratory solvents	40,000

Source: Council on Environmental Quality, *7th Annual Report* (1976). Washington, D.C.: Government Printing Office.

create health risks both in the workplace and in the general environment. Such commonly used meat preservatives as sodium nitrate and nitrate are suspected of leading to the formation of nitrosamines in the human body —and nitrosamine is a known carcinogen. Certain additives in animal feeds used to stimulate growth—i.e., DES, diethylstilbesterol—are also carcinogenic. We have previously noted in Chapter 7 the potential long-run damages—including a higher incidence of skin cancer—that may result from the use of fluorocarbons through the modification they may cause in the ozone layer of the atmosphere.

At least eight federal laws currently exist to regulate and even prohibit the production, use, and/or discharge of hazardous substances.[4] The administration of these laws involves four federal agencies—the Environmental Protection Agency, the Food and Drug Administration, the Occupational Safety and Health Administration, and the Consumer Product Safety Commission. It is not surprising that overlapping jurisdiction, confusion, inconsistency, and unevenness have accompanied some of the federal efforts to control hazardous substances. Moreover, the burden of proof is usually on the government to establish that a substance endangers public health. This burden is not easy to sustain, particularly when the effects of many chemicals are only manifested after long time lags, during which population mobility and the myriad of other factors that affect human health have often obscured the link between exposure and disease. Testing procedures to establish a substance as a carcinogenic are lengthy and costly, although recent scientific advances promise to reduce both time and money costs sharply with no loss in accuracy. Finally, the legislation treats each substance as if it had equal value to society and contains either no, or very vague, instructions to the federal agencies to balance the benefits and costs of their control efforts. All of these problems—multiple laws, multiple administering agencies, the burden of proof, and no reliance on economic incentives to strike a net economic balance—are likely to result both in difficulty of achieving effective control over these dangerous substances and gross economic inefficiencies from the controls actually imposed.

C. SOLID WASTES

The relationship between economic prosperity and environmental problems is probably most evident in the area of solid wastes. In 1970,

[4] Toxic Substances Control Act, Safe Drinking Water Act, Resource Conservation and Recovery Act, Occupational Safety and Health Act, Federal Water Pollution Control Act, Clean Air Act, Federal Insecticide, Fungicide and Rodenticide Act, and the Food, Drug and Cosmetic Act.

national trash collections amounted, on average, to 1 ton of solid wastes per person. Readers can visualize the dimensions of the problem by considering the volume of trash generated by each of their households in a single week and multiplying by 50 million. All the bottles, cans, paper, and plastics used as containers for consumption goods are discarded regularly by the average household and end up as refuse. Some scattered data indicate the magnitude of the waste disposal problem. New York City generates a daily solid waste load of 30,000 tons. Paper consumption in the United States is estimated at 576 pounds annually per person. Estimates of current per capita consumption of plastics show an enormous increase over 1950 levels. These wastes, and others, place great burdens on the generally antiquated solid waste collection and disposal systems of the United States.

Table 8–2 indicates the magnitude and components of the solid waste problem in the country. These wastes are usually generated, collected,

TABLE 8–2   POSTCONSUMER RESIDENTIAL AND COMMERCIAL SOLID WASTE GENERATION AND RESOURCE RECOVERY, BY TYPE OF MATERIAL, 1973
(quantity in millions of tons, wet weight)

Material Categories	Gross Discards	Material Recycled		Net Waste Disposal	
		Quantity	Percent	Quantity	Percent
Paper	53.0	8.7	16.5	44.2	32.8
Glass	13.5	0.3	2.1	13.2	9.9
Metals	12.7	0.2	1.6	12.5	9.3
Ferrous	11.2	0.2	1.4	11.0	8.2
Aluminum	1.0	0.04	4.0	1.0	0.7
Other nonferrous metals	0.4	0.0	0.0	0.4	0.3
Plastics	5.0	0.0	0.0	5.0	3.7
Rubber	2.8	0.2	7.1	2.6	1.9
Leather	1.0	0.0	0.0	1.0	0.7
Textiles	1.9	0.0	0.0	1.9	1.4
Wood	4.9	0.0	0.0	4.9	3.6
Total nonfood products	94.8	9.4	9.9	85.4	63.4
Food waste	22.4	0.0	0.0	22.4	16.6
Yard waste	25.0	0.0	0.0	25.0	18.5
Miscellaneous inorganic waste	1.9	0.0	0.0	1.9	1.4
Total waste	144.0	9.4	6.5	134.8	100.0

Source: U.S. Environmental Protection Agency, Office of Solid Waste Management Programs, Resource Recovery Division, *Third Report to Congress: Resource Recovery and Waste Reduction* (Washington, D.C.: Government Printing Office, 1975), p. 10.

and disposed of in populous areas and, consequently, have the potential to affect large numbers of people.[5]

The collection of solid wastes is the obvious initial problem for waste management, and in areas where refuse collection has been halted for some reason—strikes or natural disasters—the need for prompt collection has been dramatically apparent. In such situations, the rapid deterioration of sanitary conditions creates considerable human health hazards. Waste collection is undoubtedly a vital service in our urbanized society. Although some technical progress has occurred in collection techniques (for example, the compactor truck), refuse collection in the United States relies almost entirely on costly hand pickups of wastes from individual waste sources.

Once the collection of solid wastes is accomplished, disposal becomes the next problem. In the United States, disposal usually means depositing the wastes in open dumps, which often creates health hazards and scenic eyesores. Dump fires occur regularly and add to air quality deterioration, particularly in urban areas. In 1970, the EPA initiated a program to eliminate 5000 of the 15,000 open dumps in the United States and to substitute properly designed landfill disposal outlets. A few progressive localities have developed advanced waste management techniques and have turned solid wastes into new land areas, parks, and open spaces.[6] Waste management of this type offers exciting possibilities of creating public benefits from sources previously considered to be only costly problems. The recent sharp increase in fuel prices promises to make resource recovery of solid wastes for use as energy sources much more economically attractive.

Waste disposal by incineration often creates adverse air quality effects. Although there are some promising technical advances in incineration techniques, the types of incinerators commonly in use combined with the relatively low fuel grades inherent in solid wastes mean that air quality problems will continue to accompany the estimated 8 percent of wastes that are disposed of via burning. Disposal of wastes at sea is only a small fraction of the total disposal (8.8 million tons in 1975). The ecological implications of this dumping, like other ocean dumping, are largely unknown but are believed to have potential significant social costs. Legislation now exists to phase in prohibition of solid waste ocean dumping.

---

[5] This does not imply that the costs of agricultural solid wastes, which are not included in Table 8–2, are negligible. Polluted groundwater supplies, eutrophication of surface waters, and health hazards are some of the effects often associated with agricultural solid wastes.

[6] For example, a ski mountain has been built in DuPage County, Illinois out of garbage and trash. The hill, nicknamed Mount Trashmore, features public facilities for winter recreation sports.

Finally, reuse of waste material, or *recycling,* is a viable disposal method that can be directly influenced by economic policies. In the case of some waste materials, particularly within the mineral and industrial classifications, the amount of recycling is considerable. Substantial amounts of lead and copper are recycled into productive processes. However, for most wastes, recycling is currently economically unattractive and Table 8–2 shows that only 6.5 percent of all consumer and commercial wastes are recycled. The problem is basically economic. Federal tax laws, for example, provide economic incentives to producers to find and use virgin supplies of many natural resources. In many situations, therefore, it is more costly to recycle materials than to use new raw materials. This situation gives little private profit incentive to develop recycling technology, and the present, relatively primitive, recycling technology ensures the continued unattractiveness of recycling as an input source. Also, markets for recycled material are often subject to boom and bust fluctuations as variations in the prices and costs of virgin materials are reflected in these secondary markets. In addition to the implications for the solid waste problem, the incentive to use raw materials over recycled ones has considerable ramifications in terms of land use, open spaces, fish and wildlife populations, and other environmental amenities. For example, of 53 million tons of paper consumed in the United States in 1973, over 44 million tons ended up as wastes (that is, were not recycled). Beyond the collection and disposal costs associated with waste paper, are the effects of relying primarily on new raw materials for paper production. These effects might include diminished forest land, loss of recreational opportunities, deterioration of water quality (the paper pulp industry is a large source of organic wastes), and poor air quality as some of the discarded paper is disposed of by burning.

The nature of the solid wastes in this country, particularly those generated by residential, commercial, and institutional sources, creates certain technological problems for recycling. In almost all cases, the collected wastes arrive at the disposal site as mixed refuse. Plastics, glass, metals, paper, rubber, and other materials all are thrown together. Efficient separation of the wastes into various elements and categories is obviously required. Hand sorting of wastes is an expensive and cumbersome method given the magnitude and diversity of waste loads. Considerable research efforts are under way to develop mechanical waste separators that will solve this problem. Obviously, any separation technology will have a cost, and the difficulty (costliness) associated with the separation of wastes is now a considerable economic deterrent to the recycling of a number of materials. Another possible answer to the sorting problem is to separate wastes into some basic divisions at the waste source. This might involve a public-spirited appeal at the household and commercial level. Another possibility is local legislation requiring the sorting of wastes before collection occurs. Alternatively, another policy might be to provide economic tax and subsidy incentives to waste sources to separate their wastes.

Economic policies can be designed to encourage the use of recycled material. The distinction between *resource* and *junk* is not absolute. It depends on existing technology and market conditions. These, in turn, depend on existing economic incentives. As noted in Chapter 1, developments in basic science point to a future in which many productive processes will not require specific inputs but simply some source of energy and mass. Changes in economic incentives, therefore, can affect both technology and prevailing market conditions to transform what was once considered *junk* into valuable *resources*.

For example, the income tax incentives now incorporated in depletion allowances could be weakened, eliminated, or even reversed by higher extractive or severance taxes, thereby encouraging the development of alternative sources of raw materials and energy. Another policy, already in effect, is for the federal government to direct its purchasing policies toward products made of recycled inputs. The General Services Administration requires all paper bought for federal government uses to contain a certain percentage of recycled paper. This policy creates considerable economic encouragement for recycled paper production because of the large amount of government purchases of this particular item. Similar policies could be implemented at other levels of government and for other types of material. Taxes on disposable containers, bottles, and cans could be levied on purchasers of such items to stimulate the production of reusable items. Such taxes have been implemented in some areas (for example, Oregon, Vermont, Maine, and Michigan have levied deposit taxes on all regular-size beer and soft drink containers) and many states are considering similar legislation and actual prohibition of nonreturnable containers. Beyond the imposition of user taxes on specific items such as beverage bottles or containers, more broad-based taxes could be implemented at the production level on materials that contribute greatly to waste loads. These taxes, in addition to creating recycling incentives, would seek to reduce the solid waste problem by lowering the amount of wastes generated or by changing their composition. Congress has considered several proposals for a *national disposal fee* to be set on all final manufacturing output. The purpose of this fee, based solely on weight for simplicity in assessment, would be to create a source of funding to improve local solid waste collection and disposal. It would also, obviously, serve as an incentive toward lighter products.

This discussion does not mean to imply that some or all of the above policies should be immediately implemented. Careful study is necessary to determine all the relative costs of alternative disposal and recycling methods before an overall waste management policy is formed. However, in the face of continued economic growth and rising consumption levels, we can expect sharply increasing external costs of disposal if the present archaic waste management techniques continue in use. Policies making use of economic incentives, therefore, should have an important role in solid waste management. Properly designed tax and subsidy policies are appropriate mechanisms for encouraging improved recycling technology, changing the nature of the input base, altering the components of solid wastes, and, ultimately, reducing the overall social costs of solid wastes.

D. NOISE

Everyday life in urban areas is exceedingly, and sometimes intolerably, noisy. Horn honking, demolition work, and jet aircraft landing and taking off are just a few instances of what one writer has called *decibel madness*. The immediate causes of noise are often painfully obvious, but the underlying source is, again, economic growth and the resulting desire by people for increased mobility, more consumption goods, and greater convenience.

The amount of noise generated, like GNP, is often a rough yardstick of economic progress. However, for many, the cliché of the *hustle and bustle* of city life no longer invokes the image of an area of thriving, throbbing, economic activity but rather an ear-shattering, nerve-bending, assaulting cacophony of sounds. The problem of noise is not confined to the downtown areas of major cities. Excessive noise is extensive throughout sprawling metropolitan regions and even invades formerly quiet rural areas.

Table 8–3 gives decibel ratings for a variety of sounds encountered in everyday activity. The decibel unit measures relative sound, and a reading of zero represents the threshold of audible sound for normal human hearing. The decibel scale is measured in logarithms and indicates that although the sound level at 10 decibels is 10 times that at zero decibels, it is 100 times as intense at 20 decibels. Experts agree that prolonged exposure to levels of sound in excess of 85 to 90 decibels results in permanent hearing damage. Unfortunately, as Table 8–3 shows, many ordinary daily sounds are considerably above this level.

Industrial activity, quite naturally, is one large source of excessive noise. The construction industry in particular is experiencing a long-run boom that is expected to continue as population, urbanization, and economic activity increase. Some estimates indicate that worldwide urban building construction in the next 50 years will exceed the total of all

**TABLE 8–3   WEIGHTED SOUND LEVELS
AND HUMAN RESPONSE**

Sound Source	dB(A) *	Response Criteria
	—150	
Carrier deck jet operation	—140	
		Painfully loud
	—130	Limit amplified speech
Jet takeoff (200 ft)	—120	
Discotheque		Maximum vocal effort
Auto horn (3 ft)		
Riveting machine	—110	
Jet takeoff (2000 ft)		
Shout (0.5 ft)	—100	
N.Y. subway station		Very annoying
Heavy truck (50 ft)	— 90	Hearing damage (8 hours)
Pneumatic drill (50 ft)		
	— 80	Annoying
Freight train (50 ft)		
Freeway traffic (50 ft)	— 70	Telephone use difficult
		Intrusive
Air conditioning unit (20 ft)	— 60	
Light auto traffic (50 ft)		
	— 50	Quiet
Living room		
Bedroom	— 40	
Library		
Soft whisper (15 ft)	— 30	Very quiet
Broadcasting studio	— 20	
	— 10	Just audible
	— 0	Threshold of hearing

* *Typical A—Weighted sound levels taken with a sound-level meter and expressed as decibels on the scale. The "A" scale approximates the frequency response of the human ear.*
Source: Department of Transportation.

existing structures. The necessary increase in the use of jackhammers, air compressors, bulldozers, cement mixers, pneumatic rock drills, cranes, and so on is not a pleasant prospect for individuals living or working near these construction sites.

Another major source of noise is transportation. Motor vehicle noise can be a frightening experience, as anyone who has been unexpectedly overtaken by a 10-ton truck on a superhighway is well aware. If we recall the data in Chapter 7 showing that over 133 million motor vehicles are in operation in the United States and that this number will increase greatly in the future, the potential noise problem from this source is apparent. Moreover, the widespread ownership of automobiles makes noise control a difficult problem. Individuals may desire the right to peace and quiet in their home and neighborhood at the same time they desire to move about quicker, farther, and more easily in their cars. These two wants often coexist without a realization that they conflict. Further, the interrelationships among the automobile, air pollution, noise, congestion, and land use make the motor vehicle issue a most pressing and complex environmental problem.

Finally, as imposing as the automobile, traffic construction, and industrial noise problems are, they are dwarfed by the projected levels of air travel and the accompanying din. Air travel has boomed in this country with domestic schedule airlines flying almost 145 billion passenger miles in 1976, up from 30 billion only 17 years previously. Over 10,000 airports now service this demand for travel and the projections of airline use are enormous (458 billion by 1982). Certain airports, such as O'Hare and Los Angeles International, average a takeoff or landing every minute. The magnitudes of the projections for air travel necessarily imply that increasing numbers of people will be exposed to jet noise. Bigger aircraft with increased passenger capacity are the result of technological progress, but they often mean longer landing approaches and more people subject to jet noise. A study of Kennedy International Airport of New York reported that a 23-square-mile area containing 108,000 people was exposed to high noise levels. Estimates of similar areas include 106,000 people at O'Hare and 129,000 at Los Angeles International.

Supersonic commercial jet planes have been developed in an attempt to exploit further the economic advantages of bigger and faster modes of air travel. The Concorde, developed by French and British efforts, is aimed at what its sponsors see as a potentially extensive commercial supersonic jet market. Supersonic commercial planes and many military aircraft feature an ability to fly faster than the speed of sound. Conventional commercial aircraft may also, at times, fly faster than sound. The result is sonic booms—loud, sudden, thunderlike sounds, affecting wide land areas. The fad aspects of sonic booms have long ago worn off on the U.S. public and have been replaced by irate damage claims. Significant government research expenditure, therefore, has been undertaken in the area of aircraft design and noise control of jet engines. However, research in this area faces a race with the projected increases in air traffic.

All these facts point to the depressing conclusion that the United States will probably become an even noisier place to live in the future. Identification and evaluation of the social effects of this flood of noise become of growing importance. Presently, we know very little about the economic effects of noise, but what we do know is alarming. Occupationally caused loss of hearing has long been a serious problem in industrial societies. The Council on Environmental Quality estimates that 16 million individuals in the United States are subject to on-the-job noise levels capable of inflicting hearing damage. Federal government estimates show a potential cost of $450 million in claims awards if only 10 percent of the eligible workers were to file for hearing loss. Beyond the dollar figures are the unmeasured costs of personal psychic losses associated with hearing deficiencies. Other studies have shown that compliance with a work place noise standard of 85 decibels would yield net benefits of almost $13 billion in lower work absenteeism and reduced workers' compensation payments.

Noise is also a contributing cause of industrial and domestic accidents because it often masks warning signals and distracts attention. A study by the Department of the Interior estimates noise-induced property and structure damages at between $35 and $85 million annually. Numerous noise suits from individuals living near airports are continually in the courts. In 1970, for example, because of growing complaints about intolerable noise levels, the city of Los Angeles was forced to buy almost 2000 homes near Los Angeles airport. The ultimate taxpayer cost of this project is estimated to be over $200 million. Many of the purchased homes were simply demolished. The project included the incredible spectacle of the purchase of a $97,000 home by the city and the subsequent payment by the city of an additional $360 to a wrecking company to destroy it. Studies show considerably more residential areas equally affected by noise in the Los Angeles area not included in the purchase program. Homeowners in these areas are forced to absorb the noise pollution damage costs of jet noise in terms of lower real estate values, frayed nerves, and unknown other physical and psychological problems. The long and bitter fight in the 1960s over the location of a fourth jet airport in the New York area and the more recent heated controversy over Concorde landing rights there exemplify the extent of public resistance to jet noise and disturbance.

Less-obvious effects of noise include the possible relation between physiological stress and cardiovascular disease. The role of noise as a causal factor of cardiovascular disease has not been scientifically established. However, it is known that noise creates emotional stress that, in turn, constricts the flow of blood circulation by reducing the diameter of blood vessels. This is the basic cause of noise-induced hearing loss, as hearing cells die from blood deprivation. Scientists have suggested that a similar phenomenon may exist in the case of cardiovascular disease and chronic exposure to high noise levels. Emotional stress has also been linked with other physical ills, but the relationship is only tentatively established. In fact, the entire relationship between emotions and physical illness is still largely unexplored. The contribution of noise to emotional stress is now only a challenging research problem for the medical sciences. The social costs of noise, in terms of health and productivity losses, may prove to be considerable.

Noise obviously disturbs sleep and rest. Sleep loss due to noise has direct economic effects in terms of work productivity, although no estimates exist of the magnitude of this effect. In addition, noise is often simply an irritating invasion of privacy.

Although the growth of noise in our society is undeniable and there are clear indications that significant social costs may be involved, noise abatement presents difficult policy problems. Modern technology is linked to economic progress and, although antinoise laws and regulations exist throughout the country, enforcement is often extremely difficult. For example, New York City's model antinoise ordinance essentially boils down to prohibition of any sound without *social utility*. Accordingly, a socially useful activity such as daytime construction is usually exempted from the antinoise regulations. Moreover, locally disturbing noises such as horn blowing and dog barking are nearly impossible to prosecute under public nuisance laws, although Chicago, for example, uses a cruising mobile decibel-measuring team that locates and tickets violators. This type of enforcement, although novel, probably is not a realistic general noise control enforcement procedure.

Zoning laws are a possible device for noise protection and for resolving the basic conflict between economic activity and noise abatement. However, the trade-off between economic activity and lower noise levels presents the familiar benefit-cost dilemma inherent in environmental issues. For example, should trucks be denied the use of certain highways at night? Should a plant located near a residential area be prohibited from operating a third shift? Should the federal government require noise control devices on industrial and construction machinery similar to the emission control requirements for motor vehicles? Should these controls be national in scope or apply only in populous urban areas? Should certain highways be rerouted or, perhaps, not even built because of the increase in noise exposure to large numbers of people? The economic implications of these questions suggest the difficulties involved in evaluating noise abatement programs.

Some states (California, Connecticut, and New York) have enacted legislation that establishes maximum noise levels for motor vehicles. In addition, most states require mufflers on motor vehicles, and these are usually checked during the routine state inspection process.

In a related policy area, the federal government controls air traffic and aircraft noise limits. Furthermore, laws exist to enable injured parties to recover the value of noise-created damages. However, court rulings have established that air space over private property is *part of the public domain.* The burden of proof concerning damages from noise rests on the plaintiff. Court proceedings initiated to recover damages are often lengthy, costly, and frustrating. As suggested in Part 2, changes in the legal framework could have immense impact on the severity of many environmental problems.

Any effective noise reduction, of course, involves an opportunity cost. Soundproofing, designing new noise-controlled industrial equipment, building different types of highways, and controlling jet engine noise all will cost somebody money. We have previously noted that there has been a considerable amount of government expense aimed at noise control in jet aircraft. The automobile industry is experimenting with the development of reduced-noise vehicles, and industrial equipment manufacturers are increasing their research into noise abatement devices. In addition to zoning and noise control laws, some economic incentive programs have been proposed for noise control. For example, one proposal calls for a one dollar antinoise tax to be levied on each passenger and cargo ton using Los Angeles airport, with the tax revenue earmarked to defray the soundproofing costs in nearby residential sections. In England, the government offers a subsidy of up to one-half of the cost of soundproofing three rooms for houses within 12 miles of London's Heathrow Airport. The Environmental Protection Agency and the National Institute for Occupational Safety and Health have been given authority to determine noise emission standards in construction, transportation, and workplaces. This form of noise control by regulation would be analogous to similar EPA policies that set air and water quality standards.

However, in general, the use of economic incentives in noise abatement programs seems to be limited. Laws, regulations, and zoning techniques have been the major instruments of noise control, and these policies have been largely ineffective. The basic causes of this failure are the diffuse and broad-based nature of noise sources, the growth in these sources, the difficulty of enforcing legal remedies, and the conflict of noise control with economic activity and modern urban life. In many situations, noise is a relative problem, and although both my neighbor and I may fight vociferously for a local prohibition of trucks from our residential streets, we may disagree considerably on the proper volume of my stereo, the all-night running of his air conditioner, the use of my child's minibike, or the barking of his dog.

In summary, noise control is one of the most difficult environmental problems. Reliance on self-imposed industrial noise abatement is unrealistic. Expanded, tighter government controls may prove the only effective remedy. Perhaps development of new technology someday will permit the use of economic incentives for noise abatement in the form of noise emission charges. A large amount of research remains to be done, first to identify, and then to quantify, the extent and incidence of the social costs of noise. Additional research is needed to estimate the costs and effectiveness of various noise abatement programs.

E. OUTDOOR RECREATION, LAND USE, AND CONSERVATION

Unlike the previous environmental problems we have considered, outdoor recreation and land use practices are not associated with a particular group of effluents, production processes, or economic activities. Nevertheless, adequate outdoor recreation opportunities and the protection of natural environments are becoming increasingly important aspects of the quality of life.

1. Outdoor Recreation and Land Use

A major national growth trend of the past two decades has been public participation in outdoor recreation. Since the end of World War II, this country has turned increasingly to the outdoors for its recreational and leisure time pursuits. New recreational activities like snowmobiling have emerged and become popular, and traditional outdoor sports such as swimming, camping, and fishing have boomed. Rough projections of recreation activity days for 25 outdoor activities estimate an increase from 12.2 billion days in 1965 to 29.8 billion days by the end of this century. National park system attendance has increased from 33 million visits in 1950 to 238 million in 1975.[7] Such statistics and everyday observation confirm the fact that the American public is engaging in outdoor recreation in large and growing numbers.

The roots of this upsurge in outdoor recreation are many. Steady population growth is an obvious reason, but changes in the age distribution, migration patterns, and mobility of the population are probably just as fundamental demographic causes of the popularity of recreation activity. In addition, continued economic growth has resulted in decreases in the length of the workweek and increased leisure time. Paid vacations are now commonplace, and their length has tended to increase. A downward trend in retirement age combined with an increase in longevity has added to leisure time. Most important, however, is the

---

[7] This rise in attendance has forced radical policy changes in some of the parks. For example, Yellowstone National Park has restricted the use of private automobiles due to extreme congestion.

steady growth of per capita real income. All available evidence indicates that demand for outdoor recreation is highly *income elastic;* as incomes increase, the purchase of outdoor recreation increases *more* than proportionally. Higher income levels have led to increased demands for leisure time, and a major share of this increase in leisure is devoted to outdoor recreation activities. Thus, the substantial increase in income in the postwar period has been a major factor in the observed growth in outdoor recreation participation.

The steady rise in the number of automobiles and their travel miles along with the completion of an extensive interstate highway system has meant easier accessibility to recreation areas. The diversity of license plates at the national parks during summer vacation time is a ready indication of the mobility of the population.

An obvious question accompanies this mushrooming national pursuit of outdoor recreation: Are adequate facilities available to accommodate the present and future demand? And, more important, how can the government efficiently plan expenditures to manage outdoor recreation demand? The economic issues involved are exceedingly complex. Recent federal attention to outdoor recreation problems has resulted in considerable activity in this area by a diverse group of agencies. The Bureau of Outdoor Recreation, the Bureau of Sports Fisheries and Wildlife, the Forest Service, the Bureau of Land Management, the National Park Service, the Corps of Engineers, and the Environmental Protection Agency are some of the agencies involved in outdoor recreation planning. In addition, state and local governments have various departments engaged in outdoor recreation management. The coordination of planning, budgets, and jurisdiction among these agencies and levels of government presents some complex administrative problems in addition to the fundamental economic question of resource allocation.

The basic economic dilemma in outdoor recreation is just one facet of the well-recognized failure of private markets to provide sufficient amounts of public goods. Social and economic changes have spurred large increases in the population's demand for outdoor recreation. The private market has responded efficiently in providing all the necessary equipment for recreation activity, from surfboards to 40-foot houseboats. The difficulty arises in the market's response in supplying the basic outdoor recreational facilities and opportunities. Beaches, wetlands, clean water and clean air, open spaces, and natural environments are obviously necessary for the proper enjoyment of many outdoor recreation activities. However, the success of the private market in providing for the immense diversity of recreational equipment is matched by its failure to supply adequately the natural areas necessary for outdoor recreation. As explained in Chapter 4, the nature of recreational facilities as a public good is the cause of this imbalance.

Private markets have been quick to develop extensive resort communities in numerous locations throughout the country. The initial attraction that spurs these resort developments is often the recreational and environmental amenities available nearby. However, the ability of private profit interests to develop a resort area frequently leads rapidly to a reduction or destruction of the very environmental amenities that provided the initial attraction! The familiar syndrome of congestion, solid wastes, water quality deterioration, and elimination of fish and game populations is a common problem in many resort areas in the United States. Basically, the problem is one of land use. Although private markets work reasonably well to develop rural areas into surburbs, shopping centers, industrial sites, sources of raw materials, and even resort communities, they fail to preserve the natural integrity of water, air, and land resources for their public recreational, esthetic, and ecological values.

There are a number if reasons underlying this failure. In Part 2, we explained how the common property basis of air and water resources is a principal cause of externalities. This common ownership of air and water resources leads directly to problems of *exclusion*. In terms of the pollutants caused by production and consumption, we have seen that it is often not possible to charge individuals and firms the full social costs of their economic activities. However, this also implies that individuals and firms are unable to collect the entire social value of protecting the quality of air and water resources. Just as they cannot be charged the full social costs of environmental deterioration, they also cannot fully exclude others from the benefits of any action to maintain environmental quality. It is this inability to capture the full benefits of protecting environmental quality that lies behind the failure of private markets.[8]

A further cause of the undersupply of outdoor recreational opportunities and natural amenities is often the capacity of such sites to accommodate large numbers of people at any given time. Therefore, the marginal costs of additional use of the site are near zero, and average costs decline over wide ranges of use. Profit-maximizing behavior, following the socially efficient rule of price equals marginal cost, would result in economic losses. Private interests would not operate in such a situation or, at best, would undersupply the amount of outdoor recreation and natural amenities relative to the socially efficient quantity.

---

[8] Of course, the ability to exclude individuals from the benefits of environmental amenities varies considerably. It is probably most difficult in the case of air quality. On the other hand, the owner of land surrounding a lake can quite readily exclude individuals from its use and, therefore, charge a fee to fishermen, and so on. Such privately supplied recreation opportunities are numerous. However, exclusion becomes much more difficult, if not impossible, when we are dealing with a river system, an entire coastline, or a scenic canyon area of hundreds of square miles.

Accordingly, the value of recreational and ecological uses of the environment has only imperfect market outlets for expression. The incentive for *free rider* behavior on the part of individuals valuing environmental amenities compounds this problem even further. It is these public good characteristics of recreational activities and ecological values that warrant government intervention to protect and augment the supply of environmental amenities.

Considerable research effort has been undertaken to provide economic guidance for government's role in outdoor recreation. The objective of this research is to estimate the social benefits associated with a given *free* recreation site or natural area. This is a thorny problem because no market provides information on the demand price for each recreational facility. However, if it can be solved, then a rational comparison can be made between recreation benefits and the opportunity costs of alternative uses of the land. Various attempts aimed at quantifying recreation benefits have met with mixed success. Initial efforts used travel distance from the recreation site as an indication of the individual's valuation of a recreation visit. When summed over all users of a recreational site, this figure provided a measure of the total benefits of recreation for that particular site. The argument is that the individual would not incur the travel costs to the site if he did not value the recreation experience at least as much. As travel costs increase with distance from the site, then the number of recreation visits decrease. Thus, a demand curve can be derived from the relation among the implicit price, the travel cost, and the number of recreation visits. The area under this curve is a measure of the total benefits of the recreation activity and can be compared with the costs of providing the recreation opportunity and/or the benefits of the site in alternative uses.

Extensions of this method incorporate other determinants of an individual's desire to engage in recreation activity in addition to travel cost (the proxy for the price of recreation). Such variables as income, socioeconomic status, and available leisure time can be added in order to obtain a more valid price-recreation quantity demand relationship.

Other attempts to estimate recreation benefits use ingeniously devised questionnaire techniques to elicit willingness to pay responses from recreation seekers and then translate the sample responses to aggregate populations. This method is a costly one in terms of research effort. As explained in Chapter 4, it can also be misleading because numerous pitfalls exist in attempting to obtain such information from questionnaires. However, carefully designed surveys can provide some of the information about the demand for public recreation activities that private markets generate for conventional goods.

Thus far, we have treated outdoor recreation as a single group of activities and described how economists attempt to calculate the economic benefits of outdoor recreation. However, outdoor recreation is not a homogeneous group of activities. A national recreation survey, for example, questioned respondents in terms of 25 different and carefully defined outdoor activities ranging from *remote wilderness camping* to *playing outdoor games and sports.* The diversity of outdoor recreation activities often implies conflict between activities that compete for the same sites or resources. Familiar examples of this situation are the general incompatibility between waterskiing and fishing or between remote camping and what is called general, or developed, camping. In the first case, waterskiing and fishing may occur with basically the same type of resource, namely, a relatively clean body of water, and the difficult question, given their incompatibility, is one of the relative social values of the water in each use.[9] In the second case, not only are the two types of camping in conflict, but they require considerably different resource bases with correspondingly different costs. It is also easy to visualize the general conflict between popular recreation activities and fragile ecological systems. Again, we face the familiar benefit-cost evaluation problem in the environmental area; this time, however, the comparison is between different recreation uses of natural resources.

2. The Economic Defense of Conservation

Preservation of natural areas and environmental quality has developed into an important national political issue. Ultimately, however, an economic rationale must be clearly demonstrated in favor of conservation if its aims are to succeed against more conventional forms of economic development. A general version of the economic argument for conservation is that although the demand for recreation activity and unspoiled natural areas is increasing, the supply opportunities are constantly shrinking, creating a steady rise in the implicit price or social value of natural environments.[10] Further, many conventional types of economic development automatically foreclose future options because the development process of a natural environment is largely irreversible. The damming of a free-flowing river, the draining of wetlands, or the use of open land for a housing community are examples of natural environments irrevocably changed by development. This irreversibility and necessary loss of future

[9] To isolate this problem, we can assume that no other uses of the lake exist and that there is a definite incompatibility in the activities. One possible solution, for example, might have zoned areas within the lake, with certain boundaries defining exclusive waterskiing zones, leaving other areas for more passive water sports.

[10] This argument draws heavily on the economic reasoning of J. V. Krutilla, in "Conservation Reconsidered," *American Economic Review,* LVII, No. 4 (September 1967).

options to use these sites as unspoiled recreational or unique ecological resources create a persuasive rationale for a careful development policy.

Maintaining future options of land use for natural unspoiled areas has economic value. This value will increase over time, due to the continued upward trend in recreation demand and also because more individuals currently enjoying the amenities of natural environments pass on the skills, attitudes, and appreciation of outdoor activities to future users and, thus, spur recreation demand even higher. The thrust of this argument is that the present population's experience with outdoor recreation results in an increase in future recreation demands. This interdependence of demand over time creates difficult research problems and may greatly complicate benefit-cost analyses of resource preservation programs.

A further economic justification for preservation is that many individuals receive satisfaction from just knowing, for example, that a wild river flows, untamed and unspoiled, through a remote and spectacular wilderness even though they have absolutely no *current* desire to *float* the river themselves and whose entire contact with water, in fact, may be presently limited to the community swimming pool. This *option demand,* as it is called, has legitimate economic value and should be properly included as a social benefit of preservation and natural areas. However, individuals cannot readily express their option demands in private markets. The recent growth of interest and membership in such groups as the Sierra Club, Wilderness Society, National Wildlife Federation, and Audubon Society suggests the validity of this preservation argument. Indeed, some private organizations have attempted on a small scale to formalize the value of option demand and preservation by actual purchases of natural areas for conservation purposes.[11]

A final economic rationale for conservation also centers on the option demand argument but involves the relation of basic research to the existence of natural biota. The natural biological environment is an ecological system of plants and animals that form a genetic pool. From this natural genetic bank has come a great variety of discoveries resulting in advances in basic scientific knowledge, development of new drugs, agricultural innovations, and so on. If this pool is diminished by the loss of a species, many future research possibilities may be foreclosed. Economic value should be assigned to the maintenance of the entirety of the natural gene pool. In addition, the research potential of the geophysical sciences is also conditional on having available the widest possible range of natural phenomena.

---

[11] This development represents an extension of the market solution of externalities presented in Chapter 3. However, all the organizational, free rider, and coordination problems discussed in Chapter 4 are relevant to this situation, and, therefore, this kind of extension of the market is, at best, an imperfect and limited expression of social values.

Considerable effort has been made to provide orderly land use and preservation of natural areas. The Wilderness Act of 1964 established a program of maintaining unspoiled natural areas, and 10 million acres are currently under its protection. Additions to the national park system also have been made. Various wildlife protection measures have gained support (for example, endangered species protection, programs to reduce or eliminate the incentives of predator control, and restrictions on pesticides uses). The Land and Water Conservation Fund provides revenues to purchase natural areas. These revenues come, in part, from taxes on motorboat fuel and user fees collected in federal recreation sites (that is, from sources using the environmental amenities associated with outdoor recreation). Annually more than half of this fund goes to state and local governments on a matching basis for the purchase and development of outdoor recreation sites. The remainder is used for federal land acquisition. The sale of hunting stamps (for waterfowl hunting) has generated considerable revenues for additions to the 30 million acre National Wildlife Refuge System.

Finally, current reviews of federal land management practices may bring a change in emphasis away from land development values and toward preservation and esthetic considerations. The National Environmental Policy Act requires all federal agencies to report on the environmental impact of any proposed projects. Although the impact statements do not contain the authority to halt or forbid any particular project, they do call for additional information that can result in the delay of project construction and raise the further possibility of executive action. This was the situation in 1971, when an executive order by President Nixon stopped the completion of the Cross-Florida Barge Canal of the Corp of Engineers. Conservation interests have also achieved delays in the development of the Tocks Island Dam on the upper Delaware River and the much publicized and fought over Alaskan pipeline, which is now completed, largely due to the pressures caused by the large price increases in oil after 1974.

In summary, society's growing desire for the amenities associated with open spaces and outdoor activities will result in an increasing social valuation of protecting the natural integrity of land and water areas. However, uses of land and other natural resources for their environmental values compete with more conventional land development interests. One distinct advantage favoring development over preservation is the relatively more complete market expressions of the value of the natural resource in its private development uses. Proper land use policy attempts to provide a more orderly use of land and natural resources by explicitly measuring the economic values of the resource in its natural state. The obvious problem arises of measuring the public recreational and esthetic values of resources preserved in their natural state relative to the opportunity costs of lost raw materials, suburban housing, plant sites, or any of the other potential private uses of the resource.

F. SUMMARY AND CONCLUSIONS

This chapter has attempted to provide a broad view of various environmental problems. The social costs of pesticides, solid wastes, and noise are significant additions to the more widely recognized water and air quality problems of Chapters 6 and 7.

The potential damages of pesticides and other chemical substances relative to their social benefits pose difficulties for both research and policy. Solid wastes are intimately related to economic growth, and economic policies have a major role to play in determining the direction of waste management in this country. Noise and its chronic human effects present formidable research challenges to the medical sciences and are a potentially large source of external costs associated with modern urban life. Finally, preservation of natural environments, wildlife populations, emphasis on scenic and esthetic values, and conservation of open spaces face the constant pressure of effluent discharges and private market land development. Economic analysis suggests that there is an increasing social value to preserving natural environments and their amenities. Government intervention is required to ensure the protection of the public interest in land uses.

Our survey of major environmental problems in Part 3 has covered a wide range of closely related problems. The one recurring theme of our discussion has been the enormous complexity of contemporary pollution problems and the amorphousness of the concept of environmental quality. Environmental problems are multidimensional, encompassing interdependent physical, chemical, biological, economic, and sociopolitical phenomena. Unfortunately, the single most important lesson to be gleaned out of this mass of complex details is that no one easy solution exists to environmental problems. Given the relatively primitive state of knowledge today about the fundamental nature of many environmental problems, optimal risk-averting social policy may call for a mix of various antipollution measures, including outright prohibitions of certain kinds of emissions. Furthermore, because many environmental problems are physically and economically interrelated, any partial equilibrium solutions aimed at individual pollution sources must somehow be centrally coordinated in an overall environmental policy. With these important considerations in mind, we next turn, in Part 4, to a more detailed evaluation of the general policy instruments available to improve and protect environmental quality.

QUESTIONS FOR DISCUSSION

1. In your judgment, are the various problems discussed in this chapter of equal importance to the air and water quality problems covered in the previous two chapters? What is the basis for your answer?

2. Some agricultural experts have argued that a ban on the use of DDT could not withstand a careful benefit-cost analysis. Identify the main benefits and costs that would enter into such an analysis, and indicate the difficulties involved in estimating the proper dollar amounts.

3. Suppose that your local government passed a law requiring every household and firm to separate its trash carefully, prior to collection. Set up a benefit-cost analysis of this law. Can you think of any better alternatives available to the government?

4. Why do not markets exist for noise abatement? Can the government provide a workable *effluent* charge solution for the externalities of excessive noise? Why or why not? Should the federal government impose maximum noise standards for new vehicles?

5. What are the difficulties involved in estimating a demand schedule for the conservation of a wilderness area? How does your answer relate to our previous analysis of public goods? How should the government allow for the interests of future generations in making decisions about investments in wilderness areas?

SELECTED REFERENCES

Pesticides
CARSON, R., *Silent Spring.* Boston: Houghton Mifflin Company, 1962. An eloquent treatment of the effects of pesticides on man and wildlife. The initial source of widespread public concern over the consequences of pesticides.
LANGHAM, M. R., J. C. HEADLEY, AND W. F. EDWARDS, "Agricultural Pesticides: Productivity and Externalities," in *Environmental Quality Analysis*, A. V. Kneese and B. T. Bower, eds. Baltimore: The Johns Hopkins Press, 1972. A study evaluating the externalities associated with pesticide use.
MELLANBY, K., *Pesticides and Pollution.* London: Collins Press, 1967. A useful description of individual pesticides and their environmental consequences.
PIMENTAL, D., *Ecological Effects of Pesticides on Non-Target Species.* Washington, D.C.: Government Printing Office, 1971. A technical presentation of the effects of pesticides on wildlife and other natural populations. Contains an extensive bibliography.
Report of the Secretary's Commission on Pesticides and Their Relationship to

Environmental Health, Parts I and II. Washington, D.C.: Government Printing Office, 1969. A comprehensive treatment of all facets of the pesticide problem. Has an excellent bibliography.

Toxic Pollutants

Council on Environmental Quality, *Toxic Substances.* Washington, D.C.: Government Printing Office, 1971. A broad view of toxic substances in the environment. Surveys sources, extent, and effects of various materials entering the environment.

Council on Environmental Quality, *Environmental Quality, Annual Report of the Council on Environmental Quality.* Washington, D.C.: Government Printing Office, annual. Provides yearly overview of developments in solid waste, toxic substances, and noise problems among other specific environmental concerns.

Solid Wastes

Council on Environmental Quality, *Ocean Dumping, A National Policy.* Washington, D.C.: Government Printing Office, 1970. Treats the waste disposal problems of ocean dumping for a variety of waste types.

LEONTIEF, W., "Environmental Repercussions and the Economic Structure: An Input-Output Approach," *The Review of Economics and Statistics,* LII, No. 3 (August 1970). Uses input-output analysis to evaluate the relationship between production levels and waste discharges.

PAGE, T., *Conservation and Economic Efficiency: An Approach to Materials Policy.* Baltimore: The Johns Hopkins Press, 1977. An excellent treatment of resource recovery issues. Highly recommended.

QUIMBY, T. H. E., *Recycling: The Alternative to Disposal.* Baltimore: The Johns Hopkins Press, 1975. A comprehensive analysis of the economics of recycling with special emphasis on paper products.

U.S. Environmental Protection Agency, *Resource Recovery and Waste Reduction, Third Report to Congress.* Washington: Government Printing Office, 1975. A survey of recycling and waste reduction with current data.

Noise

BERLAND, T., *The Fight for Quiet.* Englewood Cliffs, N.J.: Prentice-Hall, Inc., 1970. A survey of the noise problem containing a good bibliography.

STEVENSON, G. M., *The Politics of Airport Noise.* N. Scituate, Mass.: Duxbury Press, 1972. A survey of aircraft noise problems with a comprehensive treatment of the legal experience with noise damage claims.

U.S. Environmental Protection Agency, *Some Considerations in Choosing an Occupational Noise Regulation.* Washington, D.C.: Government Printing Office, 1976. The technical issues and problems of noise regulation.

U.S. Department of Labor, *Economic Impact Analysis of Proposed Noise Control Regulations.* Washington, D.C.: Government Printing Office, 1976. A benefit-cost analysis of noise control regulations.

Outdoor Recreation

CICCHETTI, C. J., *Forecasting Recreation in the United States.* Lexington, Mass.: D. C. Heath & Company, 1973. A detailed treatment of recreation projection methods.

CICCHETTI, C. J., J. J. SENECA, and P. DAVIDSON, *The Demand and Supply of Outdoor Recreation*. Washington, D.C.: Bureau of Outdoor Recreation, 1969. An empirical study attempting to quantify the demand factors and supply responses influencing individual recreation activities.

CICCHETTI, C. J., and V. K. SMITH, *The Costs of Congestion: An Econometric Analysis of Wilderness Recreation*. Cambridge, Mass.: Ballinger Publishing Company, 1976. An ingenious analysis of modeling recreation usage of wilderness areas in order to estimate demand and benefits. Advanced.

CLAWSON, M., and J. L. KNETSCH, *Outdoor Recreation*. Baltimore: The Johns Hopkins Press for Resources for the Future, 1966. A comprehensive treatment of the economic issues of outdoor recreation backed by quantitative descriptions of the problem.

DAVIDSON, P., F. G. ADAMS, AND J. J. SENECA, "The Social Value of Water Recreational Facilities Resulting from an Improvement in Water Quality: The Delaware Estuary," in *Water Research*, A. V. Kneese and S. C. Smith, eds. Baltimore: The Johns Hopkins Press, 1966. A benefit-cost study of water-based recreation and water quality in the Delaware River.

KNETSCH, J. L., AND R. K. DAVIS, "Comparisons of Methods for Recreation Evaluation," in *Water Research*, A. V. Kneese and S. C. Smith, eds. Baltimore: The Johns Hopkins Press, 1966. A useful summary of the benefit estimation problem for outdoor recreation with an interesting comparison of the travel cost and willingness to pay solutions.

KRUTILLA, J. V., "Conservation Reconsidered," *American Economic Review*, LVII, No. 4 (September 1967). The classic presentation of the economic reasoning for the preservation of natural environments.

KRUTILLA, J. V. (ed.), *Natural Environments, Studies in Theoretical and Applied Analysis*. Baltimore: The Johns Hopkins Press, 1972. A selection of studies concerned with natural resource issues. Highly recommended. Advanced.

IV

The Vehicles of Collective Environmental Action

9

REGULATION AND PROHIBITION

Part 4, consisting of this and the next two chapters, analyzes the main alternative strategies available to society in its efforts to improve environmental quality. Part 2 of the book was limited almost entirely to pure economic theory, and Part 3 concentrated on the technical biological and physical aspects of the major environmental problems facing our nation. Part 4, in turn, is intended to survey the major issues in government environmental policies, with a preponderance of facts and institutional details over abstract theory. Each of the chapters of Part 4 covers one of the three broad classes of government proenvironmental actions. The present chapter analyzes the economics of government regulations and prohibitions. Next Chapter 10 discusses government fiscal measures affecting polluters: taxes, including effluent charges, and subsidies. Finally, Chapter 11 takes up the issues involved in direct government provision of environmental services.

PUBLIC POLICY AND THE ENVIRONMENT

The theme common to this and the previous parts of the book is the notion that the fundamental factor underlying most environmental problems is the failure of the private market system to allocate resources efficiently because of pervasive external spillover effects of production and consumption. Given this premise, it follows that the main justification for government intervention in the private market system for environmental purposes should be to deal, directly or indirectly, with these external effects—to somehow *internalize* for society those effects that are *external* to individual firms and households. It is relatively simple to spell out theoretically how an enlightened, efficiency-oriented government agency should behave in a world where full information is available at very low cost in order to improve the workings of the private market system. We have already stressed the point in Chapter 4, however, that the phenomenon of government failure parallels the concept of private market failure. In fact, many activities of government agencies often cause environmental disruption. We shall attempt, therefore, to make some realistic assessments of the potential for *effective* government actions in the following discussion.

Some preliminary distinctions between the various classes of government action may be useful to the reader as part of an introduction to our discussion of social environmental policies. We confine ourselves to a consideration of (1) regulation and prohibition, (2) fiscal incentives and disincentives, and (3) direct government production of environmental services. We specifically do *not* discuss a government policy that consists merely of exhortation to better behavior by individual polluters. The authors doubt that such exhortations are effective in altering mass tastes and behavior in the long run unless they are backed up by more concrete economic policies.

Regulation in the United States conventionally means some degree of control by regulatory commissions over the services provided and the per unit rates charged by firms. Regulatory commissions are the creation of the legislative branch of government, but commissioners are appointed by the executive branch and their activities are subject to judicial review. As a rough generalization, the commissions allow regulated firms to make the great majority of decisions involving their own business affairs, subject only to pricing and service guidelines set down by the commissions in attempting to implement their conception of the public interest. More generally, and as is the case in environmental policy, regulation could mean any government directive controlling or limiting the actions of firms or households in the private sector.

In contrast, government *prohibition* means outright legislative bans on various activities. Congress, state, and local legislatures pass laws forbidding a specified activity, and the laws are subsequently enforced by the police and the judicial system of the state. Prohibition can be permanent as in the federal ban on most uses of DDT, or it can be temporary, such as legislation granting authority to environmental regulators to close industrial plants during emergency air pollution situations.

Government *fiscal measures*—taxes and subsidies—also are implemented through laws passed by the legislative branch of government. Such measures do not directly control or prohibit private economic activities. They may, however, entail an addition to, or subtraction from, the benefits (costs) of conducting private market activities in specific ways. To have an effect, they rely on altering the incentive structure of economic behavior.

Government production of environmental services involves transactions between the agencies of the state and the private owners of productive resources. The government pays the firms and households that own certain resources a mutually agreeable price or, in certain cases, uses its overriding legal right of eminent domain to compel sale at the government's price. Even in the latter case, however, the government must, in our society, pay *fair market value* for the property, with the price subject to judicial review. It then uses these resources to produce a variety of environmental services, very much as private firms hire resources to produce private sector goods and services. Alternatively, government actions may contribute to environmental deterioration and the issue becomes how to ensure that public decision making accounts for all the costs of any project undertaken by the public sector.

The distinctions between these various classes of government intervention are clear enough in principle, but in certain borderline cases it may be difficult to place a particular government action in just one or another category. Regulation and prohibition are the most difficult to distinguish, because regulation, as practiced in this country, consists essentially of piecemeal prohibitory measures by quasi-legislative agencies. That is, the regulatory commission generally sets a *maximum* rate of return and prescribes certain *minimum* standards of service for a regulated utility. The firm may then conduct its business as it sees fit, subject to the limitation that it is *prohibited* from charging rates above the regulated maximum and from allowing the quality of its service standards to fall below the regulated minimums.

Even the contrast between a tax and a prohibition is not so clear as it may seem on first encounter. A tax of $\$t$ per unit on a pollutant P may seem to differ in kind from a prohibition against the emission of any units of P, for example, but, in fact, the effect of both measures is to raise the cost of conducting a business in such a way as to allow the emission of P. The tax per unit of P adds directly to the firm's unit or average costs by a determinate amount $[= \$(X/Q) \cdot t]$, where X/Q is the number of units of P emitted per unit of output Q, but a prohibition adds to the firm's costs only indirectly. If the firm is prohibited from emitting P, it must either switch to another, more expensive technique of production,[1] shut down or ignore the prohibition and continue to emit P, thereby accepting the legal penalties for doing so. The latter alternative is by no means farfetched in the common situation in this society in which comprehensive environmental law enforcement is very costly and the penalty for breaking the law may be small relative to the firm's total costs of production. In a probabilistic sense, the firm may thus consider that a law forbidding the emission of P is equivalent to a tax of a given amount per unit of P emitted, subject to the proviso that violation of the law involves a perhaps significant moral onus in addition to pecuniary considerations. Abundant evidence exists that laws regulating, or even forbidding, various forms of pollution in the United States have been openly disobeyed or complied with only after extensive and purposeful delays.

In addition, note the close relation between a regulated maximum rate on the firm's sales of its output and a tax per unit of output. Both measures may have roughly comparable effects in reducing the firm's actual revenues below potential maximum levels.

Finally, government production entailing the use of privately owned resources may be considered as an ultimate form of prohibition on the private use of property within the private market system. Instead of taxing or prohibiting a specific use of land, for example, the government may attempt to effect the socially optimal use of the land by purchasing it and thereby removing it entirely from the vagaries of the private market system.

Preview of this Chapter

The most frequent response by the average layman who perceives the seriousness of environmental problems is to urge that the legislature pass a law forbidding or regulating polluting activities, and indeed this approach has characterized all major federal environmental legislation in the United States. Such a response is in keeping with a long American

---

[1] If an alternative technique of production were *not* more expensive, presumably the firm would have used it in the first place in order to minimize costs of production and thereby maximize profits. Admittedly, the passage of the prohibition on the emission of P may have the effect of causing the firm's management to seek cheaper techniques of production that do not involve the emission of pollutants.

tradition of attempting to solve complex social problems through prohibitory legislation. A good analogy is the antitrust legislation of the turn of the century that attempted to prohibit certain practices by giant corporate monopolies. Also, the reader may recall the Prohibition Amendment as a typically American reaction to the perceived threat of internal pollution by alcohol. In contrast, most economists argue that prohibition and regulation are inefficient mechanisms of collective action relative to the alternative of various fiscal incentive and disincentive techniques. This chapter spells out the economic argument behind this negative attitude toward legalistic solutions to environmental problems but also indicates those special circumstances in which the prohibitory strategy makes good sense.

Section A discusses the role of regulation in a national environmental policy. It considers, first, the possibility of extending the scope of the authority of the existing regulatory commissions and, second, the regulatory activities of the Environmental Protection Agency, including the specifics of its major air and water quality regulation programs. Section B then examines the role of prohibitions. It presents the benefit-cost approach to the economic effects of prohibitions. Section C discusses a special and important form of regulation and prohibition, zoning. A final Section D gives a brief summary of the chapter.

A. REGULATION

The Present Regulatory Commissions

Regulatory commissions currently operate in the United States at both the state and federal levels of government. Many of the industries regulated by these commissions are public utilities, including mainly the various transportation, communications, and power industries. Public utilities may be characterized roughly as *natural monopolies,* or industries in which only one or a very small number of firms can operate efficiently in a single market because of large fixed costs of production. The telephone industry is a good example of a public utility according to the above characterization. Enormous fixed costs are required to build up a basic network of transmission facilities in order to provide telephone services between any two points, but once such costs have been absorbed, additional services can be provided to consumers at only small marginal costs. From society's standpoint, competition in the telephone industry would be wasteful in that it would necessitate the costly duplication of the basic network of transmission facilities. Society therefore tolerates and even demands monopolistic control of the industry but at the same time establishes regulatory commissions as watchdogs over the monopolistic firm in order to forestall possible abuse of monopoly power.[2]

The five federal regulatory commissions in the United States other than the Environmental Protection Agency whose activities may be relevant to environmental quality include the Interstate Commerce Commission (ICC), the Federal Power Commission (FPC), the Federal Communications Commission (FCC), the Federal Aviation Administration (FAA), and the Nuclear Regulatory Commission (NRC). The ICC has jurisdiction over interstate transportation and oil pipelines; the FPC, over power projects and interstate transmission of electricity and natural gas; the FCC, over telephone, telegraph, radio, and television transmission; the FAA, over civil aviation, and the NRC, over nuclear energy. In addition, in 1977, Congress created the Department of Energy. Although this department is not strictly a regulatory agency, it is certain that its activities will have important environmental implications. Various state commissions have roughly corresponding jurisdictions with the ICC, FCC, and FPC within individual states.

Regulatory commissions have, in the past, been mainly concerned with regulating the rates charged by regulated firms, but they have also had the responsibility of maintaining the quantity and quality of services provided, including the public safety aspects of quality. Control over rates is obviously not sufficient to prevent potential abuses of monopoly power, because a regulated firm could, in the absence of other controls, circumvent maximum rate schedules and earn monopoly profits by cutting costs through allowing deterioration in the quality of its services.

The Environmental Policy Role of the Present Regulatory Commissions

What role, if any, can the existing regulatory commissions play in an overall environmental policy? Some of the most serious environmental problems of our society can be traced directly to the various effluents produced by regulated public utilities, in particular the gas and electric power companies regulated by the FPC and by state and municipal commissions. For example, the federal government has estimated that about half of the total sulfur oxide pollutants and one-fourth of the particulate and one-fourth of the nitrogen oxide emissions in the United States can be attributed to the discharge of fossil-fueled electric plants. One important part of a national environmental policy could entail consciously

---

[2] Not every regulated industry falls as neatly into the public utility-natural monopoly niche as does the telephone industry, which is to say that all regulation, as it is practiced today in the United States, cannot be justified by the rationale given in the text.

extending the activities of the regulatory commissions to include a major concern with the environmental problems traceable to regulated firms.

The regulatory commissions already have become involved in environmental policy, due to mounting public protests and litigation over the location of new power plants and to various other activities of regulated firms. But the environmental role of the commissions could be greatly increased either within their present mandates or under new legislative authority granted them by Congress. The FPC, for example, might redefine quality of service to include the external costs of power generation and enforce its new quality standards by setting maximum permissible levels for each effluent for regulated firms. The ICC might take into account the environmental consequences of different modes of transportation and their impacts on land and resource uses in approving rate schedules; the FCC might concern itself directly with the esthetic external costs imposed on society by existing transmission lines and force consideration of possible alternatives; and the FAA might impose more rigid noise controls at various airports. The NRA already attempts to ensure human safety from nuclear energy uses and might pursue these activities more vigorously. The state regulatory commissions could undertake similar steps within their own jurisdictions. Ideally, all these activities and more could, if undertaken, enhance the quality of the environment in our society.

Yet few economists would express much enthusiasm for greatly extending the activities of the regulatory commissions further into environmental policy. Even granted that such activities could succeed in helping to alleviate serious problems of pollution, the real issue is whether the benefits would be worth the costs. In part, the economists' doubts about the potential environmental role of the regulatory commission follow a general bias against social economizing through prohibition. In addition, however, economists fear that environmental regulation through the commission mechanism would compound the inefficiencies inherent in social control through prohibition. If a commission prohibits an activity by a regulated public utility that apparently harms the environment, the result will almost certainly be to add to the costs of providing the regulated service. These additional costs likely then will be passed directly on *in full*, in the form of a higher price for consumers, because the commission will almost certainly not deny allowing the costs it has mandated on the firm to be added to the cost base for the regulated rate schedule. Unfortunately, however, the regulatory mechanism provides no incentive to the regulated firm to minimize total social costs of production. In contrast, prohibition under conditions of market competition still leaves incentives to minimize the costs of pollution abatement unimpaired.

To elaborate on this basic point, let us suppose that a state public utilities commission bars the burning of dirty (high sulfur content) fuel for the generators of electric power companies. The regulated firms will respond to this directive by replacing the dirty fuel with more expensive clean fuel. The resulting increase in the costs of providing electric power will then be the basis of requests for higher consumer charges for electricity, requests that, as we have already observed, can hardly be denied by the state commission. In evaluating the net social outcome of this environmental *solution* by regulation, the following points should be stressed.

Most regulatory commissions in the United States have, in the past, been notoriously sympathetic to the interests of the firms they are supposed to regulate. An innocent observer from another planet might legitimately infer from the behavior of most commissions that they have perceived their major task as guaranteeing an adequate rate of return on the invested capital of regulated public utilities. On the basis of the historical record, most economists would predict that the commissions will, in general, be reluctant to enforce any antipollution measures that the regulated firms strongly oppose and accede to any requests for rate increases to compensate firms fully for the increased costs of any such measures that cannot be avoided. Such a prediction might, of course, turn out to be incorrect if the new conservation movement is successful in putting countervailing political pressures on the regulatory commissions.

As noted above, the additional costs of any genuine antipollution measures imposed on regulated firms are likely to be passed on in full to consumers without the usual corresponding market pressures on firms to reduce such costs over time by the adoption of advanced technology. In our example, the firm responds to the clean fuel directive of the commission by purchasing cleaner fuel at whatever price obtains on the market and charging its customers a correspondingly higher price for electricity. Unlike an unregulated firm, it has virtually no profit incentive to seek more efficient alternatives as, for example, more efficient combustion technology or emission control devices that would reduce a large proportion of the sulfur emissions. The profit motive fails to operate if the firm has unexploited monopoly power *and* if the commission allows the firm to use the costs of new antipollution regulations to take advantage of this monopoly power.

Under the circumstances assumed in this example, the regulated firm has virtually unlimited market power in its efforts to bid clean fuel away from unregulated competitive users. As it knows it can pass on the higher costs of clean fuel to its customers, it can bid the price of the fuel to whatever level is necessary to force previous users to switch to the relatively cheaper dirty fuel or to do without fuel entirely. In addition, the general inelasticity of demand for energy ensures that quantity demanded will not decline sharply. Under these conditions, there can be no presumption of social efficiency in the allocation of different grades of fuel between competitive users by the market system, because as observed above, the high bid price of the regulated firm merely reflects its protected monopoly position and not the relatively high value of the fuel to the customers it serves. The displaced users of clean fuel now will be forced to switch to the consumption of dirty fuel, and pollution problems will tend to be transferred from the regulated to the unregulated sector of the economy, with no presumption of any improvement in the total environment. Such ambiguous environmental outcomes of regulation are possible under the circumstances assumed above whenever substitution of polluting substances is technically feasible between the regulated and unregulated sectors of the economy.

One beneficial consequence of the regulation in our example should be added to round out a full analysis. The regulation will, as noted already, shift demand away from dirty fuel toward clean fuel. This demand shift will cause the relative price of clean fuel to rise, which will, in turn, induce a supply response of relatively more clean fuel production. Because it takes time to adjust production techniques and to complete investment in new capital equipment, the supply response could be expected to be of greater magnitude in the long run than in the short run. Thus, the regulation does seem to be of long-run value to society in helping to internalize the external costs of burning dirty fuel. But the real issue is whether or not society could engineer the same relative price changes and supply responses by alternative techniques that do not involve the inefficiencies of the regulatory process.

Regulation by the Environmental Protection Agency

Major regulation of polluting activities now is the responsibility of the U.S. Environmental Protection Agency (EPA), acting through the states and by its own authority. The EPA has already entered in an important way into the list of regulatory agencies. The EPA has a great advantage over the older regulatory commissions in that it can potentially provide a broad overview of the interrelatedness of all environmental problems. In contrast, an agency like the FPC can deal only with one narrow aspect of the environment. Furthermore, the EPA has only environmental quality as its responsibility and can devote full attention to it without being diverted by the more immediate public concerns of prices, quality of service, allocation of routes, etc., of the existing regulatory commissions. We shall attempt to describe the general regulatory approach of the Environmental Protection Agency (EPA). The authority of the EPA extends over a broad spectrum of environmental problems—air, water pesticides, noise, ocean dumping, solid wastes, toxic substances, resource recovery, land use—and it would require a whole book to detail its operations in each of these areas. Instead, we shall describe the regulatory characteristics that are common to many of the environmental issues under EPA jurisdiction, paying special attention to the major provisions of air and water quality regulations.

Legislative authority for the EPA stems, of course, from Congress, which in the 1960s and 1970s passed a series of major environmental laws —e.g., the Clean Air Act Amendments (1970), the Federal Water Pollution Control Act Amendments (1972), the National Environmental Policy Act (1969), the Federal Insecticide, Fungicide, and Rodenticide Act Amendments (1975), the Marine Protection, Research, and Sanctuaries Act (1972), the Noise Control Act (1972), the Resource Conservation and Recovery Act (1976), and the Solid Waste Disposal Act Amendments (1970). These laws and others provide the legislative authority for the EPA's activities. Typically, in such legislation Congress sets broad environmental objectives, often phrased in ambiguous language, and then instructs the EPA to develop and enforce any policies necessary to achieve the goals of the law.

In all areas where Congress has given the EPA discretion, the EPA has chosen a regulatory approach in designing environmental policy. Although there is a wide range in the precise nature of these policies, they usually involve the EPA—or the individual states on EPA authority —specifying what each individual discharger must do with respect to waste emissions. For example, the EPA can set a ceiling on the physical amount of a particular pollutant emitted into the atmosphere or water bodies. This ceiling may vary with the residual in question and the type of production process which generates it. Other regulations imposed by the EPA require individual polluters to add a specific end-of-line waste treatment technology or to change an existing production process in such a way as to generate less wastes. Typically, regulations of this type allow for a phase-in period over several years. In other situations, regulations specify the nature of inputs—new automobiles can use only lead-free gasoline, or utilities in certain areas can burn only low-sulfur fuel.

Performance requirements for final products represent another regulatory device. The best example is in the case of automobiles where federal law and EPA regulations specify minimum fuel efficiency, emission testing procedures, and some aspects of the auto's warranty. The Energy Policy and Conservation Act of 1976 requires that car manufacturers achieve an average mileage of 18 miles per gallon on their 1978 model cars, and by 1985 this average must increase to 27.5 miles per gallon. Labeling and terms of use requirements on pesticides are another example of final production regulations.

Once the regulatory policies are determined, the EPA is called on to monitor the waste discharges for violations and to determine whether the required technological changes are being made. Enforcement procedures with appropriate legal sanctions must also be established.[3]

Water Pollution Regulation [4]

Water quality has the longest history of federal involvement in environmental problems. In fact, the Rivers and Harbors Act of 1899, discussed briefly in Chapter 3, represented the initial federal concern with waste discharges into the nation's waters. The current basis for the EPA's water quality regulations derives from the sweeping provisions of the Federal Water Pollution Control Act of 1972 (FWPCA), which was a major departure from previous water pollution legislation. The broad intent of the act is no less than the complete elimination of "the discharge of pollutants into navigable waters." This is supposed to be achieved by 1985, but as an interim goal Congress also declared that by 1983 the nation should have, "wherever attainable . . . water quality which provides for the protection and propagation of fish, shellfish and wildlife and provides for recreation." One of the key provisions of the act is a time schedule whereby all waste dischargers are to install "the best practicable pollution control technology" (BPT) by 1977 and "the best available technology" (BAT) by 1983. With this objective, the law instructs the EPA to determine the specifics of precisely what constitutes "best practicable" and "best available" technology after accounting for various factors— e.g., the particular production process and the age of the existing capital equipment. Moreover, several broad statements in the law require the EPA to consider other general economic factors before developing guidelines for BPT and BAT. For example, the word "practicable" in BPT has obvious economic implications, and the law also says that the EPA's determination of BAT should be conditional on what is "economically achievable."

In addition, the EPA is instructed to establish waste performance standards for *all new sources* of emissions within comprehensive industrial classifications. Finally, in a major departure from previous legislation, the act requires the EPA to develop specific effluent standards for existing waste sources via a system of permits covering all waste discharges, private and public.

---

[3] The legislation specifies penalties—usually fines—and the EPA determines who is prosecuted, how frequently prosecutions are made, where they occur in the country, etc.

[4] For a comprehensive critique of current air and water laws and regulations on which we draw, see A. V. Kneese and C. L. Schultze, *Pollution, Prices and Public Policy* (Washington, D.C.: The Brookings Institution, 1975).

The EPA is responsible for issuing permits to each pollution source, and a typical permit will specify the amount of each pollutant that can be legally discharged and a time schedule for pollution reduction. Additional provisions of the law specify an equivalent procedure for municipal waste sources and continue the tradition of providing substantial federal subsidies—up to 75 percent—of capital construction expenditures for municipal waste treatment plants.

Opportunities for extensive public participation in the EPA's fact-finding process are provided and encouraged by the act. Finally, the law sets heavy fines for violations, with the EPA and the individual states charged with enforcement responsibilities.

Air Quality Regulation

The Clean Air Act Amendments of 1970 are the basis of the EPA's regulation of air pollution. This law requires the EPA to identify "each air pollutant which has an adverse effect on public health and welfare" and subsequently to establish for each such pollutant two threshold values—a national primary standard which will protect the public health with "an adequate margin of safety" and a national secondary standard which will protect public welfare. These are to be *ambient* standards—i.e., they refer to pollution levels in the general atmosphere and are not specific to individual waste sources. The standards are also national, applying uniformly throughout the country—they are identical in rural Kansas and New York City. In response to this broad congressional mandate, the EPA to date has identified and set standards for six air pollutants—particulates, sulfur dioxide, carbon monoxide, nitrogen oxides, hydrocarbons, and photochemical oxidants.

Once the standards are determined, the law requires each state to submit to the EPA an air pollution control plan for existing pollution sources which would achieve the primary standards by July 1, 1975 and the secondary standards by July 1, 1977. The state plans are subject to EPA approval, and if they are inadequate, the EPA has the authority to develop and implement its own plan for any state. Plans specify emission limits on individual dischargers and can also include parking and traffic flow restrictions on automobiles if further control is required to reach the standards.

In addition to the air pollutants covered by the ambient standards, the law requires the EPA to develop a list of any "hazardous pollutants" which may cause severe health damages and then to establish control regulations for all sources. To date, the EPA has issued emission standards for four hazardous pollutants—asbestos, berylium, mercury, and vinyl chloride.

Using similar language to the FWPCA, another important provision of the act requires the EPA to set emission performance standards for all *new* industrial sources of air pollutants using the criterion of "the best adequately demonstrated technology."

The final major, and perhaps most controversial, feature of the law is the imposition, beginning in 1975, of progressively stiffer emission requirements on all new cars. Standards are set—by the act—for carbon monoxide, hydrocarbons, and nitrogen oxides, and the EPA is required to monitor, test, and certify that new vehicles comply with the emission standards.

The law establishes draconian penalties for violations—a $10,000 fine for each vehicle sold that does not comply with the emissions limits. But, as previously mentioned, the law requires that the EPA must first certify that a car meets the standards *before* it can be shipped in interstate commerce. This raises the clear legal possibility that the EPA can effectively close down the automobile industry—the single largest manufacturing industry in the country!

Problems of EPA Regulation and Existing Environmental Laws

Many of the EPA's recurring problems stem from vague legislative objectives. Phrases such as "best practicable," "best available," or "best adequately demonstrated" technology generate severe difficulties when specific content must be substituted for Congressional ambiguity. The enormous complexity of the EPA's tasks—e.g., to develop emission limits for each water discharger, approve state air quality plans, establish waste performance standards for all new air and water pollution sources for numerous industries with widely differing technologies, issue water discharge permits to all existing polluters—has led to delays, confusion, and the inevitable frustrations. As a result, individual dischargers have frequently sought judicial review to contest EPA decisions. Large case backlogs and court delays follow, bringing uncertainty as to the ultimate results of the EPA's regulations.[5]

Little in the existing environmental laws or in the EPA's regulations provides economic incentives for dischargers to comply with environmental objectives. The use of the courts is therefore a rational course of action for businesses facing the substantial costs of complying with the EPA's directives. On the other hand, because of the number of dischargers and the comprehensive aims of the laws, legal enforcement by the EPA must necessarily be a selective process with reliance on major,

[5] We shall discuss the use of judicial review in more detail in Chapter 11.

attention-generating cases combined with use of the stiff penalties of the law to create a general deterrent effect on other polluters. Questions of equity are raised, however, when a single polluter must pay large fines when similar, but less visible polluters may escape prosecution altogether. In this connection it should be noted that the EPA is required to regulate a huge number of firms and other waste sources. In contrast, the older regulatory commissions have had an easier task in that their jurisdiction has been limited to a relatively small number of firms in either one industry or a few closely related industries.

In the case of automobiles, the use of the $10,000-fine provision represents a prohibitive penalty that, if systematically applied, could close down all automobile production. In fact, a new annual Washington event, similar to the predictable yearly Congressional rite of raising the ceiling on the public debt, is for Congress or the EPA to suspend or change the automobile emission requirements so that the automobile industry can legally continue to produce and sell cars. Thus, the politically appealing "hard-line" penalties of the law actually become a hindrance to improvement of automobile emission performance since their use would cripple a very major part of the U.S. economy. The penalty is so drastic that nobody believes it will ever be applied, and thus it has little credible deterrent effect.

Another basic problem of the environmental laws is their failure to take into account the materials balance problem discussed in Chapter 3. For example, the FWPCA's stated objective of eliminating all waste discharges into the nation's waters ignores the effect that such a result— if it could, in fact, ever be achieved—would place on other environmental media. Large and increasing amounts of sludge, for example, from water treatment operations would have to be disposed of by other means— burning, or dumping on lands.

Finally, economists have two major criticisms of regulation in general. First, and most central, is that regulation is simply inefficient. We shall develop this point in more detail in Chapter 10. For the present, however, we can note that the requirement in much of the EPA—or Congressionally mandated—environmental regulations that each and every waste source meet the same emission standards precludes realizing the significant cost savings available from allowing differences in waste treatment levels among waste sources according to their pollution control costs. While there may be overriding political and equity reasons that require uniform waste limits on all dischargers, there is clear evidence that such requirements significantly raise the total costs of meeting any given environmental quality target. Related to this basic efficiency point is the fact that Congress has unfortunately provided the EPA with only the vaguest, and at times contradictory, requirements to balance costs and benefits *before* determining environmental standards or emission limits in the first place.

The second general objection to regulation is that it does not provide any incentive for industry to develop new and more effective waste control technology. It is the EPA's responsibility to determine what technology is "best." Businesses, on the other hand, often will have an incentive to see that any new technology does *not* become standard and hence the benchmark for waste control practices throughout the industry. We shall return to this criticism of regulation in more detail in Chapter 10.

B. PROHIBITION

The economic case against prohibition as an environmental policy instrument has already been made implicitly in the elementary benefit-cost analysis presented in Chapter 1. A ban on polluting activity may or may not be preferable to a continuation of some existing level of pollution, but, in general, society need not be forced to choose one extreme alternative or the other. Instead, society, in effect, can trade off some potential gains in environmental quality in return for more than compensating gains in the production and consumption of goods and services.

Figure 9–1 illustrates the choices open to any society in determining environmental policy. As in Figure 1–1, the *MSB* and *MSC* schedules are drawn in reference to the units of pollution abatement for some hypothetical pollutant. The schedules represent the marginal social benefits and marginal social costs, respectively, associated with each level of pollution abatement and the corresponding level of environmental quality. As demonstrated in Chapter 1, *OA* is the optimal level of output of pollution abatement within the framework of benefit-cost analysis. For all the reasons given in Chapter 1, the exact level *OA* is extremely difficult for the government to determine, but this complexity is not, in general, a valid argument for a ban on all polluting activity. Rigidly enforced prohibitions may move society along the horizontal axis as far as *OB*, that is, to absolute purity, which people do not value and may not even be able to perceive. As drawn in Figure 9–1, the marginal social cost of achieving perfect purity may be extremely large, as it could involve the complete shutdown of some industrial firms or public utilities. Economists observe, moreover, that the costs of achieving environmental quality will, in general, be widely shared throughout the whole society. Despite the claims of some popular journalists, the burden of the costs of any prohibitions on polluters will not be limited to just a few firms or individuals.

Thus the economist's benefit-cost analysis provides a strong argu-

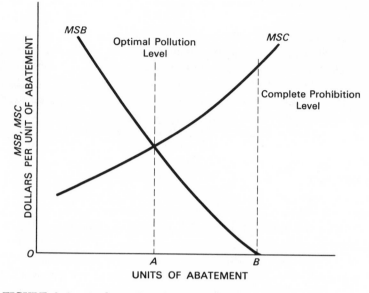

FIGURE 9–1.   Analysis of Prohibition.

ment against prohibition as a general environmental policy instrument. Nonsystematic, piecemeal prohibitions are open to much the same objections as regulation, on the grounds of the difficulty and inefficiency of effective enforcement. In general, alternative policy measures can reduce pollution levels to an acceptable degree and do it more efficiently than prohibition.

However strong the general efficiency case against prohibition, it may still be the best of several less than ideal alternatives available to society in specific circumstances. First, alternative environmental policy measures, such as regulation and effluent charges, must rely on the monitoring and measurement of emission flows. In contrast, prohibition requires only the determination of *on or off* for potential polluters. It is at least conceivable that the administrative costs of measuring effluent flows to the necessary degree of precision may be too high relative to the environmental benefits derived from the abatement of pollution levels. If such is the case, society will then have to face the all or nothing choice between inaction and complete prohibition. The reader should be aware, however, that prohibitions do not enforce themselves. If the potential gains to violators of pollution bans are sufficiently high, the laws will not stop polluters. Extremely high statutory penalties for violations are not necessarily a sufficient deterrent. As the history of the prohibition of marijuana in the United States has recently demonstrated, judges, juries, and the police are most reluctant to act against wrongdoers if penalties appear to be out of proportion relative to the social consensus about the seriousness of the offense.

Second, prohibition could possibly be justified in special circumstances on equity grounds. Suppose, for example, that the optimal use of some environmental resource calls for a very high price to ration its use among only a few consumers. Assume that naturalists determine that only 100 visitors a year can visit a wilderness area without inflicting irreparable damage to its fragile ecology. The price system could be used to ration entry to the appropriate number by setting the entry fee high enough to exclude all but the very wealthiest nature lovers. Justice in such a circumstance is not necessarily best served by reliance on the price system, however, even if intensity of desire to visit the wilderness area is accepted as the criterion of equity. Willingness to pay a high entry fee reflects *both* intensity of desire to enter the wilderness area and the distribution of wealth. If society judges that wealth should not, in fairness, count in the allocation of some scarce resource, it must opt for an alternative rationing device in preference to a price system. In this specific example, entry into the wilderness area could perhaps be made a prize, to be awarded by a carefully selected panel of distinguished citizens for meritorious social service in conservation. Otherwise, entry would be prohibited. In general, however, such nonprice allocative mechanisms are cumbersome, inefficient, and prone to fall under political influence, leading to discriminatory practices perhaps more inequitable than the workings of a price system.

Third, legislative authority to ban temporarily certain pollution activities during environmental emergencies—e.g., prolonged air stagnation conditions—offers an immediate solution to alleviate potentially disastrous health effects in large urban areas.

Finally, permanent prohibitions also make sense under extreme circumstances when potential environmental damage is so large that the marginal reasoning underlying benefit-cost analysis cannot legitimately be applied. If emission of some pollutant threatens widespread loss of life or catastrophic disruption of ecological systems, marginal trade-offs between environmental quality and consumption of other goods and services are not meaningful. Under some circumstances, the emission of certain pollutants threaten the entire ecological balance supporting human life. At the present state of knowledge, *uncertainty* about the complex long-run effects of different concentrations of such pollutants makes nonsense of any attempts to determine an optimal balance between the marginal benefits and costs of different hypothetical levels of pollution. Complete prohibition (at least in populated areas), strictly enforced, is the only rational social policy. The EPA ban on most uses of DDT is an example of this reasoning. Similar arguments are used by individuals calling for a ban on the nuclear breeder reactor.

The reader should be cautioned, however, that arguments for prohibition based on this reasoning can be pushed to ridiculous extremes. Almost every industrial process involves the emission of substances whose long-run effects are not yet fully understood and that may conceivably be a threat to human health and to present and future ecosystems. To live is to take risks, and it is fatuous to argue that man should attempt to purify his environment at all costs just because our knowledge is incomplete. The cost of achieving complete environmental purity and eliminating uncertainty about all long-run consequences of pollution is the abandonment of our industrial civilization. The alternative is to limit prohibitions to those cases in which serious danger is imminent and simultaneously to pursue research on the long-run effects of various pollutants and to encourage the development of the technology required to deal with environmental problems.

C. THE ECONOMICS OF ZONING

Zoning is the most important of the various governmental controls exercised over the use of land in the United States. Traditionally, the power to zone land—that is, to classify sites according to permissible uses and to *prohibit* all other uses—has been delegated by the states to local governments. The federal government has extensive land holdings of its own but has traditionally had little influence over private land use. In addition to zoning ordinances, other government regulations, such as subdivision controls, sewer and water permits, and the use of the power of eminent domain (the sovereign power of the state which authorizes it to appropriate all or any part of private property for necessary public use, reasonable compensation being made), are employed to exercise social control over the workings of the private market in the development of land and its allocation among alternative uses. For our purposes here, however, we shall lump these various measures used in social planning for the use of land under the general rubric of *zoning*.

The Economic Rationale for Zoning

For an economist, zoning can be justified, in principle, as a necessary means of internalizing for a community the potential external costs that might follow from unregulated private development of land. In the absence of zoning, each site would tend to be devoted to a use that maximized the profit of the individual owner, but the aggregate of such individual maximizing behavior would not result in the most efficient use of all sites because of the importance of external costs in land development. In many cases, external costs increase with proximity. For example, if land in a pleasant residential neighborhood were not zoned strictly for residential use, the owner of a slaughterhouse might find it profitable to move his plant into the area or at least threaten to do so and then allow himself to be dissuaded by a sufficiently large bribe paid by the threatened homeowners. In general, zoning is an essential component of an overall social planning process that attempts to take into account the proper balance between amenity and economic development. Ideally, the zoning process would allocate large tracts of land among well-coordinated residential, industrial, commercial, and recreational uses and then permit the private market system to allocate individual sites *within* each of the zoned tracts. Thus, proper social planning would prevent the occurrence of the most serious external costs of unplanned development but would allow the market mechanism scope for achieving allocational efficiency within the regulated framework.

Problems of Zoning

Unfortunately, zoning does not always work well in practice to foster the amenity of urban life while promoting orderly economic development. First, zoning inherently involves some degree of allocational inefficiency in the absence of costless perfect information. In the process of avoiding external costs of land development, zoning boards necessarily bar socially advantageous uses of land as well. To illustrate this point, suppose that, in the absence of zoning, a retail store could profitably locate in a residential neighborhood even after paying full compensation for all external costs it imposes on homeowners in the area. (Of course, no compensation for externalities would be paid, which means that the private gains to the firm from locating in the area would exceed net social gains by the amount of the uncompensated external costs.) Zoning prevents such socially profitable uses of land from taking place and, therefore, inevitably involves some efficiency losses as well as efficiency gains. As the example above also indicates, it clearly involves significant *distributional* considerations as well; zoning, in the hypothetical case outlined above, yields welfare gains to the owners of homes in the area but imposes large opportunity losses on the retail merchant who cannot locate in the neighborhood.

Local Politics and Zoning Policy

Probably because of the importance of its distributional effects, zoning in this country has been an intensely *political* subject at local levels of government. Considerations of economic efficiency—especially with respect to environmental quality—are too often distinctly subordinate to the issue of the distribution of potential gains and losses among competing groups and individuals. The typical zoning board in urbanized areas is heavily influenced by the dominant political forces within its jurisdiction in making decisions concerning zoning ordinances. Business and real estate interests, in particular, can threaten any one community with loss of valuable taxable properties if they move to another community with less-restrictive zoning regulations. They can play one community off against another because of the heavy fiscal dependence of local governments on industrial and commercial properties and, as a result, can often succeed in obtaining variances from any existing ordinance that prohibits the desired development of some site.

The discussion, thus far, has been limited to the effects of zoning within a single, small community, but the more important problem is the net social outcome of zoning at the community level. Within a large metropolitan area, zoning by each of a great number of independent communities will not, in general, promote environmental quality. Zoning, at best, internalizes the external costs of land development within a given jurisdiction, and any such costs spilling over from one area into another tend to be ignored. Zoning, at the local government level, tends to result in small clusters of industrial and commercial property, whereas optimal land use from society's standpoint may call for more centralization of such properties across jurisdictional lines. Similarly, each community is likely to have its own small park and recreational areas, whereas, without political fragmentation, economies of scale considerations might make large parks and playgrounds socially preferable. State and national parks partly substitute for the lack of large-scale recreational areas in some communities. Unfortunately, the distribution of these facilities is unsatisfactory. Most national parks, in particular, are remote from the average urban dweller in the East and Midwest. In general, the fragmented structure of local government results in uncoordinated planning concerning social environmental quality. The apparent solution to this problem is for the states to reallocate zoning power from local communities to area-wide planning agencies.

Centralization of zoning power is a most unlikely political development in the short run, however, because the distributional aspects of zoning dominate the efficiency aspects. Relatively well-off communities use the zoning power as an effective but apparently impersonal and non-discriminatory mechanism for excluding the poor. The common device employed by wealthy suburban communities in urban areas is minimum acreage requirements for construction of new single-family houses and a prohibition on the construction of multifamily dwellings. In recent years, these restrictive practices have sometimes been defended on "environmental" grounds. Zoning ordinances have contributed to the isolation of the poor in the older, urban core areas and have been instrumental in prohibiting the movement of racial minorities into suburban communities. Civil rights organizations have increasingly attacked extreme zoning ordinances in the courts, but the distribution of political power suggests that current practices will be hard to change. Recent attempts at comprehensive national land use legislation have failed in Congress.

D. SUMMARY AND CONCLUSIONS

This is the first of three chapters on the public policy aspects of environmental economics. The chapter began by introducing and defining several alternative strategies available to the government for internalizing the various externalities that produce environmental problems. These alternatives include regulation and prohibition, fiscal measures, including various kinds of taxes and subsidies, and government production of environmental services. These strategies pose clear alternatives for the main thrust of government environmental policy.

Regulation may be considered in two contexts. First, it is possible to conceive of extending the activities of existing federal and state regulatory commissions, especially with respect to the environmental problems associated with public utilities generating electric power. The benefits available from extension of traditional regulatory techniques in this area seem to be inadequate to balance the costs. This conclusion rests, in part, on economic efficiency arguments and, in part, on the observed behavior of the various regulatory agencies in the past—behavior that is heavily influenced by political traditions that are most difficult to modify.

Regulation may also be considered in the more promising context of a separate regulatory agency, the *Environmental Protection Agency* or EPA that has extensive powers to deal specifically and directly with all environmental problems. Our analysis of the EPA and basic air and water pollution control legislation leads again to pessimistic conclusions. Despite exclusive reliance on regulation to cope with environmental problems, economic efficiency, equity, and administrative problems make the regulatory solutions an unattractive environmental policy.

Outright legislative prohibitions on polluting activity are another environmental policy alternative. A benefit-cost analysis of the prohibition strategy demonstrates that it is, in general, economically inefficient in that it ignores possible trade-offs between different levels of environmental quality and other valued goods and services. On the other hand, prohibition makes sense either if administrative problems do not permit the adoption of other policy alternatives or under conditions in which benefits and costs are not continuous and trade-offs are not meaningful. The latter situation would appear to be pertinent, for example, under circumstances of extreme uncertainty about the effects of growing concentrations of some pollutants on human health.

The economics of zoning and planning of land use was then examined as another special case of both prohibition and regulation. Our discussion centered on how zoning actually works in the United States today as a policy for fostering urban amenity. The discussion of zoning concluded that the potentially large benefits of enlightened zoning practices are difficult to realize, largely because the administration of zoning remains at local levels of government and is preoccupied with the distribution of income and wealth.

QUESTIONS FOR DISCUSSION

1. Some writers have suggested that regulations and prohibitions would place the subject of environmental quality outside the scope of petty economic considerations. Do you agree or disagree, and why?

2. Suppose that it was already agreed to lower emission levels of a certain pollutant in a given area by a total of 10 percent. If you were an economic consultant to the responsible regulatory commission, what guidelines would you give the commissioners to help them in allocating the total emission reduction among all different firms and households?

3. "The same economic logic that favors effluent charges over prohibitions in the case of pollution should also favor excise taxes on heroin over the present prohibitory policy." Do you agree or disagree, and why?

4. The Clean Air Act sets precise performance standards for automobile emissions. What effects do you think this type of specific regulation of one particular technological process has on research incentives for alternatives to the internal combustion engine?

5. Some wealthy communities in rural New Jersey have established 1-acre or even 2-acre minimum lot sizes for new single-family houses and have prohibited the construction of multifamily dwelling units. One rationale for such zoning practices is to preserve the amenity of the areas and to prevent ecological disruption. Why do you think these zoning regulations have been challenged in the courts? Do you favor such regulations?

SELECTED REFERENCES

ACKERMAN, B. A., S. R. ACKERMAN, J. W. SAWYER, JR., and, D. W. HENDERSON, *The Uncertain Search for Environmental Quality*. New York: The Free Press, 1974. An excellent case study of regulatory efforts, within the federated structure of government, to improve water quality in the Delaware River. Highly recommended.

Ecology Law Quarterly, 4, No. 3 (1975). An entire issue devoted to analyses of the operation of the Clean Air Act.

HEALY, R. G., *Land Use and the States*. Baltimore: The Johns Hopkins Press, 1976. A discussion of issues in state control of land use decisions with several case studies.

JOHNSON, N., and J. J. DYSTEL, "A Day in the Life: The Federal Communications Commission," *Yale Law Journal*, 82, No. 8 (July 1973). A sobering account of the work load and decision-making process in a typical regulatory agency.

KNEESE, A. V., "Natural Resources Policy 1975–1985," *Journal of Environmental Economics and Management*, No. 3 (1976). A thorough, informative review and analysis of federal natural resources policy with innovative suggestions for improving its effectiveness.

KNEESE, A. V., and C. L. SCHULTZE, *Pollution, Prices and Public Policy*. Washington, D.C.: The Brookings Institution, 1975. A comprehensive critique of regulatory policy for air and water quality. Argues for more reliance on economic incentives. Highly recommended.

MISHAN, E. J., *Technology and Growth, The Price We Pay*. New York: Praeger Publishers, Inc., 1969. A lively and skillful discussion of zoning policy applications to environmental problems.

WHITE, L. J., "American Automotive Emissions Control Policy: A Review of Reviews," *Journal of Environmental Economics and Management*, No. 2 (1976). Provides an analysis of the results of several major studies of the automobile emissions problem and demonstrates the considerable existing informational obstacles to efficient policy design.

ZERBE, R. O., "Optimal Environmental Jurisdictions," *Ecology Law Quarterly*, 4, No. 2 (1974). An interesting discussion of ways to improve the effectiveness of local governmental units in addressing environmental problems.

10

TAXES, SUBSIDIES, AND EFFLUENT CHARGES

This chapter continues our discussion of the alternative broad policy instruments available to a government attempting to improve or protect environmental quality. The previous chapter presented the strategy of regulation and prohibition, which makes use of the fiat authority of government to restrict private property rights pertaining to the use of water, air and other environmental resources. This chapter covers the alternative strategy of using various taxes and subsidies designed to encourage private economic behavior conducive to improved environmental quality. The ultimate objective of these broad policy strategies is exactly the same, and the real issue is which of the two is a more effective means to the common end. The choice between them involves many complex considerations: their relative allocational efficiency, as measured by the ratio of total social benefits to total social costs; their effects on the distribution of income; the differences in enforcement problems associated with each; and their relative political acceptability.

Economists can make a valuable contribution to resolving some of these issues.

Government tax, subsidy, and expenditure policies play a number of important roles in influencing economic activity. On the macro level, they are the stabilization weapons of fiscal policies that attempt to move the economy to a full-employment level of output. Taxes, subsidies (transfer payments), and expenditures providing free collective services are also major social instruments for redistributing income. These same fiscal instruments allocate resources between the public and private sectors of the economy. Finally, and most important for our present purposes, taxes and subsidies can be used to reallocate resources *within* the private sector. Specifically, these fiscal weapons can internalize the externalities underlying environmental problems and thus cause changes in both consumer and firm behavior to take into full account the total social costs and benefits of their activities. In this way, the government can redirect private sector behavior to produce beneficial effects on the quality of the environment.

This chapter analyzes aspects of the fiscal approach to environmental policy. Section A discusses the theoretical foundations of tax and subsidy policy and contrasts this policy with the regulation and prohibition alternative. It also demonstrates the symmetry between taxes and subsidies. Effluent charges are the particular form of tax policy most directly applicable to environmental problems and deserve detailed analysis. Section B discusses some of the institutional obstacles to the implementation of systems of effluent charges in the United States. It goes on to chronicle examples of domestic and foreign experience with various fiscal incentives to improve environmental quality. Section C provides a brief summary of the chapter.

A. EFFICIENCY ASPECTS OF TAX AND SUBSIDY POLICIES

Review

In Part 1 we discussed the use of taxes to eliminate the difference between the marginal social cost and marginal private cost schedules of a firm responsible for an external diseconomy. The tax, when correctly set, internalized the full external costs of production to the firm. This induced the firm to decrease output, which led, in turn, to a cleaner environment, and also implied increased production of other goods. Moreover, this adjustment was made in response to straightforward economic incentives and did not require extensive government supervision or enforcement.

We can conceive of this rudimentary example of the use of tax policy to correct for environmental externalities as a benefit-cost problem. Initially, the price of the particular good in our example is below the full marginal costs of production, that is, the costs inclusive of the externalities associated with its production. Equivalently, the consumption benefits, as given in the price willingly paid by consumers, are less than the marginal social costs. This imbalance between benefits and costs indicates an oversupply of the good. Imposition of the tax forces the firm to consider the full marginal costs of production, and, when extended to an industry level, the tax on all firms reduces total quantity supplied and increases price. We further demonstrated that the quantity adjustment results in a *reallocation* of resources from production of the good with the externality to the production of all other goods, thereby restoring the maximum social welfare result of a private market system.

Effluent Charges as a Special Case of Tax Policy

In general, properly designed tax and subsidy schemes are viable methods of influencing resource allocation and environmental quality. They rely on creating economic incentives that, in conjunction with profit motives, alter economic activity. The potential targets of taxes as a general fiscal weapon are varied and could include such items as specific products, factors of production, incomes, or effluents. Any specific tax acts as an economic penalty and a deterrent not only to the taxed activity but to related ones as well.

Within this general category of tax weapons, effluent charges are the particular form of taxation having the most direct application to the problems of environmental quality. A per unit tax on effluent discharges removes the zero price tag associated with the use of air and water resources for waste disposal purposes and thereby narrows the unrestricted property rights implicit in the free use of the environmental media. With a policy of effluent charges, the government formally establishes its property rights to air and water resources and determines the price that must be paid for their use. Firms and individuals are thereby forced to consider effluent charges as another cost of doing business (that is, they must lease the rights granting them use of the waste disposal media). An effluent charge, therefore, creates an incentive for firms to evaluate the alternative costs associated with avoiding the tax. Profit motives induce the waste discharger to adopt a minimum-cost solution. This solution may involve a combination of waste treatment, output reduction, and payment of the effluent charge.

Figure 10–1 depicts the familiar example of an effluent charge. The firm's marginal cost schedule of avoiding the discharge of wastes into the environment reflects the least-cost combination of presently available

FIGURE 10–1. Effluent Charge or Subsidy Policy.

methods. With an effluent charge of OF dollars per unit of waste discharged, the firm takes action to not discharge its first OX waste units, saving AFB dollars relative to paying the effluent charge for discharging this amount of wastes. To the right of point B, the firm will pay the effluent charge and discharge wastes rather than incur the higher costs of not discharging. Thus, the firm acts along the heavily shaded line ABC, taking internal actions to avoid waste discharge from A to B (that is, the first OX waste units) and if the waste load exceeds OX units, electing to pay the OF per unit effluent charge on the remainder. For example, suppose the firm's total waste load is OW. The firm would then choose to reduce OX waste units and discharge XW units into the environment. However, the firm would be required to pay the effluent charge of OF dollars per unit of waste for a total cost of $XBZW$ dollars. This amount exactly compensates society for the external damages imposed by the XW waste units. (Recall that, by assumption, the MSC of each unit of waste discharged is OF.) Under the effluent charge program, the total costs to the firm are then $OABX$ (waste reduction costs) plus $XBZW$ (effluent tax payments). Changes in waste treatment technology, factor costs, and prices of final output will shift the marginal cost curve, and the interested reader can trace through these effects on the analysis.

Subsidies Compared to Effluent Charges

In Chapter 3, we noted that an offer by the party (or parties) affected by the externality of OF dollars per unit of waste *not* discharged would achieve the identical result. We argued, however, that real world conditions favored the effluent charge system over an attempt to create a private market for avoidance of pollutants.[1] Nevertheless, the basic approach of an offer not to discharge pollutants need not be confined to a private market correction for externalities. Equivalently, the government could offer a *subsidy* of *OF* dollars per unit of waste not discharged. This policy would be symmetrical to the effluent charge policy in terms of waste reduction. The firm would reduce wastes up to *OX* units because it is profitable to do so, earning a net profit of *AFB* dollars on the *OX* units of wastes treated.

However, a fundamental difference in economic incentives exists between the subsidy and the effluent charge methods. In the case of an effluent charge, the firm reacts to the potential economic penalty of a tax per unit of waste discharged into the environment. The firm takes action to minimize the net revenue effect of this tax by avoiding waste discharges if it can do so for less than the *OF* dollars per unit and paying the tax for all other waste units. An ultimate effect of the effluent charge is to increase the overall costs of operation and thereby reduce the quantity of final output offered at each price. If the effluent charge is applied throughout the industry, the final result is to increase the market price of the product and to reduce the quantity sold. Thus, the improvement in environmental quality is paid for by the consumer of the product via higher prices and by the society, in general, through a decrease in output.

On the other hand, a government offer of a subsidy of *OF* dollars acts as a *bribe not to discharge wastes*. The subsidy is an opportunity cost in terms of foregone revenue and also has the effect of internalizing the social costs of waste discharges. A subsidy scheme implies a markedly different structure of property rights in the air and water media from that of an effluent charge policy. With a subsidy offer, the property rights of discharging wastes into the environment implicitly accrue to the polluter. The government, in effect, offers a payment to the polluter not to exercise this right. Therefore, the polluter treats waste reduction as another potentially *marketable* good (that is, the selling of rights to discharge waste) and attempts to maximize profits when given the government offer. Normal profit incentives will operate as in any other market, and the more efficient the firm is in its waste reduction, the greater the profit opportunities. We can conceive of the firm selling its pollutant rights for the first *OX* units in Figure 10–1 at *OF* dollars per unit and not discharging these wastes untreated into the environment. Beyond *X* units of wastes, the firm will utilize its implicit rights to discharge wastes rather than sell them because the selling price is less than

---

[1] These reasons involved the unwieldy and costly nature of multiple contractual arrangements when the incidence of the externality was widespread and uneven. The *free rider* problem, discussed in Chapter 4, is also a considerable deterrent to the feasibility of this approach.

the per unit costs of waste reduction. For example, again assume that the firm in Figure 10–1 generates OW units of waste. Under a subsidy policy, the firm will elect to reduce the first OX waste units, incurring $OABX$ dollars in costs. In return, however, the firm receives $OFBX$ dollars in government subsidy payments for a net profit of AFB dollars. Beyond the Xth unit the firm will not accept the subsidy and will choose instead to discharge the remaining XW waste units into the environment, imposing uncompensated external costs of $XBZW$ dollars on society.

One objection to a subsidy policy such as the one outlined above is that it creates incentives to generate wastes if the costs of reducing or treating wastes are less than the per unit waste subsidy. Some firms may go into the *waste-making business* in response to the perfectly elastic demand schedule for treated waste created by the government's offer of a flat per unit subsidy.[2] The distinct possibility of this type of behavior is an obviously unwanted perversion of the original intention of the subsidy policy and a strong argument against its implementation. However, waiving this objection to a subsidy policy, a comparision of a government effluent charge policy with a policy of a subsidy per waste unit avoided yields several conclusions. First, both methods provide the same amount of waste treatment, ignoring the possibility of blackmail behavior, discussed above. Second, the *distributional* differences between the two methods are profound. In the example in Figure 10–1 the effluent charge method directly increases the costs of polluters ($OABX$ plus $BZWX$), and this increase in costs is passed on throughout the industry in the form of higher prices and lower quantities sold and consumed. In the subsidy scheme, government expenditures ($OFBX$)— representing subsidy payments to the firm—to purchase the implicitly owned pollution rights of the waste discharger must be offset by increased taxes and/or reduced government purchases in other areas. The incidence of the costs of obtaining the same level of waste treatment (OX units) is thus likely to be more diffuse throughout the economy with a subsidy policy than with effluent charges. Finally, with an effluent charge policy, the government formally establishes its ownership of the property rights in the environmental media, but a subsidy scheme implicitly creates producers' property rights to use the media for waste disposal.

Dynamic Adjustments of Effluent Charges

Suppose an effluent charge is imposed that initially is just equal to the external costs associated with a firm's output. How should the effluent charge be adjusted in response to changes in economic conditions?

---

[2] The reader may recognize some striking analogies of similar perverse effects of certain government agricultural subsidy policies.

First, suppose that the demand for environmental quality increases over time because of general increases in per capita income. In such circumstances, the level of the effluent charge should be raised to conform to the new higher value society collectively places on environmental quality. Consider this situation as depicted in Figure 10–2. The original effluent charge—equal to the per unit marginal social benefit of water treatment—is again drawn as the horizontal line OF, and the marginal cost schedule of treatment remains as MC. However, with the increase in demand for environmental quality, the increase in the external costs of pollution raise the OF schedule to OF', where OF' is now the new per unit value. As drawn, OF' is higher than OF at any given level of waste, reflecting our assumption of the increased ability and willingness of society to pay for environmental quality. The efficient waste reduction level increases from OX units to OI units, where the new marginal benefit schedule intersects the MC schedule. If the effluent charge remains at OF, the firm has no incentive to decrease its level of waste discharge. From Figure 10–2, it is clear that the effluent charge must be raised by FF' dollars, to a new level of OF' dollars. The higher effluent charge will induce the firm to reduce OI units of wastes rather than OX units in order to minimize its total waste disposal costs.

As demands for environmental amenities of all kinds can be expected to increase over time in response to sustained increases in per capita income, firms could expect with reasonable certainty that the optimal level of effluent charges would also increase over time in conformity with these increased demands. The existence of effluent charges and the expectation of increases in their level over time would provide incentives for firms to develop more efficient methods of pollution reduction. In Figure 10–2, the marginal cost schedule would be expected to shift to the right over time as firms developed more efficient techniques of waste reduction. Thus, the major strength of a taxation policy is that the imposition of effluent charges, expected to rise over time, would promote innovation and efficiency in the use of environmental resources just as secular increases in wage rates now induce firms to invest in the development of technically more advanced capital equipment in order to economize on the use of labor. As a footnote to this discussion, the reader should recognize that there is a close analogy between the appropriate effluent charge response by governments to changes in demand for environmental resources and the automatic response of prices to changes in demand in competitive markets. The important difference between the two situations is that the government must invest resources to discover the true external costs of pollution at any point in time, whereas changes in demand are reflected more directly in markets through the automatic signals of shortages or surpluses persisting at existing price levels.

FIGURE 10–2. Increase in Value of Environmental Quality.

Imperfect Knowledge, Fiscal Incentives, and Regulation

Thus far, we have tacitly assumed that the informational problems associated with either environmental policy are of manageable proportions.
This assumption is highly unrealistic, particularly with respect to ascer-
taining the marginal benefit curve of waste reduction. The informational
requirements necessary to determine such benefit functions are exceedingly complex in the situation of externalities that affect large numbers
of firms and individuals. The considerable environmental research problems discussed in Part 3 provide some perspective on the difficulties of
isolating and quantifying the full social costs of various pollutants. Moreover, portrayal of a constant benefit function in Figure 10–1 is also
unrealistic, and it is more likely that such a function would exhibit a
downward slope, indicating decreasing damages as the level of waste
reduction rises.[3] The informational difficulties associated with establishing this curve have important implications for the efficiency effects of a
tax or subsidy policy.

Suppose, for example, in Figure 10–3, that the downward-sloping
line UR is the true benefit function per unit of waste reduction. However,
because of research difficulties stemming from the complex nature of

---

[3] The argument here is that the demand curve for environmental quality (waste reduction) has, like other demand relationships, an inverse relation between price and quantity.

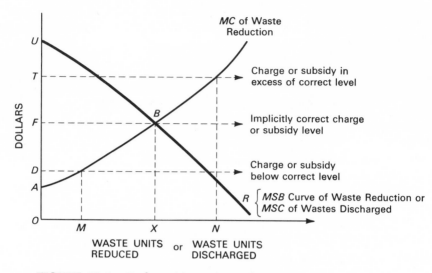

FIGURE 10–3. Realistic Marginal Benefit Curve.

the effects of this particular pollutant, the effluent charge (or waste reduction subsidy) is set lower at *OD* dollars than the implicitly correct value of *OF* dollars. The result, under either policy, will not be socially optimal; that is, waste reduction is *less* than *OX* (*OM* units). Alternatively, if the charge (or subsidy) is set in excess of the true marginal benefit function (for example, at *OT* dollars) then too much waste reduction will occur (*ON* units). In general, the difficulty of obtaining the proper marginal benefit function raises the distinct possibility of either of the above situations. In the case of *full* information about the marginal benefit and cost functions, this problem would not arise, and the efficient setting of the *OF* tax on each unit of waste discharged or as a subsidy per unit of waste *not* discharged could be made.

In fact, with an assumption of full knowledge of the marginal benefit and cost functions, either a tax or subsidy scheme would be identical in allocational effects to a policy of regulation. Knowing the benefits of avoiding wastes and the costs of waste reduction, the government could readily set *OX* units as the waste treatment quota for the firm represented in Figures 10–1 and 10–3. The firm, facing a legally enforceable requirement to treat *OX* units of wastes, incurs the same cost as in the effluent charge or subsidy method (*OABK*). The effects on final output price and quantity will also be identical to that of the effluent charge scheme. A regulation policy such as this formally appropriates for the government the waste disposal rights inherent in the first *OX* units of wastes. Thus, with perfect knowledge, regulation becomes an attractive policy and can achieve the identical efficiency results of a correctly set subsidy or effluent charge.

To be realistic, accurate knowledge of the relevant benefit and cost functions is unlikely. In addition, once we move away from the case of a single firm and recognize that numerous pollution sources are likely to exist, then a regulation scheme rapidly becomes unwieldy. Chapter 9 discussed the general efficiency aspects of regulations, but we can now explore these in more detail as they relate to policies of effluent charges and subsidies. Let us take, for example, a simple case of only two firms, each emitting the same effluent and each having differing waste reduction costs. This situation is portrayed in Figure 10–4, where the horizontal axes measure identical types of wastes for each firm. However, the waste reduction costs of firm 2 exceed those of firm 1 at any given level of waste reduction. Suppose, for simplicity, that these are the only two firms located in this river basin and that the local government has instituted a regulation policy which sets a target of a waste reduction of X pounds of BOD equivalent for the river.

The first problem that arises is how the total amount of waste reduction should be allocated between the two firms. Equity criteria might suggest that each firm share the targeted reduction equally, and thus each firm would be required to reduce wastes by $\frac{1}{2}(X)$. This equal reduction quota is what J. H. Dales calls an *across-the-board policy,* in which each and every waste source must reduce wastes by the same

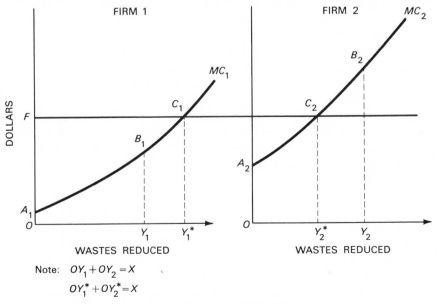

Note: $OY_1 + OY_2 = X$

$OY_1^* + OY_2^* = X$

FIGURE 10–4. Interfirm Efficiency and Equality.

amount (or same percent) regardless of any underlying cost differentials. In Figure 10–4, an across-the-board policy would mean an equal quota of OY units of wastes to be reduced by each firm (assume $OY_1 + OY_2 =$ the overall target of X). Accordingly, firm 1 incurs a cost of $OA_1B_1Y_1$ to meet its quota, and firm 2 has a cost of $OA_2B_2Y_2$. An obvious result is that the costs of reducing the X units via this across-the-board scheme are not the minimum possible costs of reducing this amount of wastes.

With full knowledge of the relevant cost functions, the across-the-board quota could be altered into what Dales refers to as a *point-to-point* scheme, which assigns separate waste quotas to each waste source. The objective of individual quotas would be to correct for the inefficiency implicit in an across-the-board scheme when waste reduction cost functions differ between sources. Thus, in Figure 10–4, costs would be minimized if firm 1 would increase its level of waste reduction above OY_1 units and firm 2 would lower its amounts below OY_2 units until the marginal cost of each firm are equal, recognizing the constraint that the X target must be maintained. This occurs at a level of OY_1^* units for firm 1 and OY_2^* units for firm 2. The costs associated with this distribution of waste quotas are minimal with respect to any other division of the X target between the firms (that is, $OA_1C_1Y_1^* + OA_2C_2Y_2^*$). Therefore, individually assigned quotas can restore efficiency to a regulatory policy. However, the obvious difficulty of achieving this least-cost solution is that complete information is required for each cost function. In our example, this would mean obtaining the technical cost information for the two sources of wastes. As we expand the number of waste sources beyond two, the required information for an efficient point-to-point regulation policy increases. This has obvious implications in terms of the costs of gathering and analyzing such data and the required bureaucratic machinery to administer individual quotas. Such considerations tend to make a point-to-point regulatory policy extremely cumbersome and costly. Accordingly, the efficiency gains of moving from an across-the-board policy of equal waste reduction to individually assigned waste quotas may be offset by the enormous increase in information costs associated with formulating and implementing a point-to-point regulatory policy.

In Chapter 9 we saw that current air and water pollution control legislation requires all *new* pollution sources to use the same—*best available*—waste control technology. Essentially this requirement represents an *across-the-board* regulatory approach, although it specifies the equipment each new firm must use rather than a uniform waste reduction target. For *existing* water pollution sources—estimated to number over 60,000—each polluter is treated separately, and the EPA's permit granting process can be individually tailored to the particular conditions existing at each waste source. As we noted in Chapter 9, and as is apparent from the above discussion, this point-to-point policy places formidable research and enforcement tasks on the EPA. For *existing* air pollution sources, the uniform national ambient standards—common across-the-board objectives—are to be translated by each state into an implementation plan which specifies emission requirements on the individual pollution sources within the state. Such a procedure approximates an attempt at point-to-point regulation.

Finally, the Clean Air Act requirement of identical emission performance standards for all new autos is a polar extreme of an across-the-board policy. It sacrifices the substantial efficiency gains available in either a two-car (or more) strategy [4] or an effluent tax based on the emissions of each model type of automobile. Both of these policies would realize some of the cost savings inherent in the spatial differences in the benefits of clean air. They would permit emission differences among automobiles but at the same time would provide ongoing incentives for consumers to buy, and manufacturers to build, cleaner cars.

A Workable Environmental Policy

Thus far, our analysis of the various environmental policies has been somewhat pessimistic. Complex informational difficulties exist when we attempt to measure the true marginal benefit and cost functions, and this militates against the likelihood of selecting the socially optimal effluent charge or waste reduction subsidy. Within the choice between a tax or subsidy policy, the perverse economic incentives inherent in setting a flat subsidy per unit waste reduction work against the implementation of this type of environmental policy. Moreover, the fiscal ramifications of such a subsidy policy create significant obstacles in addition to the equity and political implications of rewarding polluters. Regulations, on the other hand, offer a theoretically identical solution to effluent charges in the presence of perfect knowledge of the cost and benefit functions. In the likely absence of this information, an across-the-board equal reduction quota aimed at some overall target of waste reduction will be inefficient once we admit the real world conditions of many polluters with differing costs of waste reduction.[5] An attempted correction of this condition by assigning waste quotas to specific sources encounters the difficult information and administration problem briefly described above.

What then remains in terms of designing a viable environmental

---

[4] In essence, a two-car policy would make emission standards differ across the country— the emission performance of a car driven in rural Montana could differ from one driven in Washington, D.C.

[5] Indeed, not only will costs differ, but the benefits of waste reduction will differ over geographic area, type of effluent, timing of discharge, and so on.

ELIM. POLL IS EASIEST ALT.

POLLS SHOW 90% of PEOPLE WANT CLEAN ENV EVEN IF MORE COSTLY

policy? Precise measurements of the social benefits of a comprehensive waste reduction program involving a variety of waste types are likely to remain elusive for some time despite the energetic efforts of researchers in the physical, biological, and social sciences. A synthesis of waste treatment and waste reduction cost data, although more manageable, poses additional formidable research problems. This information represents a crucial missing link for the design of a socially optimal environmental policy—be it taxes, subsidies, or regulations—in terms of the resource allocation criteria presented in Part 1.

If, however, a social agreement can be reached on some overall target of environmental quality and, hence, a rough idea of the required reduction in wastes can be obtained, then a viable policy can be put together. Suppose we return to Figure 10–4 and now assume that there exists a socially determined objective of reducing wastes by X units, recognizing that this target is unlikely to reflect the optimal waste reduction implicit with full knowledge of all the relevant cost and benefit schedules. We know that an across-the-board enforcement of regulations to meet this objective will be inefficient, and a point-to-point policy presents insurmountable practical difficulties. A further possible solution is to subsidize polluting sources up to the amount necessary to achieve the stated across-the-board reduction. This will eliminate some of the costs inherent in a policy of a flat subsidy per waste unit reduced and prevent some of the perverse economic incentives of this policy previously discussed. It will still be inefficient, however, and in addition, it may not fully eliminate the incentives for polluters to overstate their waste reduction costs even with a fixed target for each waste source.

Probably a more efficient policy approach, given the goal of a waste reduction of OX units, is to implement an effluent charge. The important difference between this effluent charge policy and our previous discussion concerns the awareness that the effluent charge is now being levied to achieve the environmental quality target and not an unknown *Pareto Optimal* amount of waste reduction. All the advantages of an effluent charge policy will remain with respect to economic incentives for efficiency, innovation, and distributional equity. Returning to our simple example in Figure 10–4, an effluent charge levied at OF will bring about the efficient reduction of X units of wastes between the two firms. This will occur without the government having to obtain detailed cost data for each waste source. Of course, it is unlikely that the OF charge will be set correctly on the first attempt. Suppose, for example, that the charge was initially levied greater than OF. This would result in a combined waste reduction of greater than OX units and an environmental quality level in excess of the targeted condition. In such a situation, the signal will be to lower the charge. Conversely, if the initial charge is set below

OF, then the achieved waste reduction will fall short of the desired amount, and this should indicate that an increase in the charge is necessary. Thus, by adjustment of the effluent charge, an efficient least-cost solution will be obtained consistent with the desired waste reduction target.

Distributional Impacts

Distributional considerations may modify the above policy prescription that is based solely on efficiency criteria. Price increases in final products would, of course, follow the effluent charge policy and make some consumers worse off. Moreover, firms and waste sources with relatively efficient treatment facilities could reduce wastes more cheaply than inefficient ones and, in some cases, force them out of business. Thus, equity considerations may be important in assessing the desirability of implementing effluent charges. However, in general, it is hard to see why the costs of using environmental resources should, in the long run, be treated any differently from the costs of using other resources. Subsidization of the costs of waste disposal resources is not called for any more than the subsidization of the wages that firms have to pay their workers. Certainly, however, federal stabilization policies should be used to offset any general recessionary effects and special regional policies implemented for badly affected localities.

Implementation of effluent charges would force waste sources with costly reduction techniques to pay relatively high effluent charges and would not allow them to escape the economic penalties of their inefficiency. The revenues generated from such charges might be used to subsidize research on waste treatment technology and the implementation of more efficient waste reduction techniques. The eventual replacement of costly waste reduction methods could result in lower effluent charges and hence lower costs to the initial least-cost firms because more of the burden would be taken up by the previously inefficient waste treatment sources.

Policy Costs

Previously we discussed the information costs imposed on the environmental authorities (and society) under both a regulation and an effluent charge policy. Uniform across-the-board regulations require only the establishment of an agreed-upon waste reduction target. In the case of point-to-point regulations where pollution standards vary over waste sources—the only regulatory policy available that can replicate the efficiency results of effluent charges—we noted that substantial information costs must be incurred. Given a common efficiency objective, we concluded that the information costs of a regulatory policy significantly exceed those of an effluent charge. However, we must add that the trial and error method of adjusting the effluent tax until the environmental standard is reached is likely to create uncertainties for the individual firms. Since each firm's response to an effluent charge—installing pollution control equipment, reducing output, changing production processes—involves a time dimension, uncertainty about what the level of the effluent charge will be 2, 3, or more years in the future may induce a less than optimal choice of waste reduction methods. This will be particularly true if the authorities make a bad guess about the initial charge and subsequently are forced to make large changes. To minimize this uncertainty, some information costs may have to be incurred in order to estimate the likely waste reduction responses of firms to alternative levels of the effluent charge. This should be done so that the initial fee will not be far off from the one that ultimately will yield the targeted reduction. Thus, some information about the pollution reduction cost functions of firms may be necessary even under an effluent charge policy. To some extent, however, the uncertainty aspect of trial and error tax adjustments can be minimized by announcing a phased-in time schedule of charges several years in advance of the effective date of the initial charge.

Information costs, however, are not the only source of differences in policy costs. Under either regulation or effluent charges, waste discharges must be monitored. Across-the-board regulations require measurement of the effluent flows in excess of any allowable base amount. With the individual requirements of point-to-point regulation, effluent measurement must be related to each firm's own particular standard or waste quota in order to determine whether the firm is violating its assigned target. In the case of an effluent charge, an accurate estimate of the average emission flow must be obtained in order to compute a total tax bill.

Under all policies a significant monitoring problem arises when emission flows vary widely over a given time period.[6] Seasonal production trends, the type of production process, the nature of the capital equipment used, and numerous other factors can influence the rate of emissions. As a result, significant variations can exist in waste flows on a daily or even hourly basis.

Sampling is the conventional method of measuring discharge flows

---

[6] A good discussion of this problem, on which we draw, appears in D. N. Dewees, C. K. Everson, and W. A. Sims, *Economic Analysis of Environmental Policies* (Toronto: University of Toronto Press, 1975), Chap. 5.

with waste samples taken directly at the outflow source.[7] Samples are analyzed for waste content and concentration, and the results are then either related to the regulatory standard to determine if a violation has occurred or used to compute the tax due. The design and frequency of the sampling procedure is of critical importance for the success of either policy. There are several factors that affect the accuracy of the monitoring results. First, a policy of announced or scheduled sampling invites distortions since the polluter, knowing when the sampling will occur, may be able to reduce waste outflows during that time. Hence, a policy of random and unannounced sampling is necessary. Second, the greater the variation in waste flows, the more frequent the sampling must be in order to estimate the average emission flow. This is particularly critical for an effluent charge policy, which requires an accurate measure of average emissions as the basis for assessing the total effluent payment. With a regulatory policy, sampling must be sufficient to uncover a high percentage of any violations of the standard—either the common across-the-board standard or the individually assigned standard of each polluter. The sampling frequency combined with the expected penalty of detection must be such to deter the polluter from risking a noncompliance strategy.

Sampling also raises certain legal questions for regulation since enforcement is usually accomplished in the courts, either directly or by allowing legal appeals of agency determinations. Evidence of violations based on sampling results necessarily involves probabilistic statements which historically have not received great credence in the courts, where rigorous burden of proof rules must be met, rules that do not necessarily accommodate the statistical laws of probability.

This issue is part of the broader question of enforcement which is vital to the effectiveness of any environmental policy. An effluent charge policy requires the environmental authority to assume certain financial functions: Total charges must be determined, a collection procedure must be developed, and a legal mechanism must be established to cope with delinquent accounts. An appeal procedure allowing polluters to contest the charge assessed is also a likely component of any effluent charge system. With a regulatory program, a prosecution policy for violators must be determined with administrative guidelines set for the targets of prosecution and the spatial distribution of proceedings brought throughout the country. No a priori judgment can be made about the relative

---

[7] For some processes, waste flows can be accurately measured by simply knowing the level of inputs—e.g., in electrical power generation, the tons of coal burned and their sulfur content can provide an accurate estimate of sulfur oxide emissions.

cost of effective enforcement under each policy, but there is no reason to expect one to be particularly more costly to enforce than the other.

In summary, it appears that effluent charges are significantly less costly than regulations in terms of information requirements. Moreover, waste flows may also be marginally easier to monitor with an effluent charge policy. Nevertheless, its should be obvious that difficult real world administrative problems accompany both policies and that the theoretical efficiency and equity advantages of effluent charges that we have discussed in some detail represent only part of the basis upon which to choose policy. The complex tasks of effective policy administration—information, monitoring, and enforcement—must also weigh heavily in the selection of appropriate environmental policies.

Prohibition Reconsidered

One final task in our comparisons of alternative environmental policy actions is to relate the tax and subsidy approach to the most severe regulation policy available, the limiting case of prohibition. A complete ban on all effluent discharges is certainly a possible policy alternative. As noted in Chapter 9, prohibition is a drastic measure in the sense that it automatically forecloses alternative courses of action. It should be obvious to the reader that a generalized prohibition policy covering all categories of effluents in all areas would be grossly inefficient, socially undesirable, and, both politically and physically impossible. Nevertheless, selective use of prohibition policies may be economically justifiable and consistent with the outcome that would follow socially optimal tax or subsidy policies.

The essential economic issue concerning prohibition as an environmental policy alternative is one of the level of social costs involved and the availability of close substitutes. Suppose that the social costs of a particular effluent are clearly known to be of enormous magnitude (nuclear wastes or powerful carcinogenic substances, for example). In such a situation, any effluent charge should properly be set so high that no discharges of wastes would occur. In our example in Figure 10–1, the OX treated waste units forthcoming from an OF charge should exceed any level of wastes actually possible in current conditions. Therefore, the effluent charge becomes redundant and would not be used. The simple solution in such a situation is to prohibit any discharge of this particular type of waste.

Although prohibition policy is obviously desirable with respect to life-threatening wastes, the decision is not nearly so clear-cut for any item such as phosphate detergent (a product where prohibition policies have been used). Here, the crucial issue is the level of private and social costs and the availability of close substitutes (that is, equally effective but readily degradable nonphosphate cleansing agents). If, at one extreme, an identical substitute does exist and is available at no additional private cost and considerably lowers or eliminates external costs, then a prohibition policy makes economic sense. At the other extreme, if no close substitutes exist to satisfy the above conditions, then a prohibition policy is inefficient. Situations lying between these extremes necessitate a return to our policy menu involving modified forms of regulation, subsidy, and/or effluent charges.

Our analysis of the economic issues involved in alternative environmental policies is now complete. The general conclusion is that an effluent charge policy is a flexible, efficient method to deal with a broad variety of environmental problems. The specifics of individual situations (for example, geographic area, type of wastes, incidence and extent of social costs) should of course influence the details of any final environmental policy. However, as we have also recognized, recent environmental policy experience in this country has not been in the direction of effluent charges but instead has relied on combinations of regulatory and subsidization policies. In the next section, we shall attempt to explain why this has occurred in terms of institutional obstacles to effluent charges. We shall also provide some background by detailing the limited examples of effluent charge policies that have been implemented or proposed in the United States and shall supplement this information with an example of a comprehensive foreign experience with a similar program.

B. INSTITUTIONAL OBSTACLES AND SOME EFFLUENT CHARGE EXPERIENCES

Barriers to Effluent Charges

Most professional economists strongly endorse effluent charges as a general environmental policy. However, as we recall from our brief surveys of actual existing environmental policies, the arguments for effluent charges have not yet had any substantial impact on environmental policies in the United States. Why such a divergence between the views of economists and the actions of government, especially in an age when economists have seen their policies put into effect in other areas of practical application? The question is a complex one, and many factors contribute to a full explanation.

The first, somewhat surprising reason is the considerable opposition to effluent charges voiced by various conservation societies and groups devoted to environmental protection. In the 1960s, environmental interests opposed effluent charges with arguments based on emotional slogans such as "they are nothing more than a license to pollute" or "the environment is not for sale." In effect, these groups were saying that the value of environmental resources was infinite. The extent of this opposition may be exaggerated, and its role in deterring a national effluent charge policy is moot. Nevertheless, it is interesting to note that this resistance stemmed from the very people most concerned with improving environmental quality and essentially involved a basic misunderstanding of the economic implications of effluent charges. Environmentalists, at one time, were inclined to rely completely on strict legal enforcement of prohibition policies or stringent regulations. By the early 1970s, however, major environmental action groups, in part motivated by the poor success of the regulatory policies of the 1960s and also due to the growing awareness of the fundamental economic roots of environmental problems, began to swing their support behind the idea of effluent charges.

Although the initial resistance of environmentalists is an interesting case study in economic literacy, the politically weighty opposition of influential business spokesmen is probably the major continuing deterrent to effluent charges. In large part, business resistance derives from the obvious distributional impact of effluent charges. Our analysis in Section A showed that under a regime of effluent charges, firms' costs will increase as a result either of actions taken to avoid the tax or of actual payment of the charge or some combination of both. Cost increases endanger profit margins, create upward pressures on price, and reduce final output. They may also raise the danger, in certain extreme cases, of outright business failure. For these cogent reasons, it should not be surprising that business opposition to effluent charges has been strong and virtually unanimous. Businessmen recognize that the days of the complete absence of an environmental policy are over. However, when forced to some position, business spokesmen opt for the weakest possible regulatory schemes backed by heavy subsidy policies.[8] As we have already seen, such policies are likely to be more costly and less effective than an effluent charge policy targeted at the same level of environmental quality. Business's adherence to these more costly policies is due simply to the fact that they offer an avenue of avoiding the direct costs of environmental improvement and thus minimize immediate fiscal effects on their own operations.

Reinforcing these straightforward distributional reasons behind industry opposition are more elemental arguments concerning the owner-

---

[8] By weakest, we mean the lowest environmental quality standards with as many exceptions as possible. Our description of the environmental policies of business conflicts with the glowing descriptions found in annual reports and advertising statements. The reader is free to draw his own conclusion on this issue.

ship of property rights. We have argued previously that effluent charges formally establish the issuing authority's rights—be it federal, state, or local government—to the environmental media. This represents a drastic change from the previously existing *de facto* ownership of rights to the waste disposal capacities of air and water resources. Although public sovereignty over these resources may have long been a matter of law, the historical absence of any overt assertion or, more importantly, *enforcement* of the rights to use the ambient environmental resources effectively created a situation where these rights reverted by default to individual ownership. Not surprisingly, industry exercised its *de facto* rights and, as observed in Chapter 4, the rights to dispose of wastes in publically owned media became traditionally costless to the firm and embodied in its capital structure. The imposition of an effluent charge would create an abrupt change in this situation, with a sudden reappropriation of environmental rights by the government at the expense of private interests. If firms desire continued use of the waste assimilative capacity of the environment, they will have to pay a fee based on the economic consequences of the desired use. The prospect of this course of events creates considerable resistance, exactly comparable to the resistance that would arise should the government threaten to appropriate *any* form of wealth previously considered private property.

From a more detached historical perspective, an effluent charge policy does not represent a radical departure from conventional fiscal experience. In fact, it is a member of the quite well-known and frequently used family of excise taxes. It is true that effluent charges are a form of excise taxes extended to a new target and a target long considered as improper, or not even conceived of as a target at all. Thus, it is the novelty of an effluent charge policy and the unexpected nature of its aims rather than any radically different fiscal features that create the resistance to its adoption. It may be useful to recall, at this stage, that the origin of the federal income tax is relatively recent (1913). Certainly, at that time, a tax on income represented a radical departure for a federal fiscal system previously dependent on excise and customs taxes for its revenues. Thus, the resistance to the federal income tax was long and bitter.

However, the familiar cliché concerning the certainty of death and income taxes and the implicit acceptance of the inherent truth in this saying suggests that income taxes, once implemented, lost their radical nature and became part of the accepted rules and boundaries of economic activity. Obtaining new taxes on previously untaxed items will be much more difficult to achieve than raising already-existing taxes. In the case of effluent charges, therefore, the hardest problem is the initial implementation. Once this substantial hurdle is cleared, effluent charges simply will become another cost of doing business and part of the existing structure of economic incentives. This does not mean, of course, that the level of the charge, particular adjustments, the degree of comprehensiveness, and so on are minor problems. However, just as numerous changes to the federal personal and business income taxes have occurred, the details and alterations that will be necessary over time in any effluent charge scheme can also be worked out.

A final objection by business to effluent charges is that they are unnecessary and redundant, once environmental quality standards have been imposed. The argument is that the legally enforceable nature of laws establishing quality standards for air and water will be sufficient to ensure compliance. Therefore, imposing fees in addition to these standards represents an unneeded *overkill* solution to the problem. Although this argument has a certain logical appeal and may be a significant force against implementation of a policy of effluent fees, it is largely fallacious. Relying on legal enforcement proceedings means undue amounts of delay in achieving the ultimate objective of improved environmental quality. The road through the courts is a long and tortuous one, often extending years before final decisions are reached. Delays of 5 years and even longer, in terms of ultimate court decisions, are not uncommon in environmental cases, and 1- or 2-year proceedings are normal. In addition, a natural bureaucratic inertia operates counter to bringing court actions against established, successful, and prominent businesses and businessmen.[9] Finally, as our discussion in Section A suggested, using a regulatory approach to achieve these standards will require masses of costly information, and, in the likely absence of these data, the environmental standards will operate inefficiently at best. Effluent charges therefore offer a direct, equitable method to achieve the objective quickly and efficiently. They are not redundant in the presence of environmental standards but act to ensure their achievement.

Up to this point, our discussion has rested primarily on the resistance of business to effluent charges on the basis of some very fundamental and obvious economic arguments. Related to the strength and origins of this resistance is the final obstacle to an effluent fee policy, legislative action. A national effluent charge program must originate with the Congress, and, in fact, a number of such proposals have come before the Congress in recent years. Like all general tax policies, any effluent charge program would be subject to partisan politics, political pressures from lobbyists, and the give-and-take compromise committee procedure

↓ ALDICARB

---

[9] This aversion to instituting legal proceedings is characterized by the statement of one highly placed government official who indicated "we are dealing with top officials in industry and you just don't go around treating people like that." *Audubon* (March 1971), p. 8.

that characterizes legislation. We can expect that, because effluent charges are elementally against the basic interests of business and, especially, very powerful industries (oil, automobiles, steel, paper, and so on), substantial political pressures will be brought against a comprehensive and strong effluent charge proposal. In addition, Congress is also susceptible to the type of "logic" which initially characterized conservation groups when presented with the idea of effluent charges. Moreover, Congress tends to consist mainly of lawyers who by training generally favor the direct control approach of coping with social problems—i.e., assign duties and requirements and provide legal enforcement to see that they are achieved. If this fails, tighten the requirements and stiffen the penalties. Finally, it is also likely that the administering agency, the EPA, may regard the reliance on the incentive approach of effluent fees as a threat to its authority of direct supervision and control over the behavior of pollution sources.

Although these political obstacles are most formidable, increasing awareness of the attractiveness of effluent charge schemes has been able to overcome some of these legislative barriers and bureaucratic resistance to change. Pioneering and continued efforts by economists such as Allen V. Kneese and others who have championed effluent charges over a considerable time period are beginning to make inroads in terms of influencing the direction of national environmental policy. We can now turn to some examples of this trend and some effluent tax proposals.

Effluent Charge Experience

Although no national effluent charge policy has been legislated in any broadly defined area of environmental concern, numerous proposals abound, and in some isolated local and state situations, effluent charge policies of various types have been implemented. Not all of the policy proposals we shall discuss fit precisely into the definition of a fee placed on the extent of discharged effluents or an output tax levied to reflect the implicit environmental costs associated with a particular product or product group. Nevertheless, a central aspect of these policy proposals is the reliance on fiscal measures to create profit incentives that result in improved environmental quality. Before we begin this discussion of effluent charge proposals and actually implemented policies, it is important to note that we are excluding those policies that involve fines for noncompliance with regulated environmental standards. Much existing national and state legislation establishes legally enforceable environmental quality standards and is armed with fines and penalties. Although the existence of fines obviously creates economic incentives for improved waste treatment, a system of legal penalties does not represent a proper example of an effluent charge policy. We should note that fines imposed for not meeting certain environmental objectives, when set on a daily basis rather than as a single lump sum, tend to merge with a policy of effluent charges. However, such fines are conceptually distinct from effluent charges in that they do not involve the formal extension of public property rights for the use of the resources of air and water and the accompanying determination of a price for purchasing these rights.

1. THE PURE AIR TAX ACT PROPOSAL. In 1972, the Nixon administration submitted the pure air tax proposal to Congress. This bill provided for a national effluent charge levied on sulfur oxide emissions. As explained in Chapter 7, sulfur oxides are a major air pollutant and cause significant health, property, and agricultural damages. Sulfur oxides primarily are emitted from stationary sources of combustion of fossil fuels —electric power generation, industrial power, and home heating. The proposed tax would be implemented on a regional basis. The Clean Air Act, also discussed in Chapter 9, requires air regions to meet primary air quality standards by 1975 (a primary standard reflects levels of air quality consistent with human health), and the tax is designed to create incentives for compliance with the national air quality standards. In regions not meeting the primary standard for sulfur oxides, the tax would be set at 15 cents per pound of sulfur discharged from all sources within the region. If the region meets the primary standard but not the more restrictive secondary standard, the tax would be 10 cents per pound. If there is compliance with both standards, no tax would be levied. The assessment of the tax within a region poses some problems. As envisaged in the proposed pure air tax, there would be regular monitoring of known, large sources of sulfur oxide emissions (power plants, industrial sites). Smaller sources would pay the tax based directly on the sulfur content of their purchased fuel.

Thus, the pure air tax represented the first seriously considered national effluent charge. It was designed to complement the national air quality standards and provide the economic incentives to comply with the air quality targets of the Clean Air Act. The immediate effects of the sulfur tax would be to encourage firms to install antipollutant technology and, at the same time, to move toward lower sulfur content fuels. This bill received some initial Congressional attention but did not gain sufficient support for enactment. However, attempts are made from time to time to revive the basic idea.

2. OTHER EFFLUENT CHARGES PROPOSED TO THE CONGRESS. Another proposal that received some attention, and that is similar to the sulfur tax, is for a tax on lead in gasolines. This tax was to be based on the extent of the lead content in gasoline and was designed ultimately

to reduce lead emissions. Instead, however, the EPA chose to regulate the allowable levels of lead in gasoline. Recent court decisions make it likely that lead will be classified as an air pollutant under the Clean Air Act. This will require the EPA to set a national ambient standard for lead.

Various other national effluent charge proposals also exist. In Chapter 8, we mentioned a proposal that Congress received for a national disposal fee set at a penny per pound and levied on the final stage of production. This policy would be an output tax whose sole criterion is weight. It is designed to make producers aware of the implict waste disposal costs of their products and to create incentives toward types of products that make less of a demand on the environment when their useful life is over. Congress has also considered a similar proposal for a tax on packaging material and for a tax on the BOD content of water-borne wastes.

3. AN AUTOMOBILE EMISSIONS TAX.   Economists E. S. Mills and L. J. White have proposed an alternative to the uniform emission requirements on all new automobiles. Instead of requiring every new car to meet identical performance standards, they suggest that any car can be produced and sold no matter how much pollution it emits. However, an effluent tax would be levied on each automobile based on its average emission performance. A sample of cars of every model type would be tested by the EPA and an estimate made of the average emissions for 50,000 miles of car use of carbon monoxide, hydrocarbons, and nitrogen oxides. Existing estimates of benefits and costs could then be used to set individual effluent charges for each of these three pollutants. A total effluent fee would be computed and assessed against each model of car. The emission test results and the effluent charge would appear on the window price list of every new automobile.

The effluent fees for each pollutants would be set 5 years in advance but indexed to the consumer price index. Any subsequent changes would take effect 5 years from the date the changes are announced. Mills and White argue that consumers would shift their purchases to automobiles with relatively low emission taxes, thereby creating incentives for manufacturers to develop and sell cleaner cars. Such incentives are absent from the current automobile emissions control policy, which, in contrast, encourages foot-dragging and producer claims of technical infeasibility.

Differential fees for each pollutant could be set according to regions of the country with higher fees in the areas of poor air quality. Alternatively, one uniform federal fee structure could be imposed, but each state would be free to levy additional fees of their own—using the same EPA estimates of average emission quantities.

A follow-up effluent fee system would also be established for cars already in use. Periodic inspection of each automobile's emission performance would be necessary—accomplished, for example, as part of the routine annual vehicle inspection procedure carried out in most states. Only New Jersey and Oregon currently test cars for emission performance. There is, however, substantial evidence to suggest that such tests lead to significant reductions in motor vehicle emissions. The results of such tests and the annual mileage driven would form the basis of the effluent fee. Using miles driven as well as emission levels to compute the fee would require a tamperproof odometer for each car. The result would be an annual, recurring user tax on each car to reinforce the initial federal fee levied on new cars. This annual tax would encourage owners to provide ongoing maintenace of the automobile's emission control equipment—an incentive that is also clearly missing in existing policy. In addition it supplements the incentive of the initial federal charge for consumers to purchase low-emission cars. The economists argue further that such a program of rewarding clean cars and penalizing dirty ones provides direct and compelling incentives for manufacturers to develop effective emissions control technology—in contrast to the delays and disagreements that have characterized the enforcement of the Clean Air Act to date.

4. REGULATORY PERMITS. The use of the 1899 Refuse Act, which mandated obtaining a permit for any industrial discharge into navigable waterways, formalized the government's property rights to the waste assimilative capacities of these waters. Under the superceding legislation of the Federal Water Pollution Control Act of 1972, any firm or individual desiring to dispose of wastes in navigable waters must obtain a permit. The application for a permit requires technical information concerning the type of wastes, the quantity of wastes, where the discharge will occur, when, and so on. The environmental consequences of these permits are evaluated either by the Environmental Protection Agency or the equivalent state agencies, and the authorities decide either to grant or to deny the permit application or recommend changes in particular treatment levels. It is interesting to note the date of the original law providing this power and to speculate on the lack of enforcement of it for over 70 years.

As noted previously, the information and data evaluation problems facing the EPA and state agencies are enormous and point to the cumbersome nature of this regulatory approach to environmental problems. The permits are not allocated by a pricing (effluent charge) scheme and, therefore, do not properly represent an example of the fiscal weapons implicit in an effluent charge policy. Nevertheless, given the existence of a permit system, a relatively simple extension would be to price these permits. The price could vary with type and amount of waste, the location, the time of year, and so on. This extension would embody all the salient characteristics of a classical effluent charge solution to environmental quality.

As an example of the potential effectiveness of such an approach, Oregon has used a permit system in combination with the threat of daily fines to achieve impressive improvements in the water quality of the Willamette River. Each year, all municipalities and industries are granted a quota of permits establishing precisely how much waste they can legally discharge. Over time, as waste sources increase, the quotas are reduced by lowering the allowable pollution per permit. The daily fine acts as an incentive for discharges to remain within the assigned pollution quotas, and the Willamette is now supporting major autumn salmon runs and extensive fishing activity for the first time in many years.

5. NONDEGRADATION AIR QUALITY POLICY. A series of EPA rulings and subsequent court decisions have said that the air quality in existing clean air regions cannot be allowed to deteriorate significantly, and in regions which currently are in violation of the ambient air quality standards, new pollution sources cannot be added without a corresponding and equivalent reduction in air pollution elsewhere in the region. These nondegradation policies, which are still being legally contested and reformulated, have had an interesting effect on business behavior. They imply that any new or expanding firm must cope with the impact of its additional emissions on the region's ambient air quality. Faced with the constraint that total regional emissions cannot increase, new or expanding firms have frequently attempted to "buy" the emissions of other existing waste sources in the same locality. The purchasing firm then incurs costs to treat and reduce these emissions in order to provide the necessary offset to the emissions it will generate by its new operation. The result is a small but growing market in pollution rights, similar to the Dales idea discussed in Chapter 3. Firms that wish to expand operations have incentives to seek the lowest cost alternatives in buying and treating pollution from existing waste sources in order to balance their own new discharges. A side effect is the development, by local and state authorities interested in promoting business growth, of the organizational and information services—characteristic of any market—that identify potential pollution sources which are available for purchase by new or expanding firms.[10]

6. STATE EFFLUENT CHARGES. At the state level, we can cite some actual instances of effluent fees and output taxes. Several states have en-

---

[10] See *The New York Times*, August 1, 1977, for some examples of typical transactions in this pollution rights market.

acted legislation that requires a deposit on bottles and beverage cans. These deposits revive the once common practice of offering refunds when beverage containers are returned to the seller. This policy is, in effect, an excise tax on a particular product and is similar in its underlying economic incentives to the proposed national disposal fee. In Vermont, the Water Resources Board has the authority to levy an effluent charge on any waste source that does not comply with the state's water quality standards.[11] Michigan has given similar powers to its Water Resources Commission by requiring all waste dischargers to pay a fee "for the cost of surveillance of industrial and commercial discharges and receiving waters." Thus, the fee can range from a simple minimum associated with monitoring the waste source to a possible maximum $9000 for each waste source *in compliance* with the Michigan standards. No limit is set on the possible fee for any discharges not meeting the standards. Maryland's Environmental Service Act allows similar open-ended effluent fees that can be determined by the social costs of waste discharges.

7. USER FEES. If the waste assimilative capacity of the environment is a public good, as we have argued in Chapter 4, then rationing it by a price mechanism—effluent charges—can lead to a more efficient use of the environment's scarce ability to absorb pollutants. Effluent charges, however, are only a subcategory of the general approach of pricing public goods via user charges—i.e., the idea that those who use the facility or service must pay for this use.

An example of a user charge is contained in recently proposed federal legislation which provides for a tax on commercial users of the country's major inland and intracoastal waterways. Economists have long been critical of federal policies for financing the nation's water transportation routes. Historically, the construction and maintenance of waterways have been provided from general tax revenues, and as a result this has effectively subsidized the private users of the waterways—barge operators and commercial shipping. The House Ways and Means Committee has approved a tax on fuel purchases by barges, tugboats, and commercial craft that use major components of the waterway system— the Mississippi River and the intracoastal waterways from Texas to Virginia. The proposed fuel tax starts at 4 cents per gallon in 1979 and rises to 6 cents by 1980. The tax will accomplish several objectives. It will help eliminate the criticism of the subsidy mentioned above—private users of public goods will have to pay for their use. Second, by moving

---

[11] Again, although not precisely a classic effluent charge policy, this method represents an enforcement of the state's water quality standards based on a tax *per unit* of effluent in excess of the standards.

toward a full cost pricing policy it will promote a more efficient allocation of freight traffic among the alternative transport modes—air, land,
and water. Other, potentially more effective taxes such as a fee based on
each ton-mile of freight on the waterways have also been proposed as
alternatives to the fuel tax.

The Council on Environmental Quality in its *Second Annual Report,*
endorsed the general policy of charges and fees to efficiently obtain
given environmental quality objectives.[12] The Council cited two examples of sewer user charges to illustrate the potency of the fee approach. In Springfield, Missouri a $1400 monthly sewage processing
fee, based on waste loads, was levied on a packaging plant using the
municipal facilities. Within a short time, the firm took various waste-
reducing actions that lowered this fee to $225. In a similar case, an over-
loaded municipal sewage treatment plant in Otsego, Michigan placed
a waste charge on an industrial firm that previously had sent 1500 pounds
of BOD daily to the municipal facility. Within a month after the charge
was imposed, the waste load was down to a 900-pound average, and after
90 days, it fell to 500 pounds. Both examples illustrate the dramatic effects
of the economic incentives contained in the effluent charge system. Confronting a full cost pricing system for waste treatment services, both
firms quickly explored alternative waste reduction techniques in order to
minimize the impact of the waste treatment fees. These examples reflect firms' reactions to full cost pricing for waste treatment. We would
expect similar rapid waste reduction responses to follow a general policy of charges based on the extent of effluent emitted into the environment.

8. THE GERMAN EXPERIENCE. Although the experience of the
United States with effluent charges has not been extensive, the highly
organized river basin authorities in Germany have developed a sophisticated institutional structure to control water pollution in one of the
world's most industrialized countries. Our interest in discussing this system concerns its use of effluent charges to allocate the costs of waste
treatment among the firms and municipalities.[13] The German approach
of a coordinating river basin authority is not a recent phenomenon but
dates as early as 1904. The general term for the river basin organizations
is *Genossenshaften,* which, in translation, means cooperative associations.
These institutions are numerous throughout Germany and derive their

---

[12] *Second Annual Report of the Council on Environmental Quality* (Washington, D.C.:
Government Printing Office, August, 1971), pp. 136–139.

[13] A comprehensive treatment of the German experiences, from which we draw heavily,
appears in B. T. Bower and A. V. Kneese, *Managing Water Quality,* Chap. 12. See the Selected
References of this chapter.

authority from broadly worded legislation. In some cases, they have only a single purpose (for example, land drainage), but in others, they have jurisdiction over all aspects of water quality. Our particular interest centers on the *Genossenshaften* of the Ruhr Valley, where a comprehensive and successful water quality management system has evolved.

The engineering details of the Ruhr *Genossenshaften* are complex but are not of primary interest here. Our basic concern is the use of effluent charges as one method of achieving a least-cost solution to water quality management. The Ruhr Valley area is heavily industrialized with concentrations of iron, steel, and related production activities, all of which have heavy waste-producing technologies. The population of the area exceeds 8 million, and the river system is a relatively small one by American standards with a combined flow measure for all five rivers in the Ruhr system significantly less than the flow in such U.S. rivers as the Delaware and Potomac. Nevertheless, this river system carries an enormous waste load while providing a water supply for domestic and industrial uses. In addition, it is a substantial source of recreational opportunities. The key element responsible for this success is the approach to water quality management taken by the *Genossenshaften*. By treating the river basin as a whole, the authorities have been able to take advantage of the many economies of scale in waste treatment technology. Numerous waste sources of differing types have funneled their wastes to central treatment facilities. Certain portions of rivers have been zoned for recreational and amenity purposes; other rivers are used solely for waste discharges. The *Genossenshaften* have also been instrumental in altering the location decisions of industries when the effects of the location were deemed undesirable for water quality. Many specialized waste treatment techniques have been practiced when consistent with least-cost achievement of water quality objectives. In the case of one authority, a technical relation expresses all effluents in terms of their effect on fish life, and both treatment levels and costs are allocated on the basis of this formula.

Of vital interest to our discussion is the use of direct effluent charges based on the type and quantity of the waste. The *Genossenshaften* have employed this policy in coordination with their overall water quality management decisions to achieve waste reduction through increased waste treatment and changes in production processes. Industrial activity is the largest source of wastes in the Ruhr Valley, and effluent charges have achieved significant reductions in discharged waste loads. The underlying philosophy of the authorities has been to allocate the costs of waste disposal to the sources of wastes. This basic decision, in combination with a sophisticated systems management operation, has resulted in a river system capable of supporting the needs of large-scale heavy industry and the water requirements of a population of 8 million. At the same time, areas within the river basin offer water quality levels capable of affording significant recreational and esthetic benefits.

The lesson of the German experience points to the desirability of a systems management approach to environmental problems and a reliance on the basic principle of seeking an efficient allocation of costs. The experience of effluent charges in assessing these costs based on the contribution to total wastes has been particularly successful.

C. SUMMARY AND CONCLUSIONS

Once a social consensus is reached to "do something about pollution," a number of possible public policy strategies exist to achieve improvements in environmental quality. The first two chapters in Part 4 have evaluated the public policies of prohibition, regulation, and fiscal actions. The outcome of this comparison suggests the overall attraction of effluent charges as a general environmental policy. The use of tax instruments such as effluent charges avoids the enormous informational requirements of an efficient point-to-point regulatory policy. In the absence of this information, an across-the-board regulation policy is grossly inefficient.

Effluent charges rely on the basic profit-maximizing behavior of firms to obtain the desired level of environmental improvement. Once implemented, taxes represent flexible instruments that can be altered according to changes in environmental objectives. In terms of equity criteria, effluent fees internalize external costs directly to the producers and consumers of products responsible for environmental deterioration. As a fiscal alternative, a subsidy program rewards pollution sources by offering to purchase the implicit environmental property rights to the polluter. In addition, per unit subsidies actually may create profit incentives to generate pollutants.

In certain situations when the social costs of a pollutant are clearly unacceptable, the effects of a prohibition policy will coincide with an optimally determined effluent charge. However, where a range of product substitutes exists and the social and private costs of these relevant products differ significantly, prohibition is not economically efficient.

Although the U.S. experience with effluent charges has been limited, several actual instances of environmental taxation policy have met with remarkable success. In addition, a growing amount of support for effluent fees has been voiced by professional economists, environmental groups, leading research organizations in the environmental field, and the Council on Environmental Quality. The showcase success of effluent charges by the *Genossenshaften* of Germany in the context of a sophisticated water quality management system also reinforces the attraction of this method of environmental control. Several opportunities readily exist within the broad regulatory framework of the EPA to use an effluent charge approach to improve the effectiveness of pollution control policies.

Nevertheless, we realistically recognize that even in light of the appealing efficiency and equity aspects of effluent fees, significant business opposition exists to any environmental taxation policy. The roots of this opposition are, fundamentally, the distributional results of effluent charges and involve a decline in output, higher prices, losses of property rights, and potential decreases in profits. The nature of the legislative and bureaucratic process in combination with the political weight of industry pose further and nearly overwhelming obstacles to the implementation of a generalized effluent charge policy.

If an effluent charge policy is implemented, it should take a systems approach to reflect the systems nature of the production process with respect to the generation of waste residuals. In addition, the use of regional tax rates versus geographically homogeneous charges raises important practical problems. The degree of the locational incentives for industry that may result from a differential effluent charge structure should be carefully evaluated. The federal government must recognize its responsibilities for correcting any adverse employment effects of environmental policies.

In conclusion, our evaluation in Chapters 9 and 10 makes a strong case for the use of effluent charges whenever possible. However, even in the unlikely event that all political and administrative obstacles to effluent taxes can be overcome, complete reliance on a pricing approach to cope with environmental problems would not be appropriate. Certain special situations call for the judicious use of the other social policies we have discussed to supplement effluent fees in order to achieve an effective reduction in waste loads. For example, a considerable amount of water pollutants—up to 50 percent in some river systems—do not originate from any clearly identifiable source. Runoff from roads and urban areas places large quantities of oil, various exotic metals, lead, and carbon into water bodies. Agriculture runoff and storm sewer overflow also yield significant amounts of pesticides, organic wastes, sediment, and fertilizers. In both cases, effluent charges could not be levied on these *nonpoint* sources of pollutants. Appropriate land use policy, zoning restrictions, and product use regulations would be more effective ways of reducing pollution of this type. Also, in emergency situations caused by extreme weather conditions, accident, or catastrophe or in cases of extremely hazardous substances, authority to issue blanket prohibition orders on polluting activities is an essential component of an effective environmental program.

QUESTIONS FOR DISCUSSION

1. "The government already gives substantial subsidies to farmers, oil companies, and others. Therefore, it would be fairer to subsidize firms to control pollution emissions than to impose effluent charges on them." Do you agree or disagree, and why?

2. Should effluent charges be set higher for new firms than for existing firms, on the ground that the former would otherwise have an unfair advantage over the latter in being able to reduce emission levels at relatively low costs by adoption of the latest antipollution technology?

3. "Once economists admit the vast uncertainty that prevails about the nature and extent of environmental costs and benefits in the real world, they have to acknowledge, in all honesty, that there is no theoretical presumption for effluent charges over alternative environmental policies." Discuss critically.

4. Refer to Figure 10–1. What are the cost savings to the firm from discharging the XW units of wastes and paying the effluent charge on these units? Does society benefit from the firm's decision to pay the charge or would it be in society's interest to require the firm to reduce all OW units of wastes?

5. One river in the Ruhr Valley, the Emscher, serves exclusively as a waste conduit and has even been completely lined with concrete. Does this fact lead you to reconsider the favorable evaluation of the Ruhr *Genossenshaften* in the text? Why or why not?

SELECTED REFERENCES

ACKERMAN, S., "Effluent Charges: A Critique," *Canadian Journal of Economics*, 6, No. 4 (November 1973). A critical theoretical assessment of effluent charges. Advanced.

ANDERSON, F. R., *et. al., Environmental Improvement through Economic Incentives*. Baltimore: The Johns Hopkins Press, 1977. A comprehensive examination of affluent charges. Highly recommended.

BAUMOL, W. J., and W. E. OATES, *The Theory of Environmental Policy*. Englewood Cliffs, N.J.: Prentice-Hall, Inc., 1975. An excellent advanced treatment of the theoretical issues in environmental policy.

BOWER, B. T., and A. V. KNEESE, *Managing Water Quality*. Baltimore: The Johns Hopkins Press, 1968. A thorough discussion of effluent charges and standards. Contains chapters on the water quality management of the Ruhr Valley authorities and several river basin planning experiences in the United States.

BURROWS, P., "Pricing vs. Regulation for Environmental Protection," in *Economic Policies and Social Goals*, A. J. Culyer, ed. London: Martin

Robinson, 1974. A comparison of effluent charges and regulation. Provides a less sanguine view of effluent charges on all accounts—efficiency, equity, and administration costs.

DAVIS, O. A., and M. I. KAMIEN, "Externalities, Information and Alternative Collective Action," *The Analysis and Evaluation of Public Expenditures: The PPB System,* Joint Economic Committee, 91st Congress, 1st Session. Washington, D.C.: Government Printing Office, 1969. A survey of alternative public policy possibilities.

DEWEES, D. N., *Economies and Public Policy: The Automobile Case.* Cambridge, Mass.: The M.I.T. Press, 1974. An analysis of automobile emissions regulatory policy. Demonstrates the superior efficiency aspects of a pricing strategy.

ETHRIDGE, D., "User Charges as a Means for Pollution Control," *Bell Journal of Economics and Management Science,* III, No. 1 (Spring 1972). An empirical study of firm reaction to sewer charges.

MILLS, E. S., and L. J. WHITE, "Government Policies Toward Automotive Emissions Controls," *Approaches to Controlling Air Pollution,* A. F. Friedlaender, ed., Cambridge, Mass.: The M.I.T. Press, 1978. Evaluates existing national efforts to reduce automotive pollution and details the argument for an emission tax policy for automobile pollution control.

PORTNEY, P. R., A. M. FREEMAN, III, E. P. SESKIN, H. M. PESKIN, V. K. SMITH, and R. HAVEMAN, *Current Issues in Environmental Policy.* Baltimore, Md.: Johns Hopkins Press, 1978. An excellent survey and economic critique of major environmental laws and regulations.

SCHULTZE, C. L., *The Public Use of Private Interest.* Washington, D.C.: The Brookings Institution, 1977. A general discussion of regulations and economic incentives in public policy with examples drawn from various federal programs. Very readable.

WHITE, L. J., "Effluent Charges as a Faster Means of Achieving Pollution Abatement," *Public Policy* (Winter 1976). Stresses the compliance incentives of an effluent charge policy.

11

GOVERNMENTAL PRODUCTION OF ENVIRONMENTAL SERVICES

A third broad environmental policy alternative available to the government is to produce environmental services itself. The prohibition and regulation measures of Chapter 9 alter the rules delimiting the scope of private market actions, and the fiscal measures of Chapter 10 change the nature of the profit incentives influencing private firm behavior. But both of these two alternatives leave the production of goods and services to the private sector. Production of environmental services in the public sector is thus a third clear alternative for the government. This chapter discusses the efficiency and equity problems that arise once the government makes a decision to adopt this most direct form of intervention in environmental problems. It also considers the potential environmental damages caused by government expenditure policies and regulatory decisions. The prospects for minimizing the adverse environmental effects of governmental programs are examined.

The U.S. economy of the 1970s is best characterized neither as capitalistic nor socialistic but rather as *mixed.* Most economic activity is carried out in the private sector in response to the profit motive, but the public sector is large, and its relative size has been increasing. Government—federal, state, and local—is the single largest employer and purchaser of goods and services in the economy and its spending in recent years amounts to over 20 percent of gross national product. All levels of government provide services directly or indirectly affecting environmental quality, and the list of additional environmental services they have been asked to provide by the new conservation movement is a long and expensive one.

The classic case of government ownership and production of services is the Tennessee Valley Authority (TVA). The TVA supplies electrical power to a wide area of the South, and, at the same time, its lakes are major outdoor recreation resources. Another example of government ownership and production is the Nuclear Regulatory Commission, which, in its role as producer and regulator of energy, has profound potential effects on the quality of our environment. The federal government has long had extensive participation in water resource development, with far-reaching implications for the quality of water resources and the supply of recreational sites. National parks, seashores, and forests are further examples of government ownership and operation of outdoor recreational resources. More generally, the policies governing the disposition and use of 760 million acres of federal government land are of crucial importance for the quality of the environment. The treatment of sewage and collection of trash are typical of the environmental cleanup programs that are important responsibilities of local government in the United States. Over 70 percent of the water supply systems in the United States are municipally owned and operated.

The examples of current government activities in the previous paragraph suggest the important role public sector ownership and production already play with respect to environmental quality. The many proposals for new environmental programs would greatly expand this role. Note, in particular, that government provision of environmental services goes beyond the objective of controlling effluents and waste residuals and encompasses far broader goals. Specifically, the primary concern of this form of government intervention is with the *expansion* and *enhancement* of recreational resources and amenity, rather than simply with the preservation of existing environmental resources.

This chapter treats the topic of government provision of environmental services within an expanded and more sophisticated discussion of benefit-cost analysis and is organized according to the following outline: Section A reexamines the technique of benefit-cost analysis and discusses its role in establishing criteria for general public expenditure programs.

Section B attempts to give a more rounded view of benefit-cost analysis by detailing some of its major conceptual and operational problems. Section C examines the National Environmental Policy Act, which established the basic framework within which the environmental effects of federal activities are examined. It also discusses the use of judicial review of government agency activities which affect environmental quality. Section D follows with an application of benefit-cost analysis to public land policy. Section E provides a brief summary of the chapter.

A. PUBLIC EXPENDITURES AND BENEFIT-COST ANALYSIS

Government expenditures have many dimensions. The amount and timing of public spending have significant impacts on aggregate output and employment. At full employment, the level of public expenditure directly determines the overall mix between public and private output. Moreover, given a fixed amount of public expenditure, the composition of public output becomes an important social question. Finally, government expenditures raise implicit distributional issues because the incidence of benefits is likely to differ from the incidence of costs (the costs being primarily paid from federal personal and business income tax revenues).

In Chapter 2, we discussed how private markets, under certain ideal conditions, allocated resources efficiently. The maximizing calculus underlying each decision by producers and consumers results in an efficient allocation of resources or a maximization of social welfare. However, because of pervasive externalities, certain goods such as environmental amenities are not produced, or are underproduced, by private markets. Consequently, government provision of these goods becomes necessary. Unfortunately, the basic problem of the efficient utilization of resources does not disappear simply because there is a need for public production of a good or service. Government production involves opportunity costs. With a fixed public budget, a decision to proceed with any one project means other possible undertakings are foreclosed. Obviously, as a first criterion, it would be useful to ascertain if the project in question generates benefits in excess of its costs to society. Simply, does the project add more output to society than it takes away? If the project passes this test, a further question immediately arises; namely, how does this project compare to all others that also meet the initial efficiency test? In other words, on what basis can we rationally choose between many worthwhile outlets for public expenditure?

Benefit-cost analysis is the method best suited to answer these questions. Chapter 1 introduced the basic idea of this technique of evaluating and ranking potential public projects. Our purpose now is to explore it in more detail. In a general sense, benefit-cost analysis attempts to proxy the criteria of private markets as they would extend to public expenditures. It involves a systematic evaluation of the social benefits generated by a given project relative to the social costs of the undertaking. Both benefits and costs are measured in dollars and are supposed to reflect the economic values of the inputs and outputs of the project. In Chapter 2 we argued that private markets fail, in certain instances, to account for the full benefits or costs of production or consumption decisions because of the common property basis of externalities, and therefore, resource allocation becomes inefficient. The identical problem recurs in benefit-cost analysis. The measures of benefits and costs must be inclusive of all relevant social values if the analysis is to avoid the pitfall of inefficient public resource allocation. For example, a federal water quality improvement project in a river basin may bestow benefits in the form of decreased water treatment costs for municipalities and industries. In addition, however, it may provide a net increase in the resources available for public recreation activity. The total benefits of such a project would be the sum of decreased treatment costs plus the incremental recreation benefits generated by the project.

Symmetrically, all input costs must also be accounted for because any resources used by the project are no longer available for alternative uses. Furthermore, any additional external costs also should be included. For example, environmental costs created by the project (natural habitat disruptions, waste discharges, and so on) properly belong in the cost total. Thus, benefit-cost analysis seeks to estimate the entire extent of a project's benefits and costs.

A benefit-cost study ultimately reduces to a ratio where the numerator expresses the total present value of all benefits and the denominator measures the total present value of all costs. If this ratio exceeds unity, the project passes the first efficiency test. That is, the project promises to make a net contribution to society's economic welfare in the sense that the output produced has a greater value than the resources used for the project would have in the private sector.

The concept of *present value* is of central importance in benefit-cost analysis. Many public projects have long lives and are characterized by substantial initial construction costs followed by recurring, but relatively low, annual operating costs. Benefits, on the other hand, tend to be distributed more evenly over the life of the project. Thus, the bulk of a project's costs often occur early in its life, but the benefits are spaced over a considerable following period.

Obviously, the decision to undertake a project must be made in the present. The problem is to express a future, uneven stream of costs and benefits in terms of its value today, or, in other words, to reduce all the costs and benefits occurring in future time periods to a common present-day value. The necessity of taking time into account centers on a basic economic tenet that a dollar received at a specified future time is not so valuable as the receipt of that dollar today. Equivalently, a dollar today returns more than a dollar in the future when it is lent at interest. Exactly how much more a dollar will be worth at the end of a specified number of years will depend on the interest rate. The higher the rate of interest, the more a dollar will return at the end of the time period. The logic can also be reversed. If an expected amount of dollar benefits is forthcoming at a known future time and the interest rate is given, we can compute the present value of those benefits today. Precisely how much would have to be lent out at the given interest rate in order to generate that particular sum of benefits at the specified future time? Formally, the relation between present and future values can be expressed as

$$PV = \frac{B_t}{(1+i)^t},$$

where PV is present value, B indicates dollar benefits, i is the interest rate, and t is the time period in which the benefits accrue. The expression can be solved for PV given values of i, t, and B. If benefits occur over a series of years and in differing amounts, then the present value of this series of benefits, PVB, is obtained by summing the PV of each component of the benefit stream as computed by the above formula. We can express this summation process as

$$PVB = \sum_{t=1}^{T} \frac{B_t}{(1+i)^t},$$

where the summation covers the life of the project (T years). By identical reasoning, the costs of the project should also be expressed on a present value basis. However, let us assume that one segment of costs, capital outlays, all occur in the initial year of the project. Accordingly, the present value of the capital construction costs is stated by their full dollar value. Recurring, or annual operating, costs are spent over the life of the project, and it is necessary to compute the present value of these costs. The present value of costs (PVC), therefore, can be given by

$$PVC = K + \sum_{t=1}^{T} \frac{RC_t}{(1+i)^t},$$

where K indicates the capital costs incurred in the initial year of the project and RC indicates recurring, or operating, costs.

The benefit-cost ratio (BCR) is computed as

$$BCR = \frac{PVB}{PVC} = \frac{\sum\limits_{t=1}^{T} [B_t/(1+i)^t]}{K + \sum\limits_{t=1}^{T} [RC_t/(1+i)^t]}$$

This ratio determines whether the present value of the estimated benefits of the project exceeds, falls short of, or equals the present value of the costs. It answers the efficiency question implicitly posed by public expenditures. Moreover, projects can be ranked according to their benefit-cost ratio. The technique can also be used to determine the efficient size of a project by computing the marginal benefit-cost ratio as project size changes and selecting the size where the benefit-cost ratio is at a maximum.

Benefit-cost analysis is an invaluable tool of social accounting. If carefully done, it offers useful information to public decision making. The systematic evaluation of the full extent of benefits and costs provides a sound basis for rational public investment decisions and, thus, an efficient allocation of society's resources. However, it is important to be aware of a number of theoretical and practical difficulties in the use of benefit-cost analysis for evaluating government programs.

B. ISSUES IN BENEFIT-COST ANALYSIS

Determination of the Social Discount Rate

The role of the interest rate in benefit-cost analysis is a crucial one. It is not surprising that it has been the center of a considerable controversy in the professional literature of economics. The simple mechanics of the benefit-cost formula reveal that the higher the interest rate, the lower will be the present value of costs and benefits. Table 11–1 demonstrates the sensitivity of the present value of benefit and cost totals to the interest rate. As higher interest rates are used, the present value decreases. Moreover, because, in many cases, costs are concentrated in the beginning of the period but benefits are either spread more evenly over time or predominate later in the project's life, the benefit-cost ratio is also sensitive to the choice of interest rate. The example in Table 11–1 gives hypothetical benefit and cost values for a project over an 11-year period. Initial costs of $20,000 are followed by much lower annual operating costs of $500. Benefits, however, gradually build from $1000 per year

TABLE 11-1   THE SENSITIVITY OF THE BENEFIT-COST RATIO

Year	Benefits	Costs
0	—	20,000
1	1,000	500
2	2,000	500
3	3,000	500
4	4,000	500
5	5,000	500
6	5,000	500
7	5,000	500
8	5,000	500
9	5,000	500
10	5,000	500
Total	40,000	25,000

Social Discount Rate	PVB	PVC	BCR
0	40,000.00	25,000.00	1.6
3	33,220.54	24,265.02	1.369
6	27,640.07	23,679.70	1.167
9	23,651.02	23,209,86	1.09
12	20,246.50	22,828.83	0.8868

to $5000 per year. The three columns below this benefit and cost listing portray the sensitivity of the benefit-cost ratio to the interest rate. In this example, a project efficient at a rate of 3 percent, or even 6 percent, turns inefficient between 9 and 12 percent. In general, more projects will become worthwhile as lower interest rates are used. Lower rates will also favor long-lived projects over short-lived ones. Accordingly, the selection of the interest rate or *social discount rate,* as it is commonly termed, is crucial because it may determine whether a project is deemed efficient or not.

Current practices by many federal agencies call for the use of discount rates that are considered too low by many economists. If this is a valid criticism, then the discount rates actually overstate the true social value of projects and may make inefficient or marginal projects appear worthwhile. The argument against using a social discount rate lower than the current market rate can be summarized as follows. Private markets represent an alternative use of the resources required by public projects.

Therefore, the return that resources are earning in private pursuits is the social opportunity cost of using resources in public undertakings. Accordingly, this private rate of return is the true opportunity cost of public investment and, hence, the relevant discount rate. This position would employ discount rates over twice the size of the ones used in many federal studies. The obvious result would be fewer projects yielding a benefit-cost ratio in excess of 1.

An opposing argument claims that private investment decisions account only for private benefits and costs. The result is market failure with respect to the allocation of investment funds yielding nonappropriable social benefits. Such social benefits include the value to the present generation of the resource legacy provided to future generations. Accordingly, this position argues that a rate below the prevailing private market rate is the appropriate social discount rate choice and will correct for private investment market failure.[1]

Comprehensive Measurement of Benefits and Costs

A further issue is, to repeat, the importance of making the benefit and cost measures as all-inclusive and as accurate as possible. This point needs to be stressed because it is central to the justification of public investments. In many instances, attempts to measure the full benefits of public investment encounter significant problems. A major difficulty is the absence of equivalent, or nearly equivalent, outputs or products in the private sector. Market prices cannot serve as measures of the benefits of many public outputs. Numerous ingenious attempts have been made to obtain benefit measures in such instances. Benefit-cost analysts must be wary of all the problems of evaluating public output discussed in Chapter 4, namely, the impossibility, or difficulty, of exclusion, the free rider aspect of public goods, and the subsequent effects on willingness to pay.

Even where similar private products and prices do exist, distortions in the structure and operation of private markets may imply that market prices are not true measures of the social value of the goods. Cost measures are subject to the same difficulties. Part 1 argued that many private production processes generate substantial external costs and, therefore, involve a misallocation of resources. If public investments involve the equivalent of external costs (that is, costs not included in the cost measures), then, by the same argument, benefit-cost analysis is guilty of the identical resource misallocation charges made against private

---

[1] It is important to note that economists are not in agreement on this issue and that many counterarguments exist. The Haveman [1969] reference at the end of this chapter provides a useful review of the various positions.

market processes characterized by externalities. That is, it may be responsible for exactly the same failures of the private markets that government programs purport to correct. Therefore, considerable effort must be made to identify and evaluate all the costs associated with public investment, inclusive of any external costs imposed by the project; that is, costs beyond the market costs for factor inputs, materials, and so on.

Abundant evidence exists that many conventional government policies and programs—highway construction, water resource development, nuclear energy production, public land policies, transportation regulations—fail to account for the full social costs of their effects. Environmental deterioration in the United States has been caused, in part, by government activities that ignore environmental costs. In Section C, we shall take up the important issue of how to improve government environmental performance by making certain that all foreseeable costs are accounted for before public programs are undertaken or policy decisions are made.

Income Distribution and Pricing

A final set of issues in benefit-cost analysis concerns the distribution of the benefits and costs of public investment. Thus far, we have treated the objective of benefit-cost analysis in terms of efficiency criteria only, that is, whether a public investment has a positive net return to the society. Implicit in the analysis has been the assumption that the dollar benefit and/or cost total is independent of the incidence of benefits or costs. Equivalently, the value of the project to society would not be altered if there were a change in the composition of the beneficiaries and/or those who pay the cost. This assumption says, in effect, that a dollar of benefits or costs is worth the same regardless of who receives or pays it and permits a comparison of total benefits and costs without having to be concerned with the identity and circumstances of those who benefit from the public investment and those who bear its costs.

If we admit, however, that the role of public investment may extend beyond efficiency criteria to include changes in income distribution, then the identity of those who benefit and those who pay becomes an important matter. If a more equitable income distribution is a social objective, benefits and costs could be assigned varying weights. The weights would be chosen to reflect the social worth of benefits and costs according to the identity of individuals receiving the benefits or paying the costs. Suppose, for example, that a project confers benefits of $10,000 on individuals with annual incomes in the upper 5 percent of the income distribution. If a government objective is a more egalitarian distribution of income, then $10,000 is not a true benefit measure but rather $W \times$

$10,000, where $W < 1.0$. The weight value W indicates a dollar's worth of benefits accruing to individuals in the upper reaches of the income distribution is not equivalent to a dollar's worth of social benefits. Rather, it is less than a dollar and exactly how much less depends on the value assigned to W. An equivalent argument could be applied to the cost side, weighing less those costs borne by wealthier segments of the society and weighing more those costs paid by low-income groups. The result of such weighting would be an entirely new benefit-cost ratio for any given project.

The idea of assigning varying weights to dollar benefits and costs has met heavy resistance from many economists. It requires benefit-cost analysts to identify precisely all the distributional impacts of public investment. A further and more considerable difficulty is the question of who determines the weights and by what process. The latter problems are likely to prove formidable in practice. Thus, the conclusion among many economists is that tax and direct income transfer programs rather than public investment should accomplish the income redistribution goals of the society.

A somewhat related issue concerns the determination of the price for public outputs. If the price of publicly provided goods is set at zero, for whatever reason, then all costs of the public good are paid via the incidence of the tax structure.

There are several valid reasons for pricing public goods at zero. In many situations, exclusion is either impossible or very costly. In addition, society often decides, on equity criteria, that some public goods should be equally available to everyone, or, at least, not allocated by price and willingness to pay, that is, not on the basis of the underlying income distribution. An alternative policy is to extend the role that price plays in private markets to situations involving public goods. Private markets are constantly allocating goods and services on the basis of price. Willingness to pay the market price determines who receives the product. Consequently, with rational behavior attributed to consumers, goods are allocated to those who value them the most. In those public good situations that lack a strong social judgment favoring equal availability and where exclusion is a practical possibility, an overt pricing policy may be desirable.

Assigning a price to public output serves several functions. First, the question of who pays for public goods is now answered precisely. The costs of the public good, in whole or in part, are paid by the individuals actually using the good or service rather than being widely distributed among users and nonusers alike through the incidence of the tax structure. In addition, equity considerations would seem to favor this solution in the sense that those who benefit from the good, public or private, bear the cost. Second, pricing public goods will yield a more efficient allocation of the available public output. Because demand curves slope downward, it should not be surprising that public goods available at zero prices are quickly depleted. Zero pricing leads to overuse, congestion, and quality deterioration if capacity is limited. Examples of public highways and free recreational facilities quickly come to mind. Pricing offers a means of reducing congestion costs and maintaining the quality of the public good by reducing the quantity demanded. At the same time, it provides a measure of demand at nonzero prices and avoids a tendency to over-expand public outputs on the basis of justifying the expansion by the size of the demand at the zero price!

Effluent charges can be reexamined in this broader context of the pricing of public goods. Effluents, or waste residuals, involve the use of a public resource, namely, the waste-absorbing services of the environment. We have argued that this use should be paid for by those responsible, instead of distributing the costs more generally throughout the society via the incidence of the externalities created by the pollutants or the tax costs of subsidizing pollution treatment. Effluent charges result in less use of the public good compared to a situation where the environment's assimilative capacity is available at a zero price. The outcome will be a more efficient allocation of resources.

Institutional Framework

Thus far, we have treated benefit-cost analysis as a scientific tool of social accounting that coldly and impartially evaluates alternative public projects and steers public funds to their most socially efficient use. It would be erroneous, however, to leave the impression that public expenditure decisions are actually reached by use of benefit-cost methodology. These decisions are deeply rooted in a complex political process. A brief description and evaluation of this process place the role of benefit-cost analysis in a considerably different perspective.

Public expenditure decisions are made in the determination of the annual federal budget. This budgetary process begins with a lengthy interchange of funding requests, arguments justifying these requests, and budget reviews among the Office of Management and Budget, the various governmental agencies, and the President and his staff. After these negotiations are completed to the President's satisfaction, a budget request is sent to Congress for actual funding. The outcome of this process reflects intense bargaining and pragmatic compromises among many competing agencies.

Congressional funding decisions involve further considerable political bargaining. Initially, the various subcommittees of the House

Appropriations Committee receive the relevant budget requests from the administration. The procedures of these subcommittees conventionally include public hearings, evaluations, and the actual writing of an appropriations bill for the particular funding area in question. The subcommittee bill is then sent to the Appropriations Committee where it may be adjusted before it is sent to the full House. At this stage, the full House may ask for further revisions before passing the bill and sending it to the Senate. In the Senate, a similar process is followed until the Senate passes its own version of an appropriations bill in each of the budget areas. House-Senate conferees adjust any differences between the two versions of the bills. This adjustment may involve significant changes in controversial areas and a return of the bill to each congressional body for substantial revision. Finally, the adjusted and passed bills are signed by the President and become law.[2]

It is obvious from this brief description that budget decisions are the end result of a long and involved political process. At every stage, the budgeting process is characterized by extensive political bargaining, feedback, and subsequent adjustment before the final appropriation of funds is made. Given our previous discussion, the obvious question arises: What is the role of benefit-cost analysis in this inherently political decision-making process? Unfortunately, the answer is that benefit-cost methods play relatively minor and isolated roles in actual appropriations decisions. Entrenched congressional traditions, the power of seniority in committee and subcommittee chairmanships, and the natural reluctance on the part of the Congress to relinquish control over such a crucial area as appropriations are formidable obstacles to the widespread use of benefit-cost techniques to direct public expenditures.

As noted in Chapter 4, in 1965, the Johnson administration made an attempt to institute a systematic evaluation of public expenditures throughout all government agencies—the Planning Programming Budgeting System, or PPBS. PPBS essentially involved the application of benefit-cost methods on a consistent basis for discretionary public expenditures in all federal agencies. PPBS foundered on the hard shores of political life in the nation's capitol. Congress refused to relinquish any of its powers over the budget decision-making process, and federal government bureaucratic agencies successfully resisted the threat to their operations posed by systematic benefit-cost evaluations. Thus, PPBS vanished from the scene in Washington almost as soon as it arrived. Benefit-cost methods are still used in the federal government to a limited

---

[2] Some theorists have characterized the process of government in terms of a behavioral theory in much the same manner that economists have used to portray the economic theory of markets. References are provided at the end of this chapter.

extent by the President's Office of Management and Budget, the Congressional Budget Office, and a few government agencies. On the whole, however, government expenditure decisions remain largely untouched by systematic evaluations of the actual value of the activities they fund.

C. IMPROVING GOVERNMENT ENVIRONMENTAL PERFORMANCE

Benefit-cost analysis provides the general framework for evaluating all potential public expenditures, and it can serve as the major vehicle of an active government policy to provide and protect environmental amenities. Carefully planned public investment decisions should not cause the same environmental problems often encountered in private markets. There is little question, however, that some actual or proposed public projects can cause adverse environmental impacts, often with the same intensity as private, profit-oriented market activities. The abortive Cross-Florida Canal project, the proposed Tocks Island Dam on the Delaware River, the SST, offshore oil-leasing policy, and lumbering and extractive activities in national forests are ready examples of government programs involving considerable harmful environmental consequences.

The National Environmental Policy Act

By passing the National Environmental Policy Act (NEPA), Congress made a major effort to incorporate environmental planning into the decision-making process of federal agencies. Section 102(C) of that act declared that "all agencies of the federal government shall

> (C) Include in every recommendation or report on proposals for legislation and other major Federal actions significantly affecting the quality of the human environment, a detailed statement by the responsible official on—
>   (i) The environmental impact of the proposed action,
>   (ii) Any adverse environmental effects which cannot be avoided should the proposal be implemented,
>   (iii) Alternatives to the proposed action,
>   (iv) The relationship between local short-term uses of man's environment and the maintenance and enhancement of long-term productivity, and
>   (v) Any irreversible and irretrievable commitments of resources which would be involved in the proposed action should it be implemented."

Accordingly, federal agencies are now responsible for evaluating the environmental effects of their programs. Prior to each significant federal government action, the agency must prepare an environmental impact statement that addresses the five requirements of Section 102(C). While the NEPA does not mandate a formal benefit-cost analysis, it embodies one of the essential elements of efficient resource allocation—namely, that the entire range of a public project's effects, inclusive of any environmental costs, should be considered before a decision is reached.

The law requires that a final environmental impact statement be submitted to the Council on Environmental Quality (CEQ) for evaluation after initial draft statements have been circulated and reviewed by other affected governmental agencies as well as by the public. The CEQ can recommend to the President that the proposed project be canceled or that certain additional modifications should be made in order to reduce adverse environmental effects. However, the main objective of the NEPA is not simply to require that federal agencies go through the motions of compiling an impact statement *after* a project has been designed or *after* a policy has been determined. Rather, it is to ensure that the planning process for all major decisions involves environmental concerns from the very start and that the project's final design or the ultimate policy decision embodies these concerns.

The NEPA became law in 1970, and there is now considerable evidence that it has been successful in integrating environmental planning into the process of federal decision making. Many projects and policies have been better designed to reduce or eliminate their environmental costs. In addition, a significant number of other federal actions entailing severe environmental effects have been canceled outright. As examples of these results, the NEPA has been credited with improving the design of the trans-Alaskan pipeline, removing environmentally vulnerable offshore oil tracts from leasing, prohibiting jet aircraft flight over certain national parks, causing questionable disposal sites for radioactive wastes to be abandoned, rerouting or eliminating proposed highway construction, and canceling certain Corps of Engineers water development projects.[3]

It is important to remember that in each of the above examples, actions proposed by *public agencies*, and not the profit-maximizing behavior of the private sector, would have led to environmental damages. The NEPA's important contribution is to provide an improved decision-making framework that forces agencies to account for (i.e., internalize) the formerly external environmental effects of their actions. Without the NEPA or similar legislation there is little reason, given the bureaucratic incentives of public agencies discussed in Chapter 4, to expect that

---

[3] For the details of these effects and others, see Council on Environmental Quality, *Sixth Annual Report*, Washington, D.C.: Government Printing Office, 1975.

federal officials would willingly provide a self-examination of their proposed activities and subsequently modify or even cancel their plans because of the adverse environmental effects of their programs.

Judicial Review

In Chapter 3 we evaluated the effectiveness of the common law as a means to internalize environmental costs and improve the allocation of resources. The primary purpose of the common law process is one of equity—to compensate for the damages created by one individual upon the other. Any ensuing resource allocation effect or general environmental quality improvement is essentially secondary to this equity objective. A legal mechanism more directly relevant to environmental concerns is the citizen suit against public agencies seeking judicial review of specific governmental decisions which affect environmental quality. The purpose of such suits by private individuals is to establish and enforce *public rights* to a clean environment and to ensure that government agency performance promotes the broad public interest. This type of litigation involves a branch of legal study known as *administrative law*.

National environmental policy is characterized by broad congressional decisions and the assignment of the necessary regulatory authority to various administrative agencies. The daily decisions of many federal agencies continually affect broad areas of environmental quality. For example, the Environmental Protection Agency suspends the automobile emission requirements of the Clean Air Act for one year; the Department of Transportation funds a federal highway construction project whose route is through an urban parkland; the Interstate Commerce Commission sets rail freight rates for scrap metals at higher levels than the equivalent rates for virgin ore; the Federal Power Commission grants a license for the construction of a hydroelectric facility on a scenic and recreationally valuable stretch of a major U.S. river; and the Departments of Agriculture and the Interior issue permits for the construction of a large-scale commercial recreation facility in a remote area of a national forest. In each of these decisions (and many others), private citizens and environmental groups have sued the government agency and asked the courts for relief: for an injunction to halt the impending construction, for a court order to remand the issue back to the agency and require it to consider environmental factors before reaching a decision, or for a court review of the procedure and evidence that led to the agency's decision and an evaluation of whether the decision is a reasonable one from the record of evidence or whether all the appropriate procedural steps were followed.

Traditionally, the private citizen's access to judicial review of administrative actions has been confined to three narrow areas. First, did the agency actually violate a law or a constitutional right or exceed its statutory authority? For environmental litigation, this approach often takes the form of searching for archaic, long-forgotten laws and applying their literal interpretation to modern environmental problems. The best example of this was the "discovery" in the late 1960s of the Rivers and Harbors Act of 1899 which categorically prohibited *any* discharge of wastes into *any* navigable river (or its tributaries) without obtaining a permit from the Corps of Engineers. Reincarnated by environmentalists and the government, the law was invoked against polluters. They argued that the act required a public agency—the Corps of Engineers—to solicit permits from all potential dischargers and evaluate the effects of the proposed discharge before a permit could be granted. Discovery of this law, ignored for over 60 years, quickly created massive confusion and the threat of litigation against the government for not carrying out its enforcement responsibilities. Congress felt compelled to enact superceding legislation regulating waste discharges into the nation's waters.

A further example of citizens suing public agencies for alleged violations of existing statutes involved a section of the U.S. Forest Service Organic and Administration Act of 1877 which prohibited the cutting of timber in national forests unless it was "dead, mature or old growth." A citizens group successfully invoked this law against the Department of Agriculture and brought all national forest timber sales to a halt in the area of the court's jurisdiction.[4] The underlying issue in this case was the general policy of public land management by government agencies, and this suit forced Congress to pass new legislation for timber management.[5]

However, not all suits alleging violations of law by public agencies depend on resurrecting old statutes. Much recent environmental litigation has centered on citizens groups claiming that various administrative decisions have violated the National Environmental Policy Act requirement of an environmental impact statement for any major federal action which significantly affects the quality of the environment.[6]

A second category of private litigation against government agencies concerns whether any procedural errors or omissions occurred while the administrative decision was being made. Here the issue centers on complying with any required procedure for making decisions rather than the merits of the decision itself—e.g., were public hearings held, did all interested parties have an opportunity to participate and to present

---

[4] Izaac Walton League v. Butz, U.S. Court of Appeals, Fourth Circuit, 1975.

[5] National Forest Management Act of 1976.

[6] For a comprehensive review of the case history in this area, see Chapters 12 and 13 of the Grad text listed in the Selected References.

evidence, etc.? However, in most cases this is not a fruitful approach to improving the performance of public agencies. Procedural form can be easily met, but the substance of the public hearing record can be ignored by the agency in its actual decision.[7] An example of this type of litigation concerned the classic case of Scenic Hudson Preservation Conference v. Federal Power Commission.[8] This long-debated issue involved the construction of a hydroelectric facility at Storm King on the Hudson River by the Consolidated Edison Company of New York. A construction license was granted by the FPC, and a citizens group sued, claiming the FPC had not, in compiling the public record for reaching its decision, considered the recreational effects of the project or the alternatives to it, as it was required to do by the Federal Power Act. The court found for the plaintiffs and remanded the issue back to the FPC with the instructions to hold new proceedings which would take these factors into account.[9]

Finally, as a third cause for citizen action, any agency decision can be set aside by the courts if it is found to be "arbitrary, capricious and an abuse of discretion" or if the decision is "unsupported by substantial evidence."[10] However, it is extremely difficult for plaintiffs to make a legal case that a decision was essentially made on a whim, and the courts have been reluctant to substitute their judgment on the merits from the given evidence for that of the administrative agency.[11] Complex

[7] See, e.g., D. A. Bronstein, "The AEC Decision-Making Process and the Environment: A Case Study of the Calvert Cliffs Nuclear Power Plant," Ecology Law Quarterly (Fall 1971), and A. B. Ferguson and W. P. Bryson, "Mineral King: A Case Study in Forest Service Decision Making," Ecology Law Quarterly (Summer 1972).

[8] U.S. Court of Appeals, Second Circuit, 1965.

[9] The court said, "In this case, as in many others, the Commission has claimed to be the representative of the public interest. This role does not permit it to act as an umpire blandly calling balls and strikes for adversaries appearing before it; the right of the public must receive active and affirmative protection at the hands of the Commission. This court cannot and should not attempt to substitute its judgment for that of the Commission. But we must decide whether the Commission has correctly discharged its duties, including the proper fulfillment of its planning function in deciding that the 'licensing of the project would be in the overall public interest.' The Commission must see to it that the record is complete. The Commission has an affirmative duty to inquire into and consider all revelant facts."

[10] Administrative Procedure Act of 1966, Section 706.

[11] For example, in a case of a citizen suit against the Atomic Energy Commission (now the Nuclear Regulatory Agency) seeking an injunction against the commission's decision to burn the gas in a cavity created by a nuclear exposion, the court said, "All that is required to establish reasonableness of the decision setting a standard under the statutory directive to protect the public health and safety is that it be made carefully in light of the best of available scientific knowledge. Absolute certainty is neither required nor possible. The law provides a strong presumption of validity and regularity when administrative officials decide weighty issues within the specific area of their authority and the burden is on the plaintiffs to overcome this presumption" (Crowther v. Seaborg, District Court of Colorado, 1970). See the preceding footnote where another court also said that it did not want to substitute its judgment for that of the administrative agency.

legal questions of law versus fact are involved here, and the scope for judicial review by private citizens seeking improved environmental protection by public agencies via these two areas is somewhat limited.

Nevertheless, the existence and frequent use of judicial review by private citizens is an important vehicle to improve administrative performance. It serves as a watchdog to ensure that public agencies do not redistribute the public resources which they are supposed to manage in the public's interest for narrower, private purposes—a frequent criticism of government regulatory performance.

In addition, recent developments in administrative law have made the use of judicial review even more effective. Since 1970, the courts have significantly liberalized the rule of "standing"—i.e., who has the right to bring suit for judicial review. This has had important implications for environmental litigation. All that is now necessary to establish standing is for the potential plaintiff to show that he has suffered "an injury in fact" and that he is "arguably within the zone of interest" protected by the law in question.[12] Moreover, the alleged injury need not be economic, and the Supreme Court has recently suggested that any potential harm to a citizen's interest in environmental quality confers standing to seek a review of administrative decisions.[13]

Some legal scholars have argued that an even further broadening of judicial review is necessary in order to free private litigants completely from the circuitous route of seeking procedural flaws, "discovering" old laws in new clothing, and the difficulties of proving irrational or unsubstantiated decisions. Rather, what is required is legislation that allows citizens to go immediately and directly to the merits of governmental decisions on environmental issues.[14]

---

[12] The number of environmental statutes is now very large and offers legal access to judicial review in all important areas of environmental concern.

[13] Sierra Club v. Morton, U.S. Supreme Court, 1972. This case involved a suit against the Secretary of the Interior for granting a permit to Walt Disney Productions to construct a recreational facility in the Sequoia National Forest in California. The Sierra Club did not claim any injury—economic or otherwise—to its members, and the court ruled that it did not have standing. It did say, however, that if injury was alleged, standing would be granted. As an indication of the breadth of the new interpretations on standing, an even more recent Supreme Court decision affirmed that a citizens group had standing in its action to enjoin a railroad freight rate increase granted by the Interstate Commerce Commission that adversely affected the costs of shipping scrap materials. The plaintiffs claimed that they were harmed by having to pay more for finished products, that local recreational resources used by group members—forests, rivers, mountains—were adversely affected by the increased rates, that the quality of air, which they breathed, was deteriorated, and that the higher rates also caused them to pay higher taxes because potentially recyclable resources were disposed of as wastes and thereby imposed additional waste handling costs on public authorities (U.S. v. SCRAP, U.S. Supreme Court, 1973).

[14] For a comprehensive treatment of the argument on which this discussion is based, see Joseph L. Sax, "The Public Trust Doctrine in Natural Resource Law: Effective Judicial Intervention," *Michigan Law Review*, 68 (1970).

The basis of this position is an extension of the common law doctrine of public trust to environmental resources. The idea of public trust is that the property rights to important environmental resources—air quality, water quality, public lands—reside in the public and that the government and its agencies simply act as trustees for the public. Accordingly, as in the private common law, any property owner—the public—can sue the government if he believes that the current management of these resources is not in the public's (i.e., the owner's) interest. Encroachment on public resources would be warranted only if it can be clearly demonstrated that the overall public interest is best served by allowing any deteriorating use. The owners of public resources have access to the courts to prevent any infringement of their property just as in the private law remedies discussed in Chapter 3.

Advocates of the public trust doctrine argue that it removes environmental issues from the bureaucratic pitfalls inherent in the administrative and regulatory functions of government agencies where decisions that affect the environment must be made in an atmosphere that requires a balancing of the interests of the agency's constituents, a consideration of the potential impact on next year's budget, and a continual awareness of the decision's effect on the agency's general self-interest.[15] As a result of such factors, critics claim that administrative decisions often damage the very interests the agency is purported to protect. The frequent use of the public trust doctrine would make government agencies much more responsive to the general public interest by providing for a judicial review on the merits—and not merely on the form—of important decisions which affect the environment. It would also make legislators more reluctant to allow the considerable discretion which currently exists for agency action in administering laws.

Reliance on a public trust approach would require new legislation to establish public rights in environmental resources and specifically permit individuals to sue for the protection of these rights. Michigan now has a comprehensive Environmental Protection Act—drafted by Joseph L. Sax, a public trust advocate—which provides the right of private citizens to seek injunctive relief from the actions of any public agency which damages the environment.[16] Several other states have recently

15 For a case study of such pressure, see R. W. Findley, "The Planning of a Corps of Engineers Reservoir Project: Law, Economics and Politics," *Ecology Law Quarterly* (Winter 1973).

16 Environmental Protection Act of 1970, Public Act 127, Section 2(1) states, "The attorney general, any political subdivision of the state, any instrumentality or agency of the state or of a political subdivision thereof, any person, partnership, corporation, association, organization or other legal entity may maintain an action in the circuit court having jurisdiction where the alleged violation occurred or is likely to occur for declaratory and equitable relief against the state, any political subdivision thereof, any instrumentality or agency of the state or of a political subdivision thereof, any person, partnership, corporation, association, organization or other legal entity for the protection of the air, water and other natural resources and the public trust therein from pollution, impairment or destruction."

passed similar laws based on the Michigan act. In addition, both the federal Clean Air Act of 1970 and the Water Pollution Control Act of 1972 allow private litigants to sue individual polluters for violating these acts or the Environmental Protection Agency for not enforcing them.

Problems with Judicial Review

As the preceding section makes clear, the process of judicial review has significant economic benefits. It also involves some significant costs. The courts are already burdened with a heavy work load of litigation. If they are faced with a rush of environmental cases, this work load could become overwhelming. Judges do not always make better decisions than bureaucratic administrators under the best of circumstances; if they lack the time for a careful review of environmental cases before them, the possibility of bad decisions becomes more likely. Congress could, of course, vote more resources for the courts to solve this problem, but the court system is expensive. More money for more judges and other resources for the courts involves significant opportunity costs for society.

An even more fundamental problem with the judicial review process is that it threatens costly delay of worthwhile government programs. Citizen suits with several appeals to higher levels of the judiciary can take years to resolve. Even if such suits fail in the courts, they can succeed in prohibiting government agencies from carrying out intended projects. If all government decisions potentially affecting the environment were to be challenged by citizen suits, government would be paralyzed (and the court system could collapse under an excessive work load). This extreme possibility will probably never come to pass. The threat of excessive litigation will likely force the Congress to do a better job in avoiding the extremely vague guidelines it has given in the past to administrators making decisions affecting the environment.

D. PUBLIC LAND POLICY

Throughout its history, the United States has had extensive public ownership of land. The apex of federal land holdings occurred in 1850, when an estimated 1.2 billion acres were under federal control. Even in 1971, there were over 400 million acres of federal land in the 49 states, excluding Alaska, amounting to 21 percent of the total land area. If Alaska is added, the total rises to 760 million acres or almost 33 percent of the land area of the entire 50 states. Within the contiguous 48 states, most federal lands are located in the western states, and, in 11 western states, federal lands constitute 47 percent of the total land area. State and local governments also own and administer large amounts of land.

Public lands range from extensive holdings of forests, unique natural sites, grazing areas, and offshore water rights to the land sites of federal buildings in major urban centers. Despite the concentration of public lands in western states, every state contains some federal land. Moreover, the ownership and administration of this land is spread among numerous agencies. The National Park Service, the Bureau of Land Management, the Bureau of Reclamation, the Department of Agriculture, the military services, and the Forest Service are some of the agencies having important jurisdiction over public lands.

To a large extent, the vast federal land holdings of the early years of the United States were not the result of an overt policy to retain land in public ownership. Rather, the enormous land areas annexed by the westward expansion, in combination with the small population of the country, placed the new lands into federal ownership by default. Federal land policy, throughout the nineteenth century, was primarily concerned with the disposal of the public lands. The effects of this policy are reflected in the decline in public land acreage reported above, although this decline bottomed by 1930 and federal land holdings have been essentially stable since then.

The disposal of public lands during the last century took a number of forms. Probably the best-known method was the homestead land grants to settlers. In addition, public lands were sold outright, given to states, and, at times, granted to private enterprises, as, for example, the extensive land grants to railroads. Gradually, in the last years of the nineteenth century and then with more force in the twentieth century, a concern developed over this single-purpose policy of disposal of the public lands. As a result, disposal was gradually replaced with a policy commitment to retain the remaining public lands in federal ownership. One of the major reasons behind this change in policy stemmed from the private uses of the disposed public land and the aftereffects of these uses on the land itself—timber cutting, grazing, and mineral extraction. The Taylor Grazing Act of 1934 replaced disposal as the dominant policy for public lands with a policy of reserving the lands in public status.

The public lands of today have many users. Although the actual sale and, hence, the outright transfer of the property rights of the land have ceased to be the prevailing policy, public lands are still used for private profit. This is accomplished by leasing the land to private individuals or business for various purposes. The primary private uses of public lands are for timber harvest, livestock grazing, and mineral extraction. Individuals and businesses purchase leases of public lands, in most cases at competitive market prices, and these leases are the exact equivalent of a lease in the private market. The government leases the property rights in the public lands for specific purposes, for stated time periods, and for certain conditions of use. In return, the government receives the revenues of the leases of public lands. In recent years, this revenue has totaled over $300 million annually. In leasing public lands for private purposes, the government is effectively acting as a supplier of factor inputs. If the prices of the leases of the public lands are determined by competitive bidding, they will equal the value of the lands in private markets.

Another major use of public land is outdoor recreation. The enormous popularity of the national park and forest system is an obvious example. We have previously discussed the dimensions of this popularity and the economic implications of the burgeoning demand for public lands for recreation. In many situations, the use of public land for recreational purposes may compete with the private uses described above. Another point worth recalling is that recreational uses of public land are often offered at zero or nominal prices. Thus, unlike a situation of competitive bidding for private leases of public lands, there is no direct, obvious measure of the value of public lands in their recreational uses.

Alternative uses of public lands do not present a land management problem until the uses begin to conflict with each other. When both the private and public demands for lands were low relative to their availability, they could be met without major problems. This situation may have characterized the public lands through the first quarter of this century. However, over the last several decades, the booming recreational uses of public land increasingly have come in conflict with private uses. Moreover, as noted in Chapter 8, conflicts are not necessarily confined to the obvious recreational or conservation versus private uses but also occur among recreational uses (for example, developed versus wilderness camping or, more generally, maintaining wilderness areas compared to their development for popular recreation activities). Under such conditions, public land management becomes a much more crucial problem and requires increasing direction from economic analysis. Obviously, a desirable policy objective is to establish efficient land practices within any individual type of land use and to encourage the development of land management practices that accommodate several diverse uses on the same land area (for example, timber harvest and recreation and watershed).

Our primary concern, however, is directed to the problem of evaluating conflicting uses of public lands. Frequent controversies have developed between environmental interests, concerned with the orderly protection of public lands, and the proponents of certain public land management policies such as clear cutting of timber in national forests, the location of the Alaskan pipeline through public lands, the lease of offshore drilling rights, and the use of public lands for livestock forage. We can expect public land policy increasingly to be confronted with the task of resolving competing demands. It is precisely this type of problem that can be treated in a benefit-cost framework.

For example, consider a benefit-cost analysis of a realistic situation involving a conflict between use of a certain tract of public land for mineral extraction and use as a recreational site. Let us assume the land has only these two mutually exclusive uses. In benefit-cost terms, an obvious measure of the benefits of using the land for mineral production would be given by either the value of the bids by private producers for the lease rights to the public land or, if the bidding is not competitive, by the value of equivalent privately owned land in mineral production. Such benefits would be measured over the time period of the lease and discounted at an appropriate interest rate. The cost measure, however, unlike the conventional treatment of costs discussed in Section A for ordinary government expenditure programs, would attempt to reflect the social value of the lost recreational opportunities and environmental amenities. In other words, the relevant cost measure is the *opportunity costs* of using the public land for timber and mineral production (the cost in terms of the foregone recreational and amenity values). An interesting aspect of treating the question of public land use in this framework is that the cost measure would not necessarily be confined to the time period of the lease. In the context of our example, suppose mineral extraction rights are leased for 5 years. The costs of using the land for mineral production, however, would be the opportunity costs of the foregone recreational values for the same 5 years *only* if recreation could resume in the sixth year as if the mineral extraction had not occurred. If this is not the case, then the costs should be measured for the time period over which recreational opportunities are lost, and this may be considerably longer than the 5-year mineral lease.[17]

Benefit-cost analysis can proceed after recognizing the necessity of the adjustment. The obvious requirement is to measure the value of the foregone recreational and environmental amenities over the appropriate time period. We have already discussed some of the difficulties of obtaining such measures in Chapter 8. Nevertheless, given necessary care, the cost measures, once developed, would be discounted and the benefit-cost ratio calculated. Studies following the outline of this hypothetical example can contribute significantly toward improving the efficiency of public land policies. An excellent example of this type of benefit-cost application is the Hells Canyon case in Idaho. The controversy centers

---

[17] Of course, any perceived increase in the value of mineral production (and hence the value of mineral land) should be built into the estimated stream of benefits to the extent this may not be reflected in the price of the lease. We also assume that the addition or deletion of the mineral production will not appreciably affect the industry price of the particular ore in question (that is, the production from this land area is small compared to the total production).

on whether the Snake River should be impounded for electrical power or whether the area is to be retained in a wilderness state for recreational and amenity values. An ingenious and sophisticated benefit-cost study of this problem has estimated the critical values necessary to assign to recreational use in order to justify preserving Hells Canyon in its undeveloped state.[18]

In summary, we can expect the pressures of population and economic growth to increase demands for use of the public lands. Although land policy can attempt to devise technically sophisticated ways to accommodate various demands on the same land, it will also increasingly be confronted with the difficult issue of choosing among competing uses of public land. To this end, benefit-cost analysis is a useful tool for improving the economic efficiency of these inevitable public land allocation decisions. It provides the means to express the value of outdoor recreational and environmental amenities and to justify the preservation and protection of public lands. In the absence of a benefit-cost framework, achievement of this protection might be considerably more difficult because the comparision would be reduced to emotional appeals *to preserve the national heritage* versus the dollar values of public resources leased to private interests or developed as public power sources.

E. SUMMARY AND CONCLUSIONS

The issue of the efficient utilization of society's resources spans both the private and public sectors. Unfortunately, government investment faces the identical resource allocation problems of private markets. Benefit-cost analysis is a general method of social accounting designed to evaluate the efficiency aspects of public expenditures. Given care and thoroughness of measurement, it can help to allocate public funds efficiently among alternative outlets.

A number of difficult theoretical issues confront the benefit-cost practitioner. The choice of the discount rate directly influences the calculation of the benefit-cost ratio. Current federal practices employ discount rates considerably below private market interest rates. This discrepancy has generated significant controversy among economists. One position, arguing in favor of higher discount rates, claims that private market interest rates provide the correct measure of the opportunity cost of public investment. Alternatively, other economists argue that market rates do not reflect the social gains and costs of investment decisions. The result is private investment failure with respect to pro-

---

[18] See the Fisher et al. reference in the Selected References.

viding nonappropriable benefits for future generations. This position calls for social discount rates below market rates.

A further issue is the determination of the prices of public output. Many public projects are characterized by exclusion difficulties. Others involve a social consensus that the benefits should be equally available to all. In both of these situations, a zero or nominal price policy is usually followed in allocating the public output. However, for projects where neither condition holds, increased use of an overt pricing policy offers significant efficiency gains in the form of protection of the quality of the available public output. It also can provide much-needed information to improve benefit estimates by revealing the actual willingness to pay of the beneficiaries of public output.

Institutional obstacles pose significant practical problems to the effective use of benefit-cost analysis. Although Congress is cognizant of benefit-cost studies, other criteria than allocational efficiency heavily influence the appropriations process. Additional resistance to systematic benefit-cost analysis also stems directly from agencies fearful of resulting budget reductions.

Many traditional government expenditure programs and regulatory policies have adverse environmental effects. Congress enacted the National Environmental Policy Act to ensure that environmental factors are accounted for in federal policies. Judicial review of governmental decisions is another means of inducing public agencies to be responsive to public environmental values.

Benefit-cost analysis can usefully be applied to the problem of allocating federal lands among alternative uses. The environmental consequences of public land policies can be incorporated into opportunity cost measures in evaluating commercial uses of these land resources. This extension of the benefit-cost framework to environmental quality issues promises to remove environmental protection projects from the weak defensive position that relies on appeals to *save our heritage*. At the same time, it should reduce the number of conventional public production programs that generate severe environmental disruptions.

QUESTIONS FOR DISCUSSION

1. Do you think that the problems inherent in benefit-cost analysis are more serious for environmental programs than for government programs in other areas, for example, defense, transportation, and education?

2. Some economists have argued that much of the benefits from public

investments in environmental resources are received *now* by people who are made better off by the knowledge that their grandchildren will benefit from the availability of such resources. Does this argument make any sense to you? What is its relevance to the determination of the social discount rate in benefit-cost analysis?

3. Hydroelectric projects are justified by externalities on the benefit side of benefit-cost analysis. Could such projects also involve some externalities on the cost side? Explain how any externalities should be treated in computing the benefit-cost ratio.

4. What efficiency and equity problems may arise as a result of the effective enforcement of the National Environmental Policy Act?

5. Consider a Department of Transportation decision to construct a highway through scenic countryside. Using the public trust doctrine, a local conservation organization sues to enjoin the construction of the highway. Is there any difficulty in saying that the environmental group's values represent the public interest? Suppose a local automobile club claims its members want the highway built?

SELECTED REFERENCES

ANDERSON, F. R., *NEPA in the Courts: A Legal Analysis of the National Environmental Policy Act.* Baltimore: The Johns Hopkins Press, 1973. A comprehensive treatment of the early legal experience with the NEPA.

BARDACH, E., and L. PUGLIARESI, "The Environmental-Impact Statement vs. the Real World," *The Public Interest,* No. 49 (Fall 1977). A description of the ongoing, daily difficulties of the NEPA.

BUCHANAN, J. M., and G. TULLOCK, *The Calculus of Consent.* Ann Arbor: University of Michigan Press, 1962. A presentation of developments in theories of government behavior.

CLAWSON, M., "Public and Private Interest in Public Lands," in *Land Use Policy and Problems in the United States,* C. W. Ottoson, ed. Lincoln: University of Nebraska Press, 1963. A summary of the economic aspects of public land issues. The volume also provides a series of further readings in public land policies.

Council on Environmental Quality, *102 Monitor.* Washington, D.C.: Government Printing Office. A monthly publication summarizing environmental impact statements received by the council in response to NEPA requirements.

FISHER, A. C., J. V. KRUTILLA, and C. J. CICCHETTI, "The Economics of Environmental Preservation: A Theoretical and Empirical Analysis," *American Economic Review,* LXII, No. 4 (September 1972). A technical analysis of preservation arguments in the context of the Hells Canyon case demonstrating that preservation values may exceed the development values for the proposed hydroelectric project. Advanced.

GRAD, F. P., *Environmental Law.* New York: Matthew Bender, Inc., 1971, 1973, 1975. An excellent treatment of environmental litigation, including a comprehensive review of the legal development of the NEPA.

HAVEMAN, R. H., "The Opportunity Cost of Displaced Private Spending and the Social Discount Rate," *Water Resources Research,* V, No. 5 (October 1969). A brief but thorough summary of the discount rate issue.

HAVEMAN, R. H., *The Economics of the Public Sector,* 2nd Edition. New York: John Wiley & Sons Inc., 1976. An introductory treatment of federal participation in economic affairs; particularly relevant are Chapters 6, 7, and 8.

McKEAN, R., "The Unseen Hand in Government," *American Economic Review,* LV, No. 3 (June 1965). Presents a competition argument in the context of a theory of government.

MISHAN, E. J., *Cost-Benefit Analysis, An Introduction.* New York: Praeger Publishers, Inc., 1971. A comprehensive treatment of the issues of cost-benefit analysis.

Natural Resources Journal, 16, No. 2 (April 1976). An entire issue of articles devoted to an examination of the NEPA.

SAX, J. L., *Defending the Environment.* New York: Alfred A. Knopf, Inc., 1971. Argues for reliance on the public trust doctrine and the courts rather than administrative agencies to protect environmental interests. Very readable.

SAX, J. L., and J. F. DiMENTO, "Environmental Citizen Suits: Three Years' Experience Under the Michigan Environmental Protection Act," *Ecology Law Quarterly,* 4, No. 1 (1974). An analysis of actual experience under the public trust legal approach of the Michigan law.

U.S. Joint Economic Committee, *Economic Analysis of Public Investment Decisions: Interest Rate Policy and Discount Analysis,* 90th Congress, 2nd Session. Washington, D.C.: Government Printing Office, 1968. Public hearing proceedings of discount rate policy providing coverage of the major discount rate positions.

U.S. Joint Economic Committee, *The Analysis and Evaluation of Public Expenditures: The PPB System,* Vols. I–III, Washington, D.C.: Government Printing Office, 1969. Previously cited in Chapter 4, these volumes contain discussions of a number of benefit-cost issues and descriptions of the problems and progress of the PPB System.

WEISBROD, B., "Concepts of Benefits and Costs," in *Problems in Public Expenditure Analysis,* S. B. Chase, ed. Washington, D.C.: The Brookings Institution, 1964. Discusses the idea of weighting benefits and costs by varying amounts according to their incidence.

V

Population,
Economic Growth
and
Environmental Quality

12

POPULATION LEVELS AND ENVIRONMENTAL QUALITY

This chapter discusses the role of the *level* of population in determining environmental quality. The relationship between population level and environmental quality may appear to be all too obvious to many readers who associate the densely populated city directly with the air and water pollution problems and with the disamenities that they observe every day. In the United States and most other economically developed countries, however, the environmental problems of densely populated urbanized areas cannot legitimately be attributed to *general* overpopulation. Crowded conditions in individual American cities coexist today with a general abundance of living space per capita by international standards. In fact, the urbanization and concentration of population in the United States have been matched by the depopulation of rural expanses in the Midwest and in other areas of the country. Many environmental problems are more severe in the United States than in India, for example, but the latter country is much more crowded and at the same time much less urbanized.

Environmental problems associated with urbanization are not, of course, completely independent of the overall level of population. If the U.S. population had grown less rapidly in the past, our cities today would be smaller and, perhaps, also less crowded, and the localized air and water pollution problems of urban areas might be somewhat less severe. On the whole, however, it seems appropriate to defer, as much as possible, the analysis of the environmental problems that result specifically from urbanization and population density to Chapter 13. In this chapter, we shall confine our attention to environmental problems that are the direct consequence of high levels of population per se.

Government policies affecting population growth involve many vital socioeconomic issues beyond that of environmental quality. For example, achievement of a lower population growth rate through a reduction in the birth rate would mean that our society would have fewer children to educate in the future and that pressures on public school budgets would ease. More resources could then be devoted to improving the quality of education or to other alternative uses. On the other hand, lower birth rates have another consequence that many people would not welcome—a population with a higher average age. This chapter will ignore such important issues in order to focus on the single, narrow issue of the relationship between population level and environmental quality. We also shall not discuss the complex moral issues involved in the use of various birth control techniques and legal abortions that are the major instruments of modern population policies. These moral issues may well be of overriding importance in determining the shape of future national population policies, but they are beyond the scope of our subject.

The chapter is organized as follows: Section A briefly reviews some important demographic facts to establish the necessary statistical background for population levels and trends, both in the United States and in the rest of the world. Section B then summarizes current economic thinking about the complex relationship between population levels and various aspects of environmental quality. Section C outlines a simple economic theory of fertility, and Section D utilizes this theory to specify the policy variables available to governments interested in influencing population growth rates. A final Section E summarizes the main points of the chapter.

A. POPULATION GROWTH IN PERSPECTIVE

The Basic Demographic Variables

The net population growth rate (PGR) of any society during any time period is equal to the algebraic sum of the excess of the birth rate (BR)

over the mortality rate (MR) and the net immigration rate (IR). In symbols,

$$PGR = (BR - MR) + IR,$$

where all rates are customarily measured as the number of births, deaths, and net immigrants per thousand of the existing population. IR can be negative, of course, if emigration exceeds immigration, and PGR can be negative if $MR > BR + IR$. The algebraic difference between BR and MR is called the *rate of natural increase*. For the world as a whole, migration results only in the redistribution of a given population among different countries, and the rate of world population growth is therefore equal to the world rate of natural increase.

Demographers distinguish between the concept natural *fecundity*, a biological measure of maximum potential reproduction, and *fertility*, the actual reproduction of a species. The fertility of man is everywhere less than natural fecundity, even in societies that have available no effective contraceptive devices. Through various methods, societies have been able to exercise at least crude control over their fertility. Fertility varies with the state of economic and cultural development of societies and involves much more than the biological nature of man. The number of births in a period of time as short as a year reflects the number of women of childbearing age at that time and other transitory and random factors as well. Demographers, therefore, regard the (crude) birth rate—the number of live births per thousand of the total population in a society—as only the simplest measure of fertility. More comprehensive measures of fertility average the short-term influences on the crude birth rate and are calculated whenever sufficiently detailed data are available.

Mortality rates in the United States and other economically developed societies are now very low, about ten per thousand of population per year, reflecting a slow and steady decline in the last few decades. Mortality rates appear to be approaching a temporary biological limit in these countries, pending scientific breakthroughs in the treatment of degenerative diseases. Mortality rates in the majority of the less-developed countries have fallen dramatically in recent decades but are still far above the levels in more advanced countries. Crude mortality rates as well as crude birth rates may reflect the age distribution of the population and temporary or random factors, and age-adjusted mortality rates can be calculated to average the short-run influences of the age distribution on the crude rate.

International migration, once a major factor in redistributing world population, has become less and less important in the twentieth century, as all economically developed countries have acted to restrict the potential influx of immigrants from poor, overpopulated countries. Immigration into the United States was sharply limited just after World War I and continues today at a relatively low level. This is true at least for legal immigration; illegal immigration is reportedly very large, but reliable statistics are not available. Within just the last 50 years or so, the remaining empty habitable lands on earth have vanished, and it now is clear that human population problems must be dealt with directly by national population policies.

The tremendous growth in world population, beginning just two or three centuries ago, and accelerating in the last half century, is the result of the growing control by man over mortality at younger ages without a corresponding control over his fertility. To appreciate the environmental consequences of continued population growth at past and present rates, it is necessary to go beyond such a qualitative generalization and to review some relevant quantitative trends.

Population Developments in the United States

The population of the United States at the beginning of 1977 was 216 million. This figure compares with less than 4 million counted in the census of 1790, some 50 million in the 1880 census, and 106 million in the 1920 census. Table 12-1 shows data on the components of U.S. population growth for quinquennial averages between 1935 and 1974. Note that net population growth rates in this country have varied widely between the average 1.72 percent per year in the late 1950s to the average 0.82 percent per year in the late 1930s and the average 0.86 per-

TABLE 12-1 THE COMPONENTS OF U.S. POPULATION
GROWTH, 1935–1974 (rates per 1000 of the
midyear population)

Annual Average	Population Growth Rate	Birth Rate	Mortality Rate	Net Immigration Rate
1935–1939	8.2	18.8	11.0	0.4
1940–1944	11.4	21.2	10.8	0.8
1945–1949	15.7	24.1	10.1	1.6
1950–1954	17.1	24.8	9.5	1.8
1955–1959	17.2	24.8	9.4	1.8
1960–1964	15.1	22.6	9.4	2.0
1965–1969	10.9	18.2	9.5	2.2
1970–1974	8.6	16.3	9.4	1.7

Source: United States Census Bureau.

cent in the early 1970s. The low birth rates in the 1930s are generally attributed in part to the extraordinary economic conditions during the Great Depression. The depressed economic circumstances during the decade were especially burdensome on young workers without secure careers and encouraged young married couples either to limit the size of their families or to postpone having children. In contrast to the 1930s are the high birth rates of the late 1940s and 1950s, the period of the so-called baby boom. Since 1958, birth rates have once again declined steadily to levels even below those of the depression. As the data in Table 12–1 make clear, the major difference between the net population growth rates of the country in the 1950s and the 1970s was due to differences in birth rates, as the mortality and net immigration rates remained relatively stable.

With given assumptions about future mortality and migration experience, census projections of the U.S. population vary widely with different plausible assumptions about fertility rates. The range between the projections based on extreme high and low fertility assumptions is large even by the end of the century—between 283 million and 246 million. By the year 2020, the range widens from 362 million to 252 million. Two conclusions can be drawn from these projections: (1) In the immediate future, population in the United States will continue to grow steadily, barring a nuclear war or some other catastrophe of similar magnitude. Even if fertility rates stabilized permanently at the level consistent with zero population growth over the long run, the population of the country would grow by some 20 percent by the year 2000 due to the age distribution of the present population. (2) Over the long run, relatively small differences in fertility rates will result in large differences in the population of our country.

The fall in the crude birth rate in the United States in the 1960s and 1970s has led some observers to project optimistically a leveling off of our population. A past history of erratic and unpredictable fertility behavior makes most demographers more cautious. One important factor explaining the fall in birth rates after 1958 has been the relatively low number of women of childbearing age, especially during the first half of the 1960s. This demographic circumstance was the result of the low birth rates during the economically depressed 1930s—a so-called echo effect. A second factor has been a tendency toward later marriage and the postponement of children by young married couples who intend eventually to have children. This development was due in part to economic difficulties resulting from the Vietnam War, such as the adverse effect of the draft on the employment prospects of young males. A third factor is a real decrease, of some unknown degree, in the *true* fertility rate. The advent of low-cost, reliable contraceptives in the 1960s has made it possible for couples to plan more effectively both the timing and the total number of births. The sum of these three factors is clearly evident in actual birth rate data, but it is impossible to disentangle the effects sufficiently to be sure of the relative importance of the last two.

Until recently, surveys of the family plans of young couples found that the expected number of children per completed family was, on average, about three. This level was significantly lower than that for older couples, but was still high enough to produce steady projected growth in the country's population. Given the relatively large number of women who are of childbearing age in the 1970s, the direct consequence of the baby boom of the late 1940s and early 1950s, the realization of these family plans would have resulted in a sharp increase in the birth rate and a corresponding resurgence in net population growth. But the most recent evidence indicates that both *actual* and *expected* fertility dropped sharply in the early 1970s to levels consistent with and even below, zero population growth. These latest developments are grounds for optimism about a gradual, painless solution to population stability in our society. But we have no conclusive evidence in hand yet that fertility will permanently decline to a level consistent with eventual zero population growth under normal, peacetime, economically prosperous conditions.

Population Developments in the World

The population of the world stood at over 3.5 billion as of 1970. Estimates of world population going back more than a century are little more than inspired guesses, but it seems likely that no more than half a billion human beings lived on earth at the beginning of the seventeenth century. Just one century ago, the world population was probably only about 1 billion. By the year 2000, world population will reach close to 7 billion, again assuming no nuclear war or some comparable catastrophe. Thus, man is today behaving as if in response to the Biblical injunction to multiply and cover the earth. The population problems of the United States, the richest and one of the least crowded of nations, are trivial in comparison to those of much of the rest of the world.

Population growth in the United States and in other countries that are now at a relatively high stage of economic development resulted from initial sustained economic advances. Economic progress set off a complicated chain of events leading to declines first in mortality rates and then, after some time lag, to declines in fertility rates. In contrast, less-developed countries today have benefited from the importation of modern health techniques from the more-developed countries and have been able to reduce their mortality rates without any prior industrial breakthrough leading to sustained economic growth. Because of this dif-

TABLE 12–2   WORLD POPULATION GROWTH RATES,
1970–1975 (rates per 1000 of the population)

Area	Rate of Natural Increase	Crude Birth Rate	Mortality Rate
World, total	18.8	32.4	13.6
More-developed areas	10.1	18.7	8.6
Less-developed areas	22.5	38.2	15.7
South Asia	25.3	40.8	15.5
Europe	6.2	16.3	10.1
U.S.S.R.	11.9	19.0	7.1
Africa	25.6	45.1	19.5
Northern America	13.2	22.6	9.4
Latin America	29.1	38.2	9.1

Source: United Nations Department of Economic and Social Affairs.

ference in the time sequence of economic growth and demographic change, we cannot predict with confidence that fertility rates in less-developed countries will follow the pattern of developed countries and decline substantially in the near future.

Table 12–2 gives estimates of rates of natural increase for different areas in the world for the period 1970–1975. The figures in this table show that the rate of natural increase in less-developed countries, 22.5 per thousand, was more than double the rate in developed countries, 10.1 per thousand. The disparity in population growth rates was due to the high birth rates in the less-developed countries, which more than offset the lower mortality rates in the developed countries.[1] The world rate of natural increase is close to 2 percent a year; at this rate, world population will double every 35 to 40 years. Demographers believe that the population of the world will reach at least 8 billion before leveling off.

Table 12–3 gives estimates of the population of selected countries in the years 1920, 1950, and 1980. The clear implication of these estimates and the comparative rates of natural increase in Table 12–2 is that the combined population of the United States and other developed countries will be a much smaller fraction of the world total in the future than now or in the past. Most of the projected 7 billion human beings in the world by the end of this century will live in countries in which the

[1] The low mortality rate shown for Latin America was due to the highly skewed age distribution of that continent. The crude mortality rate reflects the very young average age of the population, but age-specific mortality rates in Latin America are much higher than in developed countries.

TABLE 12–3   POPULATION ESTIMATES OF SELECTED COUNTRIES: 1920, 1950, 1980 (population in thousands)

Country	1920	1950	1980
Mainland China	475,000	560,000	843,000
Japan	55,391	82 900	111,064
India	250,500	359,250	682,300
France	38,750	41,736	53,250
Italy	37,006	46,603	56,400
United Kingdom	43,718	50,616	57,250
Norway	2,635	3,265	4,250
South Africa	6,842	12,447	26,800
United Arab Republic	13,277	20,448	46,750
Israel	480	1,258	3,141
United States	106,782	152,271	240,893
Brazil	27,554	52,328	123,716
Mexico	14,500	25,826	70,581
Australia-New Zealand	6,641	10,127	18,237

Source: United Nations Department of Economic and Social Affairs.

demand for rapid economic growth dominates most other concerns. The significance of this trend is that it will not be sufficient just to double total world output levels in order to meet the demands of an expanding world population. In Chapter 14 we shall take up the environmental implications of this point.

B. POPULATION LEVELS AND ENVIRONMENTAL QUALITY

This section attempts to specify the relationship between the level of population in a society (or in the whole world) and the quality of its environment. The important policy question is to what extent a lower population growth rate in the future would ease the various threats now evident to specific environmental resources. In other words, should birth control be a weapon in the government's arsenal of antipollution measures, together with effluent charges, regulation, and direct government provision of environmental resources? If so, how important should its role be, relative to these alternative measures? The reader should remember that the following discussion concentrates on population *levels* and thus abstracts from the largely separate issue of population *concentration* in urbanized areas, which is the main topic of the next chapter. Finally, our discussion of the relationship of population level to environmental quality is most directly applicable to an advanced economy such as the United States. Population growth in less-developed countries involves somewhat different issues, which we postpone for the time being.

Growth of Population and National Output

The most obvious consequence of population growth in any society is that more babies today mean more potential workers in the next generation. That is, the higher the fertility rate in a society, the higher will be the rate of growth of its potential labor force. Growth of the labor force, combined with growth in the supply of other productive factors and with improvements in technology, result in a sustained rate of growth in the level of output of an economy. But, as observed throughout the book, levels of the flow of pollutants have been a function of levels of output. Thus, growth in population levels is most directly related to deterioration of environmental quality via the link between population growth and labor supply and the relationship of labor supply to the level of output and pollution in an economy.

The quantitative importance of population growth as a factor affecting environmental quality depends on the importance of labor force growth relative to other factors that determine the rate of growth of output. Economists have attempeted to explain statistically how much labor force growth and other factors each contribute independently to the total growth rate of ouput. After adjusting for growth in the capital stock, including both physical capital such as plant and equipment and human capital of education and training embodied in workers, surprisingly little economic growth remains to be explained by growth in labor force and population—perhaps one-fourth to one-third of the average 3 to 4 percent annual growth rate in total output. Similar studies done for other advanced economies appear to be consistent with this basic conclusion.[2] Thus, this method of estimation implies that population growth by itself is responsible for only a small fraction of the total growth rate of output or of the growth rate of effluent emissions in developed economies.

Noneconomists have approached this problem from a different perspective. They have attempted to factor the growth of specific effluents into the separate effects of population growth and all other factors. Such disaggregated studies are valuable because they show how population policies contribute to changes in the composition, as well as to the total

---

[2] The authoritative source on the determinants of economic growth is Edward F. Denison, *Why Growth Rates Differ* (Washington, D.C.: The Brookings Institution, 1967). See also his *Accounting for United States Economic Growth 1929–1969* (Washington, D.C.: The Brookings Institution, 1974).

level, of effluents. For example, growth in human wastes is certainly more directly related to population growth than is the total level of effluents.

Studies done from this perspective yield different conclusions, however, about the relative importance of population growth as a factor in determining effluent levels. Barry Commoner, who has done some of this work, has concluded that only between 12 and 20 percent of the total change in his various *environmental impact* indices is due to population growth. For example, he reported that after adjusting for the effects of technological change and changes in per capita output, the independent effect of population growth could account for only about 20 percent of the environmental impact of synthetic pesticides between 1950 and 1967. Paul Ehrlich and his coworkers have disputed the work of Commoner and claim to be able to show a much more important role for population growth in causing the growth of effluent levels.[3] Their results are based on the notion that the impact of total consumption of some good or resource can be factored into growth of the per capita consumption level and growth in the consuming population. This methodology appears to make the implicit assumption that growth of output and effluents is proportional to growth of population. But as we have seen, such an assumption is clearly refuted by the evidence. Population growth appears to be responsible for only a fraction of growth in total effluent levels in this and other developed economies.

The implications of the above discussion for environmental quality are quite strightforward. If population growth were stabilized by a permanent drop in fertility, the growth rate of total output would fall, eventually to perhaps 75 percent of the rate that would occur under the continuation of past fertility rates. This conclusion assumes that advanced economies such as the United States could adapt their economic and social institutions successfully to a zero population growth rate situation. With a slower growth rate of output, pollution problems would be correspondingly less severe, other things equal. Of course, the above analysis is not limited to restraining population growth alone but applies equally well to *any* measure that inhibits economic growth. Population control is unique, however, in that it is the only one of the set of growth-inhibiting policies that will not, in the long run, effect the growth rate of per capita output and consumption. Expectations of improvements in per capita economic well-being are deeply ingrained in the culture of economically developed societies in the world today, and it seems most unlikely that explicit sacrifices of consumption per capita will receive much popular

---

[3] For a debate between Commoner and Ehrlich on the relative importance of the population factor in explaining environmental problems and related issues, see *Environment*, XIV, No. 3 (April 1972).

backing for the sake of the modern conservation cause. But a zero population growth rate policy does have the attraction of promising to lower
output and effluent growth rates without a corresponding reduction in
anticipated per capita consumption standards.

The discussion thus far has implicitly taken all other policies affecting the environment as given. But our analysis implies that a population
policy is both a potential substitute and a potential complement of
alternative environmental policy measures, such as effluent charges, that
deal with environmental problems directly. Economists are generally
biased in favor of specific solutions to specific problems. That is, if environmental pollution is caused fundamentally by failure to take into
account external costs of production and consumption, then the straightforward solution to this problem is to take into account those externalities
directly through a system of explicit charges for the use of environmental
resources. In contrast, attempting to solve the problem indirectly by
limiting population growth seems a clumsy, inefficient alternative. In
this connection, the reader should note again that population growth
per se is a relatively modest factor in contributing to the growth rate of
output and, therefore, to growth in the level of emissions of pollutants.

The case of the automobile and its attendant environmental problems provides a good example of the contrast between population policies
and alternative environmental measures. Some writers take the present
ratio of motor vehicles to people in the United States (approximately
one motor vehicle to every two people) as given and project the horrible
prospect of perhaps 25 to 100 million more vehicles on the roads in
the next century. Society can avert such a development by use of
the blunt instrument of population control to control the denominator
(people) of this ratio. But the government can also work on the numerator (vehicles) by more direct policies. For example, higher excise taxes
on the sales of automobiles will raise their price and reduce their consumption. So will regulations requiring expensive air pollution controls,
an alternative that directly alleviates the worst environmental consequences of mass automobile consumption. Higher tolls on highways and
more reliance on mass transit in congested urban areas are other direct
environmental measures that are alternatives to population control. All
of these measures get directly at the root of the externalities associated
with automobiles in contrast to reliance on the birth control solution to
the problem.

As noted in the introduction to this section, our analysis is most applicable in the context of developed economies, in which consumption
levels are already relatively high and the process of sustained economic
growth leading to ever higher per capita consumption levels is well established. All the developed countries taken together account for less than

one-third of the present total world population, and this fraction is expected to decline to about one-sixth by the year 2000. Paradoxically, it is population growth in the relatively sparsely populated, developed economies that poses the immediate threat to the *world* environment. This is the case because less than one-third of the world population, in the relatively well-off countries of Europe, North America, and Japan, accounts for more than five-sixths of the consumption of available world resources, including the waste-absorbing services of the earth's waters, land, and atmosphere for various effluents.

Ironically, then, the immense problems of population growth in poor countries are for the present largely localized (economically, if not politically), but the the much less serious population problems of the affluent countries may contribute significantly to world environmental problems. Some polluting activities of developed countries may seriously hinder the development possibilities of poor countries. If water pollution destroys the world fisheries, for example, the less-developed nations will lose an important potential source of inexpensive calorie and protein supply. This could change if the less-developed countries of today perform the miracle of surmounting all their problems and succeed in achieving an economic breakthrough to Western per capita consumption standards. In solving their own domestic economic problems, however, they would likely join the ranks of developed countries as major sources of the despoilment of the earth's environment. We shall return to this problem in Chapter 14.

Population Growth and Unique Natural Resources

Let us return to the context of economically developed societies and consider a distinct, less obvious consequence of population growth for the quality of the environment. An ominous threat to environmental quality, broadly conceived, in the United States is the overutilization of certain scarce, unique resources. These resources include the small areas of the earth that are ocean beaches, mountain lakes, and other natural facilities ideally suited for recreational purposes. Other closely related examples are the even fewer sites of surpassing natural beauty, such as the Grand Canyon or San Francisco Bay. In addition, a few remaining wilderness areas are unique resources in that they shelter rare species whose survival depends on the preservation of their natural habitats free of the intrusion of human beings. These resources are unique because they have no good substitutes and they cannot be augmented or replaced if ever they are destroyed, however advanced the level of technology.

Unfortunately, many of the most precious unique resources in the United States are increasingly threatened by the *combination* of population growth and rising per capita income levels. Only a decade or two ago, places such as Glacier Park were the preserves of a small, wealthy elite. Today they are visited by a much larger cross section of our larger and wealthier population. Crowding of these natural resources occurs because every year a larger population with a higher per capita income level seeks to share their benefits. But the essential characteristics of these resources are such that crowding threatens to destroy their fragile ecosystems and to degrade their quality to the point where their consumption value will fall to zero for all potential consumers. Note that this kind of crowding is quite distinct from the crowding that occurs as a consequence of urbanization. Even if we could miraculously end the current degree of urbanization in the United States and spread our population evenly throughout the hinterlands, the problem of crowding in unique sites would remain as long as population growth and the spread of affluence continue to make such sites available to ever larger numbers of pleasure seekers.

Population and affluence have already reached levels in the United States to produce crowding that threatens specific unique natural resources. Ocean beaches near large metropolitan areas are highly congested on sunny, weekend days to the point that the net pleasure of many sunbathers and surfers is moot. As Casey Stengel once observed about a popular restaurant, "It's so crowded that nobody goes there anymore." Yellowstone Park and Yosemite Canyon are fit at times only for people who enjoy bumper-to-bumper traffic and a Coney Island atmosphere. Similar population *cum* wealth pressures face the few remaining wilderness areas in this country. The very term *wilderness area* loses all meaning when the rate of utilization reaches high levels during peak tourist seasons that threaten disastrous results to fragile ecosystems. The progressive deterorioration of some of the most beautiful natural resources in the United States has occurred at a frightening pace in the last two or three decades. Projections of population and income growth rates through the end of this century point to a pessimistic conclusion about the possibility of preserving the quality of these resources.

In many instances, such unique natural resources can be rationed effectively by charging a high enough entrance fee or user charge. Unfortunately, fees and charges may be expensive to administer because of the problem of enforcing exclusion. In addition, it may be politically objectionable on distributional grounds to ration these resources. What politician would care to defend the denial of entry to beaches and national parks to poor children? Another means of rationing these resources would be to limit access to them by not allowing automobiles to approach closer than, say, 10 miles from the entrance to parks and beaches. Or visitors may be limited to the *capacity* of a site on a first-come, first-serve basis. It is not obvious whether such rationing schemes are fairer than a system of rationing by money prices. In any case, no rationing scheme is a panacea for the basic problem. Again, population control is both a substitute and a complement to more direct environmental policies.

C. AN ECONOMIC THEORY OF FERTILITY

Population growth is the sum of natural increase—the excess of births over deaths—and of net immigration. Government policies that would attempt to manipulate mortality in order to control population are, of course, unthinkable. As of this date in history, it is also unrealistic to expect that further restrictions on legal immigration into the United States will significantly affect population growth. Immigration into the United States has already been reduced by restrictive legislation to low levels. The current level of immigration today is far below what would be necessary to meet the demands for entry, and any further cutback in immigration levels faces persuasive humanitarian and economic objections. Furthermore, as already noted, migration between nation states can no longer be an important factor in solving the *world* population problem. Thus, bv a process of elimination, only birth control remains as a realistic vehicle for government intervention in the process of population growth.

Variables Affecting Fertility

The point of departure in an economic theory of fertility is the presumption that the number of children born to families reflects a considerable degree of rational choice by the parents. The empirical basis for this presumption is the fact that everywhere in the civilized world, but especially in more economically developed societies, fertility is considerably less than fecundity. The presumption of rationality does not deny that a great many births are the result of irrationality or of accident, but it does assert that, on average, fertile couples tend to have close to the number of children they desire to have. We shall attempt to outline a theoretical framework within which rational family planning decisions take place.

Following the pioneer in this field, Professor Gary Becker, we can conceive of a couple's demand for children as being a demand for a unique type of consumer durable good. (We admit that any profession that thinks of the desire for children in this framework deserves to be called the *dismal science*.) That is, we shall consider the desire to have children in the same analytical framework used to analyze a family's decision to buy a durable good such as an automobile, a stereo set, or a washing machine. In common with these other consumer durables, children presumably are expected, before their acquisition, to make the consumers—their parents—better off or happier over an extended period of time in the future. This expected happiness may derive from a pure love of children, or from a desire to propagate the race, or from the need to assert masculinity or femininity, or in order to acquire symbols of maturity and respectability, or from any other motive, however noble or base. To use the terminology of economics, we say that children are expected to yield a flow of *consumption services* to their parents over time, much like the consumption services expected from other consumer durables. Some parents, especially in less-developed societies, may also expect their children eventually to help support them in their old age, and if this is the case, these direct income support payments should be added to the expected value of the consumption services of children to obtain the total benefits of children. All or some of these benefits may involve a great deal of uncertainty, but such uncertainty is a feature shared by all consumer durables that are supposed to yield net benefits to the owner over an extended period of time into the future.

Most couples expect the benefits of children to be large enough to justify "acquiring" a limited number of them.[4] But just as most people buy only one or two automobiles, most couples have less than the maximum number of children they could have. It is a straightforward economic problem to explain why people limit their purchases of automobiles; in brief, limited incomes force families to ration their purchases of automobiles and of *all* desired consumer goods and services. By analogous reasoning, couples must limit their purchases of children. Families have limited incomes, and the bearing and raising of children involve considerable costs. A rational couple will have one more child only if the present value of the expected lifetime stream of benefits from the child exceeds the present value of the expected lifetime stream of costs of the child.[5] The additional cost incurred in having another child may best be thought of as an opportunity cost—the automobiles, stereos, trips to Europe, and so on that a couple must forego once it chooses

---

[4] To be more precise, the theory refers only to the *demand* for children, or the number of children couples desire to have. Some couples are unable to have as many children as they desire.

[5] To be formally correct, only the prices of the goods and services a couple buys for the support of a child are fixed in the market. The quantities of these goods and services actually purchased by the couple are subject to its discretion. Thus, the cost of the child (the sum of all prices $\times$ quantities) is a variable, subject to some control by the family. A given family can choose to purchase large quantities of goods and services for its child, thus producing a "high-quality" child, and another family can skimp on its child and end up with a "low-quality" product. The obvious analogy here is the choice between a Cadillac and a Chevrolet; a higher level of expenditure presumably yields a better product.

On the plausible ground that families in a given socioeconomic class have virtually no discretion over the "quality" of child they must raise once the child is born, we shall assume for simplicity that the cost of a child is fixed for any given couple. This assumption implies that families do not choose, for example, between having either two high-quality children or three low-quality children. It also implies that they do not choose between having either a high-quality child or a low-quality child *and* a more expensive automobile.

to have the child. According to this theory, all couples continually make joint decisions on their consumption of children and their purchases of all substitute and complementary goods and services in their total lifetime budget.

From this brief outline of the economic approach to the theory of fertility, we can hypothesize that the significant forces determining the number of children demanded by a couple are (1) its tastes for children, (2) family income, and (3) the costs of children *relative to* the prices of alternative goods and services in the family budget.

Tastes for children vary from couple to couple, but it is evident that a meaningful, if somewhat vague, norm is determined by various social pressures operative within a given socioeconomic class. For example, young, highly educated professionals today tend to choose to have one or two children if they want children at all, and couples with larger families are becoming increasingly rare. The norm varies considerably, of course, across different socioeconomic groups.

Family income, defined to include both current and expected future incomes, sets the limit or budget constraint to all lifetime consumption expenditures by any family, including its expenditures on children. Families with high lifetime incomes can afford to have more children than poorer families, just as they can afford to purchase more of every good and service. This pure income effect on fertility is very weak, however, and is generally more than offset by factors such as education level and birth control knowledge that are highly correlated with income.

The cost of a child relative to the prices of alternative goods and services affects the allocation of any given income between children and all alternative forms of consumption. A fundamental theorem of microeconomics says that, given tastes and incomes, an increase in the relative cost of children will cause couples to have less children and to shift their expenditure toward more of the now relatively cheaper alternatives in order to maximize their economic well-being. The crucial empirical issue is the elasticity, or quantitative sensitivity, of this relative price response. That is, if the relative cost of children rises by 10 percent, will the number of children demanded by all families fall by 20, 10, or perhaps only 0.001 percent? Economists and demographers have as yet reached no consensus on this elasticity parameter. The answer to this question may be crucial to the eventual success of population control policies.

The Costs of Having Children

To return our discussion closer to the realm of practical policy applications, let us now consider, concretely, the costs of children. The total cost of a child includes both *upkeep costs* and *human capital costs*.

Upkeep costs include expenditures on food, clothing, medical care, and other necessities for the child. Human capital costs, on the other hand, involve outlays on such items as schooling, private music lessons, and summer camp. The difference between the two kinds of costs rests on the usual economic distinction between current and capital expenditures. Upkeep expenditures are those necessary to maintain life for the child at some socially determined acceptable level, but human capital expenditures are intended to enhance the *value* of the child by bringing him up to the norm level of some socioeconomic class. It is largely by means of such human capital investment in children that the upper middle classes in this country are able to pass on their advantageous positions in society to their offspring.

To measure the relative cost of children, the economist ideally should have available current measures of the cost of children and a corresponding index of the prices of the closest substitutes for children. Such data are not available, but it seems reasonable to assume that the two most important variables in the determination of the relative cost of children are the job opportunities available to women with and without children and the relative cost of education.

A significant cost of children for most families today is the opportunity cost of the foregone earnings of the wife who must leave the labor market once she becomes a mother. The decision to have a child means the loss of valuable continuity and experience in a career and places the mother at a severe competitive disadvantage on the job market, relative both to men and to women without children. In addition, women tend to move either when they marry or when their husband moves to a new job. These two factors, reinforced by sex discrimination, result in low wages and poor career opportunities available to women. If job opportunities for most women are relatively poor, it follows that the opportunity cost of having children is relatively low in terms of the foregone earnings of married women.

If the recent movement in the United States to end sex discrimination is successful, the opportunity cost of having children will rise directly with the improvement in the relative wage rates and career opportunities of women. Reinforcing this purely economic factor, of course, will be the changed attitude of women toward their appropriate roles in society, including their roles as mothers and housewives. Any government program that successfully reduces the impact of sex discrimination, therefore, should tend to decrease fertility rates in the future. On the other hand, if the women's movement is successful in its demand for government provision of free, or highly subsidized, child day care facilities, the result may be to encourage higher fertility rates. With child care centers available, new mothers would no longer have to forego labor market attachment to care for their children, and the opportunity costs of having children would largely disappear. Thus, the net effect of greater sexual equality, on balance, may turn out to be either significantly pro- or antinatal.

In the United States, elementary and secondary education is provided "free" by the government in the form of compulsory public schooling up to varying ages, but usually extending to about age 16 in urbanized areas. For the middle classes, however, education through 4 years of college has now become virtually a felt necessity, and a large fraction of total college costs is borne directly by the student and his parents. The relative cost of education has apparently been rising over time in the United States, presumably because of the failure of educational institutions and other service industries to achieve productivity gains comparable to those experienced in manufacturing industries. The increase in the relative cost of education has been most evident in the rapid rise in college tuitions in the United States since World War II. Elementary and secondary school costs have also risen sharply, but these costs are somewhat masked because they are financed largely by local property taxation within individual school districts in most areas of the country.

An economic theory of fertility predicts that the rising relative cost of education should decrease the number of children demanded, provided that the increased relative cost is fully reflected in the budgets of individual families. In most communities, increased educational costs are reflected in higher property taxes that vary only with the real estate value of a family's house, not directly with the number of children it sends to the local schools. Nonetheless, a mechanism does exist that, in an imperfect way, makes a couple take somewhat into account the incremental educational costs of a child. A childless couple might be able to escape high real estate taxes by living in a community with poor schools. If it decides to have a first child, it can then move to a community with a good school system and incur the additional property taxes required to support the better schools. This mechanism works imperfectly, however, because of the great inequalities in average income and wealth levels across school districts and because the psychic and pecuniary costs of moving are high relative to the benefits for many people.

The mechanism also is imperfect because it works only for the first child. If a family decides to have its first child and consequently accepts the higher tax costs of a community with good public schools, this tax cost remains invariant to the number of *additional* children it may choose to have. The decision to have a second, or higher-order, child will not, in general, be influenced by the consideration of any additional public education tax costs, because its tax liability is determined solely by the value of the real estate it owns. In other words, no mechanism exists that makes families pay the additional or marginal costs of educating an extra child and, therefore, the rising relative cost of elementary and secondary education has probably had little effect on the number of children demanded in the post-World War II United States.

The example of education is representative of the more general phenomenon that the total social marginal costs of children exceed the private marginal costs of children for the individual family. The federal personal income tax provides a modest direct subsidy for children through the personal exemption granted the taxpayer for each dependent child. The effect of the children's exemption is to shift some of the costs of children from the individual family to the general taxpaying public. Another subsidy for children in the personal income tax allows the deduction of child care expenses for some working mothers. In addition, child expenses for poor, and near-poor, families are heavily subsidized by federal, state, and local governments through welfare programs providing free school lunches and other goods and services and through various other welfare programs providing cash support varying directly with the number of children. Children from families at all income levels are provided free, or below-cost, recreational services by governments and by civic groups in local communities throughout the country. Some communities also provide subsidized medical, transportation, and other kinds of services specifically for children. All such subsidies reflect the healthy tradition in this country of broad social responsibility for the proper care and education of children. They have the unintended side effect, however, of reducing the marginal cost of additional children for the individual couple to well below the total social marginal cost per child and, therefore, are clearly pronatal.

Even if all such subsidies were ended immediately, however, the private marginal cost of a child could still be below the total social marginal cost, because each additional child involves external costs to society in the form of more crowding. (Some people make the parallel argument that there are significant external benefits to society from more children.) No individual family will rationally take into account the additional environmental problems for society that results from its decision to have one more child. Even if a couple is fully aware of the effects of population growth on the environment, it knows that its child has a negligible effect on the total population, and it also knows that the family planning decisions of all other families are not affected by its own decision. The aggregation of all families acting according to such individually rational considerations could result in a rate of population growth that may make everyone in society worse off. Thus a *perfectly contraceptive* society, in which no undesired children are born, should not be confused with a society that enjoys optimal population growth, in which the marginal social costs of children, including all external costs, are equal to the marginal social benefits.

D. POPULATION POLICIES

The analysis of the previous section suggests that governments desiring to control population growth can attempt to manipulate one of three variables: (1) tastes for children, (2) family incomes, or (3) the relative cost of children.

Any attempt by the government to influence tastes for children would encounter strong opposition in the United States today as being unwarranted propaganda and interference in what have traditionally been private family concerns. To avert such criticism, the federal government thus far has tended to limit itself to advocacy of the concept of *family planning,* the notion that each family should be helped to have exactly the number of children that it desires. Family planning does not necessarily mean moving in the direction of lower fertility. If every couple should be able to achieve its family plans, then the government should logically help otherwise childless couples to find some means of having children, perhaps by subsidizing expensive research in the problems of sterility. At this time it seems unlikely that the government would go much further than to endorse family planning in attempting to reduce fertility. Indeed, the bitter, unresolved controversy over legalized abortion illustrates the depth of feeling in this country over the full implementation of a family planning policy.

A second strategy theoretically open to the government in controlling fertility is to limit the growth rate of family incomes. As noted in the previous section, however, virtually no public support yet exists for a policy of zero, or even of slower, economic growth. Furthermore, the income effect on fertility is probably very small. The one variable that apparently remains as a realistic possibility for government manipulation is the relative cost of children.

The policy implication of the preceding discussion seems to be that if the government wants to reduce fertility, it should end all subsidies directly or indirectly reducing the individual family's cost of bearing and raising children. It could even levy a child excise tax on parents (perhaps only on the third and higher order children) to force them to take into account the full social costs of children in making their family planning decisions. Such a policy would explicitly treat the third- and higher-order children in a family as if they involved the same spillover costs for society as industrial effluents. To complete the analogy, an effluent charge would be required to achieve a socially desirable allocation of resources.

Professor Kenneth Boulding has suggested an ingenious solution to population control that carries the idea outlined above to its logical end. To stabilize population, he would have the government issue marketable licenses for children. In one version of his scheme, each mature female would be given, say, 2.11 child certificates. The government would demand a full certicate from each mother at the birth of a child. (Woe to the mother of triplets!) Any woman who had 2 or less children could sell her unused certificates on the market for such licenses to women who desired 3 or more children. The forces of supply and demand would establish the price of licenses at any time. Thus, people who wanted to have more children than the number consistent with zero population growth could have them as long as they were willing and able to pay the market price. Such a scheme is certainly a logical extension of Becker's conception of children as consumer durable goods. Unfortunately, Boulding does not address himself to the critical issue of how to enforce his plan. That is, what does the government do when a woman has a child without being able to pay for the necessary licenses in the market? The answer to this question is crucial for the workability of his scheme, but Boulding only notes in passing that its implementation would require some kind of income grants to the poor.[6]

Even if such a proposal ever overcame its political problems, more fundamental humanitarian concerns would still persist. Any program intended to punish overly fertile parents involves the likelihood of punishing the children instead. A child excise tax or a child license scheme would reduce the spendable income of the family and force it to reduce its total consumption, but this reduction is all too likely to come at the expense of the children. The circumstance that poor families in the United States tend to have relatively large numbers of children further aggravates the problem. Poor families with many children find it difficult today to provide sufficient food and other necessities for their children even with the aid of child subsidies. The only possible evasion of this difficulty is for the government to guarantee a minimum standard of consumption for all children. Such a guarantee could be enforced either by requiring parents to prove that they provide the standard level of child support, perhaps at the cost of depriving themselves of necessities, or by taking children away from their parents and providing direct government support in institutions or through a foster-parent type of arrangement. Such drastic steps are unacceptable in the United States today, even to advocates of strict population control policies. Such currently unthinkable government interference in the most intimate of family matters would gain political support only if population problems become much more severe than they are today.

At the present time, population policy in the United States em-

---

[6] See Kenneth E. Boulding, *The Meaning of the 20th Century* (New York: Colophon Books, Harper & Row, Publishers, 1956), Chap. VI.

braces much more limited programs. The federal government has only recently given tentative approval to a limited program of aid to family planning—a euphemism for birth control. In an attempt to minimize political opposition, such aid is rationalized on the basis of the traditional liberal dogma that each family should be able to implement its own plans for the number and spacing of its children. In keeping with this rationale, government programs go no further than to provide basic sex education information, including information about birth control techniques. These programs are not supposed to coerce couples to limit the size of their families. Optimistic supporters of present family planning program nonetheless expect great benefits in the form of sharp fertility reductions in return for the very low outlays currently in the government budget. According to some estimates, about 10 percent of all children born in the United States are unwanted by their parents. Similar programs have been undertaken in some foreign countries, sometimes with limited American aid, but it is still premature to assess the general success of such programs in reducing fertility rates over the long run.

One country in which government population policies have had notable success, however, is Japan, which has greatly reduced its high pre-World War II fertility. Japan's success has been due in part to provision of cheap, legal abortions upon demand, a step that has just gained limited grudging acceptance in this country. But fertility reduction in Japan may also be due to widespread public acceptance for the need for population reduction in an overcrowded country with pollution problems that, in some areas, dwarf those of the United States. It should be noted in this connection that despite its unprecedented achievement of a radical reduction in birth rates, Japan expects its population to grow from a level of about 100 million in 1970 to over 120 million by the year 2000. In contrast to Japan, the population problems of the United States today appear to be relatively minor.

In conclusion, the prospects for population stabilization in the United States are most promising as of this date. Fertility rates have already fallen below (perhaps only temporarily) the zero population growth rate level of 2.11 children per mature woman. In any event, the population growth rate is at a very low level relative to the past and relative to other societies today, and population growth does not appear to be one of our society's most pressing problems. Fertility rates have been volatile and unpredictable in the past and circumstances may change for the worse in the future, but if they do government population policies can adapt to the new situation. Thus, demands for more drastic population control measures for the purposes of environmental policy make little sense today. Slower rates of population growth do produce some environmental benefits, but, as we have noted in this section, measures to reduce fertility also involve substantial social costs and equity problems. Most important of all, for our topic in this book, there exist many good alternative policies that can substitute for population policies to alleviate environmental pollution.

E. SUMMARY AND CONCLUSIONS

The net population growth rate of any society is the sum of its rate of natural increase—the excess of its birth rate over its mortality rate— and the rate of net immigration. Of the three components of population growth, the largest changes in the United States in recent times have occurred in the birth rate. The crucial variable in determining United States population growth in the future will probably be the fertility rate —a measure of the birth rate that averages out the transitory factors affecting births in any short period of time.

Population growth in the United States is currently less than 1 percent a year, a very low rate relative to past experience and relative to most other societies in the world today. The net growth rate fell steadily in the late 1960s and early 1970s after the end of the baby boom of the immediate postwar period. The most recent evidence available on fertility developments suggests that our society may be approaching a state of zero population growth, but it is still too soon to make any firm predictions about long-run population trends under normal economic and social circumstances. Population growth in other developed countries is comparable to U.S. experience, but growth rates in the majority of less-developed countries are much higher, reflecting high fertility and progress in reducing mortality. Thus, population growth problems are relatively minor, or even negligible, in the developed economies with widespread environmental concerns.

The environmental consequences of population growth must be distinguished from the problems of population crowding in urban areas, although the two are, of course, somewhat related. Postponing the problems of urbanization until Chapter 13, we note that the remaining environmental problems of population growth are (1) the impetus given to total economic growth by population growth through growth in the labor force and (2) the crowding and eventual degradation of unique natural resources, especially sites of great, but fragile, natural beauty. Both these problems involve the interaction of increases in income and output levels with a growing population. Population control is a substitute and a complement to other environmental policies, such as effluent charges, directed at the solution of these problems.

Possible government intervention to control and stabilize population can best be investigated within the framework of an economic theory of fertility. Such a theory emphasizes the role of rational choice of family size by a couple, given its tastes for children, its family income, and its perceived private cost of additional children. Various circumstances in our society combine to make the private marginal cost of an additional child to its parents diverge from its marginal social costs, including all the eventual negative effects of higher population levels on environmental quality. Because additional children involve external costs to society, the aggregation of individual family decisions does not necessarily lead to an optimum rate of population growth, even if all private costs of children were borne by the parents.

Present government programs in this country to control fertility so far have stressed only the elimination of unwanted births through the dissemination of modern birth control techniques. Although such a limited family planning policy does not guarantee success in the long run for population stabilization, present fertility developments are promising as of this date. Unless fertility rates unexpectedly turn upward again in the future, the United States may be fortunate enough to be able to achieve population stability without resorting to more drastic alternative policies toward population control.

QUESTIONS FOR DISCUSSION

1. Many writers on population problems have made the point that population growth must end someday because the available space on earth is finite. How relevant is this point for current U.S. population policies? (Suggestion: Look up population density estimates for different developed countries in some recent years.)

2. Suppose that the level of emissions of a particular pollutant rises from E_0 in year 0 to E_t after t years. During the same time period, population grows from N_0 to N_t. Also assume that per capita emission levels remain constant; that is, $E_0/N_0 = E_t/N_t$. Is this information sufficient to conclude that growth in population explains the growth in pollution emissions? Explain.

3. Human wastes may be assumed to vary proportionally with population. Does it follow that birth control is the best environmental policy to deal with pollution due to human wastes? Explain.

4. Is optimal population growth equivalent to zero population growth? Would either result if family planning policies successfully achieve a perfectly contraceptive society?

5. Suppose that Congress enacted a Boulding child license scheme and at the same time enacted a generous negative income tax program providing substantial cash transfers to all poor families? Would the negative income tax program offset the intended effects of Boulding's plan on fertility rates? Explain.

SELECTED REFERENCES

BECKER, GARY S., "An Economic Analysis of Fertility," in *Demographic and Economic Change in Developed Countries*, Universities—National Bureau for Economic Research. Princeton, N.J.: Princeton University Press, 1960. A pioneering article in expounding the economic theory of fertility. This same volume includes other outstanding articles on various aspects of demography.

COALE, ANSLEY, J., "Man and His Environment," *Science*, 170 (October 9, 1970). A lucid statement by an eminent demographer of the view that population is a negligible factor affecting environmental problems.

EHRLICH, PAUL R., and JOHN P. HOLDREN, "Impact of Population Growth," *Science*, 171 (March 26, 1971). Argues that population growth causes a disproportionate impact on the environment. Intended as an answer to the Coale article cited above.

ENKE, S., "Population Growth and Economic Growth," *The Public Interest*, No. 32 (Summer 1973). A summary discussion of the trade-off issues.

FISHER, ANTHONY C., "Population and Environmental Quality," *Public Policy*, XIX, No. 1 (Winter 1971). A readable statement by an economist about the subject of this chapter.

HAUSER, PHILIP M. (ed.), *The Population Dilemma*, 2nd ed., Englewood Cliffs, N.J.: Prentice-Hall, Inc. 1969. An excellent collection of essays providing an introduction to the field of demography.

Population and the American Future, The Report of the Commission on Population Growth and the American Future. Washington, D.C.: Government Printing Office, 1972. Gives a variety of views on U.S. population problems.

United Nations Department of Economic and Social Affairs, *World Population Prospects as Assessed in 1963*. New York: United Nations, 1966. A convenient source for world population data. For more recent data, see the latest edition of the annual *United Nations Statistical Yearbook*.

U.S. Bureau of the Census, *Current Population Reports*, Series P-25, various numbers. Washington, D.C.: Government Printing Office, various dates. A series of publications providing basic U.S. population data, projections, and interpretations.

13

ENVIRONMENTAL PROBLEMS AND URBANIZATION

Most of the serious environmental problems the United States faces today are concentrated in our giant urban agglomerations. The most notorious example of air pollution is the smog of Los Angeles and its surburbs. Water pollution is most apparent in urban areas, where concentrations of industrial plants emit enormous, concentrated amounts of pollutants. Problems of the quality of life, or amenity, are especially associated with modern city life. The dirt, and noise, and hectic pace of life in cities are contrasted by social critics with the relative peace and tranquility of the farm and small town. Indeed, it is remarked that we need to preserve recreation, rest, and rehabilitation areas outside the cities in order to allow urban dwellers to survive continued exposure to the unnatural environment of the modern city. This chapter examines these problems of the modern urban environment. No new analytical concepts are necessary for our discussion—urban environmental problems are essentially the same in substance as all other environmental problems. But this chapter will approach these problems from a somewhat different perspective than we have employed previously in the book.

The chapter proceeds according to the following outline. Section A first surveys the present and projected future levels of urbanization in the United States and then goes on to make some tentative generalizations about the relationship of urbanization to various environmental problems. It poses the important question of to what extent *concentration* of people and industry in urban agglomerations is a causative factor in the creation of environmental problems. The analysis in Section A is the basis for evaluating appropriate government policies toward population and industry dispersion in Section B. Section C next provides a brief economic analysis of urban congestion as an environmental problem, with special attention given to urban transportation policies. Section D then looks at environmental programs as one of a competing set of programs on the budget agenda of urban area governments. It argues that some of the shortcomings of government environmental policy are due to the fragmented structure of local government in metropolitan areas. Section E summarizes the main points of the chapter.

A. THE URBAN ENVIRONMENT: AN OVERVIEW

The Level of Urbanization in the United States

Over two-thirds of our nation's population now live in urban areas, as delimited by the Census Bureau's definition of standard metropolitan statistical areas (SMSAs). This definition of urbanization includes rural parts of partly urbanized counties and excludes small cities, but it is sufficiently precise as a measure of the concentration of population for most purposes. Urbanization has grown steadily over our nation's history. Probably only 5 percent of the population lived in urban areas prior to the nineteenth century. Today about two-thirds of the population are included in SMSAs, and the great majority of the population lives along the coast lines of the two oceans, the Gulf of Mexico, and the Great Lakes.

Several studies carried out in the 1960s projected that the trend to greater urbanization in the United States would continue and that the country would be 80 percent or more urbanized within a decade or so. Population developments in the 1960s appeared to confirm this prediction as population grew 16.6 percent in SMSAs and only 6.8 percent outside SMSAs. Relative rates of population growth changed dramatically in the next decade, however. Between 1970 and 1976, population growth in SMSAs was only 4.0 percent, while it was 8.2 percent outside SMSAs.

Population growth continued at rapid rates in the SMSA suburbs in the 1970s, but central cities within SMSAs actually lost population, and population density *within* urban areas has decreased. Furthermore, in the 1970s urban agglomerations in the North lost population while cities in the South and West grew rapidly. The fastest-growing states in the United States in the last decade include Arizona, Florida, and Nevada, which all experienced population increases of more than 20 percent between 1970 and 1976; during the same period, the heavily urbanized states of New York and Rhode Island actually lost population.[1] Thus, the projections of past studies have proved to be completely wrong. This experience suggests that it is unwise to hazard predictions about the future course of population distribution patterns in the United States.

Water Pollution and Urbanization

Most large cities are situated next to important water resources. New York City grew up around the magnificent natural harbor at the mouth of the Hudson River. Chicago is located at the extreme southern tip of Lake Michigan. It is difficult to name a large urban area not contiguous to some important body of water. The proximity of cities to water resources is, of course, no accident. Water transport and travel have historically been cheap relative to overland alternatives. Cities naturally developed first as *entrepots* for water-based transportation and, in many cases, later expanded as industrial centers as well. But cities historically found adjacent bodies of water valuable resources in five additional respects: first, as sources of power (a factor of negligible importance today); second, as sources of fresh drinking water; third, as waste disposal resources—natural sewers in the case of rivers; fourth, as an input in production processes; and fifth, as recreational or amenity resources.

The waters adjacent to most major cities in the United States are currently badly polluted. The waste disposal function of water resources has been chosen by society in almost every instance where it conflicts with the recreational or amenity function. (Nevertheless recreational uses of water resources are still extremely important in many cities despite high pollution levels.) Society's choice has not been explicit in most cases. Pollution has occurred largely by default—for lack of an effective social decision to halt polluting activities. In the absence of explicit policies inhibiting emissions of water pollutants, or at least without effective enforcement of the laws governing such emissions, rising levels of eco-

---

[1] See U.S. Bureau of the Census, *Current Population Reports,* Series P-20, No. 307, "Population Profile of the United States, 1976" (Washington, D.C.: Government Printing Office, 1977).

nomic activity in the cities inevitably caused the pollution of our most important water resources.

Without contradicting the facts given above, economists do not agree unanimously that water pollution is an *urban* environmental problem per se. In fact, some even argue that the social costs of water pollution outside urban areas are greater than the social costs of urban water pollution. This dispute cannot be fully resolved in this chapter, but we can raise the following pertinent issues.

The first point to recognize is that the social costs of water pollution in a hypothetical less-urbanized society than our own would not necessarily be less than the costs we now actually incur. Assuming a given degree of industrialization and a given level of technology, the main advantage of a less-urbanized society over our own would be the technical circumstance that the natural self-cleansing abilities of bodies of water are generally more effective if the amounts of pollutants are low relative to the amount of water in a given area. For example, little pollution may result if 100 factories emit pollutants into a river over a 200-mile stretch of water. But if the same 100 factories are all located within a 1-mile length of the same stream within a city, pollution may become a serious problem. The importance of this technical point will, of course, vary greatly with the characteristics of different water resources and with the type of pollutant. We conclude that the main direct impact of urbanization within a modern industrialized society on the social costs of water pollution is the result of concentration of pollutants within a relatively small geographical area.

But this point does not settle the question at issue. On the other side are some cogent arguments that urbanization is not a fundamental cause of water pollution. First, it is not clear that a given amount of damage to water resources in urban areas involves the same degree of external costs to society as it does in rural areas. On the contrary, concentration of water pollution damage downstream in urbanized areas may result in significantly less foregone social benefits than if the damage were spread evenly throughout a whole river basin. The benefits foregone because of water pollution in urban areas seem to be limited for the most part to esthetic considerations, or loss of amenity, and to increased travel costs. Good substitutes for the water resources immediately adjacent to cities are often available for recreational and drinking water purposes, provided that upstream (rural) water resources remain relatively unpolluted. That is, transportation costs for city people to rural recreational water resources and for rural drinking water supplies to city people may be low relative to the costs of pollution prevention or pollution damage avoidance in the cities themselves. Moreover, it may be socially more efficient to transform polluted water into safe drinking water by conventional treatment methods than to prevent the pollution in the first place. Some evidence indicates that treatment costs for municipal and industrial uses are relatively insensitive to the degree of water pollution over wide ranges of pollution concentrations. Thus, the greater concentration of pollution in urban areas may be relatively unimportant in affecting the treatment costs required to produce economically useful water. A closely related point is that if society does choose to treat water discharges into water resources, there are likely to be significant economies of scale in water treatment processes if the sources of pollution are highly concentrated in urban areas. All of these points suggest that under some circumstances spreading a given amount of pollution evenly over a large area is *not* obviously better than concentrating it in just a few locations and leaving most of the area relatively unpolluted.

Finally, as we have already observed, some urban recreational uses of water—boating, in particular—are apparently compatible with a high degree of water pollution. Again, there is doubtlessly some unknown degree of loss of amenity when people have to swim or boat in the middle of beds of algae and industrial wastes. Treated drinking water is not necessarily the same thing esthetically as untreated water, and this difference, too, has to be recognized in assessing the full social costs of water pollution. More generally, the fact that people have to live in close proximity to foul-smelling and filthy water clearly diminishes the amenity of urban life to some extent.

On the whole, these points suggest that water pollution as a social problem may not be primarily a result of urban agglomeration, even if the deterioration of water resources is most evident in the vicinity of cities. On the other hand, none of these points justify the conclusion that water resources in urban areas are sufficiently clean today. The important policy issue is, however, whether the social policy mix of water quality control measures should include any of a number of governmental measures to discourage urban agglomeration or whether government efforts should be confined to the more direct measures analyzed in Part 4. Our discussion above does suggest that policies that would intentionally disperse people and industry more widely might have little impact on the total social costs of water pollution.

Air Pollution and Urbanization

Air pollution, like water pollution, is most evident in urbanized areas. The arguments we have just gone through for the problem of water pollution showed that this fact by itself does not suffice to identify the factor of urbanization as the fundamental cause of air pollution. Let us again perform the conceptual experiment of comparing air pollution in our economy with the same problem in a hypothetical economy that is significantly less urbanized than our own but is otherwise identical in every respect. As a first approximation, the total quantity and composition of pollutants emitted into the atmosphere could be taken to be identical in this comparison. Following our argument in the case of water resources, it seems reasonable to posit that only the relative dispersion of pollutants would be affected by the differences in the concentration of people and industry in urban agglomerations between the two economies. The social costs of air pollution are clearly greater in our own society than they would be in a hypothetical less-urbanized economy.

Just as in the case of water pollution, the concentration of air pollutants is an important factor in determining how well the natural processes of the air can cleanse themselves in a given area. But, in sharp contrast to the case of water, dispersion of air pollutants is probably all-important in determining the total social costs of a given level of air pollution emissions. Unlike water pollution, air pollution in a small area results in significant social costs because man has not yet discovered any good, relatively cheap substitutes for clean air in the cities where he must live and work. Low concentrations of many gases or particulates in the atmosphere seem to have virtually no harmful consequences to man, but high or chronic concentrations can have all the insidious, economically damaging effects detailed in Chapter 7. People can avoid unclean air in cities only by the very costly expendients of commuting long distances to work, quitting their jobs, or purchasing air filtration systems for their homes and venturing outside as little as possible. Therefore, public policies affecting population concentrations seem, on first consideration, to have a significant role to play in minimizing the net social costs of air pollution. We shall take up this issue in more depth in Section B.

Amenity and Urbanization

Urbanization necessarily involves the crowding together of people in small areas. The resulting congestion produces a special kind of external cost, which differs in one fundamental respect from the external costs of water pollution or air pollution. The latter kind of externality results from individuals or firms emitting waste products into socially owned environment media. The externality is *nonreciprocal;* the victims of air or water pollution do not inflict external costs back on the polluter. In contrast, congestion in cities involves *reciprocal* external costs. People and goods simply get in each other's way, and everybody is a loser.[2] For

---

[2] The distinction between the two kinds of externalities is due to Jerome Rothenberg, "The Economics of Congestion and Pollution: An Integrated View," *American Economic Review, Papers and Proceedings,* LX, No. 2 (May 1970).

example, when 1000 automobiles are crowded together on a city street built to accommodate only half that number, every one of the 1000 drivers inflicts congestion costs on the other 999. All 1000 shares responsibility for the externality equally, and all bear the costs according to how much they value the time they lose waiting for the traffic jam to clear. Other external costs directly associated with congestion costs in cities include the noise, dirt, and hectic pace of modern life.

Beyond the relatively straightforward problem of congestion costs, virtually nothing of objective validity can be said about the connection between degree of urbanization and the general level of amenity in a society. High densities of population and industry in cities inevitably lead to all sorts of externalities, both good and bad. In Manhattan, for example, one man's activities impinge on another man's welfare to the maximum degree possible in this country. When Mr. X plays his radio in Manhattan, Mr. Y, in the adjacent apartment, listens whether he wants to or not. Mr. X and Mr. Y litter the streets at each other's expense, and they constantly are in each other's or somebody's way during rush hours. Compared to Manhattan, the pace of life is slower and more relaxed in less densely populated areas, and certainly smaller towns are cleaner and quieter. Some evidence exists that the extent of mental illness in New York is astoundingly high, and some people would ascribe this fact to the disamenity of life in an overcrowded metropolis.[3] These observations tempt the authors, and perhaps the readers, to conclude that high levels of urbanization cause much of the disamenity of modern life.

The case for making urbanization the villain responsible for disamenity is not very persuasive, however. The first point to the contrary is simply that much of the evidence linking urbanization to disamenity is limited to the United States. For example, London is almost as big and densely settled as New York City but is notably quieter, cleaner, and more relaxed. Other cities in Europe appear to manage to preserve amenity much more successfully than their American counterparts. (But recently, traffic conditions in Paris and Rome seem to have matched the worst conditions in our cities.) These observations suggest that something special in American culture, rather than urbanization per se, is the fundamental cause of urban disamenity. Second, we must recognize that tastes differ radically as to what is an external economy or an external diseconomy when it comes to questions of amenity. Very few people like dirty air or water, but some people—especially the young— like the noise, excitement, and crowds of cities. Although Y may hate liv-

---

[3] See L. Srole, and A. Fischer, eds., *Mental Health in the Metropolis, The Midtown Manhattan Study* (New York: Harper & Row, 1975).

ing in such close proximity to X, X may love being close to Y and may dread, above all, the isolation of the farm or even of the suburbs. Given the above complications, economists can obviously make few safe generalizations about the functional relationship of urbanization and amenity.

B. POPULATION DISTRIBUTION POLICIES AND ENVIRONMENTAL QUALITY

The issue we shall analyze in this section has already been foreshadowed by our informal discussion in the preceding section. That is, should the government consciously attempt to control growing urbanization and to redistribute population and industry more evenly throughout the country to help alleviate environmental problems. Several European countries, including Britain, France, and the Netherlands, have attempted to restrain growth in densely settled areas and to stimulate new investment in depressed areas. These measures have been motivated by a number of considerations, including environmental quality. Some social planners believe the United States should follow similar policies to stimulate a less concentrated distribution of jobs and people.

Our analysis thus far helps us to identify air pollution and urban congestion as the two environmental problems most directly linked to urbanization in our society, and we shall therefore concentrate our attention on them. Our goal in this section is to assess the usefulness of population dispersion as an environmental policy relative to the more direct environmental policy alternatives discussed in Part 4.

Arguments for a Government Role in Population Decentralization

The case for population redistribution rests on a variant of a familiar theoretical premise—external diseconomies. In Chapters 2 and 3, we presented the theoretical case for the proposition that industries producing external diseconomies as a by-product tend to be too big, in the sense that everybody's economic welfare could be enhanced if the output of such industries were made to go down and the output of other industries were made to go up. Some writers hold an analogous view of population concentration in cities. They argue, in effect, that high-density levels in urban areas produce external diseconomies in the form of air pollution and congestion. From this argument, they conclude that cities tend to be too big in the absence of government intervention and call for various government policies to decentralize and disperse population and industry. Such policies might include the following specific measures: (1) special income tax allowances for people living in low-density areas or, alternatively, special surtaxes for people living in high-density areas; (2) subsidies to industries that locate new plants in low-density areas or, alternatively, additional taxes on industries that locate new plants in high-density areas; and (3) the construction of new government installations in low-density areas or, alternatively, a ban on construction of government installations in high-density areas. By this point in the book, the reader can doubtlessly think of additional measures that would have much the same effect as the specific measures outlined above. The basic notion is simply that the government could provide positive and negative incentives for population decentralization.

Arguments for Laissez-Faire in Population Distribution

Many economists strongly oppose the arguments given above, even though they accept the premise that urbanization is the cause of some external diseconomies. Their views are based on some simple economic principles of urbanization, which we must summarize briefly here to present the other side of this issue effectively.

The basic premise of urban economics is that the growth of cities is a phenomenon that cannot be ascribed either to historical chance or to government policies. Instead, they originate, persist, and grow for solid economic reasons. The high correlation between degree of urbanization and the level of economic development across societies strongly suggests that the causes of urban agglomeration are basically economic in nature. Urban economists conclude, on the basis of many different kinds of evidence, that the economic rationale for urbanization is that higher densities of people and firms make possible significant cost savings—economies of agglomeration—in the production and distribution of goods and services in a modern, highly developed economy. Economies of agglomeration come in many forms, some obvious and some more subtle. Just one example of such economies are the cost savings in communication and transportation to a business firm that locates in close proximity to its suppliers, bankers, accountants, lawyers, and customers.[4] One important piece of evidence supporting this contention is the concentration of industries in large cities despite the fact that wage levels are significantly higher in these cities than in more sparsely settled communities. If economies of agglomeration were *not* important, the forces of competition should induce firms to move operations to less densely populated areas. But the *net* movement of economic activity and

---

[4] The reader who desires a more extensive discussion of this subject should refer to Edwin E. Mills, *Urban Economics* (Glenview, Ill.: Scott, Foresman and Company, 1972).

people is, of course, in the opposite direction from rural areas to cities and has been for hundreds of years.

The evidence is most persuasive that economies of agglomeration associated with urbanization are an important source of productivity increases and of higher real incomes in developed economies. Granted this basic point, it follows that policies designed to control the growth of dense urban centers may have the harmful side effect of making the production of goods and services less efficient and lead to lower real incomes for the population over time. In other words, such policies may involve significant social costs.

Air Pollution and Urbanization

The assertion that the process of urbanization is an imporant factor in explaining productivity growth does not, by itself, dispose of the possibility that cites grow *too* big in the absence of government intervention because of air pollution or other similar external diseconomies of urban density. Let us analyze the relationship between air pollution and urbanization within a highly simplified framework. Suppose that total air pollution costs can be measured and that the functional relationship between such costs and urban density in a given site is known and can be represented by Figure 13–1. The diagram assumes, first, that up to a critical density, N_0 persons per square mile, air pollution costs in a city

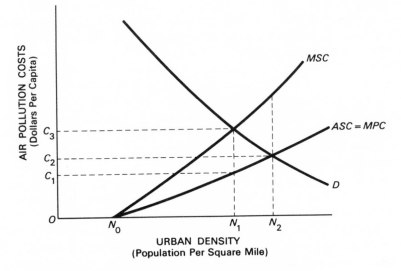

FIGURE 13–1. Air Pollution Costs and Urban Density.

are zero. At densities greater than N_0, however, everyone in the city incurs the welfare costs of air pollution in different forms of damage to health and property. High density is the cause of air pollution in the sense that it is responsible for high densities of automobiles and other sources of emissions of pollutants into the air in the city. These costs are assumed to vary directly with population density, which has the important implication that the marginal social costs of air pollution, MSC, exceed the average social costs, ASC.

The relationship between the MSC and ASC curves in this case of reciprocal externalities can best be explained by the use of a simple numerical example. Suppose that density level N_1 in Figure 13–1 corresponds to a population of 1 million persons in a given area and that C_1, the ASC corresponding to N_1, is $10 per capita. Let us assume that an additional person in the city raises average air pollution costs per capita along the ASC curve by 1 cent per capita. A potential migrant to the city could rationally ignore his own marginal contribution to average pollution in the city because 1 cent is negligible relative to the $10 existing average cost level. In making his decision whether or not to move to the city, the potential migrant therefore takes $10 to be the air pollution "price" of moving to the city, which is why we state that $ASC = MPC$ in Figure 13–1; average *social* costs are equivalent to marginal *private* costs. But note that the marginal social cost C_3, at density level N_1, is greater than the average social cost C_1. Average pollution costs rise by 1 cent for each of the existing 1 million inhabitants of the city when the million and first person moves into the city. And 1 million persons times 1 cent per person is not a negligible marginal social cost; it equals $10,000. Thus, we see that the marginal social costs in this kind of situation can greatly exceed average social costs.

We are now in a position to give some economic content to Figure 13–1. An individual contemplating migration to an urban area with density N_1 faces a level of per capita air pollution costs of C_1, or the average air pollution cost level associated with density N_1. If he moves to the city, he will have to pay an amount C_1 (plus 1 cent) either in the form of pollution prevention costs—expensive and time-consuming journeys to his work, for example—or in the form of outright welfare damage to his health or property. Therefore, he will rationally migrate to the city at this density level only if a sufficiently high wage differential and other net advantages of living in the city compensate him by at least an amount C_1. But the price of C_1 he faces for moving to the city is *too low*. When he moves to the city, he inflicts marginal air pollution costs on all people already living in the city of an amount C_3. The marginal social cost C_3 is the price he should pay for moving to the city.

Because the price he takes into account, C_1, is less than C_3, the true marginal social cost, it seems that we can conclude, on the basis of our arguments in Chapters 2 and 3, that cities will grow too large in the absence of government intervention. In Figure 13–1, we can see that if we interpret the D curve to be a demand (or marginal social benefit) curve for living in the city related to its air pollution price, equilibrium city size will be N_2, where $D = ASC = C_2$. Optimal city size, however, is only N_1, where $D = MSC = C_3$.

The flaw in the above argument for policy purposes is that it implicitly assumes that the only effective antipollution measures in these circumstances is to limit population densities. But, as the reader surely knows by this point in the book, such an assumption is almost certainly wrong. If air pollution is a problem in densely populated cities, why not simply resort to some system of effluent charges on various kinds of waste emissions? Or even prohibit some kinds of emissions, if necessary? After all, for most people, it is not population density itself that is objectionable but the side effects of population density, such as air pollution. Therefore, the most logical public policy measures are those directed squarely at the undesirable side effects. This kind of reasoning leads many economists to prefer direct antipollution measures, such as effluent charges, to indirect measures involving government interference with population distribution.

Incidentally, if effluent charges are instituted, the net effect on city sizes is not clear on a priori grounds. An efficient system of effluent charges would make all city dwellers pay, directly or indirectly, the full marginal social costs of external diseconomies due to high population density. This effect by itself would tend to make cities less densely populated, of course. On the other hand, cities will become more pleasant places to live once pollution is dealt with directly, and this factor will tend to make cities larger. The net effect of these two offsetting factors on urban densities cannot be predicted without knowledge of the relative costs of pollution abatement in areas of high density as compared to areas of low density. But urban density in itself is not an important policy target. In terms of economic efficiency, the important argument is that direct policy measures such as effluent charges are generally preferable to indirect measures, such as the population redistribution measures discussed previously. Finally, the reader should note that our arguments concerning population *redistribution* in this chapter closely parallel our arguments concerning population *levels* in Chapter 12. Economic analysis suggests some skepticism as to whether either type of population policy could pass a benefit-cost test except in circumstances of extreme population pressures and lack of feasible alternative policies.

C. THE PROBLEM OF URBAN CONGESTON

Congestion is the one disamenity problem that is uniquely urban in nature. Indeed, this must be true by definition, for what else does urbanization mean if not high population densities and crowding? For this reason, we single it out of the large number of special disamenity problems in urban areas for a brief analysis in this chapter.

Urban congestion problems are closely linked to urban transportation policy issues. The travel of people from the home to the job and back to the home, shopping and recreational journeys, and the transportation of raw materials, intermediate products, and final goods between firms all compete for the scarce space of city streets and of other urban transportation facilities. The resulting congestion is an important source of the disamenity of urban life for many people.[5] This section briefly summarizes the economic approach to the problem of urban congestion.

Let us begin our analysis with the simplifying assumptions that the locational structure of cities and their basic transportation systems are given. That is, we assume that the nature and extent of necessary trips both for people and goods are already virtually fixed by previous locational and capital investment decisions in order to concentrate most effectively on the demand for the facilities of an existing transportation network. With this assumption, what can we say about the social costs of urban congestion? Specifically, what is the economic sense of the term *too much congestion?*

This question can best be answered by reference to Figure 13–2, which depicts the relationship between congestion costs and the number of automobile (or any highway vehicle) trips on the highway network of a typical urban area. Given our simplifying assumptions for this example, we may take the number of trips on the horizontal axis to be proportional to the population in the urban area. Congestion costs per automobile trip on the vertical axis include the costs of time wasted for both people and goods delayed by traffic jams and the amorphous but significant psychic costs of the frustration and discomfort individuals suffer when stalled in traffic. The average social costs of congestion per trip, *ASC* in Figure 13–2, are shown to rise more than proportionally with the number of trips to reflect accurately a fact that is well documented and probably well known to the reader. The marginal social costs of congestion, *MSC*, rise much more rapidly than the average social costs, and the *MSC* curve lies above the *ASC* curve at any level of trips.

---

[5] Congestion in city streets caused by too many automobiles in a limited space also aggravates urban air pollution problems, as already noted in Chapter 7.

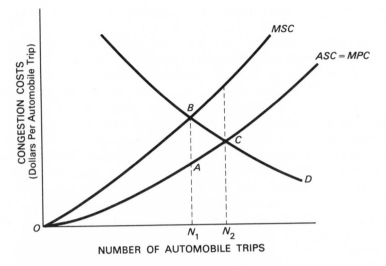

FIGURE 13–2.   Congestion Costs and Optimal Tolls.

The explanation of the divergence between the ASC and MSC curves in Figure 13–2 is completely parallel in the congestion costs case to our previous explanation in the case of air pollution costs in Figure 13–1. An additional automobile on a highway raises average congestion costs not just for the additional individual person in the automobile but also for everyone else on the highway. The difference between the ASC and MSC curves in Figure 13–2 measures the external congestion costs an additional trip imposes on all other individuals or firms. If we interpret the D curve in Figure 13–2 as the demand for travel related to its implicit congestion cost price, we can read off the diagram that too much travel—resulting in too much congestion—will result, in the absence of any intervening government policy.

Individuals take the congestion costs of their own travel into account only as it affects them as individuals but do not concern themselves with the external congestion costs they impose on other travelers. That is, they take the congestion price of travel to be the marginal private cost of congestion, MPC, which they perceive to be equal to the average social cost. Therefore, the equilibrium level of travel in Figure 13–2 will be N_2, where $D = ASC = MPC$. The N_2 level of travel is too large for efficiency in the use of the highway network, because D, which measures the marginal social benefits of travel to individuals, lies below MSC, the marginal social cost of travel, at this point. Efficient or *optimal* congestion calls instead for a travel level N_1, where $D = MSC$. In other words, the usual efficiency criterion that the value of the last unit of anything to all consumers be equal to its marginal *social* cost will not be satisfied in the case of urban travel and transportation.

The reader should note that it is good economics to call a nonzero level of congestion efficient or optimal. Common sense can be completely misleading on this point. Zero congestion costs may be efficient in rural Kansas but definitely would not do in midtown Manhattan! Densely urbanized areas exist because they provide great potential benefits for the interaction of people and goods. Society can *purchase* zero congestion in crowded city streets only at the cost of giving up some of these large benefits of communication and commercial transactions. Additional congestion, like any other real cost, is worth bearing by society up to the point where its marginal costs just become equal to its marginal benefits. Unfortunately, as we have just shown, the market system by itself will tend to produce too much congestion in cities to satisfy the maximum efficiency criterion.

By this point in the book, the reader can readily anticipate the policy implications of our discussion, for we are back on a very familiar track. Too much congestion is a result of the externalities of private decision making concerning travel and transportation. A *congestion charge* or toll on the use of urban highways (and of other transportation facilities) should therefore be levied on the users of this scarce resource. In Figure 13–2, the optimal toll ideally should be equal to an amount AB to attain optimal travel and congestion levels at N_1. With a toll of AB, the sum of the marginal private costs (equal to the money cost of the toll AB and the nonmoney congestion costs) would just be equal to the marginal social benefits on the D curve at N_1 trips. The optimal toll is theoretically identical to an optimal effluent charge in the case of externalities due to pollution.

Economists long have advocated efficient pricing of transportation facilities, and some of them have put their ingenuity to work to propose the appropriate pricing mechanisms.[6] For example, extra tolls could be levied during peak-load rush hour periods on urban highways, bridges, and tunnels; mass transit fares can also be varied according to differences in usage and congestion costs; and differential charges can be placed on alternative routes to encourage traffic to shift from highly congested to less-congested roads. Such tolls can improve air quality by reducing traffic volume and density. The EPA plan for improving New York City's air quality has included heavy tolls on all bridges and tunnels into Manhattan. The tolls would supplement more direct measures to reduce emissions into the atmosphere.

---

[6] See, for example, William S. Vickrey, "Pricing in Urban and Suburban Transport," *American Economic Review, Papers and Proceedings,* LIII, No. 2 (May 1963).

All the above measures are called for on the grounds of efficient resource allocation; whether they will conflict with the income distribution objectives of society will vary from case to case. Economists have to admit, however, that with the present state of technology, transportation pricing schemes face severe practical limitations. Times Square may be overcrowded, but attempting to charge motorists or pedestrians for the use of this space is not practicable. Establishing new tollbooths on already overcrowded roads may create more congestion (and more air pollution) than it dispels. Thus, even if the strong political opposition to charging for the use of free city streets should miraculously vanish, it would be impossible to reduce congestion costs everywhere to optimal levels until the technology of administering congestion charges makes significant advances.

In the real world, of course, transportation facilities are not simply given, as we have assumed above, and the pricing of transportation facilities should be coordinated with public investment in new facilities. The great urban transportation policy dispute of our age is between the proponents of more urban highways, with the implied reliance on buses and private automobiles, and the advocates of more and better mass transportation. The implementation of rational pricing of *all* transportation facilities might help to narrow ideological differences on this dispute. If charges were levied on all transportation media to cover full marginal social costs, the resulting pattern of consumer demand could be taken as a more reliable guide to future public investments in urban transportation than existing demands, which are a function of haphazard pricing or zero pricing. The urban transportation pricing problem for the government is immensely difficult. Automobiles and express highways in cities involve additional externalities beyond congestion costs in the form of air pollution, noise, land use, and various types of disamenity, and the same is true, to some extent, for some types of mass transportation. Such externalities should be taken into full account in optimal pricing schemes in urban transportation, but nobody, as yet, pretends to be able to estimate the various external cost functions with any accuracy.

Finally, we should take note of a strong, persistent argument against urban highways and the automobile that transcends the conventional economic analysis in this section. Urban locational patterns are undoubtedly a function of existing transportation systems that, in the main, were established long ago by governments that could not foresee the age of mass automobile ownership. If we acknowledge that urban location patterns and urban transportation systems are intimately interrelated, then we must leave the comfortable world of marginal analysis altogether to consider urban systems as an integrated whole. Optimal pricing schemes, as investment signals for urban transportation systems, can be defended on allocational efficiency grounds only if we take as given the present locational structure of cities. But some less-conventional economists and city planners argue that optimal modern cities and their transportation systems have to be built together from the ground up. Many such critics strongly believe that *New Towns* should be built entirely without access for automobiles in order to provide maximum amenity and efficiency in the use of space. Economists are generally skeptical about such grand schemes and want to be shown concrete results, but conventional marginalist analysis is not sufficient in itself to prove these ideas wrong. As the reader can see, much about the fundamentals of urban life remains an open question.

D. ENVIRONMENTAL QUALITY AND PRIORITIES IN LOCAL GOVERNMENT BUDGETS

State and local governments spend twice as much as the federal government on all nonmilitary programs. The dominance of state and local governments in the all-governments civilian budget is even greater in resource allocation activities, as much of the federal government budget is devoted to income redistribution.[7] Expenditures related to environmental quality are today a small but growing share of state and local government budgets. The main issue we shall raise in this section concerns the appropriate role of state and local governments in a total national environmental strategy. Specifically, we ask whether more responsibility for environmental quality should flow downwards to the local level of government or upwards to the state and federal governments.

The United States, in contrast to Western Europe, has a strong tradition of relying on local governments to provide government services unless such services clearly must be provided at higher levels of government. Ideally, strong local governments provide maximum responsiveness to the wishes of a diverse citizenry. Unfortunately for the proponents of maximum reliance on local governments, the advantages of providing government services at the local level are offset to some extent by disadvantages that have increased in importance over time. These disadvantages are in part distributional—the segregation of rich communities and poor communities to the advantage of the former. They could, in principle, be solved by equalizing grants either from the national or state governments. But the disadvantages also, in part, involve issues of allocational efficiency; local governments may be too small in some cases

---

[7] For details, see Dick Netzer, *Economics and Urban Problems* (New York: Basic Books, Inc., Publishers, 1970), Chap. VII.

to take advantage of economies of scale in providing government services, and they may be too small also in the sense that spillovers or externalities among political jurisdictions lead to significant inefficiencies.

One important spillover among small political jurisdictions is pollution in various forms, and the problem seems to be particularly acute in urban areas. Specifically, economists venture the generalization that local governments in urban areas will spend too little and do too little to deal with environmental problems in the absence of intervention by the state or federal governments. The basic reason for the low priority given environmental problems in local government budgets in urban areas is straightforward. The central fact of life for both central city and surrounding suburban governments in urban areas today in the United States is that they face enormous pressures both to provide more services (spend more money) and to keep tax rates down. Urban local governments all face the problem of invidious comparisons with their neighboring jurisdictions. If tax rates relative to the level of services provided get out of line in any one local jurisdiction, both people and business firms will tend to migrate out of that community to some other part of the urban area, taking valuable tax resources with them. It is relatively unimportant how strong the incentives to migrate really are in response to local fiscal incentives and disincentives; it is all-important that local government officials fear that the incentives to migrate are strong and act in response to these fears.

Such intergovernmental fiscal competition has beneficial aspects in inducing cost minimization in the provision of government services, but if spillovers are important, efficiency in resource allocation may be badly served. The case of air pollution best illustrates the nature of the problem. Air pollution within an urban area is typically most serious in the older, heavily industrialized central city. But the central city government likely will do and spend too little in attempting to deal with the problem unless the state or federal government intervenes. The benefits of air pollution abatement in the central city will be shared, in general, among residents and taxpayers of the central city and residents of surrounding suburban communities. But the benefits flowing outside the central city will be regarded by the central city officials as external to their decisions, because these officials respond only to the wishes of their own taxpayers. Therefore, they will ignore such extracentral city benefits and will spend and do too little about metropolitan-wide air pollution. Exactly the same considerations will affect the decisions of suburban governments, with the result that air pollution levels in the urban area will be too high. The smaller the individual geographical areas included in each political jurisdiction, the less will be the resources expended on air pollution abatement.

A closely related consideration reinforces the factors outlined in the previous paragraph. If a single local government places an effluent charge on emissions of a local industry or even prohibits some emissions, it raises the cost of doing business in the city for that industry just as any other tax would. The benefits of pollution abatement from an effluent charge or a prohibition in emissions will, on the other hand, provide few direct benefits for the affected industry because its stockholders are likely to be widely dispersed throughout the country.[8] Industries threatened by local government antipollution measures will likely threaten, in turn, to curtail or even close down operations in the city. Few fiscally hard pressed city officials will call their bluff, especially if the industry is vital to the local economy.

A third factor may further weaken local government antipollution activities. The middle class and the rich can often respond to the problem of air pollution and congestion in an urban area by moving far away from the central city, but the poor generally do not have this option. To the extent that this is possible, air quality is not a pure public good, even within a given air shed. However, the outmigration of the well-off and the concentration of the poor in central cities may weaken political pressures for improving environmental quality where it is poorest. As we argued in Chapter 4, demand for environmental quality is probably highly income elastic; the poor have more urgent economic priorities than clean air or amenity. For all the reasons above, we conclude that the present fragmented structure of government in urban areas is inadequate to solve various environmental problems.

A narrow concern with environmental quality would argue for an obvious solution—consolidation of local governments into a metropolitan government. Such a solution ignores the cogent arguments for strong local government, and it also poses the issue of where consolidation logically should end. Environmental spillovers and intergovernmental competition are not limited to sharply identifiable urban areas. If metropolitan government is good, would not elimination of *all* local governments and consolidation of government functions at the state level be even better? But the modern megalopolis spreads out over several states, so the same arguments would call for consolidation at the national level. And, recently, economists have called attention to the problems of international spillovers, with the seeming implication, by this same logic, that protection of environmental quality calls for an all-powerful international government.

Consolidation of governments at any of these levels seems a remote

---

[8] Pollution abatement could aid the industry indirectly if it makes the urban area a more attractive place to live and thereby aids in the recruitment of a labor force. Business firms are unlikely to find this kind of indirect effect on their costs persuasive, however.

possibility, politically, at this time, and we must recognize the dilemma this fact presents for environmental policy. One possible alternative solution is the creation of special metropolitan, or regional, agencies whose jurisdiction is limited to narrow environmental concerns. More extensive use of regional airshed or watershed authorities, such as the existing Delaware River and Ohio River Basin Commissions, may be helpful in this regard. The political advantage of such agencies is that they leave local governments with their sovereignty unimpaired in nonenvironmental areas, but such agencies may have their political disadvantages as well. Another possible solution is voluntary agreements between governments with common environmental concerns. Unfortunately, such agreements are notoriously hard to negotiate in the first place and unstable in the long run, because local government officials are jealous of their independence. The federal government may be able to play a creative role in this area by providing generous financial support for environmental purposes but making the money available only after the creation of metropolitan environmental protection agencies or of some workable scheme of cooperation between local governments. Otherwise, the major alternative would seem to be further centralization of environmental policy measures at the federal level of government. For example, many cities today have instituted strict air codes in response to federal standards. Further intervention by the federal government may be necessary to ensure effective enforcement of these codes.

E. SUMMARY AND CONCLUSIONS

Most serious environmental problems in the United States are to be found in urban areas. Some of these problems, notably air pollution and congestion, are a direct consequence of urbanization. Others, water pollution, for example, are not so clearly the result of urbanization and might be even more severe in a hypothetical industrially developed economy with more dispersion of people and industry.

Arguments for government policies to redistribute population by dispersing it more widely rest on the concept of the reciprocal externalities associated with urban crowding. The external costs of air pollution and urban congestion lead to the growth of cities that are too large for optimally efficient resource allocation. Arguments for laissez-faire with respect to population distribution concede the point that reciprocal externalities in urban areas lead to too much air pollution and congestion but maintain that direct solutions to those problems are preferable to government tinkering with population distribution. Such direct solutions would include effluent charges on emissions of pollutants into the atmosphere and higher tolls on roads that are excessively congested. More drastic solutions, involving basic changes in the transportation networks of urban areas, may also be required.

The fragmented structure of local government in urban areas may result in too low a priority for environmental programs in government budgets. The basic problem is that environmental benefits and costs spill over from one local political jurisdiction to all others in urban areas. This circumstance creates a kind of political externality that must be solved, directly or indirectly, at some higher level of government. The same political spillover problem exists to some extent at the international level and may call for some form of international cooperation with regard to problems such as pollution of the oceans.

QUESTIONS FOR DISCUSSION

1. If the total amount of pollution emissions in our country is given, is it better, in general, to concentrate these emissions in just a few small geographical areas or to disperse them much more evenly?

2. How would the levying of effluent charges on air pollutant emissions affect the curves in Figure 13–1? How would the construction of mass transit facilities affect the curves in Figure 13–2?

3. Suppose that advances in technology made it feasible to impose optimal congestion tolls on the highways in large cities. Would the burden of such tolls fall more heavily on high-income or low-income groups?

4. What is the fundamental difficulty in measuring actual congestion costs of urban highways (as depicted in Figure 13–2)? Can you think of any indirect methods for measuring such costs?

5. Urban highway construction requires enormous amounts of land. When governments decide to build new highways, they measure the costs of this land as the dollar costs of acquiring it. What is wrong with such a measure? Explain how you would value such land if you were doing a full benefit-cost analysis of a proposed urban expressway.

SELECTED REFERENCES

BAUMOL, WILLIAM J., *Environmental Protection, International Spillovers and Trade*. Stockholm: Almqvist and Wiksell, 1971. A discussion of the problem of spillovers across political jurisdictions.

EDEL, MATTHEW, and JEROME ROTHENBERG, (eds.), *Readings in Urban Economics*. New York: The Macmillan Company, 1972. An excellent set of readings.

MILLS, EDWIN S., *Urban Economics*. Glenview, Ill.: Scott, Foresman and Company, 1972. An excellent urban economics text.

MILLS, EDWIN S., "Economic Aspects of City Sizes," Commission on Population Growth and the American Future, *Population, Resources and the Environment, Research Reports*, V. Washington, D.C.: Government Printing Office, 1973. The best discussion of the issues covered in Section B of this chapter.

NETZER, DICK, *Economics and Urban Problems*. New York: Basic Books, Inc., Publishers, 1970. An elementary treatment of urban policy problems.

OWEN, WILFRED, *Transportation for Cities*. Washington, D.C.: The Brookings Institution, 1976. An analysis of modern urban transportation issues and their relation to the urban environment.

Population Growth and the American Future, The Report of the Commission on Population Growth and the American Future. Washington, D.C.: Government Printing Office, 1972. Contains recent viewpoints on some of the population issues discussed in this and the previous chapter.

SUNDQUIST, JAMES L., *Dispersing Population*. Washington, D.C.: The Brookings Institution, 1975. Advocates government policies for redistributing population away from densely populated areas. Includes accounts of European experience with such policies.

WATSON, P. S., and E. P. HOLLAND, "Congestion Pricing—the Example of Singapore," *Finance and Development*, 13 (March 1976). A description of a successful pricing program aimed at reducing central city traffic congestion.

ZERBE, R. O., and K. CROKE, *Urban Transportation for the Environment*. Cambridge, Mass.: Ballinger Publishing Company, 1975. An analysis of urban transport problems. Recommended.

14

ECONOMIC GROWTH AND ENVIRONMENTAL QUALITY

This is the final chapter of an introductory textbook treatment of the economics of environmental quality. Despite the length of the book, some important material remains to be covered. Previous chapters have concentrated on the theory and factual evidence revelant to specific, current environmental policy issues. In this chapter, we shift gears somewhat by introducing the reader to some of the broader social issues involved in the economics of the environment. The central theme of our discussion will be the relationship between economic growth and human welfare, for it is on this question that traditional economists and their conservationist critics differ most sharply.

The chapter is organized according to the following outline: Section A first presents a restatement of the traditional economic view about the relationship of economic growth and the progress of human welfare.[1] Briefly summarized, this view essentially involves a strong en-

---

[1] We call this view of the world *traditional* for convenience, but it has dominated Western thought only in the last two or three centuries. The *no-growth* or *antigrowth* views of the world are really much more traditional in a broad time perspective on human history.

dorsement of continued economic growth as a *prerequisite* for the good life. Writers in the mainstream of economics tend to accept this basic precept as self-evident and generally limit their qualifications to an acknowledgment of the knotty problems of measuring economic growth accurately and making wise use of the additional output available to society. Section B then presents the essence of assorted radical critiques of the traditional economic position on this question. These critiques are radical not so much in the political as in the philosophical sense of the word, for they go to the root of matters to question the most fundamental premises of the traditional view. The critiques are diverse, but they have one theme in common; they deny that economic growth will improve the lot of man. Section C attempts what may appear to be the impossible: a (partial) reconciliation of the two fundamentally contradictory positions outlined above. It suggests the major features of a hypothetical society in which many of the important divergences between the two ideological camps might well disappear. Section D is an addendum to the main body of the chapter in that it sketches the nature of the research frontiers in the infant science of environmental economics. But it belongs in the main body of the chapter because some of the problems on these research frontiers are closely related to the issues raised in Sections A, B, and C. Finally, Section E is a brief summary of the chapter.

A. ECONOMIC GROWTH AND WELFARE: THE CONVENTIONAL WISDOM

Economists generally accept as self-evident the optimistic proposition that sustained economic growth in the last 200 years has increased human welfare.[2] Human welfare is a most difficult notion to quantify, and, therefore, its connection to the level of economic development in a society can never be proved to skeptics. But certain kinds of persuasive evidence may convince all but a few hard-core doubters. First, we can compare some objective circumstances of the same society at different stages of its economic development. Data about economic and social conditions prior to industrialization are scarce and unreliable, but nonetheless it is clear that life expectancies and health, in general, in all developed societies, have improved dramatically over their levels of two centuries or more ago. Sustained economic growth must be credited for this revolution in the human condition, both directly and indirectly—directly through the adequate food, housing, and shelter available to the average man today

---

[2] See, for example, the epigraph to Chapter 38 in Paul A. Samuelson, *Economics*, 10th ed. (New York: McGraw-Hill Book Company, 1976).

but not to his great-grandfather, and indirectly through advances in medical technology, which were part of the renaissance in all the sciences that was a by-product of the Industrial Revolution.

Economic growth has done much more than raise the levels of consumption of goods and services in the developed countries; it is also directly responsible for easing the tremendous toil required of men, women, and children alike before industrialization just to sustain a bare existence. People in the labor force in the United States today average less than 40 hours of work a week, and, for the most part, they work under relatively pleasant conditions. Furthermore, they go to work only after the enforced leisure of an extended formal schooling and prior to a retirement age that is slowly but steadily declining below the traditional age of 65. Even during their working years, they enjoy additional leisure during weekends, numerous holidays, and paid vacations. In brief, man today enjoys higher consumption standards and a healthier, longer life at the cost of less toil over his lifetime than his ancestors. Other clear benefits to man of economic progress could be detailed, but the above are sufficient to make a strong *prima facie* case.

Similar comparisons can be made between conditions in rich and poor countries today. Most of the world still lives close to the edge of hunger in the 1970s, but the privileged minority in the developed countries worry about putting on too much weight. Despite the wide diffusion of modern medical technology to the less-developed countries of the world, people in the developed countries enjoy much better health and longer lives than their counterparts in the poorer countries. Comparisons of rich and poor individuals within our own general affluent society underscore the same basic point. Some well-off college students may conceive of poverty as romantic, but the poor themselves in this country have no illusions about the advantages of material prosperity.

Most people, and especially most professional economists, conclude from such historical and international comparisons that economic growth is obviously the means to the end of greater human welfare. Probably the most eloquent statement of this conventional wisdom was given by a man considered by many to be a most unconventional economist, John Maynard Keynes. Keynes speculated, in a famous essay written in 1930, about the economic possibilities of our (his) grandchildren. He noted that *sustained* economic growth had become possible only since the Industrial Revolution but could be expected to continue indefinitely, even though it might be interrupted from time to time by short-term cyclical fluctuations, wars, or natural disasters. A sustained growth rate of output per capita of 2 percent a year—a realistic figure in a society such as the United States with projected low growth rates of population —implies a doubling of output per capita every 35 years. Keynes therefore speculated about the economic and social consequences of a probable eightfold increase in potential output per capita over the next century.

His basic conclusion was that the successful achievement of sustained economic growth would solve the basic economic problem of man —scarcity. He greeted this possibility with enthusiasm. In his view, satisfaction of all of humanity's important material wants would finally free the creative, artistic, and intellectual talents of man for their fullest development. He proclaimed that once this happy day was attained —in only a century or so, by his calculation—materialism and economizing would die an unmourned death. In Keynes's view, the need to economize—to work hard, save, and strive for material prosperity—had a legitimate *social* function only in the transitional stage of rising from general poverty through scarcity to a final happy satiety. Once man achieved material satiety, the unnatural and unesthetic habits of economizing could happily be dropped, for they no longer would have any useful social function. Thus, Keynes saw economic growth as a good thing *not in itself* but rather as a *prerequisite* for the good life for all of mankind.

Measurement Problems

The great majority of economists probably still agree with the views of Keynes, although with some philosophical qualifications of the naive optimism of a more innocent age prior to concentration camps and the widespread deployment of thermonuclear weapons. The one major economic qualification to Keynes's arguments involves the more mundane issue of accurate measurement of changes in the level of *net* economic output over time. The analytical problem is basically straightforward. Conventional measures of output, such as those implicitly referred to by Keynes, cannot be used as accurate measures of true changes in economic welfare. Many reasons can be given for this generalization, but for our purposes in this book, we shall concentrate only on the accounting issues involving environmental quality.[3] Net national product (NNP), probably the best conventional measure of economic output, is defined as the market value of gross *final* output of goods and services (gross national product) net of estimated depreciation charges against capital equipment. NNP is also defined to be equal to the sum of all the factor costs incurred to produce this output (except for depreciation charges). When most people talk about economic growth, they, either explicitly or im-

---

[3] For a collection of critiques of the conventional national income accounts, see "The Economic Accounts of the United States: Retrospect and Prospect," Part II, *Survey of Current Business*, LI, No. 7 (July 1971).

plicitly, refer to increases in the value of *real* NNP over time, that is, increases in NNP adjusted for changes in the purchasing power of money.

Real NNP is clearly a deficient measure of net output because it does not take into account all the external costs of environmental pollution. *Pollution prevention costs* are accounted for in the national income accounts, as are *pollution damage avoidance costs*. That is, government expenditures undertaken to enforce a ban on emissions or to clean up pollutants in the atmosphere or water are appropriately part of NNP because they enhance the quality of the environment and because the resources used for such purposes are diverted from other kinds of potential collective or individual consumption.[4] However, much of the remaining portion of total pollution costs—the welfare costs of actual pollution damage—are not accounted for in NNP because they are external to the marketplace transactions that enter into the national income accounts. For this reason, NNP will be *overstated* by the amount of such welfare costs. (But see footnote 4 for an accounting problem that tends to *understate* true NNP.) Not accounting for the welfare costs of environmental damage overstates true NNP for two distinct reasons. First, and most obvious, the flow of environmental *bads* to individuals, such as the daily breathing of polluted air, should be subtracted from gross consumption of goods and services to derive the net consumption of goods and services included in NNP. Second, to the extent that pollution reduces the economy's stock of environmental capital resources, some amount of *capital consumption allowances* should be added to the estimated depreciation of physical capital stocks in going from gross national product to net national product. In other words, it is proper national income accounting practice to measure *net* output as net of all the loss in value of an economy's capital resources, and these capital resources should logically include environmental capital resources.

All economists acknowledge the problem of accounting for environmental pollution in measuring NNP, although they may differ somewhat concerning the technical accounting details. We know very little, however, about how much difference there would be to measured growth rates of net output if we could make the desired adjustments to conventional measures of NNP. Only one major study to date has been published concerning the *quantitative* importance of accounting for pollution in measuring growth rates. Professors William Nordhaus and James Tobin of Yale University have attempted to measure the disamenity costs

---

[4] Such expenditures undertaken by private business firms are incorrectly deducted from NNP as current costs instead of being treated as final outputs of capital or consumption goods. They are conceptually equivalent to government or individual expenditures to improve the environment or to counteract environmental pollution. This problem qualifies the main point developed in the text.

of economic activity indirectly by estimating the income differential required to induce people to live in cities rather than rural areas over time —what they call *a disamenity premium*. Because urbanization has increased over time, they adjust conventionally measured NNP for the additional disamenity costs borne by city dwellers over time. Their adjustment for disamenity costs is of significant magnitude—8 percent of disposable family income in 1965. However, it does not have any effect on the measured *rate of growth* of output between 1929 and 1965, the years covered by their study. Income growth over these years has been sufficiently high to keep the disamenity costs of more urbanization roughly constant as a percentage of income. This is certainly a most unexpected result.

Although the Nordhaus and Tobin study is an impressive pioneering effort, its conclusion does not settle the basic problems of properly accounting for pollution costs in the measurement of net output. As the authors themselves recognize, their measure of disamenity costs at best includes only a portion of the total welfare costs of environmental pollution. Moreover, their procedure can not take into account the possibility that environmental conditions may have worsened just as rapidly in rural areas as in urban areas over the period covered by their study. Also, it does not allow for the possibility that the cultural and entertainment advantages of cities have been responsible for attracting people away from rural to urban areas. If such is the case, their results would clearly understate the effects of environmental deterioration. Thus, the quantitative significance of environmental pollution in affecting measures of the growth rate of net output still remains very much an open question.

Whatever the effect of environmental costs on measured growth rates eventually turns out to be, it will not alter in the slightest the basic philosophical stance of those who believe in the welfare-enhancing effects of economic growth. Carefully restated, this position holds that economic growth, properly measured to take into full account the welfare costs of environmental pollution, is a prerequisite for improving the lot of man.

B. ECONOMIC GROWTH AND WELFARE: THE RADICAL CRITIQUE

A minority—but apparently a growing minority—of economists argue that economic growth has not increased the welfare of human beings and that further economic growth will just make matters much worse. This antigrowth position appears to be held even more strongly among influential noneconomists and may become a new "conventional wisdom." The logical policy position of those who hold such a belief is to call for an end to growth. As noted previously in Chapter 12, the cause of zero growth (of output) is not likely to be a part of the platform of any successful political party in the foreseeable future, but its political unpopularity does not in itself make zero growth a bad idea. Arguments against economic growth tend to touch upon a wide variety of social issues. In our discussion below, we shall confine our attention to the arguments involving environmental issues.

One traditional conservationist argument against the continuation of growth of population and output is that such growth will eventually mean the extermination of many species of flora and fauna. The amount of habitable space on earth is virtually fixed, and sites become increasingly scarce as economic growth proceeds. Increased demands for food by a larger and wealthier population cause farmers to make much more efficient use of their land by applying more capital per acre, including the application of more advanced and efficient fertilizers and pesticides. Increased demands for outdoor recreation lead to pressures to achieve higher productivity of the sites suitable for recreational purposes. Military needs for various kinds of facilities even create demands for some of the most unattractive and inhospitable sites on earth. All of these interrelated phenomena follow from the fact that the number of sites is fixed and population and output growth continually bid up the prices of these sites and induce landowners to increase productivity per acre.

One consequence of the increasing scarcity of habitable space is that the survival of species other than man often becomes an apparently dispensable luxury, even in the most affluent society. A farmer attempting to maximize the productivity of a fixed number of acres will not tolerate pests such as coyotes or mountain lions that prey upon his stock or, in any way, hamper his commercial operations. The almost extinct grizzly bear in Glacier Park turns vicious when people seeking to escape the crowds of fellow humans venture far away from normal tourist areas and begin to crowd him in his former wilderness habitat; therefore, he must be destroyed to ensure the safety of this recreational area. Nuclear testing causes ecological disaster and threatens the survival of desert flora and fauna. The increasing scarcity of space as a result of continued economic growth thus threatens to make many species extinct, with the consequent loss of irreplaceable gene pools to future generations. Conservationists have traditionally viewed the prospect of the unnecessary destruction of other species with horror. Their view has never been expressed more eloquently than in a famous passage by John Stuart Mill, which deserves to be quoted in full:

> There is room in the world, no doubt, and even in old countries, for a great increase of population, supposing the arts of life to go on improving, and

capital to increase. But even if innocuous, I confess I see very little reason for desiring it. The density of population necessary to enable mankind to obtain, in the greatest degree, all the advantages both of cooperation and of social intercourse, has, in all the most populous countries, been attained. A population may be too crowded, though all be amply supplied with food and raiment. It is not good for man to be kept perforce at all times in the presence of his species. A world from which solitude is extirpated, is a very poor ideal. Solitude, in the sense of being often alone, is essential to any depth of mediation or of character; and solitude in the presence of natural beauty and grandeur, is the cradle of thoughts and aspirations which are not only good for the individual, but which society could ill do without. Nor is there much satisfaction in contemplating the world with nothing left to the spontaneous activity of nature; with every rood of land brought into cultivation, which is capable of growing food for human beings; every flowery waste or natural pasture ploughed up, all quadrupeds or birds which are not domesticated for man's use exterminated as his rivals for food, every hedgerow or superfluous tree rooted out, and scarcely a place left where a wild shrub or flower could grow without being eradicated as a weed in the name of improved agriculture. If the earth must lose that great portion of its pleasantness which it owes to things that the unlimited increase of wealth and population would extirpate from it, for the mere purpose of enabling it to support a larger, but not a better or a happier population, I sincerely hope, for the sake of posterity, that they will be content to be stationary, long before necessity compels them to it.[5]

More recent arguments against the benefits of economic growth go beyond the conservationist issues raised by Mill. The modern radical critique of economic growth centers on the *fixity* of the environmental resources of earth. The basic point is quite straightforward. The assimilative and absorptive capacities of the earth's air, water, and land resources are finite, and, therefore, sustained economic growth producing ever-higher levels of effluents must sooner or later overwhelm these resources. Some writers have developed this point simplistically as a trivial exercise in high school algebra proving that any positive number (effluents) growing forever at a positive compound rate must eventually exceed some other fixed positive number (environmental resource capacities).[6] Of course, it is true that the level of effluents cannot keep on growing forever, but this point evades the real issues of *how* and *when* effluent levels should cease to grow. The answer depends, of course, on

[5] John Stuart Mill, *Principles of Political Economy*, Book IV, Chap. VI (New York: D. Appleton & Co., 1884). Note that Mill talks about the consequences of *population* growth. But since he wrote, it has become clear that *output* growth is the much more important factor in destroying amenity, at least in a relatively sparsely populated society such as the United States.

[6] Examples of this approach are numerous, but perhaps the most publicized is the book by Dennis L. Meadows, Donella Meadows, Jorgen Randers, and William Behrens, *The Limits to Growth: A Report for the Club of Rome's Project on the Predicament of Man* (New York: Universe Books, 1972).

benefits and costs. Such arguments also tend to miss the critical point that the rate of growth of effluents does not necessarily *have* to match the rate of growth of output; society has available techniques, such as effluent charges, to control effluent level emissions within broad limits and tax incentives to encourage the recycling of materials.

On the other hand, the same basic truism can be the starting point for a deeper analysis of the relationship between economic growth and environmental issues. Probably the most sophisticated analysis from this point of view is the *Spaceship Earth* vision of the economist and philosopher Kenneth Boulding. The Spaceship Earth concept is, in part, just a global analogue to the materials balance concept discussed in Chapter 3. That is, Boulding argues that man must begin to see earth as a closed system, in contrast to the older conception that natural resources are boundless and that man can develop and exploit them without limit. In Boulding's perspective, earth's environmental resources should be viewed as essential, irreplaceable social capital, and the major purpose of economic activity should be to conserve this *stock* of capital intact for future generations. In contrast, the more traditional economic view has always been that society should maximize the *flow* of current output. According to the traditional view, the stock of capital society passed on to future generations is determined both by the private market system and by government policies in response to the wishes of the current generation about the allocation of resources between present and future uses. Boulding's analysis is particularly useful in focusing on the issue of whether current market and nonmarket institutions are sufficient to provide for the survival of enough of our precious environmental capital for transmission to future generations. Boulding concludes pessimistically that our society expends environmental capital recklessly in pursuit of the wrongheaded goal of maximizing current output. If he is right, society must alter its basic philosophical position toward the meaning of economic growth. The overriding social goal would be maintenance of environmental resources and would entail acceptance of a lower rate of growth—even a zero rate—of current output toward this end.

One other general criticism of economic growth concerns its harmful effects on amenity, broadly conceived to include all social and cultural factors affecting the quality of life. It is alleged that economic growth has, either directly or indirectly, destroyed the best aspects of life found in less economically advanced ages, in particular the pleasures of solitude, contemplation, leisurely conversation, creative art, and the like. According to this line of argument, economic growth inundates these civilized pursuits by glorifying materialism and requiring too hectic and frenzied a style of life. To cite just one example, it is clear that the pleasures of a leisurely, solitary stroll are considerably less in modern Manhattan than in a less economically developed time and place. Among the famous economists associated with this view of the amenity consequences of economic growth, the names Fred Hirsch, Bertrand de Jouvenel, Staffan Burenstam Linder, and Tibor Scitovsky are prominent. But the most thoroughgoing reactionary (radical?) in his opposition to economic growth is the brilliant English economist E. J. Mishan.

Mishan postulates a sharp dichotomy of tastes between what we may call the *modernists* and the *environmentalists*. The modernists desire maximum consumption of goods and services and, therefore, favor all policies that increase the rate of growth of industrial production. They do not mind the disamenity of modern life and, in fact, even thrive on its noise, confusion, and excitement. The environmentalists, on the other hand, stand willing to sacrifice many of the comforts and conveniences to be derived from modern production techniques in order to enjoy greater amenity. Mishan poses the question of how society can best reconcile the divergent interests of these two groups.

The answer Mishan suggests is the logical extreme case of zoning, *separate facilities*. The separate facilities solution to amenity problems is the social analogue to the smoking and no-smoking car solution of railroad passenger trains. Instead of either allowing or not allowing smoking in all cars and thereby guaranteeing the dissatisfaction of either one group of passengers or the other, railroads often provide separate facilities so that smokers and nonsmokers can choose the environment in which they desire to travel. Why not, Mishan asks, provide separate facilities for everybody in a society in virtually all aspects of the environment? A large area with tentative boundaries in each state could be set aside initially for people who wished to live in a pollution-free environment. The equilibrium size of the environmentalists' area could be determined by migration over the long run, either expanding or contracting. In this area, total bans on automobiles, power lawnmowers, overhead jet flights, transistor radios, functional architecture, and other disamenities of modern life would be strictly enforced. Outside the environmentalists' area, life would go on for the modernists just as before, except that progress would no longer be hindered by the criticisms of the environmentalists.

Mishan's separate facilities solution to environmental problems is so appealing on its face that only a professional economist could attempt to find fault with it. Who among rational men would not opt to live in the environmentalists' zone, once separate facilities were established? The answer is that only those people willing to pay the unknown costs of amenity would choose to enjoy its environmental benefits. Our guess is that the costs would be unacceptable to all but a few thoroughly dedicated environmentalists. One cost of unknown dimensions of living in the environmental zone would be commuting costs. With automobiles banned

—a crucial requirement of Mishan's environmental zone—travel to work could well take up the full working day for those who had to work in the kinds of ecologically disruptive industries that would have to be relegated to the modernists' zone. (Also, emergency transport to expert medical care in hospitals would have to be entrusted to horse and buggy). Employment for the people who lived in the environmental zone would have to be both compatible with the amenity of the area and tightly integrated spatially with residential areas. All industry dependent on the input of electric power would be uneconomic, given the alternative of locating in the modernist zone. Industries dependent on high-speed and convenient transportation and communications would be ruled out as well. We may speculate that the environmental zone, in equilibrium, eventually would include only universities and the professors and students associated with them, a few similar industries, and, perhaps, a few wealthy retired people. Consumption levels would likely be very low except for those families whose incomes were derived from assets owned in the modernists' zone.

The fundamental problems with Mishan's ingenious proposal lie even deeper, however, than the transportation and related economic difficulties cited above. First, not all environmental problems can be segregated neatly by politically drawn boundaries. Whole regions, encompassing several states, are intimately linked in their ecological balance. It is often economically unfeasible to limit provision of clean air and water to one isolated tract in each state; as public goods, once they are provided for one person or for one small area, they can be provided for all within broad regions at negligible marginal costs. Thus, to achieve true environmental quality within the environmentalists' zone alone would be impossible without the close political cooperation of the modernists. Boulding's Spaceship Earth concept rightly emphasizes the point that all of mankind sinks or swims together in one small planet's ecosystems.

Even if we could abstract from the fact that it is impossible to escape from environmental problems on this earth, Mishan's scheme would still be unworkable because it would surely lead to a division of our country into two *societies* as well as two *facilities*. The environmentalists, leading a life of relatively low consumption and high amenity, would have virtually no interests in common with the modernists and their high consumption-low amenity life-style. What possible links could unite the two zones as part of one political entity, with the exception of interests in national defense? At best, the relationship between the two zones would be marked by antipathy and contempt for clashing life-styles and values. In addition, it is difficult to imagine how a zone of suitable size and convenience could be set aside for the environmentalists without severely hampering the activities of the modernists. Transportation and communications networks in the modernist zone would inevitably impinge on the environmentalists' zone with subsequent political conflict. At the least, noisy and dirty activities in the modernists' zone at the boundaries of the environmentalists' zone would present a source of continuing friction. In short, the coexistence of two such different cultural and economic zones within the same national state does not appear to be politically feasible.

Besides the above practical considerations, Mishan's basic assumption of a distinct dichotomy in tastes has unfortunate elitist overtones; it is more plausible to assume both that tastes for amenity vary continuously over broad ranges and that these tastes are socially conditioned and subject to change through education and experience. This point is closely related to our previous assertion that the cause of environmental quality involves some potential conflicts between the rich and poor in our society. Schemes to improve environmental quality should not blithely assume that *everybody* is affluent enough to give up the material benefits of economic growth.

The ease with which holes can be picked in Mishan's extreme proposal should not blind us, however, to its fundamental merits in more limited applications. The spatial organization of modern urban life is manifestly unsatisfactory and affords society ample scope for fundamental changes that could benefit everybody. Much can be done to shield human beings from the ugliest, dirtiest, and loudest aspects of the modern city. Although most individuals will have to continue to endure some disamenity as the cost of making a living, enlightened zoning practices can secure greater amenity both on and off the job. Separate facilities can be established to some extent for all people, not just for university professors and wealthy conservationists, by recognizing that individuals, to some extent, compartmentalize their lives as workers, commuters, consumers of goods and services, and consumers of leisure activities at different hours of the day and on different days of the year. Spatial segregation of different activities has enormous potential as a mechanism for general improvements in amenity.

C. CAN GROWTH AND ENVIRONMENTAL QUALITY BE MADE COMPATIBLE?

Sections A and B have presented two sets of apparently irreconcilable views on the desirability of continued economic growth. But the arguments in both sections have intentionally been presented without the usual academic qualifications in order to highlight the conflict between the progrowth and antigrowth camps. This section attempts a partial reconciliation of the two views by suggesting, in bare outline, a hypothetical society in which continued economic growth and high environmental quality would be compatible or, at least, much more compatible than past experience would suggest.

An Environmental Policy
for Economically Developed Countries

Suppose that, by some miracle, the present members of Congress were replaced by a random drawing from the membership files of the American Economic Association. (This is a textbook example, not a political program!) Such a Congress would undoubtedly soon pass legislation that would provide for a system of effluent charges and for new or higher extractive (severance) taxes on all materials that can be recycled. It would also pass legislation providing subsidies to encourage states and local governments to implement workable supplementary environmental measures such as noise abatement programs, marginal cost (including congestion costs) pricing of transportation facilities, and strict enforcement of existing antilittering laws. Such legislation also would encourage these government units to band together in regional environmental organizations wherever possible to take into account all spillovers across political jurisdiction. The economists' Congress also would establish experiments to find the best mechanisms for efficient allocation of scarce outdoor recreational facilities, and it would provide funds for heavy investment in new facilities, especially for new wilderness areas set aside to preserve scarce species for the future. It might also fund experiments designed to discover wholly new urban spatial arrangements that might increase the overall amenity of life in cities. Let us further suppose that the economists' Congress would discover effective means of making various government bureaucracies effective agents for carrying through the new environmental policies. Perhaps this could be done by designing a complex set of incentives and disincentives for government officials that would lead them to respond effectively to the public interest. Finally, we must suppose that the populace accepts this revolution from above and gives the new environmental measures enthusiastic support.

If we make the further critical assumption that fiscal and monetary policies would be effective in maintaining aggregate demand at a level close to full-employment output, then the major impact of the environmental package outlined above would be a massive realignment of relative prices. To be more specific, the successful implementation of all these environmental policies would mean that the prices of all outputs would have to include the full external (marginal) costs of environmental pollution. The Congress, well aware of the problems of adjustment, would be careful to make these large changes occur gradually and as painlessly as possible. We can speculate about a few of the more important expected changes in relative prices.

First, the prices of *goods*, especially heavy consumer durable goods, would rise sharply, relative to the prices of personal *services*. The reason for this expected change in relative prices is simply that external costs of production are significant for most goods and small for most personal services. The production of automobiles, for example, involves heavy use of environmental resources largely because of its utilization of steel, other metal, and rubber inputs. The production of medical services, in contrast, is much more labor intensive and involves relatively less use of capital and energy inputs that generate large amounts of effluents.

Second, the price of *energy* to both household and firms would rise sharply, relative to other prices. This price change would be due, first, to the fact that Congress would repeal the present depletion allowances and levy extractive taxes on the mining of such fossil fuels as oil and coal to ensure that the full external costs of fossil fuel combustion or the generation of nuclear energy would be included in the final price of energy. For example, the heavy taxes on the sulfur content of fuels, called for on environmental grounds, would add to fuel costs, either directly or through the mechanism of the costs incurred by firms to remove the sulfur from fuel prior to use. The day of much higher energy costs has already arrived in the United States; if the environmental measures discussed in this section were implemented, the cost increases would be greater still.

Third, use of *private automobiles* would become much more expensive. The first reason for this prediction was given above—the heavy use of key raw materials and energy at all stages of the production process for automobiles. A second reason would be the higher price of fuel, as all energy costs rise after the implementation of the new environmental program. A third factor would be the new heavy tolls imposed on automobiles using congested highways. Finally, fewer new highways would be built once highway authorities were forced to take into account all the environmental consequences of proposed construction, and the lessened availability of good highways would make automobile use correspondingly less valuable, or more expensive per mile of desired travel.

What is the relationship of these predicted relative price changes, in a new proenvironmental regime, to economic growth? Assuming again that fiscal and monetary authorities would succeed in maintaining full employment of resources, economic growth would resume after absorbing the shock of the revolution in relative prices, but in much different directions. We take the optimistic view that the pattern of economic growth in this new regime would be compatible with the maintenance of high-quality environmental resources and improved amenity or, at least, much more compatible than under the present system of relative prices.

To be specific, we foresee, first, a reallocation of resources away from goods to services, as consumers respond to the expected change in relative prices. This would mean, for example, less production of consumer durables, such as automobiles and color television sets, and more production of health, education, and welfare services.

We also predict a similar reallocation of resources away from the production of goods and services requiring relatively large energy inputs. Higher market prices for energy would be signals for firms and households to conserve on the use of energy in all forms. We would expect for example, a steady contraction of heavy goods industries and a diminished use of privately owned household appliances in response to higher energy prices. Instead of every household owning one washing machine with an expected life of less than 5 years, several households might share the use of one very efficient machine with an expected life of 10 years. In general, economic pressures might induce much more communal sharing in the consumption of the services of consumer durable goods.

Third, we predict a revolutionary reduction in private automobile use in response to the change in its relative price. People would have to substitute mass transit, jitney service, bicycles, and even walking for the automobile. Instead of every household owning two big cars, two or more households might share the use of one small car. In the long run, urban agglomerations would have to be rebuilt to accommodate the revolution in transportation wrought by the new environmental regime's impact on use of the private automobile.

Fourth, recycling of materials would become a major service industry in the new regime. Extractive taxes and the heavy environmental tax costs on the production of such basic materials as steel and rubber would afford opportunities for large profits to firms that could successfully cope with the technological problems of recycling used materials. The same economic pressures would increase the incentives for individuals to become expert in the repair and maintenance of their own consumer durables. Goods of high quality and relatively great durability would command higher market premiums than they do today.

In brief, these specific predictions lead us to expect that economic growth under a proenvironmentalist regime would be service-oriented rather than goods-oriented, as in the past. Because about 60 percent of the American labor force already is employed in service industries, such a shift in the pattern of growth would not be so revolutionary, in its employment aspect at least, as it may appear on first encounter. In contrast to goods-oriented growth, service-oriented growth would take the form of *improvements in quality* rather than increases in quantities produced. In compensation for less growth or even no growth in per capita consumption of many goods, people could expect to receive higher-quality medical care, better educations, and improved services of all kinds. We suggest that such a shift in consumption patterns would not only conserve on scarce environmental resources such as air and water but would also move society toward providing amenities of the kind so deeply desired by Mill, Boulding, Mishan, and others who share their traditional humanistic values.

Is such a revolution in our economic life *politically* feasible in this or any society? The authors do not pretend to know the answer. Much will depend on the environmental education of the next generation of Americans. A great deal will also depend on how successful our society is in redistributing its material prosperity more widely and ending poverty. The cause of a better environment will not gain widespread popular support as long as one-fourth or one-third of the people in our society consider themselves deprived of the material necessities of life. As noted previously, the issues of environmental quality and income distribution are closely linked.

Is such a revolution in our economic life *economically* feasible? Some (politically) radical economists argue that the modern capitalist economy could not cope successfully with a massive reallocation of resources away from heavy goods industries to service industries. Perhaps they are right, although the successful massive reallocation of resources in the post-World War II conversion from military to civilian production suggests that dogmatism on this issue is unwise. And, of course, the full environmental regime would have to be implemented gradually over a period of years rather than all at once. In our view, social engineering of changes in relative prices is not an environmental panacea but rather a prerequisite for any substantial progress against environmental deterioration.

The Special Problems of Underdeveloped Countries

If the above discussion leaves an optimistic impression, it is because it considers the circumstances of only the economically developed countries in the world. The United States, Canada, most of Europe, Russia, Japan, and Australia-New Zealand all belong to the developed part of the world. Most of the rest of the world can be classified as economically underdeveloped. The developed countries *can* solve the bulk of their environmental problems without sacrificing too much; if they fail to do so, it will be the result of the inadequacy of their political institutions. The underdeveloped countries, however, face much bleaker prospects.

As Chapter 12 documented, these countries already include most of the world's population, and if present population growth trends continue, only a small minority of the people alive in the world in two or three decades will live in the developed countries.

Per capita annual output of goods and services is over $7000 in the United States and less than $500 in some of the poorest countries of Asia and Africa. As noted in Chapter 12, the underdeveloped countries as a group are experiencing extremely rapid population growth that puts enormous pressure on their governments to stimulate economic growth. High rates of growth of output are required in these countries just to maintain existing consumption standards and to keep a growing, youthful labor force fully employed. The universal expectation of higher living standards, based on the model of the United States and other developed countries, creates demands for still higher economic growth. These pressures for rapid economic growth cannot be expected to abate in the next few decades. The momentum of high fertility is difficult to reverse in the short term, and the huge gap between living standards in the developed and underdeveloped countries cannot be narrowed appreciably by the end of the century (except by a catastrophe such as an all-out nuclear war). In short, every government in the underdeveloped part of the world now feels that it must strive for the highest possible growth rate of goods and services. This policy requires massive industrialization and urbanization now and for the indefinite future.

In light of the circumstances outlined above, the quality of the environment is at best a secondary consideration for most people in the underdeveloped world. The attitude of government officials in underdeveloped countries may be crudely characterized as "Damn the pollution, full speed ahead!" or "When we become rich like you, then we will worry about the environment." The environmental consequences of this stance have already proved to be locally devastating in some urban areas in underdeveloped countries. The environmental degradation that has occurred so far is, however, just a small part of what is still to come. Underdeveloped countries have already accepted many of the environmental consequences of high-risk industries and technologies that the developed countries have begun to shun. For example, new oil refineries are now often built outside environmentally conscious developed countries that will ultimately consume the bulk of the refined products. Similarly, underdeveloped countries are willing and eager to accept nuclear power installations with only minimal safeguards to solve their energy problems. They will also use dangerous pesticides and farm marginal land that is in recurring danger of desertification for the sake of increasing food supplies in order to feed their growing population. All of these developments and more threaten to devastate the environment both locally and throughout the world.

The following scenario may help the reader envision the dimensions of the problem: Suppose that the underdeveloped countries of the world successfully industrialize and grow to the point where, by the end of the century, their populations reach *present* U.S. consumption standards. Now envision the demands on all resources, especially the effluent-absorbing capacity of the atmosphere and waters of the earth, when the same per capita production levels of today in this country for a little more than 200 million people obtain on a worldwide scale for some 7 *billion* people. On top of this, add the further demands on resources caused by increases in the output levels of the developed countries beyond the present level in the United States. Also, as noted above, underdeveloped countries will resort to technologies which ignore environmental damage in order to achieve maximum economic growth. If this scenario is realistic, it is hard to escape the conclusion of environmental degradation on a mass scale throughout the world—very likely to a point that threatens human existence.

What developments might qualify this pessimistic prognosis? First, of course, is the possibility of unforeseen technological breakthroughs to save the world from man's pollution of his environment. If this appears to be just hoping for a miracle, it must be said that past predictions of disaster have proved dead wrong precisely because of a failure to foresee technological advances. Second, either birth rates may fall drastically or industrialization and growth plans may be abandoned in the underdeveloped world. Third, the developed and underdeveloped countries of the world may agree on a successful joint program of development aid from rich to poor and international environmental protection instead of each country following its own narrow, nationalistic self-interest. Neither of the latter two possibilities appears likely at the present time.

D. A NOTE ON THE RESEARCH FRONTIERS OF ENVIRONMENTAL ECONOMICS

This is a textbook, which means that the material presented herein summarizes and synthesizes existing knowledge about environmental economics. But much new exciting work is being done, even as we write, that is expanding the frontiers of this infant social science. This note is directed especially at those readers who have mastered the material in the text and are eager now to think about the major unsolved problems in the field.

The outline of the whole book can serve as an outline for this brief discussion of ongoing research. Chapter 1 (Part 1) introduced the reader to the benefit-cost approach to environmental problems, and the four chapters of Part 2 then fleshed out the theory of determining environmental costs and benefits. This theory is standard microeconomics and was essentially well worked out before the advent of major environmental problems. Economists have found it readily applicable to these problems with few modifications. Further advances in this theory can be expected, but they will probably not be of critical importance in increasing our ability to cope with environmental problems. The partial equilibrium price theory that we developed in Part 2 is already sufficient to give us the theoretical answers to partial equilibrium problems of the environment. The main frontier for economic theory applicable to the environment is in the area of general equilibrium or systems analysis. As noted throughout the book, environmental problems are linked by complex ecological relationships that are not yet well understood. Physical and biological scientists have to work out these relationships, and environmental economists have to utilize the results in their own models.

Vast problems remain virtually untouched on the *empirical* side of environmental economics. As noted in Chapters 6, 7, and 8 of Part 3, we are just beginning to get a grip on the meaning of the complex quality dimensions of air, water, and other natural resources. Benefit-cost *theory* may be well worked out, but benefit-cost *analysis* is worthless unless we can give some empirical content to the concepts of benefits and costs. Outstanding among the many empirical gaps in environmental economics are identification and quantification of the costs of long-term human exposure to various concentrations of different pollutants in the atmosphere and in food substances. Some of the evidence just recently available on the effects of substances such as asbestos is extremely frightening and appears to call for drastic government measures. But we still know very little about the effects of many other potentially dangerous pollutants. For many substances, there appear to be crucial thresholds for human tolerance; that is, marginal social costs become extremely high over some minimum concentration.

Facts are crucial also in filling in the gaps in our discussions of policy issues in Parts 4 and 5. At this point, we can only hazard intelligent guesses about how well various environmental programs will work, once put into effect. We badly need the social science laboratory of actual experience to put these guesses to the test.

To conclude, environmental economics is still in a primitive stage, especially with regard to its empirical content. We hope that the reader will not regard this fact with dismay but rather will accept it as a personal challenge.

E. SUMMARY AND CONCLUSIONS

This chapter assessed the relationship between economic growth and human welfare. Economists have, until very recently, generally accepted as self-evident the proposition that growth enhances welfare. This judgment is based on widespread evidence relating growth to vastly increased consumption per capita, greater longevity and better health, and freedom from ceaseless toil.

A growing underworld of radical criticism contests this conventional view of the beneficial effects of growth. Part of this criticism is based on the purely technical point that conventional measures of growth are faulty by their own criteria. But, more fundamentally, the revisionists' case is based on arguments that growth inevitably destroys environmental quality. Some versions of this view argue simplistically that continued geometric growth of output means geometric growth of effluents and, therefore, that effluent levels will inevitably overwhelm the finite absorptive capacities of environmental resources. More sophisticated radical critics of growth point to its harmful effects on other species, the environmental resource legacy to future generations, and various aspects of amenity.

We have suggested implementation of a full-fledged environmental program that might mollify some of the critics of growth. This program would consist of a coordinated package of environmental measures that would drastically alter relative price relationships throughout the economy. We predict that growth would continue after such a program went into effect, but along service-oriented lines in contrast to the goods orientation of traditional economic growth. The new pattern of growth would meet many of the criticisms of the radical critics. The outlook we have presented is optimistic for developed countries; for underdeveloped countries obsessed with the need for rapid industrialization and growth, the prospects for environmental quality are grim. Moreover, the global interrelatedness of many environmental problems—pesticides, nuclear wastes, carbon dioxide buildup—will threaten both the developed and underdeveloped nations.

Finally, we have concluded the book with a brief discussion of the research frontiers of environmental economics. The outstanding theoretical gap in the field is in general equilibrium or systems analysis that could deal with the complex ecological relationships relevant to most environmental problems. Probably more important is the lack of empirical knowledge about the costs of environmental pollution, especially the long-run effects of various pollutants in the atmosphere and in our foods. Until further research fills these gaps in our present knowledge, environmental economics will remain an underdeveloped science.

QUESTIONS FOR DISCUSSION

1. "The United States is now affluent enough to be able to afford zero economic growth for the sake of preserving the quality of its environment." Discuss critically.

2. Probably the single most important factor causing sustained economic growth is applied technological change. If the government seriously undertook to achieve zero economic growth, it would have to take measures to inhibit scientific research or at least to prevent the application of scientific advances. Would such measures really improve environmental quality?

3. "Government expenditures to clean up the environment should not be included in NNP because they just alleviate *bads* rather than produce *goods.*" Evaluate the logic of this statement. Should household expenditures on aspirin be included in NNP?

4. Some social critics argue that, in the past, too much of the potential benefits of economic growth has taken the form of increased market production and too little has been in the form of more leisure and other nonmarket uses of time. Would you expect this historical pattern to change if the proenvironmental program outlined in Section C were implemented? What would be the effect of an increase in the relative consumption of leisure on environmental quality?

5. Suppose the American people were given a clear either-or choice between two futures: one a simple extrapolation of the past and the other the kind of political economy described in Section C. Which do you think they would choose? Why?

SELECTED REFERENCES

BOULDING, KENNETH E., "The Economics of the Coming Spaceship Earth," in *Environmental Quality in a Growing Economy*, Henry Jarrett, ed. Baltimore: The Johns Hopkins Press, 1966. A concise statement of Boulding's ideas. Full of wisdom.

DENISON, EDWARD F., "Welfare Measurement and the GNP," *Survey of Current Business*, LI, No. 1 (January 1971). An authoritative treatment of how environmental problems are related to the official national income accounts.

DRECHSLER, L., "Problems of Recording Environmental Phenomena in National Accounting Aggregates," *Review of Income and Wealth*, 22, No. 3 (September 1976). A discussion of integrating environmental effects in the national accounts.

EASTERLIN, R. A., "Does Money Buy Happiness?," *The Public Interest*, No. 3 (Winter 1973). An international comparison of survey results on the relationship between income levels and human happiness.

HIRSCH, F., *Social Limits to Growth*. London: Routledge and Kegan Paul Ltd., 1977. An innovative analysis of social constraints on continued economic growth. Highly recommended.

KEYNES, JOHN MAYNARD, "Economic Possibilities for Our Grandchildren," in *Essays in Persuasion*. New York: W. W. Norton & Company, Inc., 1963. A beautifully written classic; well worth reading.

MISHAN, E. J., *The Economic Growth Debate*. London: Allen & Unwin Ltd., 1977. A readable statement of the views of a very original English economist.

NORDHAUS, WILLIAM, and JAMES TOBIN, "Is Growth Obsolete," in National Bureau of Economic Research, *Economic Growth. Economic Research: Retrospect and Prospect,* Fiftieth Anniversary Colloquim V. New York: Columbia University Press, 1972. A quantitative analysis of factors that might cause the *true* economic growth rate to diverge from the officially measured rate. Squarely in the traditional, progrowth tradition.

OLSON, M., and H. H. LANDSBERG (eds.), *The No Growth Society*. New York: W. W. Norton & Company, Inc., 1973. Presents pro- and antigrowth arguments. Comprehensive and very readable.

SCHUMACHER, E. F., *Small is Beautiful*. New York: Harper and Row, 1973. A critique of modern economic institutions, suggesting that many of our problems today, including pollution, are due to the overly large scale of production.

SCITOVSKY, T., *The Joyless Economy*. New York: Oxford University Press, 1976. A thought-provoking critique of economic growth.

SMITH, V. K. (ed.), *Scarcity and Growth Reconsidered*. Baltimore: The Johns Hopkins Press, forthcoming. A series of articles on natural resource scarcity. Attempts to broaden the definition and analysis of resource scarcity to include common-property resources. Advanced.

Index